T0325198

Integration and Implementation of the Internet of Things Through Cloud Computing

Pradeep Tomar
Gautam Buddha University, India

A volume in the Advances in Web
Technologies and Engineering
(AWTE) Book Series

Published in the United States of America by
    IGI Global
    Engineering Science Reference (an imprint of IGI Global)
    701 E. Chocolate Avenue
    Hershey PA, USA 17033
    Tel: 717-533-8845
    Fax: 717-533-8661
    E-mail: cust@igi-global.com
    Web site: http://www.igi-global.com

Library of Congress Cataloging-in-Publication Data

Names: Tomar, Pradeep, 1976- editor.
Title: Integration and implementation of the internet of things through
    cloud computing / Pradeep Tomar.
Description: Hershey : Engineering Science Reference, [2021] | Includes
    bibliographical references and index. | Summary: "This book explores
    various applications, techniques & use of IoT and cloud computing by
    exploring the new technical, functional, non-functional future by
    identifying and discussing future aspects and research perspectives of
    Internet of Things and the critical technology and solutions"-- Provided
    by publisher.
Identifiers: LCCN 2021019270 (print) | LCCN 2021019271 (ebook) | ISBN
    9781799869818 (hc) | ISBN 9781799869825 (s/c) | ISBN 9781799869832
    (eISBN)
Subjects: LCSH: Internet of things. | Cloud computing.
Classification: LCC TK5105.8857 .I527 2021 (print) | LCC TK5105.8857
    (ebook) | DDC 004.67/82--dc23
LC record available at https://lccn.loc.gov/2021019270
LC ebook record available at https://lccn.loc.gov/2021019271

This book is published in the IGI Global book series Advances in Web Technologies and
Engineering (AWTE) (ISSN: 2328-2762; eISSN: 2328-2754)

Advances in Web Technologies and Engineering (AWTE) Book Series

ISSN:2328-2762
EISSN:2328-2754

Editor-in-Chief: Ghazi I. Alkhatib, The Hashemite University, Jordan & David C. Rine, George Mason University, USA

MISSION

The **Advances in Web Technologies and Engineering (AWTE) Book Series** aims to provide a platform for research in the area of Information Technology (IT) concepts, tools, methodologies, and ethnography, in the contexts of global communication systems and Web engineered applications. Organizations are continuously overwhelmed by a variety of new information technologies, many are Web based. These new technologies are capitalizing on the widespread use of network and communication technologies for seamless integration of various issues in information and knowledge sharing within and among organizations. This emphasis on integrated approaches is unique to this book series and dictates cross platform and multidisciplinary strategy to research and practice.

The **Advances in Web Technologies and Engineering (AWTE) Book Series** seeks to create a stage where comprehensive publications are distributed for the objective of bettering and expanding the field of web systems, knowledge capture, and communication technologies. The series will provide researchers and practitioners with solutions for improving how technology is utilized for the purpose of a growing awareness of the importance of web applications and engineering.

COVERAGE

- Integrated Heterogeneous and Homogeneous Workflows and Databases within and Across Organizations and with Suppliers and Customers
- Integrated user profile, provisioning, and context-based processing
- Metrics-based performance measurement of IT-based and web-based organizations
- Radio Frequency Identification (RFID) research and applications in Web engineered systems
- Case studies validating Web-based IT solutions
- Mobile, location-aware, and ubiquitous computing
- Data analytics for business and government organizations
- Web systems performance engineering studies
- Knowledge structure, classification, and search algorithms or engines
- Human factors and cultural impact of IT-based systems

IGI Global is currently accepting manuscripts for publication within this series. To submit a proposal for a volume in this series, please contact our Acquisition Editors at Acquisitions@igi-global.com or visit: http://www.igi-global.com/publish/.

Titles in this Series

For a list of additional titles in this series, please visit:
http://www.igi-global.com/book-series/advances-web-technologies-engineering/37158

Design Innovation and Network Architecture for the Futur Internet
Mohamed Boucadair (Orange S.A., France) and Christian Jacquenet (Orange S.A., France)
Engineering Science Reference • © 2021 • 478pp • H/C (ISBN: 9781799876465) • US $225.00

Challenges and Opportunities for the Convergence of IoT, Big Data, and Cloud Computing
Sathiyamoorthi Velayutham (Sona College of Technology, India)
Engineering Science Reference • © 2021 • 350pp • H/C (ISBN: 9781799831112) • US $215.00

Examining the Impact of Deep Learning and IoT on Multi-Industry Applications
Roshani Raut (Pimpri Chinchwad College of Engineering (PCCOE), Pune, India) and Albena Dimitrova Mihovska (CTIF Global Capsule (CGC), Denmark)
Engineering Science Reference • © 2021 • 304pp • H/C (ISBN: 9781799875116) • US $245.00

Result Page Generation for Web Searching Emerging Research and Opportunities
Mostafa Alli (Tsinghua University, China)
Engineering Science Reference • © 2021 • 126pp • H/C (ISBN: 9781799809616) • US $165.00

Building Smart and Secure Environments Through the Fusion of Virtual Reality, Augmented Reality, and the IoT
Nadesh RK (Vellore Institute of Technology, India) Shynu PG (Vellore Institute of Technology, India) and Chiranji Lal Chowdhary (School of Information Technology and Engineering, VIT University, Vellore, India)
Engineering Science Reference • © 2020 • 300pp • H/C (ISBN: 9781799831839) • US $245.00

For an entire list of titles in this series, please visit:
http://www.igi-global.com/book-series/advances-web-technologies-engineering/37158

701 East Chocolate Avenue, Hershey, PA 17033, USA
Tel: 717-533-8845 x100 • Fax: 717-533-8661
E-Mail: cust@igi-global.com • www.igi-global.com

Editorial Advisory Board

Table of Contents

Chapter 15
Shifting Legacy Robotic Manufacturing Towards Industry 4.0: Using Cloud

Detailed Table of Contents

Chapter 1

Harshit Bhardwaj, USICT, Gautam Buddha University, India
Pradeep Tomar, USICT, Gautam Buddha University, India
Aditi Sakalle, USICT, Gautam Buddha University, India
Taranjeet Singh, G. L. Bajaj Institute of Management, India
Divya Acharya, iNurture Education Solutions Private Limited, India
Arpit Bhardwaj, Bennett University, India

Fog computing has latency, particularly for healthcare applications, which is of the utmost importance. This research aims to be a comprehensive literature analysis of healthcare innovations for fog computing. All of these components involved special abilities. In sequence, developers must be qualified to write stable, healthy IoT programs in four distinct fields of software production: embedded, server, tablet, and web-based. Furthermore, the distributed results, IoT structure essence, dispersed abilities in programming play a deciding position. This chapter discusses the difficulties in creating the IoT method and summarizing findings and observations. Experiences of the need for and co-presence of various kinds of skills in software creation in the construction of IoT applications are discussed.

Chapter 2

Kirti Kangra, Guru Jambheshwar University of Science and Technology, India
Jaswinder Singh, Guru Jambheshwar University of Science and Technology, India

The internet of things (IoT) model connects physical devices to the virtual world and enables them to interact. It enables smart devices to communicate with other devices to exchange information. To link a wireless network or cloud network, it takes the help of several technologies such as radio frequency identification (RFID), wireless sensor network (WSN), near field communication (NFC), ZigBee, and others. The IoT requires a standard architecture and protocol stack to establish links between the devices. This chapter provides a brief introduction, pillars, the evolution, architecture, application of IoT, and issues related to IoT implementation in real life.

        Iram Abrar, University of Kashmir, India
        Sahil Nazir Pottoo, I. K. Gujral Punjab Technical University, India
        Faheem Syeed Masoodi, University of Kashmir, India
        Alwi Bamhdi, Umm AL Qura University, Saudi Arabia

Internet of things witnessed rapid growth in the last decade and is considered to be a promising field that plays an all-important role in every aspect of modern-day life. However, the growth of IoT is seriously hindered by factors like limited storage, communication capabilities, and computational power. On the other hand, cloud has the potential to support a large amount of data as it has massive storage capacity and can perform complex computations. Considering the tremendous potential of these two technologies and the manner in which they complement one another, they have been integrated to form what is commonly referred to as the cloud of things (CoT). This integration is beneficial as the resulting system is more robust, intelligent, powerful, and offers promising solutions to the users. However, the new paradigm (CoT) is faced with a significant number of challenges that need to be addressed. This chapter discusses in detail various challenges like reliability, latency, scalability, heterogeneity, power consumption, standardization, etc. faced by the cloud of things.

        Nipun R. Navadia, Dronacharya Group of Institutions, India
        Gurleen Kaur, Dronacharya Group of Institutions, India
        Harshit Bhardwaj, USICT, Gautam Buddha University, India
        Taranjeet Singh, G. L. Bajaj Institute of Management, India
        Aditi Sakalle, USICT, Gautam Buddha University, India
        Divya Acharya, iNurture Education Solutions Private Limited, India
        Arpit Bhardwaj, Bennett University, India

Cloud storage is a great way for companies to fulfill more of their data-driven needs and excellent technology that allows the company to evolve and grow at a faster pace, accelerating growth and providing a flexible forum for developers to build useful apps for better devices to be developed over the internet. The integration of cloud computing and the internet of things creates a scalable, maintainable, end-to-end internet of things solution on the cloud network. By applying the infrastructure to the real universe, it generates sources of insight. Cloud computing and IoT are separate technology but are closely associated and are termed as 'cloud-based IoT' as IoT has the ability to create intelligent goods and services, gather data that can affect business decisions and probably change the business model to boost success and expansion, and cloud infrastructure can be at the heart of all IoT has to deliver.

Chapter 5

Anthony Bolton, University of South Africa, South Africa
Leila Goosen, University of South Africa, South Africa
Elmarie Kritzinger, University of South Africa, South Africa

The purpose of this chapter is to address challenges related to the integration and implementation of the developing internet of things (IoT) into the daily lives of people. Demands for communication between devices, sensors, and systems are reciprocally driving increased demands for people to communicate and manage the growing digital ecosystem of the IoT and an unprecedented volume of data. A larger study was established to explore how digital transformation through unified communication and collaboration (UC&C) technologies impact the productivity and innovation of people in the context of one of the world's largest automotive enterprises, General Motors (GM). An analysis and exploration of this research milieu, supported by a critical realist interpretation of solutions, suggested that recommendations can be made that the integration and implementation of digital transformation, delivered via UC&C technologies, impact productivity and opportunity for driving innovation within a global automotive enterprise.

Chapter 6

Dimpal Tomar, USICT, Gautam Buddha University, India
Pooja Singh, Shiv Nadar University, India
Jai Prakash Bhati, Noida International University, India
Pradeep Tomar, USICT, Gautam Buddha University, India

Today, everything is progressing to 'Smart' to enhance the environment via technological progress including IoT, big data, AI, ICT, and so on. But, in this whole process, the sustainability of being 'smart' is implemented by the cloud-based technology, which also acts as an engine. Smart society is another live example of this era that makes potential use of digital technology and sensor devices to improve people's lives through the internet. It also incorporates cloud computing, which significantly benefits them by offering a sustainable environment to access the computing power at large scale, which they could not previously access due to lack of resources. This chapter provide a broad overview of smart society that covers the scope and services, technological pillars, features necessities to be titled as 'smart', and a sustainable development. Also, it broadly covers the role of cloud computing, related technologies, and generic architecture for the sustainability of smart societies followed by applications with a case study and challenges.

Chapter 7

Indu Malik, Gautam Buddha University, India
Sandhya Tarar, Gautam Buddha University, India

The cloud-based smart city is a way to provide resources and data on demand. Two technologies used to build cloud-based smart city, IoT, and cloud computing are explored. Using smart sensors can capture the movement of the environment, humans, and city infrastructure like building maintenance, traffic control, transportation, pollution monitoring. This is possible through IoT. Future movement could be predicted based on present and past data. Cloud computing is used for cloud storage. Using cloud, users can access resources in virtual mode at any time or anywhere. It can be accessed at different locations at the same time through high speed internet. Cloud is managed by a third party. Users don't have any knowledge regarding resource location and data, such as where user data is stored. Users use cloud service in virtual mode. Basically, cloud is a service provider platform that provides resources and data storage facility in a virtual way; users don't need to purchase resources.

Chapter 8

Ruchi Garg, Gautam Buddha University, India
Harsh Garg, Delhi Technological University, India

Internet of things (IoT) is leading towards revolutionary applications with huge potential to improvise the efficiency multifold. IoT with the use of sensors has opened a huge window for applications in almost every area of life, and its penetration is endless with wireless connectivity. In this chapter, a wireless sensor-based solution for smart access control system for telecom sites is proposed and implemented. This project is initially implemented for 10 sites for a leading telecom operator, which will later on be scalable. This solution provides smart access to site engineers on the telecom site. Also, this system helps to remotely monitor multiple sites simultaneously, which protects the site from any forced entry and vandalism. The proposed solution and its implementation are given in detail in the chapter.

Chapter 9

  Prerna Sharma, Jagan Institute of Management Studies, Guru Gobind
      Singh Indraprastha University, India
  Piyush Jain, Jagan Institute of Management Studies, Guru Gobind
      Singh Indraprastha University, India
  Latika Kharb, Jagan Institute of Management Studies, Guru Gobind
      Singh Indraprastha University, India

In this chapter, an attempt has been made to develop a hardware-based remote water quality monitoring system using a single-chip microcontroller, Atmega328P, in synchrony with some sensor technology and GSM/GPRS module for long-distance data transmission. The proposed system is able to perform a qualitative test on the water, taking into consideration both the chemical behavior as well as physical properties exhibited by the latter. The fluid will be analyzed in terms of its ph value (i.e., the molar concentration of hydrogen ions, the haziness caused by the major suspension of minute particles). The device aims to transmit all the deliberated parameters of the wastewater along with the longitude and latitude information to the concerned authorities for real-time monitoring of that data. The subject aims to devise a robust solution that can be used to analyze the quality of large water bodies and send the analysis report to the authorities of pollution control for further implication.

Chapter 10

  Payel Guria, Vidyasagar University, India
  Aditya Bhattacharyya, Vidyasagar University, India

IoT and cloud computing are the novel fields that are rapidly progressing in the world of internet technology. A huge and massive amount of data are communicating via IoT and cloud devices. Along with the highly configured devices, IoT and cloud also empowered many resource-constrained devices to communicate and compute information through network. But the major problem that they face is how to provide data security through conventional cryptographic algorithms in such resource-constrained devices having smaller size, limited memory spaces, low computation capabilities, and limited power. In this scenario, the biggest driver towards the problem is lightweight cryptography (LWC). This chapter discusses thoroughly the LWC, different schemes of LWC, and cryptanalysis of different LWC schemes.

Chapter 11

Taranjeet Singh, IFTM University, India
Devendra Singh, IFTM University, India
S. S. Bedi, Mahatma Jyotiba Phule Rohilkhand University, India

A device composed of actuators is the internet of things. The internet of things (IoT) should be used for enhancing agricultural efficiency in precision agriculture. The bedrock of the Indian economy, agriculture, is adding to the country's total economic performance. Nevertheless, the efficiency contrasts with world norms. Regardless of the usage of minimum agricultural advancements and farmers from villages today for other productive enterprises, regions move to a metropolitan region, and they cannot rely on agriculture. Farming creativity is not new, but smart farming is expected to be pushed to the following internet level by IoT, a unit made up of actuators or sensors. This chapter demonstrates IoT's role in agriculture and its use in identifying plant diseases through leaf images. Several researchers' works in the domain are also outlined, and future perspectives of IoT in recognizing plant diseases are discussed briefly.

Chapter 12

Rishabh Verma, Jagan Institute of Management Studies, Guru Gobind Singh Indraprastha University, India
Latika Kharb, Jagan Institute of Management Studies, Guru Gobind Singh Indraprastha University, India

Smart farming through IoT technology could empower farmers to upgrade profitability going from the amount of manure to be used to the quantity of water for irrigating their fields and also help them to decrease waste. Through IoT, sensors could be used for assisting farmers in the harvest field to check for light, moistness, temperature, soil dampness, etc., and robotizing the water system framework. Moreover, the farmers can screen the field conditions from anyplace and overcome the burden and fatigue to visit farms to confront problems in the fields. For example, farmers are confronting inconvenience while utilizing right quantity and time to use manures and pesticides in their fields as per the crop types. In this chapter, the authors have introduced a model where farmers can classify damaged crops and healthy crops with the help of different sensors and deep learning models. (i.e., The idea of implementing IoT concepts for the benefit of farmers and moving the world towards smart agriculture is presented.)

The IoT (internet of things) is a network of people and stuff at any moment, anytime, for anyone, with any network or service. IoT is therefore a major complex worldwide network backbone for online service providers. The smart grid (SG) is one of IoT's main applications. SG is an interconnected data exchange network that gathers and analyzes data obtained from transmission lines, generation stations, and customers through the power grid. The internet of things has risen as the basis of creativity for energy grids. The chapter is based on the idea that, if one grid station transmitting electricity to customers is cut off due to some defects of IoT-based systems, all grid station loads can be connected to another system so that power is not disrupted. The authors discuss the IoT and SG and their relationship in this chapter. The best advantages for SG and specifications can be addressed in the SG works, creative innovations using IoT in SG, IoT software, and facilities in SG.

The worst natural catastrophes occurring in well-settled intelligent cities are earthquakes. A framework of earthquake warning minimizes destruction and protects countless lives. A system built on IoT to identify the earthquake in the S waves and then to warn people by showing them an alert and where the earthquake happened is proposed. An early warning system is generated by a seismic wave survey. The larger the earthquake, the heavier the tremor. The waves are also breaking down the driveway. So the earthquake in the S wave is safer to find. Therefore, determining the extent of the early warning system is essential for creating an earthquake. The chapter addresses the detection of the frequency of earthquakes by identifying the size of earthquakes. In this chapter, we will discuss the elevated processors and IoT (internet of things) that can efficiently deploy an early warning device that can capture and transmit data over networks without manual interference. The early earthquake warning system (EEW) can be used to support smart urban planning, making earthquake areas less sensitive to disasters.

    Hadi Alasti, Purdue University Fort Wayne, USA

The mission of this chapter is to review and investigate the requirements and applications of using cloud-based internet of things (CIoT) for shifting the legacy robotic manufacturing towards Industry 4.0. Sensing and communications are two requirements of Industry 4.0. In the chapter, the legacy robotic manufacturing equipment collaborate with the environment, where it supports sustainable manufacturing. An implementation example of the proposed scenario will be discussed in this chapter.

Preface

The IoT has drawn great attention from both academia and industry, since it offers challenging notion of creating a world where all the things, known as smart objects around us are connected, typically in a wireless manner, to the Internet and communicate with each other with minimum human intervention. Another component set to help IoT succeed is cloud computing, which acts as a sort of front end. Cloud computing is an increasingly popular service that offers several advantages to IoT and it is based on the concept of allowing users to perform normal computing tasks using services delivered entirely over the internet. Cloud computing as a paradigm for big data storage and analytics, while IoT is exciting on its own, the real innovation will come from combining it with cloud computing. The combination of cloud computing and IoT will enable new monitoring services and powerful processing of sensory data streams. These applications alongside implementation details and challenges should also be explored for successful mainstream adoption. IoT is also fuelled by the advancement of digital technologies. The next generation era will be cloud based IoT systems.

Recently, IoT and cloud computing have been widely studied and applied in many fields, as they can provide a new method for intelligent perception and connection from M2M (including man-to-man, man-to-machine, and machine-to-machine), and on-demand use and efficient sharing of resources, respectively. A novel paradigm where Cloud and IoT are merged together is foreseen as disruptive and an enabler of a large number of application scenarios. In this book we will focus our attention on the integration of Cloud and IoT named Cloud IoT paradigm. We try to cover various aspects of Cloud IoT system, the need for integrating them, the challenges deriving from such integration, and how these issues have been tackled. Apart from them we will try to describe various application like cloud based smart cities, smart grids, smart homes, smart farming and smart e-health services etc. We will try to explore various communication technologies. Apart from that major emphasis will be given to energy efficiency of the cloud based IoT system. Overview of publications is about Cloud based IoT, standards, protocols, IoT architecture and system design for Cloud based IoT, integration with existing standards and protocols with Cloud based

IoT, data management and technology involved in Cloud based IoT, Applications of Cloud based IoT with challenges and Solutions of Cloud based IoT.

This book aims to explore various applications, techniques & use of IoT and cloud computing by exploring the new technical, functional, non-functional future. This book aims to identify and discuss Future Aspects and Research Perspectives of Internet of Things, demonstrating critical technology and solutions. The ultimate objective of this book is to determine whether these its integration with Cloud Computing: Challenges and Open Issues, Applications of Cloud-Based Internet of Things, The Integration and Implementation of the Internet of Things Through Digital Transformation and Blockchain of Internet of Things - Based Earthquake Alarming System in Smart Cities, agriculture and farming.

The chapters of this book are written by experienced researchers and specialists from all over the world, providing a unique gathering of information relating to the role. The significance and impact of Cloud-Based Smart City Using Internet of Things, Internet of Things Enabled Smart Entry System for Telecom Sites, Lightweight Cryptography in Cloud-Based Internet of Things: An Analytical Approach and Shifting Legacy Robotic Manufacturing Towards Industry 4.0, Using Cloud IoT are also discussed very effectively. This book will provide valuable knowledge and insights to a vast spectrum of readers at different hierarchical levels, from graduate to researcher students, and also beneficial to incorporate all the discussed systems into practical use. This book is divided into fifteen chapters where each chapter has a distinct focus.

Chapter 1: Future Aspects and Research Perspectives of Internet of Things

A globally dispersed fog computing architecture that involves several at the end of a network, heterogeneous systems are ubiquitously linked to collaboratively have Variable and customizable facilities for connectivity, computing, and storage. Fog computing has latency, particularly for healthcare applications, is of the utmost importance. This research's aim a comprehensive literature analysis of healthcare innovations for fog computing is discussed. All of these in components for their growth, involved special abilities. In Sequence, developers must be qualified to write stable, healthy IoT programs. In four distinct fields of software production, and learned in: Embedded, server, tablet, and web based. Furthermore, the distributed results, IoT structures' essence, dispersed abilities in programming Play a deciding position. This article discusses the difficulties in creating the IoT method and summarizing findings and observations of other. Experiences of the need for and co-presence of various kinds of Skills in software creation in the construction of IoT applications.

Chapter 2: Internet of Things and Its Relevance

The Internet of Things (IoT) model connects physical devices to the virtual world and enables them to interact. It enables smart devices to communicate with other devices to exchange information. To link a wireless network or cloud network, it takes the help of several technologies such as Radio Frequency Identification (RFID), Wireless Sensor Network (WSN), Near Field Communication (NFC), ZigBee, and others. The IoT requires a standard architecture and protocol stack to establish links between the devices. This chapter provides a brief Introduction, pillars, the evolution, architecture, application of IoT, and issues related to IoT implementation in real life.

Chapter 3: On IoT and Its Integration With Cloud Computing – Challenges and Open Issues

Internet of things witnessed rapid growth in the last decade and is considered to be a promising field that plays an all-important role in every aspect of modern-day life. However, the growth of IoT is seriously hindered by factors like limited storage, communication capabilities, and computational power. On the other hand, Cloud has the potential to support a large amount of data as it has massive storage capacity and can perform complex computations. Considering the tremendous potential of these two technologies and the manner in which they complement one another, they have been integrated to form what is commonly referred to as the Cloud of things (CoT). This integration is beneficial as the resulting system is more robust, intelligent, powerful, and offers promising solutions to the users. However, the new paradigm (CoT) is faced with a significant number of challenges that need to be addressed. This chapter discusses in detail various challenges like reliability, latency, scalability, heterogeneity, power consumption, standardization, etc faced by Cloud of things.

Chapter 4: Applications of Cloud-Based Internet of Things

Cloud storage is a great way for companies to fulfill more of their data-driven needs and excellent technology that allows the company to evolve and grow at a faster pace, accelerating growth, and provides a flexible forum for developers to build useful apps for better days devices to be developed over the internet. The integration of Cloud Computing and the Internet of Things creates a scalable, maintainable end-to-end Internet of Things solution on the cloud network. By applying the infrastructure to the real universe, it generates sources of insight. Cloud computing and IOT are separate technology but are closely associated and are termed as – 'Cloud-based IOT' as –IoT has the ability to create intelligent goods and services, gather data that can affect business decisions, and probably change the business model to boost success and expansion, and cloud infrastructure can be at the heart of all IoT has to deliver.

Chapter 5: The Integration and Implementation of the Internet of Things Through Digital Transformation – Impact on Productivity and Innovation

The purpose of this chapter is to address challenges related to the integration and implementation of the developing Internet of Things (IoT) into the daily lives of people. Demands for communication between devices, sensors, and systems are reciprocally driving increased demands for people to communicate and manage the growing digital eco-system of the IoT and an unprecedented volume of data. A larger study was established to explore how digital transformation through Unified Communication and Collaboration (UC&C) technologies impact the productivity and innovation of people in the context of one of the world's largest automotive enterprises, General Motors (GM). Analysis and exploration of this research milieu, supported by a critical realist interpretation of solutions suggested that recommendations can be made that the integration and implementation of digital transformation, delivered via UC&C technologies, impact productivity and opportunity for driving innovation within a global automotive enterprise.

Chapter 6: Sustainability of Cloud-Based Smart Society

Today, everything is progressing to 'Smart', to enhance the environment via technological progress including IoT, big data, AI, ICT, and so on. But, in this whole process, the sustainability of being 'smart' is implemented by the cloud-based technology which also acts as an engine. Smart society is another live example of this era that makes potential use of digital technology and sensor devices to improve people's lives through the Internet. It also incorporates cloud computing which significantly benefits them by offering a sustainable environment to access the computing power at a large scale; which they could not previously access due to lack of resources. This chapter provides a broad overview of smart society which covers the Scope and Services, technological pillars, features necessities to be titled as 'smart', and sustainable development. Also, broadly cover the role of cloud computing, related technologies, and generic architecture for the sustainability of smart societies followed by applications with case study and challenges and finally, conclude the chapter.

Chapter 7: Cloud-Based Smart City Using Internet of Things

Cloud-based Smart City is a way to provide resources and data on demand. Two technologies used to build a Cloud-based Smart City, IoT and cloud computing. Using Smart sensors can capture the movement of the environment, humans, and City infrastructure like building maintains, traffic control, transportation, pollution monitoring this is possible through IoT. Future movement could be predicted, based on present and past data. Cloud computing is used for cloud storage. Using the cloud, users can access resources in virtual mode at any time or anywhere, it can access different locations at the same time through high-speed internet. Cloud is managed by a third party. Users don't have any knowledge regarding resource location and data, such as where user data is storing. Users use cloud service in virtual mode. Basically, the cloud is a service provider platform that provides resources and data storage facilities in a virtual way; users don't need to purchase resources.

Chapter 8: Internet of Things-Enabled Smart Entry System for Telecom Sites

Internet of things (IoT) is leading towards revolutionary applications with huge potential to improvise the efficiency multifold. IoT with the use of sensors has opened a huge window for applications in almost every area of life and its penetration is endless with wireless connectivity. In this chapter, a wireless sensor-based solution for a smart access control system for telecom sites is proposed and implemented. This project is initially implemented for 10 sites for a leading telecom operator, which will later on scalable. This solution provides smart access to site engineers on the telecom site. Also, this system helps to remotely monitor, multiple sites simultaneously, which protects the site from any forced entry and vandalism. The proposed solution and its implementation in detail are given in the chapter.

Chapter 9: Internet of Things-Based Water Quality Control and Monitoring System for Urban Society

In this chapter, an attempt has been made to develop a hardware-based remote water quality monitoring system using a single-chip microcontroller, Atmega328P in synchrony with some sensor technology and GSM/GPRS module for long-distance data transmission. The proposed system is able to perform a qualitative test on the water, taking into consideration both, the chemical behavior as well as physical properties exhibited by the latter. The fluid will be analyzed in terms of its ph value i.e. the molar concentration of hydrogen ions, the haziness caused by the major suspension of minute particles. The device aims to transmit all the deliberated parameters of the wastewater along with the longitude and latitude information to the concerned authorities for real-time monitoring of that data. The subject aims to devise a robust solution that can be used to analyze the quality of large water bodies and send the analysis report to the Authorities of Pollution Control for further implication.

Chapter 10: Lightweight Cryptography in Cloud-Based Internet of Things – An Analytical Approach

IoT and Cloud computing is novel fields that are rapidly progressing in the world of Internet technology. A huge and massive amount of data are communicating via IoT and cloud devices. Along with the highly configured devices, IoT and Cloud also empowered many resource-constrained devices to communicate and compute information through the network. But the major problem that they face is how to provide data security through the conventional cryptographic algorithm in such resource-constrained devices, having a smaller size, limited memory spaces, low computation capabilities, and limited power. In this scenario, the biggest driver of the problem is Lightweight Cryptography (LWC). This chapter discusses thoroughly the LWC, different schemes of LWC, and cryptanalysis of different LWC schemes.

Chapter 11: Monitoring and Detecting Plant Diseases Using Cloud-Based Internet of Things

A device composed of actuators is the Internet of Things. Sensors or both that have Internet access either consciously or implicitly. The Internet of Things (IoT) should be used for enhancing agricultural efficiency in precision agriculture. The bedrock of the Indian economy, agriculture, is adding to the country's total economic performance. Nevertheless, our efficiency contrasts with world norms. Regardless of the usage of minimum agricultural advancements and farmers from villages today for other productive enterprises, regions move to a metropolitan region, and they cannot rely on agriculture. Farming creativity is not new, but smart farming is expected to be pushed to the following Internet level by IoT, a unit made up of actuators or sensors. This chapter demonstrates IoT's role in agriculture and its use in identifying plant diseases through leaf images. Several researchers' works in the domain are also outlined, and future perspectives of IoT in recognizing plant diseases are discussed briefly.

Chapter 12: Smart Farming Using Internet of Things – A Solution for Optimal Monitoring

Smart Farming through IoT technology could empower farmers to upgrade profitability going from the amount of manure to be used to the quantity of water for irrigating their fields and also help them to decrease wastage. Through IoT, sensors could be used for assisting farmers in the harvest field to check for light, moistness, temperature, soil dampness etc. and robotizing the water system framework. Moreover, the farmers can screen the field conditions from anyplace and overcome the burden and fatigue to visit farms to confront problems in the fields. For example, farmers are confronting inconvenience while utilizing right quantity and time to use manures and pesticides in their fields as per the crop types. In this paper, authors have introduced model where farmers can classify damaged crops and healthy crops with the help of different sensors and deep learning models i.e. the idea of implementing IoT concepts for the benefits of farmers and moving the world towards smart agriculture is presented.

Chapter 13: Smart Grid Using Internet of Things

The IoT (Internet of Things) is a network of people and stuff at any moment, anytime, for anyone, with any network or service. IoT is therefore a major complex worldwide network backbone for online service providers. The Smart Grid is one of IoT's main applications (SG). SG is an interconnected data exchange network that gathers and analyzes data obtained from transmission lines, generation stations, and customers through the power grid. The Internet of things has risen as the basis of creativity for energy grids. The project is based on the idea that, if one grid station transmitting electricity to customers is cut off due to some defects of IoT-based systems, all grid station loads can be connected to another system so that power is not disrupted. We are discussing the IoT and SG and their relationship in this chapter. The best advantages for SG and specifications can be addressed in the SG works, creative innovations using IoT in SG, IoT software, and facilities in SG.

Chapter 14: Blockchain of Internet of Things-Based Earthquake Alarming System in Smart Cities

The worst natural catastrophes occurring in well-settled intelligent cities are earthquakes. A framework of earthquake warning minimizes destruction and protects countless lives. A system built on IoT to identify the earthquake in the S waves and then to warn people by showing them as alert and where the earthquake happened. An early warning system is generated by a seismic wave survey. The larger the earthquake, the heavier the tremor. The waves are also breaking down the driveway. So the earthquake in the S wave is safer to find. Therefore, determining the extent of the early warning system is essential for creating an earthquake. The chapter addresses the detection of the frequency of earthquakes by identifying the size of earthquakes. The proposed technique, along with elevated processors and IoT (Internet of Things), can efficiently deploy an early warning device that can capture and transmit data over networks without manual interference. The Early Earthquake Warning system (EEW) can be used to support smart urban planning, making earthquake areas less sensitive to disasters.

Chapter 15: Shifting Legacy Robotic Manufacturing Towards Industry 4.0 Using Cloud IoT

The mission of this chapter proposal is to review and investigate the requirements and applications of using cloud-based Internet of Things (CIoT) for shifting the legacy robotic manufacturing towards industry 4.0. Sensing and communications are two requirements of industry 4.0. In the proposed chapter, the legacy robotic manufacturing equipment collaborate with the environment, where it supports sustainable manufacturing. Implementation example of the proposed scenario will be discussed in this chapter.

This book will also highlight outputs of research and development (R&D) projects, which include smart farming technologies, products, information systems, methods, and approaches to make farming operations more productive, sustainable, efficient, convenient, and competitive. Scientists, researchers, and experts from related disciplines will be contributing their book chapters related to Technologies for Farm Modernization and Mechanization, Smart Nutrient Management for Corn Production, Food 4.0, Smart Water Management Strategies, Smart Crop, Smart Crop Monitoring System and Sustainable farming, Wireless Sensor Network for Smart Agriculture, etc.

Pradeep Tomar
USICT, Gautam Buddha University, India

Chapter 1
Future Aspects and Research Perspectives of the Internet of Things

Harshit Bhardwaj
USICT, Gautam Buddha University, India

Pradeep Tomar
ⓘ https://orcid.org/0000-0002-7565-0708
USICT, Gautam Buddha University, India

Aditi Sakalle
USICT, Gautam Buddha University, India

Taranjeet Singh
G. L. Bajaj Institute of Management, India

Divya Acharya
iNurture Education Solutions Private Limited, India

Arpit Bhardwaj
Bennett University, India

ABSTRACT

Fog computing has latency, particularly for healthcare applications, which is of the utmost importance. This research aims to be a comprehensive literature analysis of healthcare innovations for fog computing. All of these components involved special abilities. In sequence, developers must be qualified to write stable, healthy IoT programs in four distinct fields of software production: embedded, server, tablet, and

DOI: 10.4018/978-1-7998-6981-8.ch001

web-based. Furthermore, the distributed results, IoT structure essence, dispersed abilities in programming play a deciding position. This chapter discusses the difficulties in creating the IoT method and summarizing findings and observations. Experiences of the need for and co-presence of various kinds of skills in software creation in the construction of IoT applications are discussed.

INTRODUCTION

It is now evident that computing environments are experiencing a significant disturbance. The significance of personal computers, mobile Computing is shrinking, and internet computing has evolved. Software as a Service (SaaS) and apps have been standardized. It brings us linked nodes (devices) that are an essential component of the realm of physicality. Advancements in hardware production and development the availability of integrated, efficient, but very inexpensive Chips would make it easier to combine networking and total connectivity digital computers and runtimes for complex languages practically everywhere. As a result, daily stuff in our world may become interconnected and programmable. The effect of this invasion of the Programmable Universe would be almost as critical as the revolution of smartphone devices, which was activated when similar technical advancements rendered it possible, Tuli et al. (2016). In this article, we concentrate on our IoT device impressions. The evolution from both technical and educational perspectives: what competencies must be learned and perfected by app developers as they start their journey into the IoT and application framework.

These impressions are focused on a continuum of IoT experiences. We have carried out efforts in product creation in the Nokia and Mozilla over the last four years Dastjerdi et al.(2016). Including applications for smartphone use. Furthermore, considering the critically essential IoT networks have a distributed structure, explicit knowledge of the A central obstacle in spreading distributed networks is necessary. In the quicker periods of deployment typical of Today, additional problems arise from cloud-based computing structures and even difficulty. A variety of IoT utilities, such as tools for Computing, storage, cloud storage, delivers attributes such as fast computational capacity, heterogeneity, and others that have ushered in a technical revolution. The cloud offers the virtualization of tools for computation at varying speeds.

Cloud networking, however, has Disadvantages in respect to high delays that have a detrimental impact on tasks on the IoT that need an answer in real-time. In 2012, Cisco's infrastructure was Fog computation, which is a recent computing phenomenon, is a paradigm named. To overcome cloud infrastructure limitations, three networking stages, fog computing is applicable, Mirjana (2017):

(1) the Data collection from machines on the periphery (sensors, cars, Roadways, and ships).
(2) Several network-connected devices and the sending of all the information.
(3) The data gathered from the devices must be analyzed and the decision in less than a second, Thota (2018).

Background

Fog computing changes cloud capabilities near to the end consumer, including storage, Computing, and connectivity edge computers, which render mobility simpler and better; privacy, protection, low latency, and bandwidth of the network, such as Fog computation, will balance real-time computing user demands, Kumari et al. (2018). Fog-computing infrastructure contains nodes called fog nodes, networks for edge applications, and Linked to these virtualized data centers or IoT computers or nodes. This is linked to the cloud to be deployed to Big data facilities. In low latency systems, and performs best.

Healthcare Care applications include vast amounts of data needing preservation Instead of relying on the available computational power in the cloud and computers for storage. The result data of healthcare apps is significant. A vast number of healthcare diagnoses, data is produced, must be analyzed, and extracted promptly and through Perfect Path. In E-Health, streaming-based broadcasts Considering the real-time criteria, implementations can be addressed. Fog computing is for modeling healthcare software.

The best approach to focus on was considered since Computing with Fog adds significantly to healthcare Applications to serve aged persons by home nursing, Xavi et al.(2016). One fog node or multiple related computing nodes linked fog computing nodes may significantly increase the Scalability, redundancy, even elasticity, and where it requires some computing. Different fog nodes may be installed. The above-stated features adhere to the healthcare technology criteria. Fog computing can be relied upon as it is due to its improvement. It better serves multiple healthcare applications Standard of operation, minimum reply period, low latency, position.

IoT END-TO-END FRAMEWORK

The Internet of Things is all about spinning actual artifacts into computer data goods, and daily services and services have historically offered fresh value and information stuff, which are lifeless. Effectively, this suggests taking until devices that are not wired, linking them to the Internet, and implementing a backend infrastructure and online and smartphone Software to view, assess, and handle all items to add fresh relevance comfort. An informal formula, in brief, the following may be provided for IoT device development, Xavi et al. (2018):

Stuff X + Internet + Provider + Applications = Thing X Smart

Typically, IoT structures consist of devices, gateways, apps, and clouds. Modules are components of hardware's physical features that capture sensor data, and actions may be done. There is a range of significant cloud positions, including Controlling computers, data collection, saving and accessing data, Data analytics, and system actuation in real-time and offline. Applications vary from a detailed simulation of web-based data to dashboards for network and smartphone applications that are incredibly domain-specific. On the surface, IoT systems software creation does. It does not vary much from any other design method as engineers focus on their first development of the IoT.

They usually target a basic framework that consists of a project. Maybe an Arduino from a single computer or board Tessel, or another variant of Tessel, a Raspberry Pi. A comparatively homogeneous mixture of such devices. It illustrates some of the IoT production chips and boards of Today. When working with appliances or with a handful of IoT, production does not stand substantially for smartphones at most Atlam et al. (2018).

In comparison to conventional embedded or smartphone development tools, dynamic cloud and multiple portal solutions, backends from analytics, the production of IoT systems at that stage is quite far from traditional web and smartphone applications. Only the creator typically involves via a single mobile device or with a single browser or screen. Most challenges emerge from the device's distributed structure and its sporadic, theoretically intermittent nature, long latencies, and unreliable communication in IoT growth. The theoretically unexpected, incredibly complex existence of the, also, the, if thousands of computers are spread globally, it is essential to upgrade them in unison. Let us first peek at certain obstacles before jumping into them Azam et al. (2016). In the E2E architecture, in each of the primary four regions, Starting with Computers (1) and advancing to (2) Gateways, (3) Apps, and (4) Cloud. Unlike several IoT posts focusing on information technology and protocols, this chapter focuses mainly on information technology and techniques in software creation. An IoT Devices Software Technology. In the traditional end-to-end, the first, leftmost part of real-time service is powered by low-end IoT devices systems with no system of service at all. Complex software is not widely needed for quality sensors of piles. Programming language for growth C or C++ is for low-end applications, but the assembly language may still be included in specific areas Kraemer et al.(2017).

The supply of affordable hardware for inventory pushes the industry towards IoT devices that are overly competent. There is no need for dynamic programming, basic IoT units, help, or third-party support for technology creation in the appliances themselves. Just the app upgrades, essentially, are given the increasingly growing hardware, however low price point capabilities, dynamic programming capabilities even though they are becoming increasingly viable and famous, in computers with a low-end. The standard Raspberry Pi, for example, boards can offer help for A complete operating environment compliant with Linux at a very affordable cost from rates. Purchasing can also be faster and more convenient for all but those solutions for IoT devices in which the smallest potential size and smallest possible size demands complete focus. Likely, power usage can be offered by stock hardware, The shortest way to achievement. For program stacks, there are several standard levels of Apps with IoT. There are several levels of stacks of Software. Based on the planned programming capabilities for IoT devices, the next step up is instruments like the Raspberry Pi that is strong enough to operate, Zahmatkesh et al.(2020).

The desire to operate a Linux-based operating system, such as the minimum RAM specifications of a system, is bumped from Platforms with high-end wearable systems, including software Stacks close to new smartphone apps. Node.js. IoT devices focused on (https://nodejs.org) are now gradually becoming common. For, e.g., the Tessel 2. Substantially the most crucial discovery here the creation of IoT devices brings back the need for the creative skills of integrated, limited memory software. This is a significant development for 10-15 years have passed by. Many universities have cut down in Europe.

A Recent Progression Survey results from Economics affirm production and demand emphasis on computer capabilities at higher levels.

IoT Gateways Software Innovations Tools for the gateway have a crucial position in Today's IoT applications. The primary function of gateways, the bridge of communication between IoT devices, is to act as and the cloud, empowering IoT devices as an intermediary. Thus, for cloud access, a gateway solution is needed. As well as managing cloud access and uploading results, Gateways can carry out data preprocessing and run Algorithms for analytics to root out and preselect the most important until data is posted data and can also produce updates. When data values surpass those ranges that have been predefined, generally, as gateways usually provide more power and processing power, tools other than IoT computers, more intensive computing features must be carried out. The gateway technologies of Today can be separated narrowly into two different solutions.

Categories that are focused on IoT device use.

(1) IoT solutions that are consumer-oriented usually use smartphones, such as gateways. IoT solutions that are tailored for customers the customer's mobile are also seen as the portal solution. Smartwatches or athletic watches, for example, are typically Balanced with the mobile of the consumer, using the smartphone.

(2) Generally, professional IoT solutions use dedicated solutions tools for gateways. IoT solutions that are skilled appear to have Specific specifications that include unique solutions for gateways. From the discussion mentioned above, as can be calculated, the software technology needed for the production spectrum of gateways from smartphone production to developing an embedded device.

Computational specifications for gateways are heavily contingent on computational requirements. Gateways are used for gathering and collection Transmission of information to the cloud or what gateways are awaited critical Computing, e.g., by running complicated computations, libraries, and algorithms for analytics. In the last decade, it has grown considerably. Computing through the cloud during the Internet in the late 1990s became a hot place. Apart from the online servers and applications for databases, nearly all the Software production had to be performed from scratch. In comparison, the use of public cloud facilities, such as (https://aws.amazon.com/), Amazon Web Services (AWS), IBM Cloud, was created by Microsoft Azure (https://azure.microsoft.com/).

The main elements of a standard IoT backend cloud solution are presented, which is focused on some of our Projects for industrial IoT production. Nowadays, virtually half of them the areas of the components can be built from open access systems. In setting up, for example, developers usually use HAProxy on the defense perimeter, NGINX data. For Apache, Kafka is a data acquisition that is a common approach.

Because of open-source availability and maturity, through such progress, the Code that the creators themselves have written shapes the code "The "peak of the iceberg" alone, while the rest of the structure comes from technology developed by third parties that are open source. Instead of building from the available IoT cloud solution, it is also possible to provide an open-source or commercial element. As a service, rent the whole IoT backend. IoTs are common. e.g., Amazon AWS IoT cloud services Nokia effect IoT Portal can be used with a monthly charge for linking IoT computers. There are IoT cloud services that may set up "white label" IoT cloud service providers. IoT clouds and run certain clouds on IoT Apps Software Technology In the popular E2E IoT method, the fourth core element is clients. The Software, or Apps for short, is architecture via Software. We apply to the Software used to visualize the data obtained by IoT devices and the control and management of monitoring the machines. It is possible to break these apps broadly into three categories: smartphone, web, and computer applications. Cellular since the internet browser has essentially been the End-User device execution environment on personal computers, the development of conventional PC applications has, in recent years, has been on the wane. Therefore, it is just the first two software types are smartphone applications and web apps. That counts these days, as most activities take place on Today, personal computers use the Internet to operate Instead of conventional configured web software, the browser.

Consequently, the IoT technology growth environment is controlled primarily via distinct mobile ecosystems. The toolchains for Android and IOS and mainstream frameworks include React.js or Angular for web creation. The prevailing technology for app creation is needed in the end-to-end IoT for each of the four design areas.

IOT IN HEALTHCARE

Based on the findings provided in the preceding portion, IoT production needs an extensive range of implementation projects to construct a complete E2E scheme. Most of these places would give staff with qualifications. Currently, most of the creators of apps have been educated to do either smartphone or web creation. All these developers seem to believe their talents are for IoT growth. This will be explicitly relevant. Furthermore, As IoT systems have several features, this is not accurate, which does not extend at all to smartphone apps or online apps. In addition to the embedded design of gateways and IoT devices, the general E2E framework's distributed design focuses on the E2E system specifications. We can peek at the following subsections in some fields beyond and above the planned subjects. A. Computing distributes IoT creators need to consider some unfamiliar considerations. Many creators of smartphone and client-side web apps keep in mind these concerns: Heterogeneity of devices and their diversity; Intermittent connectivity, possibly unreliable; The extremely complex, dispersed, and theoretically migratory Software's nature; Computations based on observed sensor readings are activated (and retriggered) and ultimately contribute to several actionable events. The systems are asynchronous and circulated in tandem.

In the 1990s, Sun Microsystems wrote down a description of Invariably, the conclusions programmers create while Writing tools for distributed networks and frameworks for the first time:

1) It is reliable to network.
2) There is zero latency.
3) Bandwidth is boundless.

4) It is safe to network.
5) It Doesn't change the topology.
6) One administrator is there.
7) The expense of transport is negligible.
8) Homogeneous is the network.

Such hypotheses commonly lead (1) to the failure of the scheme to act as expected, (2) a significant reduction Scope of the method, and (3) major unplanned expenditures. It was essential to overhaul the structure to fulfill its original objectives by implementing technologies in the E2E architecture for each region. Famous examples include, e.g., written applications. According to some research, verification and confirmation operations and Checks constitute up to 75 percent of technology's overall production cost. As a consequence of the requisite additional Code, An order to brace for the fallacies of distributed computation, The applications' actual reasoning is hidden under a tonne of "boilerplate" Code, rendering systems even more challenging to comprehend And upkeep. There are no good options except for educating IoT developers about the fallacies in this field, Breaks, and drawbacks related to distributed computation.

DEPLOYMENT PROCEDURES

Compared with conventional computing systems, IoT programs may be made up of tens or even hundreds of thousands of people, Computing Units Going. The vast amount of the IoT appliances and their dynamic topologies, connections, and partnerships various networking processes raise fascinating problems for creating apps, e.g., finding it impossible to execute data format or API changes in a synchronized manner.

In order not to disturb the whole system's conduct (e.g., A factory or greenhouse processes monitoring sensor system), Security upgrade deployments will have to be tiered and then postponed and coordinated, such as upgrading apparel, do not occur until it is understood that all the impacted devices the updates have been issued and analyzed. Often, it needs to be bear in mind that certain systems can have sporadic communication. Therefore, for prolonged and could be unreachable or offline duration periods, certain systems cannot access alerts before a lot longer. Those forms of conditions face problems not for software creation only but also for device activities. Innovative Software further complicates IoT Approaches' production to growth and conclusions that depend on rapid cycles of deployment and tiny increments that are continuously Built to use. Continuous technologies for distribution and implementation. The methodologies and DevOps redefined the planned software device actions, resulting in updates. This could theoretically happen many times a day. What sort of a solution is focused on an automatic pipeline originating from a pipeline. The world for creation where programmers render adjustments, culminating with the latest system's public deployment, with everything that was immediately checked along the way. The different one's compilation, integration, checking, steps of this pipeline include staging, deployment (possibly to a significant volume of computing machines operating independently), and eventually activities, Dubey et al. (2015). This manner of functioning is well known Today in the web-based Internet Resources background. Nonetheless, the absolute it can be challenging and harder to implement advanced IoT programs. Related to process automation applications' problems, those difficulties present in traditional PCs are Software deployment or mobile. Other important new developments and predictions while our attention is on the Software created in this article, technologies, and the overall design of the IoT framework, and we wish to illustrate significant developments in communication in a fast way technology that is going to have a huge effect on the overall software infrastructure and the IoT framework. Radio technology for cellular IoT would reduce the need for around gateways. In certain cases, gateways' nature in It is possible to consider IoT devices as an annoyance. IoT computers, preferably, are all meant to work everywhere, and out-of-the-box without IoT structures have traditionally been rather cloud-centric. For the bulk of computations locally taking place, this will lift technology's significance for mesh networking that unlocks IoT Apps for conducting acts and peer-to-peer processing Fashion for very short latencies (P2P). The emergence together Anticipates that LPWAN and mesh networking technologies will significantly change the topologies and overall design in IoT structures. Isomorphic architectures for the IoT framework will appear. Earlier stuff We also argued in this paper that the creation of apps needed technologies for various IoT systems is quite separate. Nevertheless, given the increasingly rising We foresee IoT computer processing and retrieval resources, IoT systems would be able to do so over the next 5-10 years. Host stacks of applications that are substantially more capable. Eventually, this can lead us to isomorphic architectures of IoT systems and operate devices, gateways, and the cloud, Enabling flexible transfer of the same apps and resources code between any variable inside the overall framework. Isomorphic designs can be used in the "holy grail" developing the IoT. Rather than studying different items, incompatible product creation processes in an isomorphic one-based technology design will suffice. They will be capable of including all facets of the production of E2E. At this point, it is still It is impossible to determine the innovations are going to "rule all of them," so talk. Architectures focused on containers like Docker (HTTPS:/www.docker.com/) or (https://coreos.com/rkt/) from CoreOS at this point, even though their memories seem like fair guesses, and the criteria for computational capacity can appear exorbitant from the experience of the IoT systems of Today. Greengrass Amazon's framework also points out (https://aws.amazon.com/greengrass/) to a paradigm in which technologies for production would be used in the cloud and IoT systems; in Greengrass, the tool for programming is Amazon's Lambda, Duey et al. (2017). Calculations will be made possible by isomorphic systems to be transferred and performed dynamically in those Components that offer optimum performance, storage, network speed, latency, and characteristics of energy efficiency, so enabling optimization of the overall behavior of the IoT system based on a "soup" of various computational elements available, diverse in the end-to-end system overall. In this situation, the system consists of smart gateways, IoT sensors, and efficient ones. Besides ECG signals, body signals, sensors collect the temperature and respiration rate and send them privacy and safety as critical. A fog-based healthcare component of healthcare applications. The framework Dastjerdi et al. (2017) was suggested, adding a layer of fog between the two cloud and end devices act as an intermediary layer. Confidentiality and anonymity usage of a security broker for Cloud Access Increased Security (CASB) at the network's edge. The system was introduced by using a modular method. Data from several sources have merged the structure, and sufficient references should be backed up by cryptographic evaluation and the system. Latency-sensitive healthcare data may affect the efficiency of healthcare applications. a mist-like fluid data for healthcare Naha et al. (2018) is a solution for working with latency-sensitive computing platforms. The detection of important trends was achieved by illustrations, which were then sent to the cloud. The Director of School for Power Fog, the purpose of this device is to process large volumes of data with minimal data resources. A smart e-health gateway was launched. As a method for supporting healthcare IoT programs and the availability of data collection, data interpretation, and real-time services, fog computing may be used where local storage is available. The e-health smart gateways are scattered and geographically located at every gateway's duty. The role involves handling a series of IoT devices that are directly linked to the patient. The machine is capable of tracking patients individually, regardless of their movement. The fog-based scheme's capacity, mobility, and reliability Issues should be settled easily. Those patients' diagnosis The Chikungunya virus (CHV) was first proposed in the 1960s. Fog-based healthcare infrastructure The proposal is split into three sections. For wearable IoT, the key layers are sensors, fog, and the cloud layer. The device is used to classify and monitor the CHV virus. The compromised patients' diagnoses were made utilizing Fuzzy-C (FCM) Warnings and evolving ones. Data for time-sensitive healthcare applications was proposed in the case of brain strokes and heart attacks. Fog computing was used to alert consumers as quickly as possible. Fog computation lowers the time it takes for these programs to operate. The network's usage and the cost of electricity use. A Cloud of Computation For chronic Computing, a distributed computational approach was suggested. Romanian healthcare laws regulate individuals with obstructive pulmonary disease (COPD) and obstructive pulmonary disease (COPD) Mild dementia. The control device is used to guarantee that the protocol is observed. Fog computing limits the volume of data that is transmitted and retrieved. Patients' data is secured. Fog computing is conducted close to end-users for large-scale distribution. There are both systems and customers who are globally dispersed. Apps, real-time connectivity, accessibility assistance, and interoperability, to name a couple. The interplay of preprocessing and variability is valued about the Internet. Fog computation has the potential to cope with several circumstances. Fog computing is a form of cloud computing that is distinct from conventional healthcare solutions. IoT networks; a fog-assisted system's design can potentially handle many healthcare networks, such as Scalability, can handle issues. As seen in the illustration, consciousness, mobility, and energy reliability are all essential considerations. Constraints, given the various advantages of utilizing common services, often have many major pitfalls in healthcare applications. Preprocessing is a costly operation as time and resources are commonly used to characterize the method. A substantial delay in the supply of customer services.

Data analytics may be fully outsourced to the network's edge. Therefore, precision and adaptability have degraded. The loss of computing power at the border is attributed to various reasons nodes, to be exact. Given the advantages of utilizing cloud-based and cloud-based applications, there are several pitfalls. Fog-based architectures have minimal usefulness due to architectural design restrictions—the net profits from all data's easy delivery. On the verge of multiple competitive programs are too much for a computer to accommodate. Owing to a shortage of commodities, resource contention occurs. Then there is additional processing latency [30]. It is fog-based middleware. There will be a slew of problems in cloud healthcare. The services are as follows: The fog layer necessitates continuing management—significant sensory data quantities in a limited amount of time and necessary response in several cases. This is particularly valid in the case of crucial incidents. The Fog Node is a location where there is a lot of fog.

Consequently, the fog nodes have a fixed power limit. Preparation for the resources may be delayed for specific projects, especially for particular assignments for fog nodes with minimal capital failure is an actual probability. The blend has been scaled with a fog device. In healthcare, Computing is used in IoT programs. The papers that were related were ordered and described in the taxonomy. This analysis is mainly concerned with employment-targeting approaches and strategies. In healthcare, fog computing is used in several projects, including infrastructure. This makes use of the mutual capital. Fog computing is defined in this post. Apps for healthcare that understand success assessments, motives, and other variables the obstacles, concerns, and potential directions are addressed.

ASSESSMENT OF RESULTS

The research's main goal was fulfilled; the goal was to survey the integration of "Internet of Things" and "Artificial Intelligence Techniques" in the detection of plant diseases. To measure the allocation of various services, In healthcare, fog/edge computing execution methods the most critical success measurement requirements for IoT applications. The following are some of the more essential methods utilized in the experiments involved in this. Examining the literature assessing resource sharing feasibility, low latency, real-time, and other considerations are considered. Processing, reaction time, and a judgment reached in less than the second Scalability, versatility, automated rollout, and dynamic setup are only a couple of available functionalities. Battery existence, network traffic, speed, and energy use are all things to remember. To preserve data privacy and reduce data volume, data is distributed one at a time, establishing a modern computational model known as "Fireworks." The goal was to make data exchange simpler, although, via fog, data protection and stakeholder dignity are maintained.

Computing is a concept used to define low latency, distributed Computing, and improved Scalability. Fault tolerance increased security, and privacy are all benefits. This function may help health-related applications. Because of their need for better efficiency and real-time processing, Mobility and meaning perception are allowed, Byers et al.(2017). Fog Computing in a significant way reduces data transfer latency, reaction time, and end-to-end time. In terms of time-sensitive data, execution time and resources, Consumption costs, and network utilization. A real-time follow-up A device that reduces the system's demand was introduced infrastructure for data transfer exchange. In a comparable scenario, the concentrate was on processing monitoring and management in the background—data in healthcare applications and its preservation and distribution. A high-level management framework was proposed in the High-Level management system. To allow effective use of the physical sensing capabilities that have been deployed equipment. Facilities are available for improved computer protection and healthcare trustworthiness. The device was illustrated. Cost-effective computing solutions the new generation of edge devices was established in the vicinity of sent-in situation distributed data-intensive processing including location-aware data and measurement positioning, duplication, and the word "recovery" were included.

The answer timeline accelerated, which cuts down on resource waste. According to an analysis, the emergency assistance response time for heart attack patients has been strengthened in-vehicle networks in an earlier period, resulting in more significant results. Heart problems may be avoided from causing car crashes. The key aim is to enhance communication protection while lowering costs—medical sensors' resource-constrained load. A previous study aimed to quantify heterogeneous Edge systems to gather data and have a minimum of resources work latency is a concept used to characterize the period it takes for a machine to the roaming of data and the offloading of data the usage of migration in the exploitation of healthcare data and remote connectivity is feasible. In the previously described work, diagnostic products assist in facilitating IoT domain context amalgamation of heterogeneous domain data and streamlined data distribution between multiple officers. The mission at hand End-user authentication and authorization is shown, as previously reported.

It offered storage as well as data mining. The mission at hand in a previous study the evidence provided helped decision-making and data analysis. Information merging and trending assist in network reduction by decreasing data submitted to the cloud and the amount of traffic and bandwidth utilized. Effortless health data aggregation and privacy security It addressed the protection of health profiles. The research aimed at achieving high-quality, adequate network bandwidth. Minimum generation reaction period and operation Real-time update. The main aim was to reduce the volume of waste.

CHALLENGES OF IOT IN HEALTH CARE

Fog and edge computing have become more prevalent in recent years. With healthcare applications to fix central processing problems in cloud computing, there are numerous positives of healthcare IoT services for fog computation, but there are also several disadvantages. Controlling capital has its drawbacks and obstacles. Among Mutual money is a significant feature that affects production. With the fog computation application, to hold the parameters in check, the fog computing infrastructure may be used in healthcare IoT networks. Be dealt with correctly the issues and problems around mutual assistance the next segment in this section addresses infrastructure. The issues that have been uncovered in the usage of money, Device-related units, provisioning, elasticity, or tools. It developed the words "pooling" and "sharing."

Similarly, necessary processing was shown to be processed in previous research. To handle a complex mission, fog computing resources. Repositioning, on the other hand, triggers technical concerns. In the plant's field, there are computer facilities. It may also create problems if not treated properly.

On the other hand, Edge computing requires researchers' resolution uncovered technical challenges in previous research ventures. As previously noted, research must become pervasive. Inefficient data mobility is a hindrance, rendering it unsuitable for many uses. Tools for dispersed-data-intensive environments can be implemented and managed located in various locations. The challenge of installing medical sensors heightens the proportions and the reaction's weight: time and financial mismanagement. Sensitivity, latency, and geographic variations are all variables to remember. There has been a debate on awareness. DDoS vulnerability risks that block sessions the resumption's emphasis was on end-to-end healthcare security. Medical energy equipment, tiny ROM, RAM, and processor Sensors used in healthcare applications also enhanced their overall performance. Connectivity by using currently installed gadgets on the computer web technology is still a problem.

DISCUSSION AND FUTURE WORK

Several lessons on fog computation were given. Without question, fog computing reduced latency about fog computing—Cloud Infrastructure in IoT applications for healthcare. Researchers show that the many benefits of simulation and experimental amounts are distributed production, protection, defense, Scalability, for instance, tolerance for errors, and low latency. Such incentives are advantageous for vital indications, including substantial patient management programs, reliability, versatility, knowledge of meaning, and real-time processing. The next critical one is the Internet of Things (IoT). A phase in the Internet's development. In the end, it will lead to the creation of a programmable environment in which even the most accessible and most commonplace items are linked to and can be regulated by the Internet and remotely programmed. Canali and Lancellotti (2019a) implemented a structured model for the issue of data source representation through fog nodes. Mostly on fog nodes, the suggested optimization issue considers both contact latency and process time. Also, we recommend a versatile heuristic focused on genetic algorithms for solving the dilemma.

Canali and Lancellotti (2019b) propose a fog computing-based approach to solve the concerns of a conventional good city situation, in which sensors or intelligent devices dispersed around a regional region generate a vast volume of data. They found out that traditional cloud architecture will converge all flow of data. Various technologies, such as intelligent transportation, smart grid, and smart cities, are explored in Rani and Ahmed(2019) to show that hierarchical clustering computing-based IoT can efficiently serve practical applications. The hierarchical clustering-based technique is used in the suggested model, and frame Relay Nodes are enhanced to choose the most favored sensor node (SN) among cluster nodes. Several technologies like Autonomic Computing Singh and Kumar(2016), Machine Learning Singh et al. (2020,2021), Genetic Programming Bhardwaj et al. (2011,2016,2020,2013), etc. can be integrated with fog computing and IoT for applications in healthcare. This will not only help to speed up the tasks but also improve the performance of existing systems.

CONCLUSIONS

The main goal of the research was fulfilled; the goal was to survey "Internet of Things" and "Fog Computing" in the domain of "health care."

- Accordingly, in summary, the development of end-to-end in its current form, perhaps the most complex Software is IoT systems evolution. Fog computing is one of the significant studies. Through serious examination and investigation of various review articles, for example, a high volume of essential data was obtained.
- The problems, challenges, difficulties, motivation, and benefits were identified for future fog computing work in healthcare applications. We have identified concerns in this study; difficulties, challenges, and suggestions were made to identify current and potential resource problems and challenges healthcare IoT systems leadership can overcome by Computing offloading, load balancing, and adopting the three primary variables.

Therefore, research studies motivate researchers to Propose (or develop) and use the healthcare fog computing framework systems for IoT.

REFERENCES

Aazam, M., Zeadally, S., & Harras, K. A. (2018). Offloading in fog computing for IoT: Review, enabling technologies, and research opportunities. *Future Generation Computer Systems*, *87*, 278–289. doi:10.1016/j.future.2018.04.057

Acharya, D., Goel, S., Asthana, R., & Bhardwaj, A. (2020). A novel fitness function in genetic programming to handle unbalanced emotion recognition data. *Pattern Recognition Letters*, *133*, 272–279. doi:10.1016/j.patrec.2020.03.005

Atlam, H. F., Walters, R. J., & Wills, G. B. (2018). Fog computing and the Internet of things: A review. Big data and cognitive. *Computing*, *2*(2), 10.

Bhardwaj, A., & Tiwari, A. (2013, July). A novel genetic programming-based classifier design using a new constructive crossover operator with a local search technique. In *International Conference on Intelligent Computing* (pp. 86-95). Springer. 10.1007/978-3-642-39479-9_11

Bhardwaj, A., & Tiwari, A. (2013, July). Performance improvement in genetic programming using modified crossover and node mutation. In *Proceedings of the 15th annual conference companion on Genetic and evolutionary computation* (pp. 1721-1722). 10.1145/2464576.2480787

Bhardwaj, A., Tiwari, A., Bhardwaj, H., & Bhardwaj, A. (2016). A genetically optimized neural network model for multiclass classification. *Expert Systems with Applications*, *60*, 211–221. doi:10.1016/j.eswa.2016.04.036

Bhardwaj, A., Tiwari, A., Varma, M. V., & Krishna, M. R. (2014, July). Classification of EEG signals using a novel genetic programming approach. In *Proceedings of the Companion Publication of the 2014 Annual Conference on Genetic and Evolutionary Computation* (pp. 1297-1304). 10.1145/2598394.2609851

Bhardwaj, H., Tomar, P., Sakalle, A., & Sharma, U. (2021). Artificial Intelligence and Its Applications in Agriculture With the Future of Smart Agriculture Techniques. In Artificial Intelligence and IoT-Based Technologies for Sustainable Farming and Smart Agriculture (pp. 25-39). IGI Global.

Byers, C. C. (2017). Architectural imperatives for fog computing: Use cases, requirements, and architectural techniques for fog-enabled not networks. *IEEE Communications Magazine*, *55*(8), 14–20. doi:10.1109/MCOM.2017.1600885

Canali, C., & Lancellotti, R. (2019). GASP: Genetic algorithms for service placement in fog computing systems. *Algorithms*, *12*(10), 201. doi:10.3390/a12100201

Canali, C., & Lancellotti, R. (2019, May). A Fog Computing Service Placement for Smart Cities based on Genetic Algorithms. In CLOSER (pp. 81-89). doi:10.5220/0007699400810089

Dastjerdi, A. V., & Buyya, R. (2016). Fog computing: Helping the Internet of Things realize its potential. *Computer*, *49*(8), 112–116. doi:10.1109/MC.2016.245

Dastjerdi, A. V., Gupta, H., Calheiros, R. N., Ghosh, S. K., & Buyya, R. (2016). Fog computing: Principles, architectures, and applications. In Internet of things (pp. 61-75). Academic Press.

Dubey, H., Monteiro, A., Constant, N., Abtahi, M., Borthakur, D., Mahler, L., & Mankodiya, K. (2017). Fog computing in medical internet-of-things: architecture, implementation, and applications. In *Handbook of Large-Scale Distributed Computing in Smart Healthcare* (pp. 281–321). Springer. doi:10.1007/978-3-319-58280-1_11

Dubey, H., Yang, J., Constant, N., Amiri, A. M., Yang, Q., & Makodiya, K. (2015). Fog data: Enhancing big telehealth data through fog computing. In *Proceedings of the ASE bigdata & social informatics 2015* (pp. 1-6). Academic Press.

Kraemer, F. A., Braten, A. E., Tamkittikhun, N., & Palma, D. (2017). Fog computing in healthcare–a review and discussion. *IEEE Access: Practical Innovations, Open Solutions, 5,* 9206–9222. doi:10.1109/ACCESS.2017.2704100

Kumari, A., Tanwar, S., Tyagi, S., & Kumar, N. (2018). Fog computing for Healthcare 4.0 environment: Opportunities and challenges. *Computers & Electrical Engineering, 72,* 1–13. doi:10.1016/j.compeleceng.2018.08.015

Maksimović, M. (2017). Implementation of Fog computing in IoT-based healthcare system. *Jita-Journal Of Information Technology And Applications, 14*(2).

Masip-Bruin, X., Marín-Tordera, E., Alonso, A., & Garcia, J. (2016, June). Fog-to-cloud Computing (F2C): The key technology enabler for dependable e-health services deployment. In *2016 Mediterranean ad hoc networking workshop (Med-Hoc-Net)* (pp. 1-5). IEEE.

Masip-Bruin, X., Marín-Tordera, E., Tashakor, G., Jukan, A., & Ren, G. J. (2016). Foggy clouds and cloudy fogs: A real need for coordinated management of fog-to-cloud computing systems. *IEEE Wireless Communications, 23*(5), 120–128. doi:10.1109/MWC.2016.7721750

Naha, R. K., Garg, S., Georgakopoulos, D., Jayaraman, P. P., Gao, L., Xiang, Y., & Ranjan, R. (2018). Fog computing: Survey of trends, architectures, requirements, and research directions. *IEEE Access: Practical Innovations, Open Solutions, 6,* 47980–48009. doi:10.1109/ACCESS.2018.2866491

Purohit, A., Bhardwaj, A., Tiwari, A., & Choudhari, N. S. (2011, June). Removing Code bloating in crossover operation in genetic programming. In *2011 International Conference on Recent Trends in Information Technology (ICRTIT)* (pp. 1126-1130). IEEE. 10.1109/ICRTIT.2011.5972430

Rani, S., Ahmed, S. H., & Rastogi, R. (2019). Dynamic clustering approach based on wireless sensor networks genetic algorithm for IoT applications. *Wireless Networks,* 1–10.

Sakalle, A., Tomar, P., Bhardwaj, H., & Sharma, U. (2021). Impact and Latest Trends of Intelligent Learning With Artificial Intelligence. In Impact of AI Technologies on Teaching, Learning, and Research in Higher Education (pp. 172-189). IGI Global.

SinghT. (2020). A Survey on Intelligent Techniques for Disease Recognition in Agricultural Crops. Available at SSRN 3616700. doi:10.2139srn.3616700

Singh, T., & Kumar, A. (n.d.). Survey on Characteristics Of Autonomous System. *International Journal of Computer Science and Information Technologies, 8.*

Singh, T., Kumar, K., & Bedi, S. S. (2021). A Review on Artificial Intelligence Techniques for Disease Recognition in Plants. *IOP Conference Series. Materials Science and Engineering, 1022*(1), 012032. doi:10.1088/1757-899X/1022/1/012032

Thota, C., Sundarasekar, R., Manogaran, G., Varatharajan, R., & Priyan, M. K. (2018). We have a centralized fog computing security platform for IoT and cloud in the healthcare system. In *Fog computing: Breakthroughs in research and practice* (pp. 365–378). IGI Global. doi:10.4018/978-1-5225-5649-7.ch018

Tuli, S., Mahmud, R., Tuli, S., & Buyya, R. (2019). FogBus: A blockchain-based lightweight framework for edge and fog computing. *Journal*, 22-36.

Zahmatkesh, H., & Al-Turjman, F. (2020). Fog computing for sustainable smart cities in the IoT era: Caching techniques and enabling technologies-an overview. *Sustainable Cities and Society, 59*, 102139. doi:10.1016/j.scs.2020.102139

Zhang, P., Zhou, M., & Fortino, G. (2018). Security and trust issues in fog computing: A survey. *Future Generation Computer Systems, 88*, 16–27. doi:10.1016/j.future.2018.05.008

Chapter 2
Internet of Things and Its Relevance

Kirti Kangra
Guru Jambheshwar University of Science and Technology, India

Jaswinder Singh
Guru Jambheshwar University of Science and Technology, India

ABSTRACT

The internet of things (IoT) model connects physical devices to the virtual world and enables them to interact. It enables smart devices to communicate with other devices to exchange information. To link a wireless network or cloud network, it takes the help of several technologies such as radio frequency identification (RFID), wireless sensor network (WSN), near field communication (NFC), ZigBee, and others. The IoT requires a standard architecture and protocol stack to establish links between the devices. This chapter provides a brief introduction, pillars, the evolution, architecture, application of IoT, and issues related to IoT implementation in real life.

INTRODUCTION

According to Yasuura et al. (2017), the "Internet of Things" (IoT) is one of the most innovative technologies of the modern era. This technology connects our real-world to the virtual world using transducers and permits them to communicate, to exchange useful information. IoT sometimes also called the Internet of Objects, is an interconnection of Transducer that smartly collaborated with other devices. It is a device that transforms one form of energy into another. It is additionally used for changing some electrical phenomenon into an associate electrical impulse.

DOI: 10.4018/978-1-7998-6981-8.ch002

Transducers are broadly classified into sensors and actuators. The function of an actuator is that the inverse of a sensor. Sensors are used to take input from the outside world and the Actuator is used to convert the system's electric signals into physical entities. It transmits, the electrical key into the physical lash. There are, different kinds of actuators implicate in systems and alternative motor devices. The sensor is employed to collects data and transfers the information to the gateway unit of IoT. The analogous commands to the sensed input are distributed once more to an actuator to manage the system. According to Cisco, the number of IoT devices has increased to 50 Billion in 2020 and will increase 1 Trillion in 2022 which is enormously large when compared with the world's population as depicted in Figure 1 according to (Evans, D. (2011)). Every day, the number of Internet of Things (IoT) devices grows. The cause for the rise of IoT devices is that they make life easier for people and perform tasks more efficiently than humans. IoT has many advantages, but it also has some drawbacks, such as ineffective management, energy efficiency, identity management, protection, and privacy. The most important problems in the creation of IoT are security and privacy. All devices in the Internet of Things are linked to the Internet because they can't function without it. On the Internet, there are numerous attackers who steal the sensitive details of items (Burhan & Rehman, 2018).

Figure 1. Number of connected devices with respect to world's population

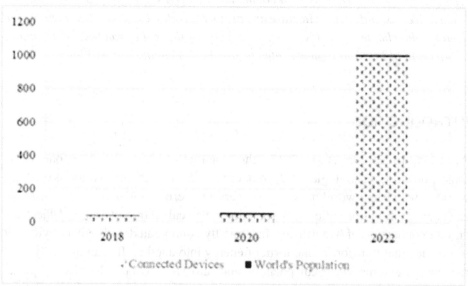

The main idea of (Madakam et al., 2015) behind IoT is to create a much better place for people to control the devices, without any physical intervention. Virtually everything becomes "smart" as a result of the Internet of Things, which uses the power of data collection, AI algorithms, and networks to enhance aspects of our lives. According to (Granjal et al., 2015), as sensor networks are an important part of an IoT system Table 1 shows the relationship between the sensor network and IoT.

Table 1. Relation between Sensor network and IoT (Granjal et al., 2015)

Sensor Network	IoT
Sensor is a type of Transducer that collects data.	Smart and Instrumented devices are connected to a wireless network to exchange data.
Senor plays an important role in building an IoT environment.	Smart objects that are connected to the internet are made from devices or objects.
Using sensors, data is collected.	Data are collected later and decisions are taken
Space, objects, and humans are especially monitored by sensors.	Here, everyday objects are made intelligent, warning of a mistake.

A human with a diabetes monitor implant, an animal with tracking devices, and so on are examples of things in the Internet of Things. Tessel 2, Eclipse IoT, PlatformIO, IBM Watson, Raspberry Pi, OpenSCADA, Node-RED, and Arduino, etc. are tools that can help in the development of an IoT device.

PILLARS OF INTERNET OF THINGS

There are four pillars of IoT as shown in Figure 2. By combining these four pillars like "Radiofrequency Identifier (RFID), Near Field Communication (NFC), Wireless Sensor Network (WSN), and Supervisory Control and Data Acquisition (SCADA)" are the latest adapted technologies that give a boost to the IoT. Now the IoT is growing more day by day and is assimilated into the future internet.

Machine-to-Machine (M2M) communication is a way of information transmission which includes more than one object and does not primarily require human involvement. Machine-to-Machine (M2M) is another term for "Machine-to-Machine communication (MTC)". M2M connects devices to a central server through a network connection, which infers the sensed events into useful information by (Verma et al., 2016).

Some key features of M2M communication system are given below:

Figure 2. Four pillars of IoT

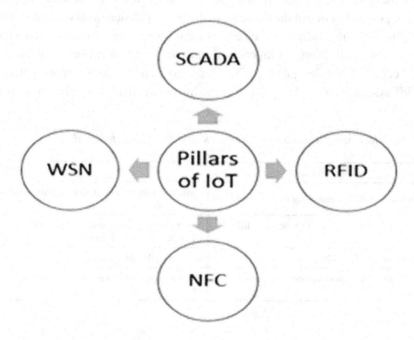

- **Limited Movement -** M2M devices are stationary, move infrequently, or only move within a small area.
- **Time Management -** Information is only sent or received at predetermined times.
- **Packet Switched -** With or without an MSISDN, a network operator may provide packet-switched service.
- **Monitoring -** This feature isn't meant to deter theft or vandalism, but rather to detect them.
- **Stumpy electricity Depletion -** To increase the system's ability to service M2M applications efficiently.
- **Location Specific Trigger -** Intentionally triggering an M2M system in a specific location, such as waking it up.

WSN entails spatially distributed independent sensors to observe physical or environmental circumstances according to (Rashid & Rehmani, 2016).
Some key features of WSN are mentioned below:

- Power usage limits for nodes that use batteries or extract electricity.
- Capacity to handle node failures (resilience)
- There is some node versatility (for highly mobile nodes see MWSNs)

- The nodes' heterogeneity.
- The nodes' homogeneity.
- Large-scale deployment scalability.

SCADA is also known as a smart system or CPS data, is a network-based system that links, tracks, and controls apparatus in a facility such as a plant or a house suggested by (Vanderzee et al., 2015). Some key features of SCADA:

- Handling of alarms
- Curves and Patterns of Trends
- Data Access and Retrieval
- Computer Processing and Networking

NFC allows wireless data transfer between two portable devices that are placed/work very near place. These days NFC is widely used in contactless payments(Lazaro et al., 2018). NFC has integrated security features like encryption that reduce the risk of snooping and other suspicious attacks. NFC tags will share data gradually even if they don't have power or an IoT link.

EVOLUTION OF INTERNET OF THINGS

The word "Internet of Things" was devised by "Kevin Ashton", the current "Executive Director of Auto-ID Labs", in 1999. It was the title of a presentation he gave at Procter & Gamble (where he was working at the time) on how P&G's supply chain could be linked to the Internet using RFID. By 2003-2004, major newspapers such as The Guardian and Scientific American were using the word IoT. During the same period, the US Department of Defence and Walmart both implemented RFID in their stores. According to 2005 report, the United Nations International Telecommunications Union recognized the influence of IoT. It was expected that the Internet of Things would assist in the development of a whole new complex network of networks. The first IoT conference was held in Zurich in March 2008. It brought together academic and industry researchers and practitioners to promote information sharing. The internet of things was named one of the six revolutionary civil technologies by the US National Intelligence Council in the same year information by (Techahead, 2021).

Cisco Internet Business Solutions Group (CIBSG) stated in 2011, a white paper that the internet of things was truly born between 2008 and 2009 when the number of things linked to the internet outnumbers the number of people who use it. According to the CIBSG, the ratio of objects to people increased from around 0.8 in 2003 to 1.84 in 2010 (Techahead,2021).

According to Jadiel (2015), there was no internet to communicate during the pre-internet stage. That time people interact with other people through short messaging or by telephone calls. As technology progresses, people start communicating using various types of protocols, like the World Wide Web (www). Here people start focusing on content or media files such as documents, video, and audio files. The next stage is more focused on providing services like selling products online. This phase is called Web 2.0. As the number of mobile devices increased, people start communicating using social media apps like Facebook, Twitter, Tumbler, YouTube, Hike, etc. But it is noticeable that communication is still between humans. As technology advances, people need to automate the services with the help of machines. Here machines automate without human intervention. This era is called the internet of things. A simplistic view of the evolution of IoT is depicted in Figure 3 (Jadoul, 2015).

Figure 3. Evolution of IoT

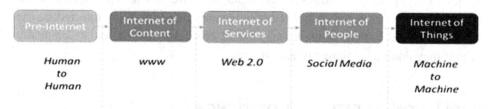

According to McKinsey, the economic impact of the Internet of Things (IoT) could range from USD 3.9 trillion to USD 11.2 trillion by 2025. Given how IoT is being used in engineering, healthcare, automotive, public safety, logistics, energy management, and organizational redesign, this does not seem to be a far-fetched estimate. IoT is used in a wide range of sectors and enterprises, and the COVID-19 pandemic has accelerated adoption because it holds the promise of allowing businesses to pivot in the new normal (Techahead, 2021).

IOT MARKET FROM GLOBAL AND INDIAN PERSPECTIVE

IoT has taken charge over the global market as well in the Indian market. **Table 2** shows growth of IoT in national as well as in the international market by (E. P. Yadav, 2018). From start to now IoT has changed the market scenario towards its devices.

Table 2. IoT Market from Global and Indian Perspective (Granjal et al., 2015)

IoT Global	IoT India
IoT has grown globally from 15.4 billion equipment to 30.7 trillion in 2020 to 75.4 billion equipment in 2015.	By 2020, the Indian IoT market is projected to increase by 15 billion dollars with 2.7 billion units from 5.6 billion dollars and 200 million connected units by 2025.
Over 2016,253 billion dollars are expected to be paid for global expenses on IoT products and services through initiatives, which will reach 16 percent of CAGR.	Throughout the period 2015 to 2020, the IoT market in Indian is expected to grow at a CAG by more than 28 percent.
In the next 20 years, IoT will increase global GDP by $ 10 to $ 15 trillion	The goal of the Indian government is to generate 15 billion dollars of IoT production in India by 2020.
In 2020, vehicles have improved globally by automated driving and IoT	Slowly reaching the top 5 industries such as electronics and telecommunications in India are generating revenue.

ARCHITECTURES OF INTERNET OF THINGS

There are billions of connection existed that communicate smartly using protocols. To make them communicate over the internet, it requires a novel reference architecture. Since old models/architecture doesn't support light packet format. So it becomes a big problem for the researchers and networking organizations. Several Architecture has been purposed and discussed below.

European FP7 scientific research project (2016) (European Commission, 2017), suggested a concrete design for IoT devices in the form of a Tree. Where roots of the tree depict smart devices and Leaves depict the core applications related to the business and healthcare sectors. By focusing on collaborative research, organizing national or European consortiums, developing research networks, and increasing individual researcher mobility, the FP7 program aimed to achieve these goals. The FP7 hoped to bring stability to the European research landscape in this way since, since the EU's establishment, this vital economic field has been fragmented, individualistic, and naturally non-cooperative among the Member States.

International Telecommunication Union (ITU) (2017) purposed a four-layer IoT architecture that encloses the Device layer where physical devices are connected/ sensing; Network layer that defines lightweight routing protocols for communication; Access layer and Application layer by (International Telecommunication Union - ITU, 2017).

The Internet of Things International Forum (IOT Forum) (2014) suggested by (Green, 2014), three-layer architecture comprised of the Application layer, Transportation layer, and Processors layer which is shown in Figure 4. Each layer acted independently.

Figure 4. Suggested IoT Architecture by IoT Forum
[Source: https://iotforum.org/]

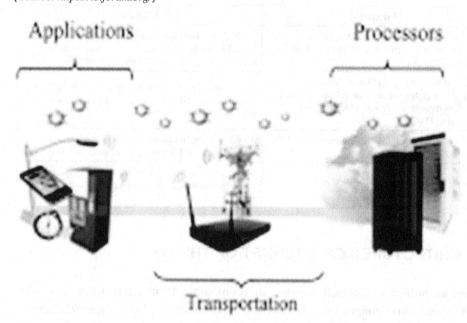

LAYERED ARCHITECTURE OF IOT

There is no universally agreed-upon architecture for IoT that the entire world and researchers will agree on. Researchers have suggested a wide variety of architectures. Some researchers believe that IoT architecture has three layers, while others advocate for a four-layer architecture.

3- LAYER ARCHITECTURE

3-layer architecture is a fundamental architecture that placates the IoT's core concept. It was proposed at the start of the Internet of Things' growth according to (Pei, L., Guinness et al., 2013; Bui et al., 2011; M. J. McGrath & C. N. Scanaill. (n.d.),2013). It is made up of three layers and the names are "Perception, Network, and Application layer".

- **Perception Layer** - Sensor layer is another name for it. It behaves similarly to a person's eyes, ears, and nose. It is in charge of identifying artifacts and collecting information from them. RFID, 2-D barcodes and sensors are just some of the types of sensors that can be connected to objects to collect data. Sensors are selected based on the applications' requirements. These sensors can collect data on position, changes in the air, the atmosphere, motion, and vibration, to name a few. They are mainly interested in those attackers who want to use their sensor with the original one according to (Burhan & Rehman, 2018).

- **Network Layer** - This layer is also known as the Transmission layer. It acts as a connection among the application and perception layers. It uses sensors to assemble and relay data from physical objects. The use of wireless or wired communication mediums is also an option. It has the authority to connecting smart objects, network devices, and networks. As a result, it is extremely vulnerable to attackers' attacks. It has serious security problems with the integrity and authentication of data being transmitted over the network according to (Burhan & Rehman, 2018).

- **Application Layer** - This layer identifies all IoT-enabled applications or those in which IoT has been implemented. Smart houses, smart cities, smart health, animal tracking, and other IoT applications are possible. It is responsible for delivering services to the applicants. Since services are dependent on information collected by sensors, services differ for each application. There are numerous problems in the application layer, with protection being the most important. When IoT is used to create a smart house, from both the inside and the outside, it faces a range of challenges and vulnerabilities according to (Burhan & Rehman, 2018).

4- LAYER ARCHITECTURE

The 3-layer architecture was the simplest one but it was unable to meet the criteria of IoT due to ongoing progress in the field. As a result, researchers suggested a four-layer architecture. Support Layer was added in architecture rest of the layers were the same.

- **Support Layer** - The protection in IoT architecture is the reason for adding a fourth layer. In a 3-layer architecture, a network layer is used to send data directly. The risk of receiving threats increases when data is sent directly to the network layer. A new layer is proposed as a result of defects in the three-layer design. Data is sent to a support layer in a four-layer architecture. A new layer is proposed as a result of defects in the three-layer design. Information from the perception layer is sent to the support layer in a four-layer architecture. The support layer is responsible for two things. It ensures that information is submitted by legitimate users and that it is safe from attacks. There are numerous methods for verifying users and records. Authentication is the most widely used form. Pre-shared secrets, keys, and passwords are used to execute them. The support layer's second duty is to transfer data to the network layer. Wireless and wired media can be used to relay data from the support layer to the network layer.

5- LAYER ARCHITECTURE

The 4-layer architecture was critical in the creation of the Internet of Things. In a four-layer architecture, there were also some problems with security and storage. To make the Internet of Things more stable, researchers suggested a five-layer architecture (Burhan & Rehman, 2018). Perception layer, Transport layer, and Application layer are the three layers, as in previous architectures. Two additional layers were added to this architecture. The processing layer and Business layer are the names of these added layers.

Processing Layer - "Middleware layer" is another name of this layer. It receives data from a transport layer and collects it. It processes data that it has gathered. It is responsible for eliminating irrelevant data and extracting the relevant data. It does, however, solve the issue of big data in IoT. A significant volume of data is received in big data. A huge quantity of data is acknowledged in big data, which can affect IoT efficiency suggested by (Burhan & Rehman, 2018).

Business Layer - It describes an application's expected actions and serves as a machine manager. It is in charge of managing and controlling IoT implementations, as well as market and benefit models. This layer is also in control of the user's privacy. It can also decide how knowledge can be produced, processed, and modified. This layer's weakness allows attackers to take advantage of an application by bypassing the business logic. The majority of security concerns emerge from vulnerabilities in an application triggered by a faulty or absent security control according to (Burhan & Rehman, 2018).

These architectures were introduced because of security aspects. The basic layered architecture was Three-layer architecture after four, five, and some enhanced architecture were also induced for the safety perspective.

PROTOCOLS OF IOT

As protocols are the set of rules. IoT communication protocols are forms of communication that shield and guarantee the information being shared between access points is as secure as possible.

Message Queue Telemetry Transport (MQTT) - Since it collects data from several electronic devices and allows for virtual network monitoring, it is a common protocol for IoT devices. It's a TCP-based subscribe/publish protocol that allows for event-driven messaging over wireless networks (Kellton tech,2020). MQTT is predominantly used in low-cost devices that need small electricity and storage. For example, smoke detectors, car sensors, smartwatches, and text-messaging apps. A subject may be published or subscribed to clients. The provider is responsible for making communication with the customer and arranging subscriptions as well as authenticating the client for security reasons. It's a simple protocol that's ideal for Internet of Things (IoT) projects suggested by (Sethi & Sarangi, 2017).

Constrained Application Protocol (CoAP) - It is a network device with limited access. The client can use this protocol to transmit its request to the server, and the server can reply to the client using HTTP. For a light-weight implementation and to save room, it employs UDP (User Datagram Protocol). The CoAP protocol is used by automation, mobile computers, and microcontrollers. The protocol requests application access points like home appliances and accepts an answer from the app's services and resources (Kellton tech, 2020). It uses the "EXI (Efficient XML Interchanges)" data format, which is a binary data format that saves a lot of space over "HTML/XML". Built-in header encoding, resource discovery, auto-setup, asynchronous message exchange, congestion management, and multicast message support are among the other features. Non-confirmable, confirmable, reset (nack), and acknowledgment are the four forms of messages in CoAP (Sethi & Sarangi, 2017).

Advanced Message Queuing Protocol (AMQP) - It is a software layer protocol for routing and queuing in a message-oriented middleware setting. It facilitates the seamless and safe sharing of data between connected devices and the cloud and is used for stable point-to-point connections. AMQP is made up of three different parts: Exchange, Message Queue, and Binding. To ensure a secure and efficient result, all three components function together. To ensure a reliable and effective message exchange and storage, all three elements function together. It also aids in the creation of a connection between two messages. This protocol is primarily used in the banking industry. When a server sends a packet, the protocol tracks it until it is sent without error to the intended consumers/destinations (Kellton tech, 2020).

Machine-to-Machine (M2M) Communication Protocol - It is an international standard protocol for controlling the Internet of Things devices from far. Low-cost M2M communication protocols depend on public networks. It provides a communication and data exchange environment between two machines. This protocol facilitates computer self-monitoring and helps systems to adjust to changing conditions. Smart houses, automated vehicle authentication, vending machines, and ATMs all use M2M communication protocols according to (Kellton tech, 2020).

Extensible Messaging and Presence Protocol (XMPP) - It sends and receives messages in real-time using a push mechanism. XMPP is adaptable and can easily integrate with changes (Kellton tech, 2020). XMPP is a presence indicator that uses open XML (Extensible Markup Language) to indicate the state of the servers or devices that send or receive messages. It links servers and allows for near-real-time communication. It facilitates near-real-time activity by acting as a link between or among servers. In the future, the protocol could enable users to send instantaneous messages to anyone else on the Internet, regardless of their operating system or browser suggested by (Sethi & Sarangi, 2017).

ZigBee - It is an Internet of Things protocol that enables smart objects to communicate with one another. It's a popular component of home automation. ZigBee is most generally associated with industrial environments, but it is also used with applications that allow low-rate data transmission over short distances. Highway lighting and electric meters in metropolitan areas use the ZigBee communication protocol to provide low-power consumption. It's also suitable for smart homes and security systems according to (Kellton tech, 2020).

6LoWPAN - 6LoWPAN stands for the new iteration of the IPv6 and Low-power Wireless Personal Area Networks (LoWPAN). 6LoWPAN enables even the minutest devices with minimal processing capacity to send data wirelessly over the IP protocol. 6LoWPAN networks use a gateway (WiFi or Ethernet) to connect to the Internet that has its own set of capabilities. Since today's installed Internet is mainly IPv4, 6LoWPAN networks are connected to the Internet through an access point (WiFi or Ethernet), which also has protocol aid for IPv4 to IPv6 reformation. As a result, the adaptation layer optimizes the packets by fragmenting them to hold only the needy data according to (Sethi & Sarangi, 2017).

IOT IMPLEMENTATION IN REAL-LIFE

There are many applications in this technology in various areas as shown in Figure 5. There are several potential areas in which the Internet of Things (IoT) can be used to solve daily problems. However, many more uses can be made.

Smart Cities - IoT can be used to increase the efficacy of cities on a broader scale. The goal of smart cities is to use IoT to improve citizens living standards through improved transport control, assessment of air quality indexes, and information on parking lots by (P. Yadav & Vishwakarma, 2018).

Figure 5. Applications of IoT

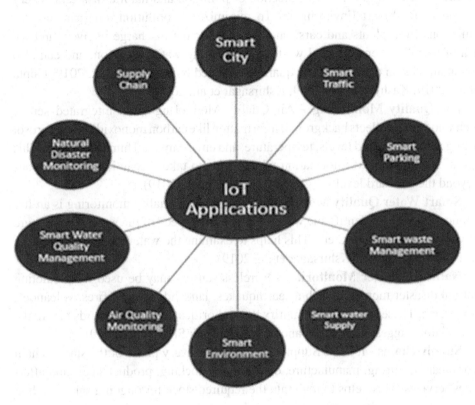

Smart Traffic - Smart traffic currently is a major issue in metropolitan cities. Managing them manually has become almost impossible. The IoT for traffic management can solve this problem. This intelligent traffic monitoring uses sensors to collect raw traffic information to aid car drivers to decide which route is best to travel on (Ghazal et al., 2016).

Smart parking - Smart car parking is Sensors placed in car-parks to see if car parks are available or not. Sensors are available. In the park application, the drivers provide their information, which then provides cost based on data collected by sensors to the nearest available parking lot (Hasan et al., 2019).

Smart Waste Management - Smart waste management is trash combined with sensors proficient in analyzing and notifying the owner when it is full and needs to be empty suggested by (Singhvi et al., 2019; Medvedev et al., 2015).

Smart water supply - Smart water supplies where clever cities need to monitor water supply to make it possible for residents and businesses to access water adequately. Wireless Sensor enables its pipeline systems to be monitored more accurately and detects water leakage and informs them about the loss of water (Water, 2016).

Smart Environment - IoT detection of pollution and natural disasters is very important for Smart Environment. To minimize air pollution, one can monitor emissions from plants and cars. one can monitor the discharge in rivers and the sea of harmful chemicals and waste, thus stopping water pollution, and can also maintain tabs on drinking water quality suggested by (Singhvi et al., 2019; Gupta et al., 2019; Kashyap et al., 2019; Kshirsagar et al., 2019).

Air Quality Monitoring - Air Quality Monitoring is an integrated sensor technology that collects background information like carbon monoxide (CO), aerosol nitrogen (NO2), sound levels, temperature, and environmental humidity levels. This gives ongoing context information which helps to take precautions when it goes beyond the standard level suggested by (Gupta et al., 2019).

Smart Water Quality Monitoring - Smart water quality monitoring is an IoT application used to identify the water quality index, speed of the water, temperature of water, pollution index, etc. This helps to examine the water resources for use in real-time information (Kshirsagar et al., 2019).

Natural Disaster Monitoring - Wireless sensors may be used for predicting natural disaster monitors, such as earthquakes, landslides, forest fires, volcanoes, floods, etc. These smart devices notify the authorities to take safeguards before the devastation suggested by (Floreano & Wood, 2015; Shah et al., 2019).

Supply-chains - It helps Suppliers to monitors every phase of the supply chain from manufacturing, manufacture, distribution, stocking, product sales, and after-sales services. This helps to maintain the required stock for ongoing sales, leading to customer consummation and increased production. According to the economic analysis by Cisco, supply chain and logistics revenue will be $1.9 billion over the next 10 years. With this, we can diagnose whether the machines need to be repaired and maintained according to (Dekhane et al., 2019; Supply Chain Council, 2012).

Smart Medical Services - Doctors can track a patient's condition outside of the hospital and in real-time by using wearables or devices linked to them. Through continuously monitoring those measurements and delivering programmed alerts on their vital signs, the IoT helps in the improvement of patient treatment and the avoidance of fatal accidents in high-risk patients. Another use of IoT technology is in hospital beds, resulting in smart beds with sensors that track vital signs, blood pressure, and body temperature, among other things.

IOT IMPLEMENTATION ISSUES

While the Internet of things (IoT) can change the way companies work, there are a variety of obstacles to the adoption of IoT:

Hardware platforms - IoT hardware platforms have only recently matured to the point where they can support a wide range of applications. This has facilitated inroads into hitherto unknown domains.

Data Planning - Even the tiniest IoT ecosystems produce a massive amount of data, which necessitates extensive strategic planning. What kind of data should be collected, how long should it be kept, and what kind of insides are required? If not properly handled, a flood of data will destroy business strategy.

Confidentiality and safety - Data protection and privacy of people who communicate with IoT systems is a major concern, and it is something that must recognize from the launch of every IoT project.

Long-term viability - All IoT devices must be powered on at all times. This necessitates a massive amount of energy. During the project planning process, consider the sustainability and environmental effects of IoT adoption.

CONCLUSION

IoT is a new technology that can connect smart devices and people via the internet using applications. Uniquely identified IoT devices work independently and communicate with other objects using a wireless network. Initially, it provides an introduction to the internet of things. Then it presents how IoT evolves and how it impacting our global and Indian economy. The IoT requires a standard architecture and protocol stack. Each Architecture describes how sensors produce data and how that data is collected, analyzed, presented. Smarter applications will be developed immediately by embedded sensors on objects. Some issues to implementing IoT in real- life are also addressed. Tessel 2, Eclipse IoT, PlatformIO, IBM Watson, Raspberry Pi, OpenSCADA, Node-RED, Arduino are some tools that can help in developing an IoT device.

REFERENCES

Bui, N., & Zorzi, M. (2011, October). Health care applications: a solution based on the internet of things. In *Proceedings of the 4th international symposium on applied sciences in biomedical and communication technologies* (pp. 1-5). 10.1145/2093698.2093829

Burhan, M., Rehman, R. A., Khan, B., & Kim, B. S. (2018). IoT elements, layered architectures and security issues: A comprehensive survey. *Sensors (Basel)*, *18*(9), 2796. doi:10.339018092796 PMID:30149582

Dekhane, S., Mhalgi, K., Vishwanath, K., Singh, S., & Giri, N. (2019, January). GreenCoin: Empowering smart cities using Blockchain 2.0. In *2019 International Conference on Nascent Technologies in Engineering (ICNTE)* (pp. 1-5). IEEE. 10.1109/ICNTE44896.2019.8946014

European Commission. (2017). *LAB–FAB–APP, Investing in the European future we want: Report of the independent High Level Group on maximising the impact of EU Research & Innovation Programmes.* Directorate-General for Research and Innovation.

Evans, D. (2011). *The Internet of Things.* Cisco. http://blogs. cisco. com/news/the-internet-of-things-infographic/

Floreano, D., & Wood, R. J. (2015). Robert J. Wood Science, technology and the future of small autonomous drones. *Nature, 521*(7553), 460–466. doi:10.1038/nature14542 PMID:26017445

Ghazal, B., Elkhatib, K., Chahine, K., & Kherfan, M. (2016). Smart traffic light control system. *2016 3rd International Conference on Electrical, Electronics, Computer Engineering and Their Applications, EECEA 2016.* 10.1109/EECEA.2016.7470780

Granjal, J., Monteiro, E., & Silva, J. S. (2015). Security for the internet of things: A survey of existing protocols and open research issues. *IEEE Communications Surveys and Tutorials, 17*(3), 1294–1312. doi:10.1109/COMST.2015.2388550

Green, J. (2014). The internet of things reference model. In *Internet of Things World Forum* (pp. 1-12). Academic Press.

Gupta, H., Bhardwaj, D., Agrawal, H., Tikkiwal, V. A., & Kumar, A. (2019). An IoT Based Air Pollution Monitoring System for Smart Cities. In *2019 IEEE International Conference on Sustainable Energy Technologies and Systems (ICSETS)* (pp. 173-177). IEEE. 10.1109/ICSETS.2019.8744949

Hasan, M. O., Islam, M. M., & Alsaawy, Y. (2019, June). Smart parking model based on internet of things (IoT) and TensorFlow. In *2019 7th International Conference on Smart Computing & Communications (ICSCC)* (pp. 1-5). IEEE.

International Telecommunication Union - ITU. (2017). *ITU-T Y.4455 - Internet of things and smart cities and communities – Frameworks, architectures and protocols Reference.* ITU.

Jadoul, M. (2015). The IoT: The next step in internet evolution. *Techzine.* Retrieved from https://techzine. alcatel-lucent. com/iot-next-stepinternet-evolution

Kashyap, R., Azman, M., & Panicker, J. G. (2019, February). Ubiquitous mesh: a wireless mesh network for IoT systems in smart homes and smart cities. In *2019 IEEE International Conference on Electrical, Computer and Communication Technologies (ICECCT)* (pp. 1-5). IEEE. 10.1109/ICECCT.2019.8869482

Kelltontech. (n.d.). https://www.kelltontech.com/kellton-tech-blog/internet-of

Kshirsagar, R., Mudhalwadkar, R. P., & Kalaskar, S. (2019, April). Design and Development of IoT Based Water Quality Measurement System. In *2019 3rd International Conference on Trends in Electronics and Informatics (ICOEI)* (pp. 1199-1202). IEEE.

Lazaro, A., Villarino, R., & Girbau, D. (2018). A survey of NFC sensors based on energy harvesting for IoT applications. *Sensors (Basel)*, *18*(11), 3746.

Madakam, S., Lake, V., Lake, V., & Lake, V. (2015). Internet of Things (IoT): A literature review. *Journal of Computer and Communications*, *3*(05), 164.

Medvedev, A., Fedchenkov, P., Zaslavsky, A., Anagnostopoulos, T., & Khoruzhnikov, S. (2015). Waste management as an IoT-enabled service in smart cities. In *Internet of Things, Smart Spaces, and Next Generation Networks and Systems* (pp. 104–115). Springer.

Pei, L., Guinness, R., Chen, R., Liu, J., Kuusniemi, H., Chen, Y., & Kaistinen, J. (2013). Human behavior cognition using smartphone sensors. *Sensors (Basel)*, *13*(2), 1402–1424.

Rashid, B., & Rehmani, M. H. Applications of wireless sensor networks for urban areas. *Journal. of Network & Computer Applications, 60*.

Sethi, S. R. S. (2017). *Internet of things: architectures, protocols, and applications.* https://www. hindawi. com/journals/jece/2017/9324035

Shah, S. A., Seker, D. Z., Hameed, S., & Draheim, D. (2019). The rising role of big data analytics and IoT in disaster management: Recent advances, taxonomy and prospects. *IEEE Access: Practical Innovations, Open Solutions*, *7*, 54595–54614.

Singhvi, R. K., Lohar, R. L., Kumar, A., Sharma, R., Sharma, L. D., & Saraswat, R. K. (2019, April). IoT basedsmart waste management system: india prospective. In *2019 4th International Conference on Internet of Things: Smart Innovation and Usages (IoT-SIU)* (pp. 1-6). IEEE.

Supply Chain Council. (2012). Supply Chain Operations Reference Model 11.0. In *Supply Chain Operations Management*. doi:10.1108/09576059710815716

Techahead. (2021). https://www.techaheadcorp.com/knowledge-center/evolution-of-iot/

VanderZee, M., Fisher, D., Powley, G., & Mohammad, R. (2015). Scada: Supervisory control and data acquisition. *Oil and Gas Pipelines*, 13-26.

Verma, P. K., Verma, R., Prakash, A., Agrawal, A., Naik, K., Tripathi, R., ... Abogharaf, A. (2016). Machine-to-Machine (M2M) communications: A survey. *Journal of Network and Computer Applications*, *66*, 83–105.

Water, S. (2016). Managing the water distribution network with a Smart Water Grid. *Smart Water*. doi:10.118640713-016-0004-4

Yadav, E. P., Mittal, E. A., & Yadav, H. (2018, February). IoT: Challenges and issues in indian perspective. In *2018 3rd International Conference On Internet of Things: Smart Innovation and Usages (IoT-SIU)* (pp. 1-5). IEEE.

Yadav, P., & Vishwakarma, S. (2018, February). Application of Internet of Things and big data towards a smart city. In *2018 3rd International Conference On Internet of Things: Smart Innovation and Usages (IoT-SIU)* (pp. 1-5). IEEE.

Yasuura, H., Kyung, C. M., Liu, Y., & Lin, Y. L. (Eds.). (2017). *Smart sensors at the IoT frontier*. Springer International Publishing.

Chapter 3

On IoT and Its Integration With Cloud Computing:
Challenges and Open Issues

Iram Abrar
University of Kashmir, India

Sahil Nazir Pottoo
https://orcid.org/0000-0002-2312-6963
I. K. Gujral Punjab Technical University, India

Faheem Syeed Masoodi
University of Kashmir, India

Alwi Bamhdi
Umm AL Qura University, Saudi Arabia

ABSTRACT

Internet of things witnessed rapid growth in the last decade and is considered to be a promising field that plays an all-important role in every aspect of modern-day life. However, the growth of IoT is seriously hindered by factors like limited storage, communication capabilities, and computational power. On the other hand, cloud has the potential to support a large amount of data as it has massive storage capacity and can perform complex computations. Considering the tremendous potential of these two technologies and the manner in which they complement one another, they have been integrated to form what is commonly referred to as the cloud of things (CoT). This integration is beneficial as the resulting system is more robust, intelligent, powerful, and offers promising solutions to the users. However, the new paradigm (CoT) is faced with a significant number of challenges that need to be addressed. This chapter discusses in detail various challenges like reliability, latency, scalability, heterogeneity, power consumption, standardization, etc. faced by the cloud of things.

DOI: 10.4018/978-1-7998-6981-8.ch003

INTRODUCTION

Internet of things (Ashton, 2011) has emerged as one of the rapidly growing paradigms that have revolutionalized the world of technology. IoT is primarily a sensor-based technology that works on the principle of establishing communication and interaction between heterogeneous smart objects that work together to achieve a common goal. According to Gartner, 20.4 billion devices will be linked through IoT by 2020 (van, 2017). A vast amount of information is generated through IoT; hence, there is a need to develop a mechanism that could store this information. Clouds are of paramount importance when it comes to storing a gigantic amount of data, and as such, it is a natural option to store the massive amount of data generated in IoT. Cloud provides a common platform for users to analyze, manage, and store the information. The primary characteristics of the Cloud include elasticity, multi-tenancy, scalability, and adaptability. Since these two technologies balance each other, researchers (Alhakbani et al., 2014; Gomes et al., 2014) have proposed their integration; as such, the resulting system is more agile, ubiquitous, and flexible as it could respond to the events in real-time from anywhere. The Cloud of things (CoT) is a novel paradigm that came into being by combining Cloud and IoT technologies, and Andriod Things (earlier known as Google Brillo) & Microsoft Azure IoT Suit are two known examples of the Cloud-IoT integrated platform. The dynamic nature of IoT can provide services in real-time to the Cloud users, and simultaneously, the latter can be used to integrate and process the huge data generated by the connected devices. Moreover, using these technologies in combination is beneficial as the loopholes of one technique can be filled by the other. However, as many IoT devices are concurrently connected to the Cloud platform in CoT, forming a massive network due to which several challenges such as reliability, latency, scalability, heterogeneity, power consumption, standardization are faced. Besides, security is a significant concern in the Cloud-IoT paradigm that can pose a severe threat to the sensitive information stored on Cloud and thus, hamper user privacy. The significant issues that are caused due to different due to application framework of CoT are listed in figure 1.

Although many solutions have been proposed to tackle these problems, yet an effective solution to addresses these issues remains an open challenge. The full potential of these two technologies can be harnessed when these issues are resolved so that uninterrupted and better services can be offered to the users. Some of the challenges of the Cloud-IoT paradigm have been discussed below.

Figure 1. Challenges in Cloud-IoT integration

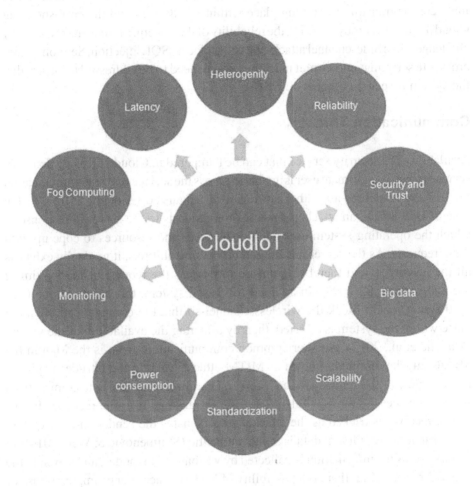

CHALLENGES IN CLOUD-IOT PARADIGM

Security and Trust

Since a colossal amount of data is generated and stored at one place on Cloud-IoT, it is more vulnerable to attackers, and hence can unfavorably influence the security of the system. In recent times various measures (Abrar et al., 2020; Bamhdi et al., 2021) have been taken into consideration in order to tackle these issues. In a Cloud-IoT paradigm, as the information captured by the IoT node is forwarded to the Cloud, there is a high risk involved as the information might be leaked because of the multi-user characteristic of the Cloud. Further, the wireless nature of IoT makes them more vulnerable to attacks (Masoodi et al., 2019), wherein the attackers intercept the transmission taking place within IoT devices and the corresponding Cloud platform, thereby affecting the reliability of the system. Moreover, new security challenges, like Side-channel attacks, Session hijacks, SQL injection, Session riding, cross-site scripting, and virtual machine escape, need to be addressed to ensure that the system is secure (Botta et al., 2016).

Communication Threats

Availability is a security service that can be hampered in Cloud-IoT using denial of services where a legitimate user is unable to access the services as the communication link, or the resources are either cut down or exhausted (Alotaibi, 2015). In the case of DoS attack, an attacker sends several requests to the server in response to which the operating system uses additional power and resources to cope up with these requests. As the server has limited processing abilities, it gradually exhausts all the resources, and thereby, is unable to process the request of the legitimate users (Jensen et al., 2009). In a Cloud-IoT based system, this attack can be used by the attackers to block the wireless channel so that the communication taking place within the system is affected, thereby affecting the availability of the system (Mahalle et al., 2012). Another common communication threat is the Man in the Middle attack commonly known as MITM attack, wherein the intruder is placed in the middle of the sender and the receiver, i.e., it interrupts the data coming from source, replaces it with fraudulent data and retransmits it to the receiver. In this way, a receiver is tricked as the attacker impersonates the sender and makes him believe that the fraudulent data is in fact authentic (Stojmenovic & Wen, 2014). In Cloud-IoT, as the information is collected by various sensor nodes, and is sent to the Cloud for processing, there is a possibility of MITM attack. For example, in case of temperature sensing, IoT based sensors can sense the temperature, and accordingly, this information is forwarded to the Cloud. However, in such a scenario, if MITM attack takes place, the attackers can send false information to the Cloud, thereby affecting the performance of the system and can cause severe physical damage to the recipient (Liu et al., 2012). Similar to MITM attack is the replay attack, where the attacker gets hold of the actual message, and then replicates it later to lure the receiver to believe that the message is from a legitimate user (Gope & Hwang, 2015). In case of Cloud-IoT, when the attacker gets hold of the information sensed by the sensor, it can be resent to the Cloud platform resulting in the wastage of essential resources. Apart from these, eavesdropping and spoofing attack are also typical in Cloud-IoT paradigm. In a spoofing attack, the attacker either mimics the operation of the network device or impersonates a legitimate user in order to launch an attack on the network with the intent to either steal the user's information or to bypass the security mechanism of the system. IP spoofing and ARP spoofing are commonly used spoofing attacks (Ferdous et al., 2016). Likewise, attackers can use eavesdropping to extract the data during its transmission from IoT devices to the Cloud by intercepting the communication link.

Data Threats

The data, when collected by the IoT device, is sent to Cloud-based centers where this data is then processed. However, when this data is transmitted from the IoTs to the Cloud, attackers might get the hold of this raw data (Roman et al., 2013), and modify it according to their own needs and benefits. For example, an attacker might deploy its own devices in the environment to generate false data in the system, which would lead to violating the security constraints of the system. Also, as nodes are more vulnerable to attacks as compared to that of computers due to their computational abilities, the attackers can fake a device to launch attacks in Cloud-IoT as the result of which malicious information can transmit to the Cloud, which can cause serious problems (Puthal et al., 2016). In order to overcome this problem, data must be received by the Cloud only when it has been sensed by an authentic source so that the security of the system is not affected, and thus, false data can be prevented from entering the system thereby, maintaining the reliability of the system. Furthermore, as IoT devices use sensor-based technologies, they have limitations in terms of computational power. Conversely, implementing a cryptographic (Masoodi & Bokhari, 2019) mechanism, which is used to enhance the security of the existing system, is quite expensive in terms of power requirements. Due to this fact, developers of Cloud-IoT are bound to employ weak cryptographic mechanisms, so that power requirements of the system do not overshoot, but due to this, the system becomes more vulnerable to the attackers, as they can easily break such cryptographic mechanisms and hamper the security of the system. However, if the data is encrypted before uploading it to the Cloud, disclosure of sensitive information can be avoided, and for the same, keys are used, which are managed by the IoT devices. Although using such approach data security can be ensured but simultaneously, it can cause an unnecessary burden to the IoT devices. For example, if data from a sensor node is encrypted before being forwarded to the Cloud and since the authorization application changes every time, new keys have to be invoked, and the process has to be repeated, which are not desirable. However, current research on homomorphic encryption, which is used to encrypt the data without actually accessing the plain text (Hrestak & Picek, 2014; Lauter et al., 2011), can provide an aid to this problem.

Access control (Anderson, 2001) is a security service that defines an action that an entity can perform on a particular data, and can broadly be categorized as authentication and authorization, both of which are essential security parameters. In Cloud-IoT, since the data and resources of a single user are controlled and coordinated by several devices, enforcement of these security parameters is quite challenging. Hence, there is a need to define and enforce flexible policies in both these dimensions. Cloud can be used to control and coordinate the IoT devices, but there should some sort of access control mechanism incorporated within the devices to prevent unwanted access of data. Moreover, the policies, which are enforced for Cloud, must be compatible with several IoT devices to ensure that they do not lead to further vulnerabilities. For example, an attacker using the Masquerade attack can forge the identity of an authentic user and cause a financial loss in a banking system.

Although the integration of these two technologies can prove to be beneficial to the users as their needs can be monitored and processed in the real-time; however, the attackers can misuse this platform for their own interest. For example, the attacker may launch an attack on this platform to inform the users of some policies that would be beneficial to the attackers. Though implementing such kind of attacks on the Cloud is somewhat tricky, it is still possible. Currently, IT industry has limited the use of services provided by the Cloud owing to its security concerns. In Cloud-IoT, on the other hand, if access to the Cloud is restricted, it can affect the operation of actuators of the IoT, and ultimately the attacker, apart from getting hold of sensitive information, will also able to control the physical objects, which is even worse. Furthermore, with the advancement in Cloud-IoT, the services of Cloud are used to manage a virtual learning environment (VLE) that engages many users in the learning process. However, unauthorized access to this platform with the intent to corrupt VLE can cause a severe threat to the security of Cloud-IoT system as well as its users, as their sensitive information is at high risk and thus would affect the overall virtual learning experience.

Trust

Trust is an essential aspect of the Cloud-IoT environment (Bhattasali et al., 2013), which is used to improve the communication between the consumer and the vendor by focusing on securing the storage, transmission, and virtualization of data. In the Cloud, service level agreement, which contains information about services, priorities, responsibilities so on, forms the basis of the trust between the entities involved in communication; whereas, in IoT, two categories of protocols are used for enforcement of trust in the system, namely distributed (Bao et al., 2013; Bao & Chen, 2012; Chen et al., 2016; Chen et al., 2018; Kamvar et al., 2003) and centralized (Chen et al., 2011; Nitti et al., 2013, 2014) trust-based protocols. Scalability is the main problem in implementing the former set of protocols, whereas, the other set of the protocols is quite tricky to implement. However, it is essential to enforce trust-based mechanisms in the system as every device is not trustworthy; for example, some of the IoT devices might be deployed by the attacker with an intent to harm the system by disrupting the Cloud services (Chen et al., 2018). Hence, it is crucial to have a trust-based mechanism in the system, but implementing the same in Cloud-IoT is challenging. Although authentication and access control mechanisms can get rid of vulnerable IoT devices, it still cannot be assured that these devices can be trusted completely. Overall, trust management for IoT devices is critical, and how to achieve situation-aware, scalable, and consistent trust management mechanisms in Cloud computing requires extensive research efforts.

Heterogeneity

In recent past, Cloud-IoT development witnessed a considerable growth (Mansour et al., 2016), yet there are several issues that need to be addressed; one of the major problems being inter-operability, which prevents various smart devices from different vendors to communicate with one another and prevents them from forming a cost-effective network. Popular vendors like Amazon (AWS IoT), Cisco (Jasper), IBM (Watson), Apple (HomeKit), Google (Brillo), Microsoft (Azure IoT), and Qualcomm (AllJoyn) have taken over the market in recent years, but as each one of them has their own standards and policies, they are incompatible with one another, and thus, cannot collaborate (Gluhak et al., 2016). According to a report (Manyika et al., 2015), a substantial threat to non-interoperability could cause a severe threat to economic value and cause its downfall. It is also estimated that about 40% of profit in the case of IoT is obtained via interoperability. Various environments must be interoperable with one another so that better services could be provided to the users (Jabbar et al., 2017). In Cloud-IoT, as different service providers have different policies, it can cause a hurdle to interoperability, i.e., the theory of service providers of one country might not be in compliance with that of another. Besides, owing to the complexity of the machine learning algorithm and cost incurred, in the present scenario, Cloud service provider do not support applications that can predict the location of the IoT devices, which could create problems in Cloud-IoT. For example, due to the lack of standardization, different IoT platform use different protocols leading to the question of interoperability, and as such, there arises a need to have standardized communication protocols (e.g., CoAP for constrained devices) (Collina et al., 2012) which could be used to enforce interoperability. Besides, it is important to ensure that these protocols are available for all devices such that the interoperability solution does not depend on network entities such as gateways as they have their own limitations. Likewise, Cloud infrastructure, except a few like

SGI Cyclone, R Systems, Amazon Cluster GPUs (Crago et al., 2011), enable users to have a limited control over the target architecture, thereby, restricting them to avail their advantages. Thus, there arises a need of interoperability which would enable various heterogeneous devices and platform to be in compliance with one another and would, hence, be beneficial for Cloud-IoT industry.

Figure 2. Popular Cloud-IoT platforms

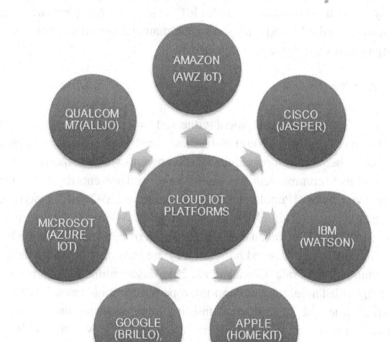

Interoperability enables various heterogeneous devices to communicate with one another, thereby improving the services by optimizing computations, which could, in turn, enhance the effectiveness of the system. In an attempt to counter the issues related to heterogeneity, efforts are being made on industrial as well as on academic level (Noura et al., 2019). Similar work is being carried out in the field of IoT interoperability (Gambi et al., 2016; Gazis et al., 2015). To enforce interoperability, standards that will integrate the existing platforms should be adopted, so that the problem of using different protocols, packet size, encryption/decryption algorithms can be solved (Jabbar et al., 2017). For the same, different vendors need to come forth to address this issue by developing a transparent mechanism that can be enforced in all the existing domains.

Interoperability faces a significant issue in terms of heterogeneity, which is not a new paradigm, nor is it limited to a particular domain. For example, people from different countries use different languages, but at the same time, they can communicate with one another using a translator. Similarly, the Cloud-IoT paradigm enables various heterogeneous devices, operating systems, and platforms to collaborate with one another to provide new and improved services. In case of Cloud-IoT, wireless networks are used for communication among heterogeneous sensor nodes. Moreover, the services are tightly coupled to a particular application based on its nature, and by analyzing its requirements, hardware and software environments are selected, and accordingly, these heterogeneous subsystems must be integrated to offer computing infrastructure and services to the users. In Cloud, heterogeneity is a severe concern owing to services being provided by various service providers and can, thus, lead to vendor lock-in. Solutions in the form of federations are suggested by Cloud providers to overcome these problems, but these are not fully resolved. Although, with the help of a Cloud service delivery model (Li et al., 2013), like platform as a service, Cloud-IoT can ease service delivery on a Cloud platform. However, their implementation can face a severe issue in terms of heterogeneity. Many solutions, such as platforms and middleware, interoperable programming interfaces (Kamilaris et al., 2010), means for copying with data diversity (Simmhan et al., 2011), are being investigated in the various research works to provide solutions to this problem.

Big Data

IoT has an immense number of applications in healthcare, agriculture, smart cities, and industries, where they enable various devices to communicate with one another. It is predicted that approximately around fifty billion devices will be linked by 2020 (Botta et al., 2016); it is, therefore, necessary that the information generated by these devices should be handled, stored, and processed correctly, and the Cloud can be used for the same. For example, in healthcare, a resource-based data accessing method, namely, UDA-IoT (Xu et al., 2014) has been developed, which can be used by the doctors to fetch and process the data from the IoT device in real-time, and this device is highly efficient on Cloud platform. Nowadays, technology giants such as Google, Yahoo, Facebook use the Cloud to store data using the concept of virtualization (Manyika et al., 2015). Even though the cost of storage is gradually decreasing, the collection and storage of such a tremendous amount of data are still quite expensive. With the advancement in technology, there is a growth in the Cloud-IoT network due to which more amount of data is being produced. According to IBM, 2.5 quintillion byte of data is being generated every day (Manyika et al., 2015), and as such, there arises a need to have a platform wherein this kind of colossal amount of data can be collected and stored from the sensor nodes, so that the issues of data flooding can be tackled (Alansari et al., 2018). Besides, the performance of Cloud-IoT is directly dependent on the data being stored on the Cloud (Aziz et al., 2019), so enforcing proper data management techniques is imperative. Big data provides aid to this problem as it enables the users to analyze the data obtained from a variety of sources to enable them to make efficient decisions. Moreover, from a business perspective, big data has the capability to generate more revenue, and is, therefore, beneficial for the business sectors. With the growth of the internet, smartphones, and machine to machine communication, big data has been revolutionized (Miraz et al., 2015). In the absence of big data, a tremendous quantity of data produced by IoT devices in Cloud-IoT cannot be analyzed, adding an unnecessary burden on the organizations, thereby creating an obstacle in its development (Alansari et al., 2018). Massive storage, high latency, and processing power are some of the requirements of big data (Lee et al., 2013). However, since IoT is limited in terms of processing power and also suffers from latency problems (Fan & Bifet, 2013; Samie et al., 2016), sufficing this need for big data using Cloud-IoT becomes a real challenge. Also, as data is unstructured (Manyika et al., 2015), due to the fact that it is collected from various applications developed by different vendors (using different standards), it can pose a problem to Cloud-IoT in processing this data.

In addition, obtaining information by data mining can be quite challenging, mainly due to the lack of adequate data mining approaches owning to the complexity of an application. Although several research works are currently being carried out in this field, the challenge lies in effectively handling the data as the effective performance of an application is directly related to data. Furthermore, to overcome this challenge of the Cloud-IoT paradigm, Cloud-driven solution used for Big Data analyses are being investigated so that a better remedy can be provided to tackle this issue(Ahmed Teli, T., & Masoodi, 2021). Despite significant research in this field, a proper or generic solution to handle this problem in the Cloud is yet to be found, and as such, it persists in Cloud-IoT (Zaslavsky et al., 2012).

Scalability

The use of sensors and actuators has rapidly increased over recent years owing to increased use of IoT, and according to recent research works in the field, this technology will continue to grow exponentially (Rodrigues et al., 2016). One of the significant challenges which can play a vital role in the advancement of this technology is scalability (Misra, 2016). It ensures data on the Cloud with high request rates is able to render services to the subscribers at low latency, and handle

Figure 3. Statistics depicting IoT devices connected to Cloud from 2012 to 2020 (Burhan et al., 2018)
Note: The figure reprinted from https://www.mdpi.com/1424-8220/18/9/2796 under open access Creative Common CC by license

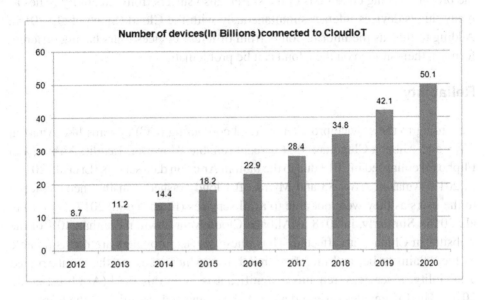

the requests from multiple tenants, i.e., system must be capable of redistributing the data (Sakr et al., 2011) automatically.

It is essential to guarantee that the system is scalable and makes efficient use of available resources (Gupta et al., 2017). However, a proper, effective, and adequate solution to this problem of scalability has not been addressed (Al-Fuqaha et al., 2015; Bao et al., 2013; Ishaq et al., 2012; Kim et al., 2015; Wu et al., 2013). In Cloud-IoT, Cloud interacts with several IoT devices because of which a large volume of data is generated. Therefore, the Cloud must be proficient at managing and scaling the gigantic amount of data generated by these devices for the proper functioning of the system. If it fails to scale the data, it can lead to the unavailability of data, which can cause serious issues that can limit data access or prevent the Cloud from workout with IoT devices. Also, IoT must be scalable to handle a significant amount of data, which means that it should be able to support various users and devices while maintaining service quality. One way to tackle the problem of scalability is to develop tools that could work well for decentralized data (Rabkin et al., 2013), and thus, could provide a promising solution by improving the coordination between IoT devices and the corresponding Cloud platform. Moreover, a hybrid approach (Singh et al., 2016) can be considered to deal with the issue of data handling, storage, and

47

processing overheads. In general, analyzing the information in a distributed system like Cloud-IoT is challenging yet unsolved, and needs further research(Pandow, B. A., Bamhdi, A. M., & Masoodi, 2020). For example, logs which are used to ensure the proper working conditions of the system also suffers from scalability issues as many things/devices interact simultaneously with the Cloud (Singh et al., 2016). Adding to this, as the information is from different devices/users having different formats, their storage on the Cloud can be problematic.

Reliability

According to the service providers, Cloud computing (CC) systems like Amazon AWS and Alibaba Cloud are 99.9 percent reliable. However, Reddit, Airbnb, and Flipboard collapsed in 2012 due to the fault in Amazon data servers (Li et al., 2013). In 2017, Amazon AWS S3 and Microsoft Cloud crashed, causing inconvenience to the users as they were not able to avail services (Etherington, 2017; Gunawi et al., 2016). Similarly, in 2018 as Alibaba Cloud went down, more than 40% of the websites in China were affected. Thus, these service providers are not as reliable as they claim to be, and therefore, reliability, which refers to the uninterrupted availability of services, remains a significant issue in this field (Armbrust et al., 2010). The IoT enables several devices to be connected, resulting in the formation of a considerable network that should be able to configure itself to adapt to changes in the environment or components (Kempf et al., 2011). There is a possibility of applications running on the network not being reliable even though the network itself is reliable. For example, the error rate in sensors of IoT may appear to be small, yet it can create problems for users while configuring their devices. Adding to this, as sensor technology used in IoT is resource constraint, the use of the Cloud can aid the computation of complex tasks for effective decision making. Cloud can enhance the reliably of system as it provides a self-healing mechanism, and enables users and operations to achieve distributed generation and demand response. Self-healing allows the system to recover from hardware or software failures without any disruption. Although reliability has shown great potential as far as Cloud is considered yet owning to the large scale of Cloud-IoT, it becomes difficult to keep track of the failures. To counter the issues of reliability, fault-tolerant mechanisms (Zhang et al., 2018) have been devised for Cloud platforms, most of which are based on virtualization or deployment of numerous redundant devices. In virtualization, snapshots of data are taken periodically, and when a failure in the system occurs, the data is recovered from the previous snapshot (Luo et al., 2019). However, as the speed of recovery hinges on the size of data and the network traffic, only critical applications can migrate this data in real-time. Thus, there arises a need for high-speed storage devices, which adds to the cost of data recovery (Luo et al., 2019).

Apart from this, numerous human resources are essential to identify new problems at the early stages and develop corrective code patches. Due to these facts, it becomes mandatory to keenly analyze the reliability issues so that these characteristics and relationships can be identified, and the system can quickly recover and avoid failures in the future.

Fog Computing

It is a classical model that encompasses cloud computing facilities to the end devices in the system. Fog computing has been intended to sustain IoT applications that have latency, mobility and geo-distribution (Liu et al., 2015) limitations. As shown in figure 4, fog computing turns as an arbitrator amongst the cloud and IoT devices that carry loading, processing and networking facilities nearer to the end devices.

Figure 4. FC and IoT integration model (CC – cloud computing and FC – fog computing)

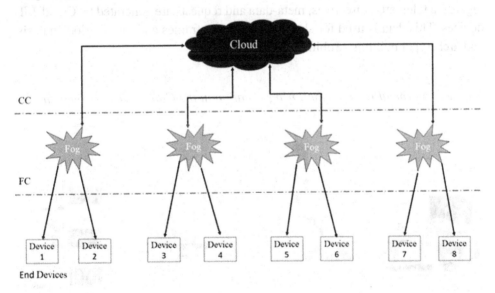

Fog computing delivers interconnection application services to end devices like cloud computing. Therefore, fog computing can be deliberated as an intercessor sandwiched among end devices and Cloud, which works for network latency issues that necessitate interruption requirements for other nodes (Sood, 2019). Fog computing has assured characteristics like position alertness and edge locality that are responsible for geo-distribution and short delay even though processing, storage and networking are the common resources between the fog computing and the cloud computing. In distinction to Cloud, fog computing offers a great number of nodes which are sustained for real-time collaboration and agility (Atlam et al., 2017). Nowadays, fog devices are manufactured in a way that they can interact directly with Cloud (Malik & Om, 2018). Certainly, the implementation of Fog-centered methodologies involves numerous precise procedures and policy allocation with the trustworthiness of the linkage of smart devices and functioning underneath explicit circumstances that enquire for lenient liability practices.

Monitoring

In the Cloud-IoT integration, monitoring is the critical action keeping in view the security issue, bulk forecasting, resource management, service level agreement (SLA) and troubleshooting (Stergiou et al., 2018). Although few related challenges exist between Cloud-IoT and cloud computing, which get affected by swiftness, capacity and diversity but both have similar monitoring necessities. Information regarding telemetry, directives, meta-data and requests are generated by Cloud-IoT devices. This data is used for short working time frames and long-period analysis and archetypal building (Sobin, 2020).

Figure 5. A typical remote monitoring situation in the Cloud-IoT environment

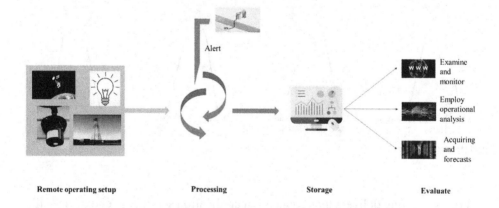

Like local monitoring in our day to day life in the form of a beeper or an alarm board on properties, Cloud-IoT devices need some sort of monitoring for both short and long stretch computing. This kind of monitoring is essentially remote monitoring that comprises assembling and scrutinizing the monitored data from a remote location using a reporting device. Such a scenario is depicted in figure 5, where a different set of operating devices record and deliver status information to a processing device, which either activates alert in case of system ambiguity or carries the information to the storage device. Data once stored undergoes monitoring dashboard serving, time series analysis called operational data (Belgaum et al., 2018), and machine learning models for data prediction. Afterwards, this data is used to recognize operational time zone, system alteration, firmware sorting, and so on (Sicari et al., 2015). Therefore, in context to Cloud-IoT, monitoring denotes to identify, repair and determine technical glitches that happen in operating network and its end devices to recover system reliability and improve link performance.

Latency

Latency in the Cloud-IoT environment can be defined as the time that the information consumes while traveling from its source to destination. Latency has always been a known issue in cloud-IoT; increased latency means that a device has to wait longer for the response, which directly affects the battery life of the device. Sometimes the end devices can manage minor deferments while in some urgent and important situations, even a little delay in judgment could cost a heavy toll on network performance. In Cloud-IoT integration, active network connectivity in real-time is highly important since devices can be located in isolated spaces producing information 24x7 (Guechi, 1955). The causes of communication latency in Cloud-IoT integration are highlighted in figure 6. Latency is caused due to delay in computing speed, inadequate storage or poor network allocation, which can be due to sudden failures in communication link resulting from wear and tear in case of fiber communication or atmospheric turbulence in free space channel or any unexpected fault in interconnecting devices or user end devices. Any network delay may result in poor user service, sluggish link performance and even connection termination.

For latency measurement in the Cloud-IoT environment, the processing latency is deliberated vital parameter (Maharaj & Malekian, 2016). Latency measurement can be realized in numerous ways (Abrar et al., 2021). One of them can be when link devices report themselves the time frame for every single operation and create a feedback loop to sync network requests and positive or negative acknowledgment timing slots (Ferrari & Sisinni, 2017).

Figure 6. Causes of network latency in Cloud-IoT services

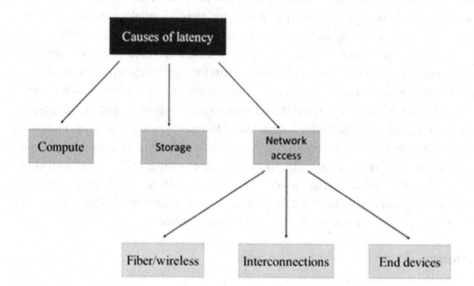

Power Consumption

Recent Cloud-IoT submissions have turned user end devices into power-hungry machines due to continuous 4k/8k data streaming. Nowadays, the challenge is to obtain power efficiency at all three stages of Cloud-IoT; computing, storage, and networking. Transfering around zita-bytes of data among all connected IoT devices means large CPU power consumption (Pottoo et al., 2018). To regulate this power drain menace, more proficient data collection methods are required (Han et al., 2018) to deliver more facilities at the same power level (Odun-ayo et al., 2018). We need to move towards energy garnering and energy management in order to address heavy power consumption by cloud-IoT devices. A typical example of an energy-efficient Cloud-IoT ecosystem is presented in figure 7. Here, the concept of green cloud computing has been introduced with resource management and sustainable resource supplies. Resource management is achieved in 4 steps; (a) Virtualization, (b) Scheduling, (c) Replica management, and (d) Power/voltage scaling. The sustainability of resources is accomplished through heat re-use, sustainable energy sources, and free cooling.

In the given scenario, when an IoT device needs the service(s), it sends a request to access the cloud, and if when acknowledged, the server requests service allocation from the cloud which when granted, the connection is established. Furthermore, to

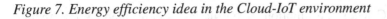

Figure 7. Energy efficiency idea in the Cloud-IoT environment

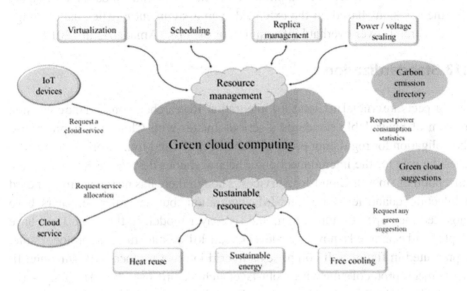

monitor carbon dioxide emission, a carbon emission regulatory service is available within the integrated system. In order to keep Cloud-IoT integrated system up-to-date with the latest self-reliant practices, a green cloud service pours the suggestions for any system up-gradation inline. In addition, some practices to overcome power consumption issues in Cloud-IoT ecosystem, as found in the literature are put-forth as under:

- RFID response in the Cloud-IoT ecosystem can be condensed by regulating the communication among readers and identifiers for ensuring the quality of service (QoS) requirements for Cloud-IoT applications (Kalyani & Chaudhari, 2019).
- Better energy efficient protocol suites should be implemented in Cloud-IoT integration such that routing devices undergo the sleep phase till the next activation to stop power drain (Kumari et al., 2018).
- The energy efficiency in the Cloud-IoT ecosystem can be augmented by means of a maximum power point tracking mechanism to decrease the power consumed by the analog and digital circuitry (Mahmud et al., 2018).
- Gamification methodology for attaining energy efficiency works by allocating the idle spectrum to secondary users (SUs), which instead belongs to primary users (PUs) based on spectrum sensing algorithm (Baktayan, 2018).

- Excess MAC level consumption of the nodes is controlled by optimizing the decisions based on the extended span assignment practice data through constraints over overhaul interruption of the task (Amadeo et al., 2019).

2.13 Standardization

Legal aspects are crucial in Cloud-IoT integration. Researchers consider the confusion problem of unavailable standards a serious matter with Cloud-IoT applications. The obligation for regulating protocols, architectures and frameworks exists and it paves the way for the interconnection of heterogeneous devices, as such assist the conception of smooth Cloud-IoT services. Though there has not been any standard architecture quantified for Cloud-IoT integration, but several researchers have suggested their specific three, four, and five-layer model. In this regard, we have adopted and examined a novel four-level Cloud-IoT architecture and protocol suite, as presented in figure 8. It comprises a hybrid internet protocol (IP) suite and IP smart objects protocol suite with a four-layer architecture, namely, (a) Link layer, (b) Network layer, (c) Transport layer, and (d) Application layer. The link-layer acts as a physical layer for IoT devices to sense and monitor the environment. The network layer is accountable for managing routing protocols that route information through

Figure 8. Cloud-IoT architecture and protocols
(Source: https://www.postscapes.com/internet-of-things-protocols/)

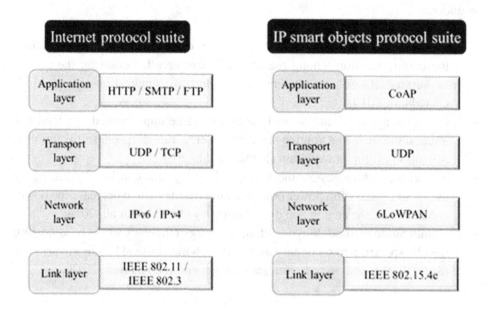

different devices. The transport layer carries out information transfer between Cloud-IoT devices. The application layer deals with user interface applications.

The involvement of users directly or indirectly into Cloud-IoT operations is being applauded to address system anomalies, thereby introducing the trust factor in what is now just machine to machine (M2M) communication (Dang et al., 2019). Such interaction facilitates engineers and designers to acquire know-how about human to machine collaboration to design user and eco-friendly technology with embedded security, privacy, and trust guarantee. For this thing to happen, human-machine interaction should be made simple and easy to open window for novel standard and economical designs (Belgaum et al., 2018).

CONCLUSION

To overcome the limitations of Cloud and IoT, researchers have proposed a combination of these two technologies leading to the formation of Cloud of Things that enables the service providers to offer improved services to the users. Though this integration can play a very vital role but a number of challenges are generated by this integration that needs to be addressed so the system can function without causing any inconvenience to the users. Since the notion of Cloud-IoT is in the initial stage of its development, no standard mechanism exists based on which they can be integrated. Likewise, as it enables various IoT devices to connect, it causes heterogeneity and scalability issues. Security, which is considered as an essential aspect as far as user privacy is concerned, can also face a severe threat in Cloud-IoT, due to which it becomes difficult for the users to trust the network with their sensitive information. Similarly, latency, reliability, scalability, power consumption, monitoring are the other vital aspects that need to be pondered upon in the case of CoT. Moreover, promising technologies, like big data and fog computing, also face several challenges.

REFERENCES

Abrar, I., Ayub, Z., Masoodi, F., & Bamhdi, A. M. (2020). A Machine Learning Approach for Intrusion Detection System on NSL-KDD Dataset. *Proceedings - International Conference on Smart Electronics and Communication, ICOSEC 2020,* 919–924. 10.1109/ICOSEC49089.2020.9215232

Ahmed Teli, T., & Masoodi, F. (2021). Security Concerns and Privacy Preservation in Blockchain based IoT Systems: Opportunities and Challenges. *ICICNIS 2020.*

Al-Fuqaha, A., Khreishah, A., Guizani, M., Rayes, A., & Mohammad, M. (2015). *Towards better horozontal integration among IoT services*. Academic Press.

Alansari, Z., Anuar, N. B., Kamsin, A., & Soomro, S. (2018). Challenges of Internet of Things and Big Data Integration. *International Conference on International Conference on Emerging Technologies in Computing 2018 (ICETiC '18)*, 1–9. 10.1007/978-3-319-95450-9_4

Alansari, Z., Soomro, S., Belgaum, M. R., & Shamshirband, S. (2018). The rise of Internet of Things (IoT) in big healthcare data: Review and open research issues. *Progess in Advances in Intelligent Systems and Computing, 564*, 675–685. doi:10.1007/978-981-10-6875-1_66

Alhakbani, N., Hassan, M. M., Hossain, M. A., & Alnuem, M. (2014). A framework of adaptive interaction support in cloud-based internet of things (IoT) environment. In Lecture Notes in Computer Science (Vol. 8729, pp. 136–146). Springer Verlag., doi:10.1007/978-3-319-11692-1_12

Alotaibi, K. H. (2015). *Threat in Cloud-denial of service (DoS) and distributed denial of service (DDoS) attack, and security measures*. Academic Press.

Amadeo, M., Ruggeri, G., Campolo, C., Molinaro, A., Loscrí, V., & Calafate, C. T. (2019). Fog Computing in IoT Smart Environments via Named Data Networking : A Study on Service Orchestration Mechanisms. *Future Internet, 11*(11), 222. doi:10.3390/fi11110222

Anderson, R. (2001). *Security engineering : a guide to building dependable distributed systems*. Wiley.

Armbrust, M., Fox, A., Griffith, R., Joseph, A. D., Katz, R., Konwinski, A., Lee, G., Patterson, D., Rabkin, A., Stoica, I., & Zaharia, M. (2010). A view of cloud computing. *Communications of the ACM, 53*(4), 50–58. doi:10.1145/1721654.1721672

Ashton, K. (2011). *That "Internet of Things" thing*. RFID Journal.

Atlam, H. F., Alenezi, A., Alharthi, A., Walters, R. J., & Wills, G. B. (2017). Integration of Cloud Computing with Internet of Things. *Challenges and Open*, (October), 670–675. Advance online publication. doi:10.1109/iThings-GreenCom-CPSCom-SmartData.2017.105

Aziz, F., Chalup, S. K., & Juniper, J. (2019). Big data in IoT systems. In M. Y. & J. Khan (Eds.), Internet of Things (IoT): Systems and Applications. doi:10.1201/9780429399084-2

Baktayan, A. (2018). *EAI Endorsed Transactions A Review on Cloud and Fog Computing Integration for IoT : Platforms Perspective.* 10.4108/eai.20-12-2018.156084

Bamhdi, A. M., Abrar, I., & Masoodi, F. (2021). An ensemble based approach for effective intrusion detection using majority voting. *Telkomnika Telecommunication Computing Electronics and Control, 19*(2), 664–671. doi:10.12928/telkomnika.v19i2.18325

Bao, F., & Chen, I.-R. (2012). Dynamic trust management for internet of things applications. *Proceedings of the 2012 International Workshop on Self-Aware Internet of Things - Self-IoT '12,* 1. 10.1145/2378023.2378025

Bao, F., Chen, I.-R., & Guo, J. (2013). Scalable, adaptive and survivable trust management for community of interest based Internet of Things systems. *2013 IEEE Eleventh International Symposium on Autonomous Decentralized Systems (ISADS),* 1–7. 10.1109/ISADS.2013.6513398

Belgaum, M. R., Soomro, S., Alansari, Z., & Alam, M. (2018). Article. Advance online publication. doi:10.1109/ICETAS.2017.8277844

Belgaum, M. R., Soomro, S., Alansari, Z., Muşa, S., Alam, M., & Su'Ud, M. M. (2018). Challenges: Bridge between cloud and IoT. *4th IEEE International Conference on Engineering Technologies and Applied Sciences, ICETAS 2017,* 1–5. 10.1109/ICETAS.2017.8277844

Bhattasali, T., Chaki, R., & Chaki, N. (2013). Secure and Trusted Cloud of Things. *2013 Annual IEEE India Conference (INDICON),* 1–6. 10.1109/INDCON.2013.6725878

Botta, A., De Donato, W., Persico, V., & Pescapé, A. (2016). Integration of cloud computing and Internet of Things: A survey. *Future Generation Computer Systems, 56,* 684–700. doi:10.1016/j.future.2015.09.021

Burhan, M., Rehman, R. A., Khan, B., & Kim, B. S. (2018). IoT elements, layered architectures and security issues: A comprehensive survey. *Sensors (Basel), 18*(9), 1–37. doi:10.339018092796 PMID:30149582

Chen, D., Chang, G., Sun, D., Li, J., Jia, J., & Wang, X. (2011). *TRM-IoT: A trust management model based on fuzzy reputation for internet of things.* doi:10.2298/CSIS110303056C

Chen, I., Guo, J., Tech, V., Wang, D., & Al-hamadi, H. (2018). Trust-based Service Management for Mobile Cloud IoT Systems. *IEEE Transactions on Network and Service Management,* 1. doi:10.1109/TNSM.2018.2886379

Chen, I.-R., Guo, J., & Bao, F. (2016). Trust Management for SOA-Based IoT and Its Application to Service Composition. *IEEE Transactions on Services Computing, 9*(3), 482–495. doi:10.1109/TSC.2014.2365797

Chen, K., Chen, K., Chang, Y., & Tseng, P. (2011). *Measuring the latency of cloud gaming systems Measuring The Latency of Cloud Gaming Systems.* doi:10.1145/2072298.2071991

Collina, M., Corazza, G. E., & Vanelli-Coralli, A. (2012). Introducing the QEST broker: Scaling the IoT by bridging MQTT and REST. *2012 IEEE 23rd International Symposium on Personal, Indoor and Mobile Radio Communications,* 36–41.

Crago, S., Dunn, K., Eads, P., Hochstein, L., Kang, D.-I., Kang, M., Modium, D., Singh, K., Suh, J., & Walters, J. P. (2011). Heterogeneous cloud computing. *2011 IEEE International Conference on Cluster Computing,* 1–8.

Dang, L. M., Piran, J., Han, D., Min, K., & Moon, H. (2019). *A Survey on Internet of Things and Cloud Computing for Healthcare.* doi:10.3390/electronics8070768

Etherington, D. (2017). *Amazon AWS S3 outage is breaking things for a lot of websites and apps.* Academic Press.

Fan, W., & Bifet, A. (2013). Mining big data: Current status, and forecast to the future. ACM SIGKDD Explorations Newsletter, 14.

Ferdous, M. S., Hussein, R. K., Alassafi, M. O., Alharthi, A., Walters, R. J., & Wills, G. (2016). Threat taxonomy for cloud of things. In Internet of Things and big data analysis: Recent trends and challenges (pp. 149–190). Academic Press.

Ferrari, P., & Sisinni, E. (2017). *Evaluation of communication latency in Industrial IoT applications.* doi:10.1109/IWMN.2017.8078359

Gambi, E., Montanini, L., Raffaeli, L., Spinsante, S., & Lambrinos, L. (2016). Interoperability in IoT infrastructures for enhanced living environments. *2016 IEEE International Black Sea Conference on Communications and Networking, BlackSeaCom 2016,* 1–5. 10.1109/BlackSeaCom.2016.7901573

Gazis, V., Manuel, G., Huber, M., Leonardi, A., Mathioudakis, K., Wiesmaier, A., & Zeiger, F. (2015). IoT: Challenges, projects, architectures. *2015 18th International Conference on Intelligence in Next Generation Networks,* 145–147.

Gluhak, A., Vermesan, O., Bahr, R., Clari, F., Maria, T. M., Delgado, T., Hoeer, A., Bösenberg, F., Senigalliesi, M., & Barchett, V. (2016). *BDeliverable D03.01 Report on IoT platform activities - UNIFY-IoT.* Academic Press.

Gomes, M. M., Da Rosa Righi, R., & Da Costa, C. A. (2014). Future directions for providing better IoT infrastructure. *UbiComp 2014 - Adjunct Proceedings of the 2014 ACM International Joint Conference on Pervasive and Ubiquitous Computing*, 51–54. 10.1145/2638728.2638752

Gope, P., & Hwang, T. (2015). Untraceable sensor movement in distributed IoT infrastructure. *IEEE Sensors Journal*, *15*(9), 5340–5348. doi:10.1109/JSEN.2015.2441113

Guechi, F. A. (1955). Secure and Parallel Expressive Search over Encrypted Data with Access Control in Multi-CloudIoT. *2018 3rd Cloudification of the Internet of Things (CIoT)*, 1–8.

Gunawi, H. S., Hao, M., Suminto, R. O., Laksono, A., Satria, A. D., Adityatama, J., & Eliazar, K. J. (2016). Why Does the Cloud Stop Computing? Lessons from Hundreds of Service Outages. *ACM Symp. Cloud Comput.*, 1–6. 10.1145/2987550.2987583

Gupta, A., Christie, R., & Manjula, R. (2017). Scalability in Internet of Things: Features, techniques and research challenges. *International Journal of Computational Intelligence Research*, *13*(7), 1617–1627.

Han, Z., Member, S., Li, X., & Huang, K. (2018). *A Software Defined Network based Security Assessment Framework for CloudIoT.* doi:10.1109/JIOT.2018.2801944

Hrestak, D., & Picek, S. (2014). Homomorphic encryption in the cloud. *2014 37th International Convention on Information and Communication Technology, Electronics and Microelectronics (MIPRO)*, 1400–1404. 10.1109/MIPRO.2014.6859786

Ishaq, I., Hoebeke, J., Moerman, I., & Demeester, P. (2012). Internet of things virtual networks: Bringing network virtualization to resource-constrained devices. *Proceedings - 2012 IEEE Int. Conf. on Green Computing and Communications, GreenCom 2012, Conf. on Internet of Things, IThings 2012 and Conf. on Cyber, Physical and Social Computing, CPSCom 2012*, 293–300. 10.1109/GreenCom.2012.152

Jabbar, S., Ullah, F., Khalid, S., Khan, M., & Han, K. (2017). Semantic interoperability in heterogeneous IoT infrastructure for healthcare. *Wireless Communications and Mobile Computing*, *2017*, 1–10. doi:10.1155/2017/9731806

Jensen, M., Schwenk, J., Gruschka, N., & Lo Iacono, L. (2009). On technical security issues in cloud computing. *CLOUD 2009 - 2009 IEEE International Conference on Cloud Computing*, 109–116. 10.1109/CLOUD.2009.60

Kalyani, G., & Chaudhari, S. (2019). An efficient approach for enhancing security in Internet of Things using the optimum authentication key An efficient approach for enhancing security in Internet of Things using the optimum authentication key. *International Journal of Computers and Applications, 0*(0), 1–9. doi:10.1080/120 6212X.2019.1619277

Kamilaris, A., Trifa, V., & Pitsillides, A. (2010). The smart home meets the web of things. *International Journal of Ad Hoc and Ubiquitous Computing*, 1–12.

Kamvar, S. D., Schlosser, M. T., & Garcia-Molina, H. (2003). *The EigenTrust Algorithm for Reputation Management in P2P Networks*. Academic Press.

Kempf, J., Arkko, J., Beheshti, N., & Yedavalli, K. (2011). *Thoughts on reliability in the Internet of Things*. Academic Press.

Kim, S.-M., Choi, H.-S., & Rhee, W.-S. (2015). IoT home gateway for auto-configuration and management of MQTT devices. *2015 IEEE Conference on Wireless Sensors*, 12–17. 10.1109/ICWISE.2015.7380346

Kumari, S., Karuppiah, M., Kumar, A., Xiong, D., Fan, L., & Kumar, N. (2018). A secure authentication scheme based on elliptic curve cryptography for IoT and cloud servers. *The Journal of Supercomputing, 74*(12), 6428–6453. doi:10.100711227-017-2048-0

Lauter, K., Naehrig, M., & Vaikuntanathan, V. (2011). Can homomorphic encryption be practical? *Proceedings of the ACM Conference on Computer and Communications Security*, 113–124. 10.1145/2046660.2046682

Lee, J., Lapira, E., Bagheri, B., & an Kao, H. (2013). Recent advances and trends in predictive manufacturing systems in big data environment. *Manufacturing Letters, 1*(1), 38–41. doi:10.1016/j.mfglet.2013.09.005

Li, F., Vögler, M., Claeßens, M., & Dustdar, S. (2013). Efficient and scalable IoT service delivery on Cloud. *2013 IEEE Sixth International Conference on Cloud Computing*, 1–8.

Li, Z., Liang, M., O'Brien, L., & Zhang, H. (2013). The Cloud's Cloudy Moment: A Systematic Survey of Public Cloud Service Outage. *International Journal of Cloud Computing and Services Science, 2*(5), 1–15. doi:10.11591/closer.v2i5.5125

Liu, J., Xiao, Y., & Chen, C. L. P. (2012). Authentication and access control in the Internet of things. *Proceedings - 32nd IEEE International Conference on Distributed Computing Systems Workshops, ICDCSW 2012*, 588–592. 10.1109/ICDCSW.2012.23

Liu, Y., Dong, B., Guo, B., Yang, J., & Peng, W. (2015). Combination of Cloud Computing and Internet of Things (IOT) in Medical Monitoring Systems. *International Journal of Hybrid Information Technology*, *8*(12), 367–376. doi:10.14257/ijhit.2015.8.12.28

Luo, L., Meng, S., Qiu, X., & Dai, Y. (2019). Improving failure tolerance in large-scale cloud computing systems. *IEEE Transactions on Reliability*, *68*(2), 620–632. doi:10.1109/TR.2019.2901194

Mahalle, P. N., Anggorojati, B., Prasad, N. R., & Prasad, R. (2012). Identity establishment and capability based access control (IECAC) scheme for Internet of Things. *The 15th International Symposium on Wireless Personal Multimedia Communications*, 187–191.

Maharaj, P. K. G. B. T., & Malekian, R. (2016). A novel and secure IoT based cloud centric architecture to perform predictive analysis of users activities. *Multimedia Tools and Applications*. Advance online publication. doi:10.100711042-016-4050-6

Mahmud, M., Kaiser, M. S., Rahman, M. M., Rahman, M. A., Shabut, A., & Hussain, S. A. A. (2018). *A Brain-Inspired Trust Management Model to Assure Security in a Cloud Based IoT Framework for Neuroscience Applications*. Academic Press.

Malik, A., & Om, H. (2018). *Cloud Computing and Internet of Things Integration : Architecture, Applications, Issues, and Challenges*. doi:10.1007/978-3-319-62238-5

Mansour, I., Sahandi, R., Cooper, K., & Warman, A. (2016). Interoperability in the heterogeneous cloud environment: A survey of recent user-centric approaches. *ACM International Conference Proceeding Series*, 1–7. 10.1145/2896387.2896447

Manyika, J., Chui, M., Bisson, P., Woetzel, J., Dobbs, R., Bughin, J., & Aharon, D. (2015). *The Internet of Things: Mapping the value beyond the hype*. Academic Press.

Masoodi, F., Alam, S., & Siddiqui, S. T. (2019). Security & Privacy Threats, Attacks and Countermeasures in Internet of Things. *International Journal of Network Security & Its Applications*, *11*(02), 67–77. doi:10.5121/ijnsa.2019.11205

Masoodi, F. S., & Bokhari, M. U. (2019). Symmetric Algorithms I. In *Emerging Security Algorithms and Techniques* (pp. 79–95). Chapman and Hall/CRC. doi:10.1201/9781351021708-6

Miraz, M. H., Ali, M., Excell, P. S., & Picking, R. (2015). A review on Internet of Things (IoT), Internet of Everything (IoE) and Internet of Nano Things (IoNT). *2015 Internet Technologies and Applications, ITA 2015 - Proceedings of the 6th International Conference*, 219–224. 10.1109/ITechA.2015.7317398

Misra, P. (2016). *Build a scalable platform for high-performance IoT applications.* Academic Press.

Nitti, M., Atzori, L., & Cvijikj, I. P. (2013). *Friendship selection in the Social Internet of Things: challenges and possible strategies.* doi:10.1109/JIOT.2014.2384734

Nitti, M., Girau, R., & Atzori, L. (2014). Trustworthiness Management in the Social Internet of Things. *IEEE Transactions on Knowledge and Data Engineering, 26*(5), 1253–1266. doi:10.1109/TKDE.2013.105

Noura, M., Atiquzzaman, M., & Gaedke, M. (2019). Interoperability in Internet of Things: Taxonomies and open challenges. *Mobile Networks and Applications, 24*(3), 796–809. doi:10.100711036-018-1089-9

Odun-ayo, I., Okereke, C., & Orovwode, H. (2018). Cloud Computing and Internet of Things. *Issues and Developments, C*, I.

Pandow, B. A., Bamhdi, A. M., & Masoodi, F. (2020). Internet of Things: Financial Perspective and Associated Security Concerns. *International Journal of Computer Theory and Engineering, 12*(5), 123–127. doi:10.7763/IJCTE.2020.V12.1276

Pottoo, S. N., Wani, T. M., Dar, A., & Mir, A. (2018). IoT Enabled by Li-Fi Technology. International Journal of Scientific Research in Computer Science, Engineering and Information Technology, 1(4).

Puthal, D., Nepal, S., Ranjan, R., & Chen, J. (2016). Threats to networking cloud and edge datacenters in the Internet of Things. *IEEE Cloud Computing, 3*(3), 64–71. doi:10.1109/MCC.2016.63

Rabkin, A., Arye, M., Sen, S., Pai, V., & Freedman, M. J. (2013). *Making Every Bit Count in Wide-Area Analytics.* Academic Press.

Rodrigues, L., Guerreiro, J., & Correia, N. (2016). RELOAD/CoAP architecture with resource aggregation/disaggregation service. *IEEE International Symposium on Personal, Indoor and Mobile Radio Communications, PIMRC*, 1–6. 10.1109/PIMRC.2016.7794607

Roman, R., Zhou, J., & Lopez, J. (2013). On the features and challenges of security and privacy in distributed internet of things. *Computer Networks, 57*(10), 2266–2279. doi:10.1016/j.comnet.2012.12.018

Sakr, S., Liu, A., Batista, D. M., & Alomari, M. (2011). A survey of large scale data management approaches in cloud environments. In IEEE Communications Surveys and Tutorials (Vol. 13, Issue 3, pp. 311–336). doi:10.1109/SURV.2011.032211.00087

Samie, F., Bauer, L., & Henkel, J. (2016). IoT technologies for embedded computing: A survey. *2016 International Conference on Hardware/Software Codesign and System Synthesis, CODES+ISSS 2016*, 1–10. 10.1145/2968456.2974004

Sicari, S., Rizzardi, A., Grieco, L. A., & Coen-Porisini, A. (2015). Security, privacy and trust in Internet of things: The road ahead. *Computer Networks, 76*(October), 146–164. doi:10.1016/j.comnet.2014.11.008

Simmhan, Y., Kumbhare, A. G., Cao, B., & Prasanna, V. (2011). An analysis of security and privacy issues in smart grid software architectures on clouds. *Proceedings - 2011 IEEE 4th International Conference on Cloud Computing, CLOUD 2011*, 582–589. 10.1109/CLOUD.2011.107

Singh, J., Pasquier, T., Bacon, J., Ko, H., & Eyers, D. (2016). Twenty Security Considerations for Cloud-Supported Internet of Things. *IEEE Internet of Things Journal, 3*(3), 269–284. doi:10.1109/JIOT.2015.2460333

Sobin, C. C. (2020). A Survey on Architecture, Protocols and Challenges in IoT. In Wireless Personal Communications. Springer US. doi:10.100711277-020-07108-5

Sood, S. K. (2019). Mobile fog based secure cloud-IoT framework for enterprise multimedia security. *Multimedia Tools and Applications*. Advance online publication. doi:10.100711042-019-08573-2

Stergiou, C., Psannis, K. E., Kim, B. G., & Gupta, B. (2018). Secure integration of IoT and Cloud Computing. *Future Generation Computer Systems, 78*, 964–975. doi:10.1016/j.future.2016.11.031

Stojmenovic, I., & Wen, S. (2014). The Fog computing paradigm: Scenarios and security issues. *2014 Federated Conference on Computer Science and Information Systems, FedCSIS 2014*, 1–8. 10.15439/2014F503

Wu, L., Xu, Y. J., Xu, C. N., & Wang, F. (2013). Plug-configure-play service-oriented gateway: For fast and easy sensor network application development. *SENSORNETS 2013 - Proceedings of the 2nd International Conference on Sensor Networks*, 53–58. 10.5220/0004271700530058

Xu, B., Da Xu, L., Cai, H., Xie, C., Hu, J., & Bu, F. (2014). Ubiquitous data accessing method in iot-based information system for emergency medical services. *IEEE Transactions on Industrial Informatics, 10*(2), 1578–1586. doi:10.1109/TII.2014.2306382

Zaslavsky, A., Perera, C., & Georgakopoulos, D. (2012). Sensing as a Service and Big Data. *International Conference on Advances in Cloud Computing (ACC)*, 1–8.

Zhang, F., Liu, G., Fu, X., & Yahyapour, R. (2018). A survey on virtual machine migration: Challenges, techniques, and open issues. *IEEE Communications Surveys and Tutorials*, *20*(2), 1206–1243. doi:10.1109/COMST.2018.2794881

Chapter 4
Applications of Cloud-Based Internet of Things

Nipun R. Navadia
*Dronacharya Group of Institutions,
India*

Taranjeet Singh
*G. L. Bajaj Institute of Management,
India*

Gurleen Kaur
*Dronacharya Group of Institutions,
India*

Aditi Sakalle
*USICT, Gautam Buddha University,
India*

Harshit Bhardwaj
*USICT, Gautam Buddha University,
India*

Divya Acharya
*iNurture Education Solutions Private
Limited, India*

Arpit Bhardwaj
Bennett University, India

ABSTRACT

Cloud storage is a great way for companies to fulfill more of their data-driven needs and excellent technology that allows the company to evolve and grow at a faster pace, accelerating growth and providing a flexible forum for developers to build useful apps for better devices to be developed over the internet. The integration of cloud computing and the internet of things creates a scalable, maintainable, end-to-end internet of things solution on the cloud network. By applying the infrastructure to the real universe, it generates sources of insight. Cloud computing and IoT are separate technology but are closely associated and are termed as 'cloud-based IoT' as IoT has the ability to create intelligent goods and services, gather data that can affect business decisions and probably change the business model to boost success and expansion, and cloud infrastructure can be at the heart of all IoT has to deliver.

DOI: 10.4018/978-1-7998-6981-8.ch004

INTRODUCTION

In the context of Cloud Computing and Internet of Things (IoT) the prototype, the Iot concept is both global and dynamically networked infrastructure based, and it operates self-configuring entities with superior intellect. It is distinguished by legitimate issues such as performance, reliability, privacy and scalability and typically includes small artifacts (things) with minimal Memory storage and computing power. Cloud Computing, on the other hand, is a huge area with nearly infinite capacities when it comes to data and computing capacity. Many IoT problems were partly solved by this technology. IoT and Cloud are two daunting developments that have been combined to transform the present and potential of Internetworking networks (Chang, et al., 2011),(Zhou, et al., 2013). The majority of the papers presented individually about Iot and Cloud, indicating concern in the trend since 2008, and there are many more journals on our analysis between 2008 and 2013 about IoT and Cloud integration. Implementation of Cloud and IoT is the most current and upcoming trend (Cloud based IoT). Cloud IoT is the name assigned to this latest concept.

Cloud computing is a technology concept that allows ubiquitous, on-demand platform access to a number of customizable computing infrastructure such as servers, software, networks, storage and services, all of which can be easily delivered and deployed with limited maintenance effort or service provider involvement. The five basic features of the Cloud Computing paradigm are Resource pooling, limited network connectivity, Rapid Elasticity, Metered Operation and on-demand self-service. Infrastructure as a Service, Applications as a Service, and Web as a Service are both part of the Cloud Paradigm. Private Cloud, public Cloud, Hybrid Cloud, and Group Cloud are some of the implementation frameworks for cloud computing (Mell, et al., 2011).

The IoT theory has developed quickly in recent time, and It recognizes the web as a collection of sophisticated and integrated artifacts in a complex, global constructing networks. Objects are individually addressable and as well as available smart devices with sensing and actuation capabilities that are widely dispersed and have minimal computational resources like Processor, network capabilities and memories. The Internet of Things (IoT) is the combination of many systems and connectivity solutions, such as RFID, actuators and cameras. The primary concept is that smart objects would be present all over people, capable of understanding, monitoring, and even controlling the world. IoT has the ability to play a vital role in e-health, smart homes and offices and smart transportation assisted living scenarios at home and at work (Vermesan, et al., 2011)(Chen, et al.,2014)(Whitmore, et al., 2015)(Da Xu, et al., 2014). Small wearable sensors, for example, are used in biomedical applications to collect patient data like readings of blood pressure. The information gathered is then submitted to physicians for medical consultation, and it may even be made accessible to medical researchers for analysis remotely. Smart Cities is one more ground-breaking IoT technology that seeks to create an effective networking and collaboration network by combining different data sources to render communities smarter (Yue, et al., 2014)(Tei, et al., 2014)(Moreno, et al., 2016). Despite recent progress in rendering IoT a possibility, there are a number of accessible concerns that will need further research and development activities to fully realize its potential (Cavalcante, et al., 2016) (Borgia, et al., 2014) (Mital, et al., 2016). One of these issues is the enormous amount of energy required to stream data generated by a so many interconnected computers with limited resources, which must be collected, analyzed, and delivered in an effective and understandable manner.

Table 1. Major difference between IoT and Cloud

IOT	Cloud
The Internet of Things (IoT) is everywhere about us (things placed everywhere).	Clouds are everywhere (resources usable from everywhere).
There are incidents that happen in the actual world.	It's all about virtual capital.
This is constrained in terms of computing power.	It has almost limitless computing power.
It has minimal storage capacity or none at all.	The cloud has almost limitless computing options.
The Internet is seen as a point of integration in this case.	It delivers services over the internet.
This is a large-scale data base.	It refers to the management of large amounts of data.

Various surveys have lately embraced cloud infrastructure as a potential alternative to some of the IoT's problems. In (Mell, et al., 2011), NIST describes cloud computing as a paradigm for allowing easy, access on request of all networks to a common reserve of computing tools which are configurable and can be quickly configured and published by service supplier with small control commitment involvement. Cloud computing also moved processing and all the activities from the laptop and desktop to the internet, allowing for nearly limitless data and computational capacity. Because of the cloud on-demand utility price structure, the usage of cloud infrastructure to manage enterprises has grown significantly over the last decade. To devise the structure, suppliers provide services to the public on a reservoir of resources, end users search for and pay to take advantage of the programmes they need, and a network of strong bandwidth link is formed between users and providers. To compensate for its technical constraints (i.e., storage, computation, and communication), IoT will take advantage of the cloud paradigm's practically infinite capability and services (Alessio, et al., 2014) (Yue, et al., 2014). According to a study published by the International Data Corporation (IDC), deployed service provider datacenter resources consumed by IoT workloads will rise by approximately 750 percent during the years 2014-2019 (Yue, et al., 2014), and over 80 to 95 percent of the information produced IoT computers will be a server in the cloud by the year 2020. According to the study, IoT would become the most significant engine of IT growth in broader datacenters, hastening the move to cloud-based computing and data network architectures.

Since IoT can access the cloud's limitless resources, it can use the model for delivering cloud infrastructure resources to make available to end-users with IoT services. The Service oriented Architecture seems a promising approach that can be outlined to IoT services of this manner that functionalities of each smart system are offered as a single service with a shared interface for correspondence. To become a "stuff," all concerned resources are labeled as input/output components. The main economic goal of this pay-as-you-go pricing technology is to help these computing tools available for consumers' needs at a certain moment. Pay-per-use would enable users to focus more strongly on IoT apps, allowing them to more efficiently and scale them up and down as required offerings within the spectrum of their needs (Baker, et al., 2015). In this case, providers of services have a bunch of IoT tools combined as online services that can be assembled by a representative to provide users with a single infrastructure that has been virtualized. In a situation when one vendor is insufficient to meet customer demand, the composition of the operation is crucial. In essence, a customer request would travel the path to the service provider, who will then return a response to the user. This situation If the number of people increases, the situation gets more complex of needed providers grows, or where only a portion of the requested service is accessible, or when performing a customer activity based on resource limitations, that a single provider cannot treat individually. The most famous examples of this are service configuration and broker-based service structures (Baker, et al., 2015), which require coordination across multiple IoT service providers. This, whether directly or indirectly, formulates the so-called Multi-clouds IoT Environment in order to provide service outputs and end effects to the customer.

Users typically prioritize service pace, response time, and expense, with little to no regard for service place, number of hybrid resources required to satisfy specifications, or energy efficiency. Cloud computing's increasingly increasing rate of electricity usage and greenhouse emissions have become a major environmental issue. When the number of IoT software customers, vendors, and datacenters grows, so will traffic on the internet and the resources needed by a massive infrastructure necessary to react efficiently and successfully to a consumer request. This power consumption problem is especially important when moving data or information to a datacenter that is situated some place on the earth that is comparatively far away from the spatial location of the customer, such as the UK and Hong Kong. Furthermore, considering the vast the quantity of service providers providing things and the enormous volume of data produced, increased network bandwidth and pace are expected to deal with worldwide cloud internet traffic and to accelerate data transfer processes (Rose, et al., 2015). As a consequence, a considerable amount of electricity is consumed. Thus, in order to meet customer needs, a major challenge is to incorporate less networks from cross-continental and dispersed vendors, which implies less data sharing and, as a result, a lower to deal with global cloud network traffic in the multi-cloud IoT setting. The energy usage of the whole application phase is influenced by the flow of large amounts of data between facilities.

BACKGROUND

IoT is a new technology that aims to incorporate machine vision into devices for the home that are a must properly managing house frameworks. Few early studies that used Modeling and simulation using Internet of Things (IoT) technologies and there have been smart homes built. seen. As per the authors of (Pandiyan, et al., 2020) created a safe home atmosphere that made use of data fusion and belief interpretation to monitor daily household behaviors by combining IoT and service are inextricably linked. technologies. According to the authors of (Sanjeevi, et al., 2017) tried to monitor residents' daily routines and behaviors in order to have a comfortable living environment.

Previous activities in this field have mainly focused on particular concerns such as providing reliable data management systems or data protection and protection. Data from interoperable smart devices stored in the cloud collection as well as study to allow make well-informed decisions has received little attention.

As per the authors of (Tseng, et al., 2014) emphasized a importance of the coherent raw data speech collected from a variety of Internet-of-Things (IoT) devices in order to make processing easier . Typically, Data from the Internet of Things is collected through physical tags, sensors, and actuators in a variety of forms, and the data cannot be interpreted as a single entity. The value of the interoperability in this field is reflected in the article. The aim of the project was to expand the Architecture of the EPCglobal system by using a standardized EPC (Electronic Product Coding) system to describe 1451- IEEE standard. compliant transducers to process more data diverse Data from IoT applications. They did not think about the difficulties of transferring Clouds and data storage effective research.

As per the author of (Moreno, et al., 2014) suggest a comprehensive Smart IoT devices climate control framework. The creators (Authors) acknowledge exponential expansion and implementation of sensors and mobile systems in our environment, as well as the variability of data generated by these devices. As a consequence, their proposed platform aims to address the issue of interoperability. problems in data collection, analysis, and manage. Their ideas are similar to ours, but They focused on mixing energy consumption with the ease of use in the smart buildings rather than considering Cloud connectivity for data collection.

Authors in (Brama, et al., 2014) propose a modular smart object inter-device communication procedure . Their paper addresses the role of interoperability and durability in data collection and analysis for Sensory objects The authors confronted these concerns on a low-level hardware level by developing flexSPI, a quick and scalable protocol for contact between devices and it is based on the Serial Peripheral Interface (SPI) that uses packet-oriented signaling to minimize routing overhead and allow modularity. Furthermore, they believe that when developing sensors for the IoT setting, low power consumption is critical. Their method, on the other hand, ignores data collection and analysis at the device level in Clouds.

To maintain anonymity, the author of (Hummen, et al., 2012) suggest a user-controlled cloud design collection and analysis of data from sensors They understood the importance of using the cloud to process data from sensors On the other side, their approach focuses on security-related issues such as data safety and access control. In view of the influx of sensor results, the author of (Aoki, et al., 2010) present a Infrastructure for the cloud that enables quick response to real-world applications. To accomplish this aim, the authors used a method of lowering network latency, but they did not suggest designing a common framework for various sensor data collection.

For real-time data collection, author of (Piyare, et al., 2013) propose a user interface for integrating Wireless Sensor Networks (WSN) with cloud services WSN is an essential model for Internet of Things, according to their approach, since it is made up of smart sensing nodes with integrated Central Processing Units (CPUs) and sensors for monitoring different conditions ,Other sensor forms were not included in this study, which focused on linking WSNs to Clouds. In (Mell, et al., 2011) (Vermesan, et al., 2011), the authors explore specific methods for collecting medical sensor results. A survey on the use of sensors was conducted in Clouds is presented by (Alamri, et al., 2013)The survey examines in this field's latest efforts and threats, revealing that many new initiatives are focused on creating abstract sensors in Clouds from real sensors.

GSN (Global Sensor Network) is a middleware system. developed by the author of (Salehi, et al., 2007) to link various sensor network technologies. The aim of this project is to create a system that allows current networked sensors to be easily integrated. The control of sensor networks is made easier with this method. Changing or upgrading components in a sensor network, for example, has little effect on connections with other sensor networks. The article, however, does not take into account the collection of information from a single sensor. Other projects, such as the Sensor Observation Service (SOS) (Emeakaroha, et al., 2015), include The Open

Geospatial Consortium is a non-profit organization dedicated to the advancement of (OGC) -compliant specifications for the detection and Geospatial data collection and exchange was used to retrieve real-time data from a number of sensors.

As a result, none of the current work, to our knowledge, offers a common Cloud-based infrastructure for monitoring, data collection, analysis, and actuating processes. In the following portion, we examine the current state of commercial and open source systems.

The writers of (Son, et al., 2016) proposed a frivolous time management scheme for home mechanization networks based on the restricted app protocol (CoAP). In the home automation network, the CoAP decision area, along with the header shim, and is recycled to include a the date and time stamp As a result, their proposed method can be used in mechanization networks that are both IP-based and non-IP-based . In their opinion, tests, they used a variety of non-IP connection devices, and preliminary findings show that their proposed solution has a standard 1 millisecond delay and a device overhead reduction of seventeen percent as compared to the service model of the network time protocol

The interface of numerous home appliances and utilities planned by various vendors has resulted in several managing and operating issues due to a lack of continuity. New services integrating existing heterogeneous cameras, home admittances, and cloud computing are all examples of home systems. for developing clouds aimed at smart homes have been spoken about as a solution to this issue. The author of (Petnik, et al., 2018) demonstrated a cloud-based method for meeting the growing demand for smart homes by allowing transfers among smart home appliances over web services to improve data transmission efficiency. Since cloud-based applications are characterized by continuous cross-platform interaction, privacy protection is a major concern. Authors in (Tao, et al., 2018) proposed an architecture integrating danger and home appliance controlling to implement scheduled data allocation by establishing risk management as a cloud service. In conclusion, the smart home industry's potential trend is to continue integrating IoT and cloud storage technologies.

The authors introduced the strategy and implementation of a smart home structure with IoT in (Gaikwad, et al., 2015). They created a classification system that is both practical and long-term, with the added advantage of reduced costs. This approach affluents the home automation job, and the consumer can access and monitor their home automation control from anywhere through the internet. Individual switch components and IoT devices can be identified by conveying a distinct individuality to them, which will electrically disconnect two circuits and hypnotically reattach them. On the host stage, this method's security has been boosted by completing three levels of Kerberos validation.

A new dissemination of resources that uses both IoT and cloud computing technologies has been developed to provide several advantages into smart home organization, thanks to technological advancements in IoT and cloud computing. Authors in (Uma, et al., 2019) propose a cloud-based solution to incorporate remote control of electrical equipment on the network in order to address home construction and sustainable power issues. Authors in (Han, et al., 2014) demonstrated a hardware pattern of lightweight authentication mechanism in cloud-based IoT setting, called LAM-CIoT, to identify resident's activity and smartly support resident's charge on power without or with slip. In (Uma, et al., 2019) authors also proposed a smart home energy management system (HEMS) framework by employing intelligence and sensing technology, and machine learning system.

They defined a real-world IoT castoff implementation for observing consistent domestic circumstances using a low-cost pervasive sensing system in (Wazid, et al., 2020). In their context, they recognize the network framework and communicating devices for the consistent calculation of constraints by sensors and the transmission of knowledge across the network. The longitudinal erudition approach offers a self-regulatory mechanism for improving the administration phase of devices. For data aggregation, the device is built on a set of widely dispersed sensing components. The results show that the incorporated network architecture improves the accuracy of sensing data transfer by 97 percent.

Authors of (Mrozek, et al., 2020) provide an overview of existing approaches for activity recognition as well as new developments and focuses of pending problems in this IoT by resident and elderly care in smart homes. Authors in (Suryadevara, et al., 2013) suggest a movement detection framework that employs a predictor and conviction mechanism to examine context-sensitive details, allowing for prompt recognition of the elderly's irregular behavior and related assistance operations. Several studies have also piqued interest in cloud and IoT-based architecture and approaches that incorporate ontology methods for activity monitoring and regulation in smart home environments (Okeyo, et al., 2014).

The data flow algorithm (DFA) (Kesavan, et al., 2016), the systems integration system for IoT devices in the cloud (SMFIC) , the data-centric framework for IoT apps in the cloud (DCFIC) , and the remote surveillance cloud platform of healthcare knowledge (RMCPHI) (Luo, et al., 2016) both disseminate a wireless overview based on network decorum to accomplish the audacious home mechanisms fluently. They assessed a home structure with the help of related devices, having been trained in this methodology. Entities may use mundane smartphones to ostensibly view home uses.

THE DEMAND FOR IOT AND CLOUD INTEGRATION

Since IoT has restricted computing capacity and storage resources, as well as issues such as Efficiency, Stability, Reliability, and Privacy, combining The Internet of

Things (IoT) is more powerful when combined with the cloud. advantageous for achieving limitless competences such as processing and storage capacity. IoT will also enable the cloud broaden its functionality by helping it to communicate with real-world artifacts in a more complex and dispersed way, allowing it to provide a wide range of resources in real time. The cloud would serve as an abstraction layer among applications and items, obfuscating many of the functionalities and nuances required for subsequent processing (Roman, et al., 2013). The system has consequences for potential application growth, as the knowledge collection and sharing processes would face new problems in a multi-Cloud world (Alberti, et al., 2016). The benefits of implementing the Cloud IoT model are described below (Roman, et al., 2013).

NETWORK ARCHITECTURES

IoT computers are often space limited, and they only use the storing and forwarding form of forwarding of packets when they have sufficiently storing. IoT nodes cannot perform computationally demanding activities, so they must be outsourced to the cloud, where both computing and processing capacity are presumed to be available. As a result, the resource-constrained environment necessitates a gentle supporting action for efficiency and practicability, notably for IoT users.

Moving IoT users (such as cars and mobile energy consumers) are dynamically categorized into various social classes dependent on their paths, velocities, and accelerations, and are believed to be evenly spread. Each group's IoT nodes are in touch with one another, broadcast their gathered content bundles on demand, and exchange a dynamically modified group key that they have all agreed. Owing to complex community structure, the group leader is positioned at the group core, is resistant to such attacks, and is updated on a daily basis.

Self-Organization: Within contact range of each other, smartphone IoT users often collect and broadcast packet bundles. The cloud is only involved where high-complexity computations must be delegated from resource-constrained IoT computers, but it is seldom involved in the development and authentication of distributed information packages.

Short-Range Communication: In mobile cloud-based IoT, there is no assured link between the origin and the final destination owing to responsiveness as well as short-range contact. Every IoT consumer is part of a delay-tolerant network (DTN). The accounting center (AC) is in charge of charging and awarding IoT users, and packet transmission is achieved by cooperation among IoT users.

APPLICATIONS

This session explores a broad variety of technologies that have been dramatically expanded by the Cloud IoT paradigm. For a vast number of applications (Mittal, et al., 2016), which are characterized by features, accessible problems, and obstacles, combining two technologies makes sense. The following are few descriptions of cloud Iot systems.

1. Agriculture

As a function, the Internet of Things (IoT) In agriculture, the Internet of Things (IoT) is bringing on new problems. As a consequence, the most profitable crops are those with the lowest output costs. Contribution of IoT in Agriculture, agricultural equipment, agricultural goods (pesticides, fertilizers, etc.) are all integrated, as are wide band networks and data base structures, culminating in a new "agricultural infrastructure" class. Using RFID to monitor food, tracking soil and plants, observing and regulating (the greenhouse effect), keeping track of livestock and food protection requirements are only a few of the advantages of agriculture with IoT. Water, dirt, nutrients, fertilizers, and other agricultural materials are controlled, which ensures they are utilized in the quantity and consistency that the crop needs. As a part of cloud computing: Farmers cannot handle administration providers on an individual basis in regional areas because it is not financially viable. They need comprehensive and financial administration vendors that can deliver a range of services. MBR Customer Services Pvt. Ltd. is one such dare to appeal to the needs of the rural market community. Rama Krishna created it in 2005. It began as a mega mart in Andhra Pradesh, with an first-time setup of around ten villages and has since expanded to 55. The above MBR is somebody who has given more India's rural farmers get edge assistance. MBR has encouraged more stuff and continues to do so certain critical products such as retail distribution, fast moving customer products, and a boost, among others. Individual farmers can be able to sell crops directly to consumers using the Internet of Things, not only in a specific location like direct selling or supermarkets, but across a wider area. This development contributes to increased crop yields, more efficient food commodity prices, and food product production, both of which support the actual world.

2. Healthcare

Some modernized hospitals use sensor networks to keep track of patient physiological data, which is used to regulate the facility, physicians, and patients, as well as to manage medication administration (Mittal, et al., 2016). IoT and multimedia systems (Moreno, et al., 2014) was the first contribution in the area of healthcare. To allow patient facilities that are both high quality and cost effective and are available anywhere, mobile internet that works, smart devices, and Cloud services are leading to indefinite and systemic health-care inventiveness (Brama, et al., 2014). Hospital and laboratories, physician networks, health insurance providers, customers, pharmacies and other organizations are some of the applications faced by the healthcare sector (Alessio, et al., 2014). This form of healthcare application produces a ton of data and information, which needs to be adequately processed for potential processing and review (Hummen, et al., 2012). In the future, mobile devices can enhance access and connectivity to health information (Roman, et al., 2013). Device reliability, streaming quality of the service (QoS), compatibility, and adaptive increasing memory have all been investigated in this sector (Brama, et al., 2014).

3. Smart City

IoT (Rose, et al., 2015), gathering information and data from sensors or devices, IoT technologies (Geo-tagging and RFID sensors), and placing information and data in a coherent about a way are examples of traditional middleware for future-oriented smart cities. It has been proposed in recent proposals to make it simpler to find, attach, and incorporate actuators and sensors. This promotes the creation of realtime technologies for the model of smart cities and universal networking. This makes it possible for third parties to build IoT plug-ins that are cloud-connected (Aoki, et al., 2010). Protection, real-time interaction, and durability are all common concerns.

4. Smart Home and Smart Metering

IoT has a lot of applications for the home setting, where embedded sensors are used, to allow the automation of routine in-home activities. Cloud is the greatest source for creating scalable software with fewer code lines and for performing complicated activities as well (Roman, et al., 2013). When a single parent household Some of the following criteria must be fulfilled before a smart home accessing reusable service can be reached over the internet. The bulk of the proposed literatures are concerned with and incorporate metered systems for appliance identification (Mell, et al., 2011), Advanced power management and wireless sensors (Mell, et al., 2011), heating, illumination, and air conditioning (Roman, et al., 2013). To increase quality, further problems must be addressed. For example, home computers must be wired to the internet, which necessitates consistent identification and service details, as well as structured contact. Effective computer machines that must be built should be given to manage tasks and communicate with IoT and Cloud.

5. Surveillance by Camera

As a tracking and self-management device, video surveillance is the most essential intelligent thing in terms of protection concerns. To meet the storage and processing requirements of the complex video study, Cloud-based solutions (Tseng, et al., 2014) were needed. The suggested approach includes detecting, saving, and handling video data from cameras, as well as increasing data transmission reliability to the amount of users via the load-balancing, internet and fault tolerance approaches.

6. Smart Mobility and Vehicles

Automobile utilities and transportation networks will benefit from the Internet of Things. Loud computing convergence systems for satellite networks, as well as wearable sensor networks, provide a way to solve the most urgent problems. IoT-based vehicular data clouds are a modern form of technologies that can be used to offer market advantages such as reducing traffic congestion, traffic control (Piyare, et al., 2013), and enhancing road protection. The Internet of Things and Cloud Storage technology are powered by a cloud-based vehicular data network. The key aim of these networks is to provide consumers with lower-cost, real-time, on-demand, and safe applications. Vehicular Clouds are planned to broaden existing Cloud storage capabilities, processing, and on-demand computing. Scalability, Standard of Operation, Efficiency, and Efficiency of IoT-based vehicular Clouds (Piyare, et al., 2013), (Salehi, et al., 2007). Implementing authorization and authentication systems that have an effect on infrastructure privacy and protection is complicated (Alamri, et al., 2013).

PRIVACY AND SECURITY IN CLOUD BASED IOT

We primarily concentrate on cloud-based IoT security risks, especially in the areas of safe packet forwarding with outsourced aggregated transmission proof generation and effective privacy-preserving authentication with outsourced message filtering. The following are the special protection and privacy standards of cloud-based IoT, in addition to the standard data confidentiality and unforgeability:

- **Identity Protection:** Conditional identity secrecy relates to the fact that the true identity of a telephone IoT device can be kept secret from the public; but, once a conflict happens in an accident, the government will track it down easily. Pseudonyms have been commonly used to accomplish this aim, but the computing expense of modifying pseudonyms and certificates on a frequent basis is too large for resource-constrained IoT nodes. More seriously, it is susceptible to the mechanically complex tracing assault on location privacy that we found.

- **Place Privacy:** Location privacy tends to be particularly essential in IoTs, since constantly revealed location privacy will show the IoT user's living habits. The most commonly employed approach is to use pseudonyms to mask its position. However, since the position data isn't explicitly secured, it can't survive a mechanically complex tracing attack. Specifically, a community of malicious IoT users may be deployed in collusion to locations where the target IoT user occasionally traveled, in order to physically capture collections of real identities of passing nodes over specific time periods through surveillance or traffic tracking footage, and then recognise the target IoT user's real identity. If the adversary learns that the goal node with pseudonym pid visits n locations Loc1, Loc2,..., Locn on a regular basis, the adversary will detect n sets of nodes' real identities moving through these n locations Veh1, Veh2,..., Vehn. The intersection will undoubtedly expose the true nature of the tar-get node as well as its private operations in other areas.

- **Node Compromise Assault:** A node compromise attack happens when an adversary removes all confidential information from resource-constrained IoT devices, such as the secret key used to encrypt packets, the private key used to produce signatures, and so on, and then reprograms or substitutes the IoT devices with malicious ones under the adversary's power. Through observing the traffic flow across all nodes in the IoT, an adversary with global monitoring capabilities will pick the IoT node carrying the most packets as the compromise target. As a consequence, the adversary is likely to receive further packets from a single agreement in order to retrieve the original message or hinder its efficient transmission by interference.

- The layer removing/adding assault happens when a community of greedy IoT users delete all forwarding layers within themselves in order to increase their compensated credits by reducing the amount of intermediate trans- mitters sharing the incentive. Layer adding, on the other side, is a malicious detour of the packet forwarding route between IoT users for enhanced credits by growing the overall obtainable utility.

- **Forward and Backward Protection:** In the Internet of Things, forward and backward security is expected due to the versatility and complex social community forming. The former indicates that newly joined IoT users can only decode encrypted messages obtained after they enter the cluster, not before, whereas the latter implies that terminated IoT users also can decipher encrypted messages received previously but not after they quit the cluster.

- **Semi-trusted and/or deceptive cloud protection:** When the cloud and IoT combine, the cloud's security and privacy specifications should be taken into consideration. The semi-trusted model suggests that the cloud can diligently obey the protocol specification while still trying to obtain sensitive knowledge from communications with IoT users; while the malicious model implies that the adversary will destroy the protocol execution at will. As a consequence, the following three protection priorities for outsourced computing should be met:

  ○ Input privacy: Even though the cloud and approved data receivers collude, the data owner's individual inputs should be well secured.

  ○ Output privacy: Only approved data receivers should be able to decode the computation outcome.

  ○ Protection of the underlying feature: The underlying function must be well shielded against both cloud collusion and malicious IoT users.

  ○ The key protection and privacy risks in cloud-based IoT, along with the related countermeasures.

FUTURE CONSTRAINTS AND DISCUSSIONS

Sensing that is available anywhere, which slices into the every day life of more places and provides the capabilities to consider Indices for the atmosphere, deduce and quantify anything from environmental assets to urban environments, enables Wireless Sensor Network technology (IoT). Cloud environments are used to process and store the information or data. Cloud computing provides internet-based technology, platform, and apps. With the aid of Wireless Sensor Network technologies, sensors are mounted in a dispersed manner to detect changes in the atmosphere and physical changes including temperature and pressure. It aids in controlling the remotely linked sensor and the information or data provided by any other sensor globally by combining Cloud Computing and the IoT. Now we'll talk about some of the unanswered questions about Cloud IoT that still need to be researched, as well as potential paths. Now, IoT6, a European research initiative, is focusing on the usage of IP-V6 and similar specifications (such as CORE and COAP) to improve the IoT environment.

- **Standards are needed:** Though the Scientific Community has contributed to the standardization and implementation of Cloud and IoT paradigms, standard protocols, interfaces, and APTs are expected in the cloud IoT paradigm. This is for connecting the development of enhanced services with heterogeneous smart artifacts in order to realize the CloudIoT paradigm (Rose, et al., 2015).

Mobile-to-Mobile (M2M) is the dominant model, with a small standard. As a result, current strategies depend on network, telephone, and cellular technology. The majority of designs suggested in the early stages of IoT come from either Cloud at the Heart or Wireless Sensor Network viewpoints.

- **Data mining on a large scale:** The current developments do not address the complexity of big data. As a significant amount of Big data is collected, the frequency of data generated increases, and the distance between data access and data organization for processing widens. To face the demands of Big data, further analysis is required. Heterogeneous spatiotemporal (geo-related and sparsely distributed) data with high-valued data combined with incorrect data is not explicitly consumed utilizing virtualization platforms derived from IoT. New schemes must be built in order to produce visually appealing and easy-to-understand visualizations [9].

- **Capabilities of the Cloud:** Protection is a big concern for CloudIoT in every networked field or climate. On both the IoT and Cloud sides, there are further chances of assaults. Encryption in IoT may maintain integrity, anonymity, and authenticity, as well as fix internal threats, and is a common activity to enforce on processor or embedded computers. Since it has a high degree of intelligence, the RFID aspect achieves high levels of protection. To address the QoS needs of a wide range of customers, as well as to ensure that programs run smoothly, domain-specific programming resources are available. Duplication of cloud scheduling algorithms should be rendered in case of malfunction management in order to provide stable resources, but QoS parameters should be focused.

- **Computing in the fog:** Fog computing is somewhat of a computing for bringing Cloud computing and applications to the network's slant. Fog, like Cloud, provides end-users with compute, application services, files, and storage. It's a form of Cloud Computing that sits between the network's edge and the cloud, dealing with latency-sensitive applications that rely on nearby in order for nodes to meet their latency criteria (Zhou, et al., 2013).

CONCLUSION

As Cloud Computing and IOT are combined, a flexible, maintainable end-to-end Internet of Things solution is created on the cloud network. It provides points of knowledge by implementing the infrastructure in the modern world. Since IoT has minimal computational space and storage facilities, as well as concerns like Privacy, Security, Performance and Reliability, and integrating Cloud with IoT is a safer choice for achieving limitless capacities like processing power and storage.

Hence, The Cloud-based IoT has enhanced the performance of IoT technology. Based on the network architecture cloud based IOT is been defined for highlighting their integrated features. The Cloud based IoT model has significantly extended a wide range of innovations in the fields of agriculture and healthcare, and it has proven to be a versatile applied technology in smart city, smart house, and certain other applications. Identity protection, node compromise assault, place privacy, deceptive cloud protection and forward & backward protection are some of the special protection and privacy standards of cloud-based IOT. The IoT and Cloud computing are potential Internet phenomena. However, IoT technology is developing at a fast rate and is not yet interoperable. Cloud storage solutions, on the other side, are dependent on service providers. The increased utilization of the Internet of Things in the cloud has assisted in the creation and implementation of scalable Internet of Things technologies and business models. IoT (Internet of Things) in the cloud has public cloud applications that can effectively assist the IoT (Internet of Things) sector by allowing third-party access to networks. Therefore, IoT (Internet of Things) data or computational components running over IoT devices can benefit from the integration. In terms of cost reduction, IoT Cloud-based solutions can include flexibility, scalability, and security. However, it is undeniable that a wired and digital future would emerge. Cloud computing can be a crucial component.

REFERENCES

Alamri, A., Ansari, W. S., Hassan, M. M., Hossain, M. S., Alelaiwi, A., & Hossain, M. A. (2013). A survey on sensor-cloud: Architecture, applications, and approaches. *International Journal of Distributed Sensor Networks*, *9*(2), 917923. doi:10.1155/2013/917923

Alberti, A. M., dos Reis, E. S., Rosa Righi, R. D., Muñoz, V. M., & Chang, V. (2016). *Converging Future Internet, "Things", and Big Data: An Specification Following NovaGenesis Model*. Academic Press.

Alessio, B., De Donato, W., Persico, V., & Pescapé, A. (2014, August). On the integration of cloud computing and internet of things. In Proc. Future Internet of Things and Cloud (FiCloud) (pp. 23-30). Academic Press.

Aoki, H., Shikano, H., Okuno, M., Ogata, Y., Miyamoto, H., Tsushima, Y., . . . Nishimura, S. (2010, September). Cloud architecture for tight interaction with the real world and deep sensor-data aggregation mechanism. In *SoftCOM 2010, 18th International Conference on Software, Telecommunications and Computer Networks* (pp. 280-284). IEEE.

Baker, T., Aldawsari, B., & England, D. (2015). Trusted energy-efficient cloud-based services brokerage platform. *International Journal of Intelligent Computing Research*, 6(4), 630–639. doi:10.20533/ijicr.2042.4655.2015.0078

Borgia, E. (2014). The Internet of Things vision: Key features, applications and open issues. *Computer Communications*, 54, 1–31. doi:10.1016/j.comcom.2014.09.008

Brama, R., Tundo, P., Della Ducata, A., & Malvasi, A. (2014, March). An inter-device communication protocol for modular smart-objects. In *2014 IEEE World Forum on Internet of Things (WF-IoT)* (pp. 422-427). IEEE. 10.1109/WF-IoT.2014.6803203

Cavalcante, E., Pereira, J., Alves, M. P., Maia, P., Moura, R., Batista, T., Delicato, F. C., & Pires, P. F. (2016). On the interplay of Internet of Things and Cloud Computing: A systematic mapping study. *Computer Communications*, 89, 17–33. doi:10.1016/j.comcom.2016.03.012

Chang, K. D., Chen, C. Y., Chen, J. L., & Chao, H. C. (2011, September). Internet of things and cloud computing for future internet. In *International Conference on Security-Enriched Urban Computing and Smart Grid* (pp. 1-10). Springer. 10.1007/978-3-642-23948-9_1

Chen, S., Xu, H., Liu, D., Hu, B., & Wang, H. (2014). A vision of IoT: Applications, challenges, and opportunities with china perspective. *IEEE Internet of Things Journal*, 1(4), 349–359. doi:10.1109/JIOT.2014.2337336

Da Xu, L., He, W., & Li, S. (2014). Internet of things in industries: A survey. *IEEE Transactions on Industrial Informatics*, 10(4), 2233–2243. doi:10.1109/TII.2014.2300753

Emeakaroha, V. C., Cafferkey, N., Healy, P., & Morrison, J. P. (2015, August). A cloud-based iot data gathering and processing platform. In *2015 3rd International Conference on Future Internet of Things and Cloud* (pp. 50-57). IEEE. 10.1109/FiCloud.2015.53

Gaikwad, P. P., Gabhane, J. P., & Golait, S. S. (2015, September). 3-level secure Kerberos authentication for smart home systems using IoT. In *2015 1st International Conference on Next Generation Computing Technologies (NGCT)* (pp. 262-268). IEEE.

Han, J., Choi, C. S., Park, W. K., Lee, I., & Kim, S. H. (2014). Smart home energy management system including renewable energy based on ZigBee and PLC. *IEEE Transactions on Consumer Electronics*, 60(2), 198–202. doi:10.1109/TCE.2014.6851994

Hummen, R., Henze, M., Catrein, D., & Wehrle, K. (2012, December). A cloud design for user-controlled storage and processing of sensor data. In *4th IEEE International Conference on Cloud Computing Technology and Science Proceedings* (pp. 232-240). IEEE. 10.1109/CloudCom.2012.6427523

Kesavan, G., Sanjeevi, P., & Viswanathan, P. (2016, August). A 24 hour IoT framework for monitoring and managing home automation. In *2016 international conference on inventive computation technologies (ICICT)* (Vol. 1, pp. 1-5). IEEE.

Luo, S., & Ren, B. (2016). The monitoring and managing application of cloud computing based on Internet of Things. *Computer Methods and Programs in Biomedicine, 130*, 154–161. doi:10.1016/j.cmpb.2016.03.024 PMID:27208530

Mell, P., & Grance, T. (2011). *The NIST definition of cloud computing*. Academic Press.

Mital, M., Chang, V., Choudhary, P., Pani, A., & Sun, Z. (2016). TEMPORARY REMOVAL: Adoption of cloud based Internet of Things in India: A multiple theory perspective. *International Journal of Information Management.*

Moreno, M. V., Santa, J., Zamora, M. A., & Skarmeta, A. F. (2014, June). A holistic IoT-based management platform for smart environments. In *2014 IEEE International Conference on Communications (ICC)* (pp. 3823-3828). IEEE. 10.1109/ICC.2014.6883917

Moreno, M. V., Terroso-Sáenz, F., González-Vidal, A., Valdés-Vela, M., Skarmeta, A. F., Zamora, M. A., & Chang, V. (2016). Applicability of big data techniques to smart cities deployments. *IEEE Transactions on Industrial Informatics, 13*(2), 800–809. doi:10.1109/TII.2016.2605581

Mrozek, D., Koczur, A., & Małysiak-Mrozek, B. (2020). Fall detection in older adults with mobile IoT devices and machine learning in the cloud and on the edge. *Information Sciences, 537*, 132–147. doi:10.1016/j.ins.2020.05.070

Okeyo, G., Chen, L., & Wang, H. (2014). Combining ontological and temporal formalisms for composite activity modelling and recognition in smart homes. *Future Generation Computer Systems, 39*, 29–43. doi:10.1016/j.future.2014.02.014

Pandiyan, S., Ashwin, M., & Manikandan, R., KM, K. R., & GR, A. R. (2020). Heterogeneous Internet of Things organization predictive analysis platform for apple leaf diseases recognition. *Computer Communications, 154*, 99–110. doi:10.1016/j.comcom.2020.02.054

Petnik, J., & Vanus, J. (2018). Design of smart home implementation within IoT with natural language interface. *IFAC-PapersOnLine, 51*(6), 174–179. doi:10.1016/j. ifacol.2018.07.149

Piyare, R., Park, S., Maeng, S. Y., Park, S. H., Oh, S. C., Choi, S. G., . . . Lee, S. R. (2013, October). Integrating wireless sensor network into cloud services for real-time data collection. In *2013 International Conference on ICT Convergence (ICTC)* (pp. 752-756). IEEE. 10.1109/ICTC.2013.6675470

Roman, R., Zhou, J., & Lopez, J. (2013). On the features and challenges of security and privacy in distributed internet of things. *Computer Networks, 57*(10), 2266–2279. doi:10.1016/j.comnet.2012.12.018

Rose, K., Eldridge, S., & Chapin, L. (2015). The internet of things: An overview. *The Internet Society (ISOC), 80*, 1-50.

Salehi, A., & Aberer, K. (2007, January). *GSN, quick and simple sensor network deployment.* In *4th European conference on Wireless Sensor Networks*, Delft, The Netherlands.

Sanjeevi, P., & Viswanathan, P. (2017). NUTS scheduling approach for cloud data centers to optimize energy consumption. *Computing, 99*(12), 1179–1205. doi:10.100700607-017-0559-4

Son, S. C., Kim, N. W., Lee, B. T., Cho, C. H., & Chong, J. W. (2016). A time synchronization technique for coap-based home automation systems. *IEEE Transactions on Consumer Electronics, 62*(1), 10–16. doi:10.1109/TCE.2016.7448557

Stankovic, J. A. (2014). Research directions for the internet of things. *IEEE Internet of Things Journal, 1*(1), 3–9. doi:10.1109/JIOT.2014.2312291

Suryadevara, N. K., Mukhopadhyay, S. C., Wang, R., & Rayudu, R. K. (2013). Forecasting the behavior of an elderly using wireless sensors data in a smart home. *Engineering Applications of Artificial Intelligence, 26*(10), 2641–2652. doi:10.1016/j. engappai.2013.08.004

Tao, M., Zuo, J., Liu, Z., Castiglione, A., & Palmieri, F. (2018). Multi-layer cloud architectural model and ontology-based security service framework for IoT-based smart homes. *Future Generation Computer Systems, 78*, 1040–1051. doi:10.1016/j. future.2016.11.011

Tei, K., & Gürgen, L. (2014, March). ClouT: Cloud of things for empowering the citizen clout in smart cities. In *2014 IEEE World Forum on Internet of Things (WF-IoT)* (pp. 369-370). IEEE.

Tseng, C. W., & Huang, C. H. (2014, April). Toward a consistent expression of things on epcglobal architecture framework. In *2014 International Conference on Information Science, Electronics and Electrical Engineering* (Vol. 3, pp. 1619-1623). IEEE. 10.1109/InfoSEEE.2014.6946195

Uma, S., Eswari, R., Bhuvanya, R., & Kumar, G. S. (2019). IoT based voice/text controlled home appliances. *Procedia Computer Science*, *165*, 232–238. doi:10.1016/j.procs.2020.01.085

Vermesan, O., Friess, P., Guillemin, P., Gusmeroli, S., Sundmaeker, H., Bassi, A., ... Doody, P. (2011). Internet of things strategic research roadmap. *Internet of Things-Global Technological and Societal Trends*, *1*(2011), 9-52.

Villars, R. L., Cooke, J., & MacGillivray, C. (2015). Impact of internet of things on datacenter demand and operations. *Special Study*, 255397.

Wazid, M., Das, A. K., Bhat, V., & Vasilakos, A. V. (2020). LAM-CIoT: Lightweight authentication mechanism in cloud-based IoT environment. *Journal of Network and Computer Applications*, *150*, 102496. doi:10.1016/j.jnca.2019.102496

Whitmore, A., Agarwal, A., & Da Xu, L. (2015). The Internet of Things—A survey of topics and trends. *Information Systems Frontiers*, *17*(2), 261–274. doi:10.100710796-014-9489-2

Yue, H., Guo, L., Li, R., Asaeda, H., & Fang, Y. (2014). DataClouds: Enabling community-based data-centric services over the Internet of Things. *IEEE Internet of Things Journal*, *1*(5), 472–482. doi:10.1109/JIOT.2014.2353629

Yue, H., Guo, L., Li, R., Asaeda, H., & Fang, Y. (2014). DataClouds: Enabling community-based data-centric services over the Internet of Things. *IEEE Internet of Things Journal*, *1*(5), 472–482. doi:10.1109/JIOT.2014.2353629

Zhou, J., Leppanen, T., Harjula, E., Ylianttila, M., Ojala, T., Yu, C., ... Yang, L. T. (2013, June). Cloudthings: A common architecture for integrating the internet of things with cloud computing. In *Proceedings of the 2013 IEEE 17th international conference on computer supported cooperative work in design (CSCWD)* (pp. 651-657). IEEE. 10.1109/CSCWD.2013.6581037

Chapter 5

The Integration and Implementation of the Internet of Things Through Digital Transformation:
Impact on Productivity and Innovation

Anthony Bolton

(iD) https://orcid.org/0000-0002-1259-7479
University of South Africa, South Africa

Leila Goosen

(iD) https://orcid.org/0000-0003-4948-2699
University of South Africa, South Africa

Elmarie Kritzinger

(iD) https://orcid.org/0000-0002-5141-4348
University of South Africa, South Africa

ABSTRACT

The purpose of this chapter is to address challenges related to the integration and implementation of the developing internet of things (IoT) into the daily lives of people. Demands for communication between devices, sensors, and systems are reciprocally driving increased demands for people to communicate and manage the growing digital ecosystem of the IoT and an unprecedented volume of data. A larger study was established to explore how digital transformation through unified communication and collaboration (UC&C) technologies impact the productivity and innovation of

DOI: 10.4018/978-1-7998-6981-8.ch005

people in the context of one of the world's largest automotive enterprises, General Motors (GM). An analysis and exploration of this research milieu, supported by a critical realist interpretation of solutions, suggested that recommendations can be made that the integration and implementation of digital transformation, delivered via UC&C technologies, impact productivity and opportunity for driving innovation within a global automotive enterprise.

INTRODUCTION

In this chapter, there will be a focus on introducing the paradigm of the Internet of Things (IoT). The role of people in the rapidly developing and emerging digital environment of the Internet of Things is investigated, highlighting changes in the dynamics of communication and collaboration between the IoT-enabled, digital, cyber and physical worlds.

This chapter establishes **background** context on the development of the technologies associated with the Internet of Things and how it overlaps with other emerging digital paradigms, such as Industry 4.0. A literature review explores these concepts, serving to provide a context for addressing questions relating to the drivers of individual innovation behavior (Ngugi & Goosen, 2018) and productivity, resulting from the integration and implementation of associated Unified Communication and Collaboration (UC&C) technologies.

The context developed through the review of the IoT and Industry 4.0 is essential to address the primary research question: To what extent can the integration and implementation of the Internet of Things through digital transformation impact productivity and innovation? To establish and evaluate the requirements of a communication and collaboration technologies framework that supports successful enterprise digitization, comprehension of the future and emerging Internet of Things applications and strategic trends, as well as technological advances related to cloud based IoT, is required.

The rapid development of the Internet of Things and Industry 4.0 is leading to not only the next generation of industrial revolution, but also the emergence in new approaches to UC&C technologies in society, businesses and enterprises.

The IoT has garnered a lot of attention based on what is known as smart objects, as well as being connected via technology, middleware and applications (Fortino & Trunfio, 2014).

Cloud computing is considered to act as a paradigm for Big Data management, storage and analytics, including, according to Tripathi (2015), Optimizing Operational and Migration Cost in the Cloud Paradigm (OOMCCP). The cloud based IoT, alongside integration, is further fueled towards the next generational era.

Target Audience

This chapter lies therein that the target audience of academics, as well as members of IoT research groups, who integrating introduction of protocols, led by developments about integration and implementation in the context of the **challenges** and implication **issues** of these on society.

In terms of the **recommended topics** for possible inclusion in the book, this chapter will consider:

- With regard to network architecture and system design for cloud-based IoT, the functional architecture of "UC&C systems are typically composed of multiple heterogeneous communications platforms, applications, digital communication mediums and" computer platforms (Bolton, Goosen, & Kritzinger, 2016, p. 5). Such platforms can "include dedicated virtual, **cloud**, desktop, mobile" computer and storage systems.
- Integration and implementation of existing IoT related technologies, standards and protocol options
- **Solutions and recommendations**
- **Future research directions**

Impacts: This chapter will therefore represent the incorporation of inputs. The chapter will also provide an introductory overview and discussion of the impact that the current uses, **issues** and inherent assumptions with regard to information being shared across 'things' and applications, as well as the possible impact that these sectors could have on the Internet of Things and vice versa. Together with studies related to the features of this chapter, the main emphasis will be placed on such social aspects.

The impact of Information and Communication Technologies (ICTs) on sustainable development towards youth employability (Alao & Brink, 2020), sustainable and inclusive quality education through research-informed practice on ICTs (Goosen, 2018a), as well as the sustainability of cloud-based **solutions** for *smart society*, will also receive attention.

Finally, unified communication and collaboration that could be achieved with **cloud** computing in terms of security and social media (Messier, 2014), as well as the impact on productivity and innovation that the integration and implementation of the IoT through digital transformation and UC&C technologies could have on the promotion of the Fourth Industrial Revolution (Bolton, Goosen, & Kritzinger, 2020b), will be investigated.

Objectives

The **purpose** of this chapter is to respond to a call, which encouraged investigations into aspects of the Internet of Things amongst various enterprises related to the:

1. Integration and implementation of existing IoT related technologies, protocols and standards involved in cloud-based options.
2. Description of both foundational and the most recent research and developments with regard to the IoT.
3. Discussion of **future** and emerging Internet of Things applications and strategic **trends**, as well as technological advances related to these.
4. Integration in the context of the **challenges** and implication **issues** of these on society.

Background

There are many **definitions** for the Internet of Things. However, it is generally accepted that the Internet of Things is a function of the broader Internet, established through the hyper-connection of devices across many different access methods (Dong-Woo, 2016). Advances in technology, such as radio-frequency identification, mobile communications, wireless connectivity, smart sensors and nanotechnology, have extended the functions of the internet beyond the connectivity of computers and host services.

These technology advancements have led to the creation of new cyber-physical opportunities, blending the digital world of the Internet with the physical realities of daily human life (Salim & Haque, 2015). The miniaturization of technologies, such as cellular and smart sensors, are facilitating the ubiquitous embedding of internet technologies into society and combined with the proliferation of commercial broadband and cellular internet access, enabling effortless always-on communication at low cost.

The integration and implementation of sensor and mobile connectivity technologies, along with the effects of combinatorial technological innovation, has not only enabled the evolution of the internet from a connectivity medium to sharing information, but also enabled enterprises to digitally transform through unified communication and collaboration technologies (Bolton, et al., 2016). It now also accelerates the integration and implementation of ICTs to facilitate the creation of context and cognitive decision making in the smart industry (Kaur & Sood, 2015).

Sensors with the ability to observe and record everything, from human wellbeing to environmental and industrial component statuses, open new opportunities for innovation and the creation of autonomous services. The Internet of Things thus paves the way to the Internet of Everything, inclusive of not just devices (things), but also cognitive data and artificial reasoning.

Definitions of the Internet of Things

Many of the **definitions**, which exist for the IoT, are aligned with the marketing of new commercial services. The International Telecommunications Union (ITU) defined the Internet of Things as "global infrastructure for the information society, enabling advanced services by interconnecting (physical and virtual) things based on existing and evolving interoperable information and communication technologies" (Pacheco-Torgal, et al., 2016, p. 414).

While the Internet of Things as a phrase was coined as recently as 1999, the concept can be traced as far back as 1926, when, in an interview with Collier's magazine, Tesla (cited in Zuckerman (2013, p. 43)) stated:

When wireless is perfectly applied the whole earth will be converted into a huge brain...We shall be able to communicate with one another instantly, irrespective of distance ... Through television and telephony...we shall see and hear one another as perfectly as though we were face to face, despite intervening distances of thousands of miles.

Cited in Sturken, Thomas and Ball-Rokeach (2004), Winner, as Chair of Humanities and Social Sciences in the Department of Science and Technology at Rensselaer Polytechnic Institute, New York, suggested that technologies, such as the Internet and the Internet of Things, have the potential to influence and embody social relations, i.e. power.

The Internet of Things is a phrase that is increasingly being used in modern society, invoking visions of pervasively connected technologies, where the cyber-digital and human-physical worlds are converging (Madakam, Ramaswamy, & Tripathi, 2015).

A *literature review* in this regard covers a wide spectrum, including, e.g. from computer lecturers integrating and implementing vodcasts in all sorts of environments, to educational technologies being integrated and implemented towards students learning programming (Goosen & Van Heerden, 2017) with qualitative perspectives (Goosen & Mukasa-Lwanga, 2017).

Such technologies are also being used in the context of ICT for Development (ICT4D) (Goosen, 2018b), as well as to facilitate students' access (Goosen, 2018e) to an ICT4D Massive Open Online Course (MOOC) (Goosen, 2015a; Goosen, 2018c; Goosen, 2019d) and/or in terms of projects (Goosen, 2015b) related to Information Systems (IS) (Goosen, 2019b) (Goosen, 2019a; Goosen, 2019c).

Finally, Vorster and Goosen (2017) also proposed considering these at the tertiary level, as Goosen (2016) and Goosen (2018d) indicated that it should be practiced.

While discourse around the Internet of Things has increased and become mainstream in recent times, its origins can be traced back to when Ashton (2009) from the Auto-ID Center at the Massachusetts Institute of Technology (MIT) coined the phrase 'Internet of Things' in a presentation, suggesting the idea of linking new Radio-Frequency Identification (RFID) technologies in the supply chain of Proctor & Gamble to the Internet (Sundmaeker, Guillemin, Friess, & Woelfflé, 2015).

The extension of data and meaning between the physical and digital worlds through sensor technologies is core to the idea of the Internet of Things (Gubbi, Buyya, Marusic, & Palaniswami, 2013). The roots of the IoT and its associated technology and service developments are linked to the development of the modern Internet itself.

The Internet: Born of a Rich Heritage of Innovation

Arguably one of the most pervasively marketed and understood buzzwords in modern times, the Internet, received its name via a simple descriptive context. Cerf (1979) is frequently credited with its invention as a term, achieved through the abbreviation of the term 'internetworking' (Meinel & Sack, 2016). In the early 1960's, thought leaders, such as Licklider (1963) at MIT, started envisioning and proposing the concept of a global network of computers (Lambert, Poole, & Woodford, 2005).

The vision of networked computers quickly gained the attention of the government of the United States (US of America) and the Defense Advanced Research Projects Agency (DARPA). Kleinrock (1961) of the University of California (Los Angeles, UCLA) Henry Samueli School of Engineering and Applied Science developed and published a mathematical theory of packet switching networks (Seel, 2012), which were to become one of the fundamental building blocks of the Internet.

Inspired by the memorandum for members and affiliates of the 'Intergalactic Computer Network' by Licklider (1963), Roberts (1967) of the MIT Lincoln Laboratory developed the concept of computer-to-computer networking with communication facilitated via 'data packets' (Hey & Pápay, 2014). Roberts (1967) is also credited with connecting two computers via dial-up telephone lines when connecting one of the computers at MIT with one in California, proving the feasibility of what has since become commonly known as Wide Area Networking (WAN) (Laudon & Traver, 2006).

From the Ashes of Failure: The Advanced Research Projects Agency Network

Driven by the conceptual developments in computer networking by pioneers, such as Kleinrock, Roberts and Licklider (1963), and a growing proliferation of incompatible computing systems, DARPA Information Processing Techniques Office (IPTO) Director Taylor took the formative steps that would lead to the realization of the modern Internet (Igarashi, Altman, Funada, & Kamiyama, 2014). Taylor is credited with questioning why multi-system access could not be achieved with one terminal, after being forced to install three different teletype terminals in a Pentagon office for access to different research computer systems. The initial goal was not to create a network of computers designed for the primary purpose of sharing and transferring data; it was the more fundamental goal of gaining access from a single access point to time-sharing resources on multiple incompatible ARPA computers. The concept of networked computer access was pitched to ARPA Director Herzfeld, who, in 1967, approved a $1 million project to develop the Advanced Research Projects Agency Network (ARPANET) (Russell, 2014).

Taylor and Roberts (1967) made three critical decisions about the development of ARPANET that hold through to key tenants in the development of the Internet today. The first came from recognizing the fact that ARPANET had limited funding. It was unlikely that a project would be funded to develop a wired network to support international network communication.

The decision was therefore taken that data transport would run through the public telephone system. American Telephone and Telegraph (AT&T) ran the public telephone system at the time and this decision led DARPA to lease many high capacity telephone lines dedicated for use by the project and linking the initial ARPA computer sites. This decision represents one of the earliest forms of 'leased lines', a core and essential building block of Internet communication (Banks, 2012).

The crucial second decision followed the direction of previous research from communication pioneers, such as Kleinrock (1961). It was decided that digital messages would be broken into individual fixed length segments, known as packets. This method acted as a safeguard from the excessive corruption of the message due to static and other anomalies on the leased telephone lines. Breaking the digital messages into smaller packets allowed for more efficient methods in terms of the detection and mitigation of data corruption through error detection and correction methods and processes.

Against the background of a post-Covid-19 era (Bolton, Goosen, & Kritzinger, 2021b), Bolton, Goosen and Kritzinger (2020a) provided further discussion of the final decision etc. in the context of such aspects (Rittinghouse & Ransome, 2016). Bolton, Goosen and Kritzinger (2021a) offered additional details with regard to the unified communication technologies utilized at this global automotive organization.

Evolution From the Advanced Research Projects Agency Network to the Internet

Over the years following its initial inception in 1969, the ARPANET grew rapidly, with some of the early highlights including:

1970 - Expansion of ARPANET to the East Coast

The introduction of the first ARPANET node to the East Coast of the USA was brought about through the addition of a computer node managed by Bolt, Beranek and Newman (BBN), the consulting company contracted to develop the first ARPANET Interface Message Processors (IMPs), which joined ARPANET in March 1970.

1970 - Foundational Network Control Protocol (NCP)

The Network Control Protocol (NCP) for ARPANET was first deployed in 1970, following development by the Network Working Group (NWG), established at the UCLA (Zelnick & Zelnick, 2013). This protocol was the precursor of the Transmission Control Protocol/Internet Protocol (TCP/IP), which formed the basis for communication on the Internet and remains as a core communication protocol today.

1971 - Introduction of Remote Access

In September 1971, the first remote access system was implemented through the creation of the Terminal Interface Processor (TIP). Khan (1972) of BBN first demonstrated the TIP at the International Conference on Computer Communications in Washington, where forty individual computers and a TIP were connectedly linked to ARPANET (Seel, 2012).

1971 - Introduction of Email Messaging

Tomlinson (2009), a BBN employee at the time, implemented the first system to transmit messages between terminals hosted on separate central processing units

(Meinel & Sack, 2016), and developed the first email program that could send and receive messages across separate systems connected to ARPANET.

1973 – The Emergence of the TCP/IP Specifications

In September, DARPA scientist at Stanford University, Cerf and Khan (1974) collaborated on the design of a new network protocol and the publication of a paper describing 'A Protocol for Packet Network Interconnection' (Murray, 2016). The paper also included a proposed open-architecture network design, which was the precursor to the transmission control protocol, allowing multiple networks to interconnect and communicate.

1974 - TCP/IP Specifications Published

Cerf, Sunshine and Dalal (1974), fellow Stanford students, published the first technical specification for the TCP/IP via Request For Comments (RFC) 675 and included a design that leveraged a thirty-two-bit IP address (Russell, 2014). This address system facilitated addressing for up to 256 networks, with each network containing up to 16.7 million unique host addresses.

1976 – The First Incorporation of TCP/IP into Unix

Upon request by DARPA, Joy, a graduate student at the University of Berkeley, first integrated and embedded TCP/IP into distributions of the Berkeley Unix operating system (Bygrave & Bing, 2009).

1977 – First Live TCP/IP International Network Demonstrated

In July, Cerf and Khan (1974) designed, implemented and demonstrated the first multi-hop network system by sending a packet of data from a host on a network in San Francisco, via a network in London on to a host on a network in the University of Southern California, Los Angeles. That same year, one of the first purpose-built multi-site networks was designed and implemented by Landweber (1992) from the University of Wisconsin - Madison (Carpenter, 2013). These events realized the promise of inter-networking.

1979 – Network Expansion through USENET

Truscott, Ellis and Bellovin developed and shared the initial designs for Usenet (Lueg & Fisher, 2012). Initially conceived by the trio in 1979, Usenet was established and deployed in 1980 at the University of North Carolina at Chapel Hill and Duke University. Usenet employed Unix-to-Unix-Protocol (UUCP) for file transport and Berkeley UNIX as host operating system.

1980 – TCP/IP Becomes a Standard

The first formal specification for the version of TCP/IP used in modern networks (version 4) was ratified in 1980. In 1982, it was decided that the TCP/IP protocol suite would replace NCP and become the standard transport protocol for ARPANET. The switchover of ARPANET to TCP/IP occurred on January 1st, 1983, facilitating the further exponential growth of the network (Bank, 2006).

1983-1984 - From ARPANET to the Internet

Also in 1983, the Internet Advisory Board (IAB) was established, to later become the Internet Architecture Board, which was created to succeed the DARPA initiated Internet Configuration Control Board (ICCB). The purpose of the IAB was to provide oversight of the development of internet standards, as well as architectural and operational needs. 1984 witnessed the development of Domain Name Services (DNS) by Mockapetris and Partridge (Denardis, 2008).

DNS remains a core element of the Internet and internet related services, enabling the mass proliferation of IoT and digital technologies beyond traditional business and academic computers, down to the smallest sensor and mobile devices (Margolis & Resnick, 2000). DNS revolutionized the management of hosts and devices on the internet through the delivery of a mechanism to quickly identify and locate systems.

1985-1990 - Internet Expansion, Governance and Establishment of Community

Overseen by the IAB, the Internet Engineering Task Force was established with the remit of driving governance through voluntary standards for the Internet (Denardis, 2008). These internet standards would include protocol suites such as TCP/IP. This period also saw increased government-sponsored activity, for example, a $600 million allocation of funding because of the High-Performance Computer and Communication Act (United States Congress Committee on Commerce, Science and Transportation, 1991) and the advent of the 'Information Super Highway'.

1991-2000 – Independent Governance, Consumer Adoption and the Advent of the Web

The period between 1990 and 2000 was critical to the formation of the modern internet from a couple of key perspectives. Firstly, the governance structure further developed into an open community approach facilitating further global expansion and collaboration on internet services development. It was during this period that mass consumer adoption started to occur outside of the government, academic and scientific communities through subscription-based dial-up services from companies, such as America Online, Compuserve, Prodigy and Genie (Vincenti, 2010). Home access to USENET, a service previously only leveraged in an academic forum, was extended to consumers of America Online in September of 1993; this marked one of the first major introductions of consumers to the larger Internet of systems and services. Luttrell (2016) highlighted the contemporary phrase 'Content is King' and the Internet served to develop value scenarios associated with digitization and the IoT.

The roots of the modern internet and arguably one of the most impactful services released on the Internet is the World Wide Web (WWW). The World Wide Web, also known as the Web, was conceived by Berner's Lee, a scientist at the European Organization for Nuclear Research (CERN) (O'Regan, 2013). Building on some internal developments within CERN, Berner's Lee placed the first openly accessible Web Server onto the Internet via a NEXT workstation in 1991.

Following direction from US President Clinton to the Secretary of the US Department of Commerce, the Internet Corporation for Assigned Names and Numbers (ICANN) was established and chartered as a non-profit independent private sector body to manage and coordinate the assignment of Internet domain names and IP number allocations (Lindsay, 2007). Formally established and recognized by the US Department of Commerce in 1999, ICANN persists as a global community and organization today with the responsibility of managing over 180 million registered domain names and 4 billion number assignments.

EVOLUTION OF THE INTERNET OF THINGS AND THE COGNITIVE INTERNET

The Combinatorial Effect of Mobile, TCP/IP and Sensor Technology

Bolton, et al. (2020b) cited Varadharajan and Bansal (2016) with regard to data security and privacy in the Internet of Things environment from a distributed computing perspective, Mavromoustakis, Mastorakis and Batalla (2016) relating to the Internet of Things in 5G mobile technologies, and Slama, Puhlmann, Morrish and Bhatnagar (2015) regarding enterprise IoT strategies and best practices for connected products and services.

In a survey on context aware applications and computing for the Internet of Things, Perara, Zaslavsky, Christen and Goergakopoulos (2014) found that when these were combined with context sensing sensor technologies, a path was provided to improve and further integrate the experiences between humans and computers, bridging the cyber-physical divide (Fortino & Trunfio, 2014).

The concept of the cognitive Internet of Energy supports the facilitation of a system whereby people, governments and commercial bodies can produce, store and efficiently leverage energy, while intelligent systems balance the supply and demand (Fiorentino & Corsi, 2014).

Content and Information Centric Networking and Communication

In Bolton, et al. (2020a), Aguayo-Torres, Gómez and Poncela (2015) were mentioned in the context of wired/wireless internet communications. Information access to Content-Centric Networking (CCN) will evolve from traditional Internet information access, as the focus will be less on access via pre-defined specific DNS and IP addresses (location-based references), and center more on requesting information from the network. The Internet will evolve from a host-centric and an end-to-end communication model, to one of receiver-driven content retrieval (Zhang, Li, & Lin, 2013).

With the Information Centric Network and Context Centric Networking approaches, data is not merely transported on or in the network; it is inherent to the network and not just at pre-abstracted layers, such as websites. The storage and caching of information becomes an embedded and integral function of the network. CCN, in combination with Software Defined Networking (SDN), hold the potential to virtualize services within the core of the network as abstracted functions of intelligent IoT application ecosystems and *smart services* (Rahman, Rahmani, Kanter, Persson, & Armundin, 2013). In the chapter by Bolton, et al. (2021a), the latter authors similarly pointed out that when building a hyperconnected society, Internet of Things research and innovation in terms of value chains, ecosystems and markets should be considered (Vermesan & Friess, 2015).

The Cognitive Internet of Things

Extending from the realization of a context-aware network with CCN, a further natural step in the evolution of the Internet, driven by the realization of the IoT, is the Cognitive Internet of Things (Wu, et al., 2014). Research, such as Smart, Heersmink and Clowes (2016), suggested that a cognitive internet or 'internet with a brain' is the next evolutionary step for the Internet, which should be viewed as an essential part of the cognitive environment within which human biological brains are currently situated. Through Context Centric Networking, the Internet will evolve new methods and approaches to generate meaning from the plethora of observational data that is generated and disseminated by context sensitive IoT sensors. Wu, et al. (2014, p. 1) argued that being "connected is not enough", meaning that objects within the Internet of Things should have the capability to think, learn, understand and, ultimately, make informed and intelligent cognitive decisions to act.

The development of the Cognitive Internet of Things intersects with many areas of human-directed sciences, such as cognitive psychology, cognitive science, cognitive neuroscience, linguistics, sociology and anthropology (Bibri, 2015). While the current evolution of the Internet towards the Internet of Things is increasing the level of available contextual information, there is still a high dependency on human cognition for processing decision making and the interpretation of sensor observation. The concept of the Cognitive Internet of Things enhances the concept of Context Centric Networking with the insertion of intrinsic human-like cognitive capabilities. It is not envisioned that the Cognitive Internet of Things would act wholly independent of humans. However, it holds the potential to raise the role of sensors to agents that can intelligently leverage captured and disseminated real-time data and act on behalf of humans with the minimum required human intervention (Moin, 2015).

Through the seamless integration of humans with the Internet of Things using digital approaches, such as unified communications and collaboration technologies to optimize action (Bolton, et al., 2021a); (Sathi, 2016), the Cognitive Internet of Things holds potential for increased cyber-physical engagement (Geng, 2016). Research, such as what was reported on by Barnaghi, Wang, Henson and Taylor (2012) on the Cognitive IoT, suggested that human engagement can become more efficient through the offload of various fundamental cognitive tasks, such as the initial analysis and interpretation of sensor-based environmental information. The integration of real-time sensory data that is analyzed and converted into 'actionable knowledge' creates more beneficial and value-generating social and commercial products and services.

Issues, Problems, Challenges

This subsection will further expand on the authors' perspectives with regard to **challenges** related to digital transformation, as well as the main theme of the book.

The vision for and **challenges** related to realizing the Internet of Things have bearing (Sundmaeker, et al., 2015), as well as **issues** and current **trends** with regard to **cloud** portability and interoperability (Di-Martino, Cretella, & Esposito, 2015).

Bolton, et al. (2020a) cited a survey on the Internet of Things by Atzori, Iera and Morabito (2010): Human integration and interaction are required to support the growing number of use cases within industry. Requirements for social integration are likely to arise in many ways, with bi-directional consequences for people and systems. These **challenges** are not new and were previously encountered in the pioneering days of computer programming, language development and compilation. The memorandum on research relating to what Simon (1963) refers to as the heuristic compiler focused on the need to bridge the gap between the explicitness and strict requirements of computer systems and languages and the inherent freedom experienced in human communication. Combining observations by Wieser (1991), on the nearly invisible nature of profound technologies, with those of Simon (1963), it is reasonable to suggest that IoT **solutions** will require consideration of integration and communication between people at psychological level, with unconscious computing systems.

SOLUTIONS AND RECOMMENDATIONS

Business-to-Business Optimization

From the perspective of the enterprise, current implementations of the Internet of Things are focused on Business-to-Business (B2B) integration and optimization (Kranz, 2016). This approach offers an opportunity for incremental engagement, in addition to existing business models, and eases into the technology strategies associated with the IoT, while also realizing incremental financial and resource **solutions** within the enterprise. The approach is therefore a significant step in the evolution of a digital enterprise.

IoT strategies are enabling optimization and business gains within, and across, commercial enterprises via numerous use cases, including convergence and the digitization of analogue processes. These two use cases are prevalent within manufacturing enterprises, where IoT is being leveraged to converge isolated analogue sensor technologies and transform associated information into intelligent data. When analyzed through predictive analytics, this data facilitates increased leverage of manufacturing assets as a collaborative network and pool of resources (Zhang & Tao, 2016).

Supply Chain Optimization

An Internet of Things-enabled supply chain further optimizes manufacturing operations and cost through the facilitation of integrated real-time 'Just-In-Time' (JIT) supplier services (Ligthart & Prasad, 2016). IoT-enabled supply chain **solutions** include the real-time tracking and utilization of resources with the integrated real-time alerting, monitoring and engagement of people, as well as supply chain systems, from distribution through production within the value chain. The leverage of sensors and intelligent Human-Machine Integration (HMI) is not limited to physical manufacturing. Similar business value and benefits are experienced through the application of these strategies within other enterprise verticals, including transport, healthcare, agriculture and utilities.

Service Oriented Architectures

This chapter makes **recommendations** that Service Oriented Architecture (SOA) should be leveraged in conjunction with Internet of Things technical strategies to take advantage of, and apply, gains associated with the IoT within *society*. The concept of SOA, commonly associated with the practice of business computing, is now being leveraged through the IoT to simplify the complexity of social and consumer services and introduce newer, more flexible systems. The connected digital nature of IoT systems provides an opportunity to recalibrate social and consumer services in a more flexible and reconfigurable way, facilitating the integration of an increasing number of loosely coupled service components (Friess, 2013).

Smart Society

Over the coming years, advancements in, and the availability of, social and commercial services are projected to grow and have significant social impact. Some of these areas and trends include:

Smart Environments

Converging technologies for *smart environments* and integrated eco-systems take care of water leaks and loss prevention, flood management, water management, urban supply chain management, in-field product management, and greenhouse management (Friess, 2013).

Smart Health

Applicable scenarios include accident and fall detection, lifestyle and health monitoring, medical inventories and dispensation, patient monitoring, dental health monitoring, surgical and clinical hygiene monitoring, and sleep monitoring and treatment.

Smart Living

In terms of start-up creation, the smart eco-efficient built environment will incorporate energy, resource and safety monitoring (Pacheco-Torgal, et al., 2016), while reasoning services enable SmartHome automation at the edge of current context networks (Rahman, et al. 2013). The associated advantages will be complimented by intelligent, personalized shopping by, and connectivity frameworks for, (even) smart(er) personal devices (Varadharajan & Bansal, 2016).

People as a 'Thing' Within the Construct of the Internet of Things

Discourse associated with the Internet of Things extends beyond machine-to-machine communication and devices talking to devices. Fixed and mobile data connectivity is an essential enabler in **cloud** and machine-to-machine **solutions**, the forms and modes of communication required to support the Internet of Things. As the application of the IoT extend, the need for communication is also expanding (Brooks, 2016). Machines are instruments designed to carry out physical operations. The Internet of Things introduced the concept of smart technologies, which now extends the potential of machine-to-machine communication through the real-time integration of sensors and people.

In his seminal paper, Wieser (1991, p. 94) pointed out that the most profound technologies are the ones that disappear and are indistinguishable as technologies in themselves. Such profound technologies are also integrated and "weave themselves into the fabric of everyday life". These technologies further seamlessly extended to marketing functions, such as digital and static billboards, where information transmits between machines and people seamlessly. Many times, this sharing occurs at a subconscious level and require only a glance. The development of theories, such as the Opportunistic IoT, highlighted the importance of the bi-directional relationship between humans and IoT services, comprising of communication technologies, devices, applications (Ajibola & Goosen, 2017), data and analytical systems. In their research associated with the opportunistic IoT, Guo, Zhang, Wang, Yu and Zhou (2013, p. 3) argued that the Internet of Things becomes "the primary media to sense and monitor human" behavior. Such behavior includes things like patterns of mobility obtained from phones and GPS systems, Wi-Fi location analytics in the home or retail stores, as well as sleep and exercise patterns. Whereas, on the one hand, the Internet of Things becomes the primary media for monitoring behavior, on the other hand, the performance of the IoT and many associated services are dependent on, and affected by, human behavior.

According to Wieser (1991), only when technology and associated **solutions** disappear from active and conscious view are people freed up to use these without thinking and truly focus, not on the technologies, but on the goals for which these were created to achieve. In addition to the redefinition of collaboration, encompassing the full spectrum of the developing cyber-physical reality, the many modalities of communication required to support interconnectivity must be considered (Brooks, 2016).

FUTURE RESEARCH DIRECTIONS

Internet of Things applications and strategic trends will be discussed, after more established ones have already been reviewed. It will further expound on the theme of the book in terms of the 'Integration and Implementation of the Internet of Things Through Cloud Computing' related to the integration and implementation of the Internet of Things through digital transformation

In terms of a vision, architectural elements, and **future** directions (Gubbi, et al., 2013), more exploration of the influence on the development of **future** connected products and services is needed, and how the Internet of Things is affecting change in modern business operations.

Bolton, et al. (2020b) cited Kanniappan and Rajendrin (2017) with regard to privacy and the Internet of Things in the modern business environment, as well as Kranz (2016), related to building the Internet of Things by implementing new business models, disrupting competitors, and transforming industry.

By providing a baseline view of the fundamental components that are facilitating the creation of products and services, many of which are influencing and changing the social, business and economic landscape, Bolton, et al. (2020b), referred to Guimaraes, et al. (2013) in the context of experimenting with content-centric networks in the **future** internet testbed environment.

CONCLUSION

This chapter introduced scholarly literature relating to the developing Internet of Things in terms of foundational roots, as well as alignment with the innovation and connected architecture of the internet.

The **background** section described contemporary **definitions** proposed by organizations, such as the ITU, to develop a commonly accepted conceptual description of the Internet of Things. It also reviewed and discussed the foundation of Internet technologies and communication through an exploration of the Internet in historical context. The concept of a hybrid cyber-physical world (Madakam, et al., 2015), enabling human and digital machine convergence through the IoT, was established, contrasting these with the originating ideas of IoT-enabled RFID supply chain systems conceptualized by Ashton (2009). The expansion of the conceptual IoT through bridging of the physical world and associated tactile data into a digital form via sensor technologies as presented by Gubbi, et al. (2013) was also discussed and aligned as a core component of the IoT digital strategy.

In the next section, the combinatorial effect of innovation in the areas of sensors and connected internet technologies was reviewed, highlighting resulting innovation developments and extensions of the IoT, such as the concept of the Cognitive Internet of Energy (Vermesan & Friess, 2015), Information and Content-Centric Networking (Aguayo-Torres, et al., 2015) and the Cognitive Internet of Things (Wu, et al., 2014). The shift of internet technologies from being transport-centric, to a data-rich platform with cognitive potential, lead to an exploration of the overlap between the cyber (digital computer) and physical (human) worlds. This overlap and the emerging consequences were discussed through the lens of the model from Moin (2015) of the Cognitive Internet of Things. The concepts of human and cyber-physical engagement and interaction were also discussed, emphasizing the growing potential for what Barnaghi et al. (2012) described as 'actionable knowledge' expanding.

A review of the work of Simon (1963) and research on computer system languages, through the lens of heuristic compilation, underlined the different explicit and literal **challenges** of computer system languages, versus the inherent freedom evident and expressed through human interaction. The theories of Simon (1963) were contrasted with the observation of Wieser (1991) that profound technologies attain maximum impact when these are integrated into society at an almost imperceptible level. The resulting integration paves the way for an expansion in research on the integration of people and things within the construct of the Internet of Things within the enterprise through digital communication and collaboration technologies.

The current focus with regard to **solutions** is mostly on business-to-business integration and optimization at enterprise level (Kranz, 2016). Opportunities for enterprise enhancement of operations was presented through the concept of supply chain optimization and the improved integration of systems and people within the framework of developing IoT-based digital Just-in-Time models (Ligthart & Prasad, 2016). The societal integration and personalization of products through IoT-enabled SOA was reviewed, focusing on the potential benefits to enterprises gained through IoT-enabled abstraction and recombination of service components (Friess, 2013).

In terms of integrating people with the IoT, the perspectives of scholars, such as Brooks (2016), and the need for enhanced communication as IoT cyber-physical use cases expand, was presented. IoT related concepts, such as smart technologies, were established, raising the question of the role of humans in enriching IoT **solutions** with data beyond binary and digital sensor information. The theories of Wieser (1991), related to profound technologies and their impact as these weave into the fabric of everyday life and society, were introduced and explored further, underscoring the potential for cyber-physical integration, even at subconscious levels. These concepts were further expanded by introducing scholars, such as Guo et al. (2013), suggesting that the IoT can become a medium for not only monitoring and controlling machines, but also for monitoring human behavior and performance.

The last section before this conclusion focused on scholarly opinions relating to the subsequent influence of IoT on **future** architectures and opportunities for industry through the progressive digital shift towards the paradigm of Industry 4.0. This section also provided a summary review and discussion on the strategic trends and emerging developments in the area of IoT use cases and applications, including discussing the importance of the IoT to new and emerging business models (Kanniappan & Rajendrin, 2017).

The chapter is closed by synthesizing these concepts into a discussion on digital human-system integration and how the IoT has the potential to influence and impact many aspects of the daily lives of people.

REFERENCES

Aguayo-Torres, M. C., Gómez, G., & Poncela, J. (2015). *Wired/Wireless Internet Communications (WWIC): 13th International Conference, May 25-27, Revised Selected Papers*. Malaga, Spain: Springer.

Ajibola, S., & Goosen, L. (2017). Development of Heuristics for Usability Evaluation of M-Commerce Applications. In P. Blignaut, & T. Stott (Ed.), *Proceedings of the South African Institute of Computer Scientists and Information Technologists (SAICSIT)* (pp. 19 - 28). Thaba 'Nchu, South Africa: Association for Computing Machinery (ACM). 10.1145/3129416.3129428

Alao, A., & Brink, R. (2020). Impact of ICTs for Sustainable Development of Youth Employability. In *Promoting Inclusive Growth in the Fourth Industrial Revolution* (pp. 148–180). IGI Global. doi:10.4018/978-1-7998-4882-0.ch006

Ashton, K. (2009). That 'internet of things' thing. *RFID Journal, 22*(7), 97-114.

Atzori, L., Iera, A., & Morabito, G. (2010). The Internet of Things: A survey. *Computer Networks, 54*(15), 2787–2805. doi:10.1016/j.comnet.2010.05.010

Bank, A. G. (2006). *TCP/IP Foundations* (2nd ed.). John Wiley & Sons.

Banks, M. (2012). *On the Way to the Web: The Secret History of the Internet and Its Founders*. Apress.

Barnaghi, P., Wang, W., Henson, C., & Taylor, K. (2012). Semantics for the Internet of Things: Early progress and back. *International Journal on Semantic Web and Information Systems, 8*(1), 1–21. doi:10.4018/jswis.2012010101

Bibri, S. (2015). *The Shaping of Ambient Intelligence and the Internet of Things: Historico-epistemic, Socio-cultural, Politico-institutional and Eco-environmental Dimensions*. Springer. doi:10.2991/978-94-6239-142-0

Bolton, A., Goosen, L., & Kritzinger, E. (2016). Enterprise Digitization Enablement Through Unified Communication and Collaboration. In *Proceedings of the Annual Conference of the South African Institute of Computer Scientists and Information Technologists*. Johannesburg: ACM. 10.1145/2987491.2987516

Bolton, A., Goosen, L., & Kritzinger, E. (2020a). The Impact of Unified Communication and Collaboration Technologies on Productivity and Innovation: Promotion for the Fourth Industrial Revolution. In S. B. Buckley (Ed.), *Promoting Inclusive Growth in the Fourth Industrial Revolution* (pp. 44–73). IGI Global. doi:10.4018/978-1-7998-4882-0.ch002

Bolton, A., Goosen, L., & Kritzinger, E. (2021b). An Empirical Study Into the Impact on Innovation and Productivity Towards the Post-COVID-19 Era: Digital Transformation of an Automotive Enterprise. In L. C. Carvalho, L. Reis, & C. Silveira (Eds.), *Handbook of Research on Entrepreneurship, Innovation, Sustainability, and ICTs in the Post-COVID-19 Era* (pp. 133–159). IGI Global. doi:10.4018/978-1-7998-6776-0.ch007

Bolton, A. D., Goosen, L., & Kritzinger, E. (2021a). Unified Communication Technologies at a Global Automotive Organization. In M. Khosrow-Pour (Ed.), *Encyclopedia of Organizational Knowledge, Administration, and Technologies* (pp. 2592–2608). IGI Global. doi:10.4018/978-1-7998-3473-1.ch179

Bolton, T., Goosen, L., & Kritzinger, E. (2020b, March 8). Security Aspects of an Empirical Study into the Impact of Digital Transformation via Unified Communication and Collaboration Technologies on the Productivity and Innovation of a Global Automotive Enterprise. Communications in Computer and Information Science, 1166, 99-113. doi:10.1007/978-3-030-43276-8_8

Brooks, T. (2016). *Cyber-Assurance for the Internet of Things*. John Wiley & Sons. doi:10.1002/9781119193784

Bygrave, L., & Bing, J. (2009). *Internet Governance: Infrastructure and Institutions*. Oxford University Press. doi:10.1093/acprof:oso/9780199561131.001.0001

Carpenter, B. (2013). *Network Geeks: How They Built The Internet*. Springer Science & Business Media. doi:10.1007/978-1-4471-5025-1

Cerf, V., Dalal, Y., & Sunshine, C. (1974, December). *RFC0675: Specification of Internet Transmission Control Program*. Retrieved from https://dl.acm.org/doi/pdf/10.17487/RFC0675?casa_token=NOnU2L4MPPEAAAAA:sC4AvMV_LpQGCPPeiOjs8bp-OBj8vcme31lEY6nwAtnHosl8qLob9FvWde7lgublhEeaZJq4dtgU65Y

Cerf, V. G. (1979). DARPA activities in packet network interconnection. In *Interlinking of Computer Networks* (pp. 287–305). Springer. doi:10.1007/978-94-009-9431-7_17

Cerf, V. G., & Kahn, R. E. (1974, May). A protocol for packet network interconnection. *IEEE Trans. Comm. Tech, COM-22*(V 5), 627-641. doi:10.1145/1064413.1064423

Denardis, L. (2008). IPv6: Standards controversies around the Next-Generation Internet. In I. Inkster & J. Sumner (Eds.), *History of Technology* (Vol. 28). Continuum.

Di-Martino, B., Cretella, G., & Esposito, A. (2015). *Cloud Portability and Interoperability: Issues and Current Trends*. Springer.

Dong-Woo, L. (2016). A Study on Actual Cases & Meanings for Internet of Things. *International Journal of Software Engineering and Its Applications, 10*(1), 287–294. doi:10.14257/ijseia.2016.10.1.28

Fiorentino, G., & Corsi, A. (2014). Cyber Physical Systems give Life to the Internet of Energy. *ECRIM News, 98*, 39–40.

Fortino, G., & Trunfio, P. (2014). *Internet of Things based on Smart Objects: Technology, Middleware and Applications*. Springer. doi:10.1007/978-3-319-00491-4

Friess, P. (2013). *Internet of Things: Converging Technologies for Smart Environments and Integrated Ecosystems*. River Publishers.

Geng, H. (2016). *Internet of Things and Data Analytics Handbook*. John Wiley & Sons.

Goosen, L. (2015a). Educational Technologies for an ICT4D MOOC in the 21st Century. In D. Nwaozuzu, & S. Mnisi (Ed.), *Proceedings of the South Africa International Conference on Educational Technologies* (pp. 37 - 48). Pretoria: African Academic Research Forum.

Goosen, L. (2015b). Educational Technologies for Growing Innovative e-Schools in the 21st Century: A Community Engagement Project. In D. Nwaozuzu, & S. Mnisi (Ed.), *Proceedings of the South Africa International Conference on Educational Technologies* (pp. 49 - 61). Pretoria: African Academic Research Forum.

Goosen, L. (2016, February 18). *We don't need no education"? Yes, they DO want e-learning in Basic and Higher Education!* Retrieved from http://uir.unisa.ac.za/handle/10500/20999

Goosen, L. (2018a). Sustainable and Inclusive Quality Education Through Research Informed Practice on Information and Communication Technologies in Education. In L. Webb (Ed.), *Proceedings of the 26th Conference of the Southern African Association for Research in Mathematics, Science and Technology Education (SAARMSTE)* (pp. 215 - 228). Gabarone: University of Botswana.

Goosen, L. (2018b). Trans-Disciplinary Approaches to Action Research for e-Schools, Community Engagement, and ICT4D. In T. A. Mapotse (Ed.), *Cross-Disciplinary Approaches to Action Research and Action Learning* (pp. 97–110). IGI Global. doi:10.4018/978-1-5225-2642-1.ch006

Goosen, L. (2018c). Ethical Information and Communication Technologies for Development Solutions: Research Integrity for Massive Open Online Courses. In C. Sibinga (Ed.), *Ensuring Research Integrity and the Ethical Management of Data* (pp. 155–173). IGI Global. doi:10.4018/978-1-5225-2730-5.ch009

Goosen, L. (2018d). Ethical Data Management and Research Integrity in the Context of E-Schools and Community Engagement. In C. Sibinga (Ed.), *Ensuring Research Integrity and the Ethical Management of Data* (pp. 14–45). IGI Global. doi:10.4018/978-1-5225-2730-5.ch002

Goosen, L. (2018e). Students' Access to an ICT4D MOOC. In S. Kabanda, H. Suleman, & S. Jamieson (Ed.), *Proceedings of the 47th Annual Conference of the Southern African Computer Lectures' Association (SACLA 2018)* (pp. 183 - 201). Cape Town: University of Cape Town.

Goosen, L. (2019a). Technology-Supported Teaching and Research Methods for Educators: Case Study of a Massive Open Online Course. In L. Makewa, B. Ngussa, & J. Kuboja (Eds.), *Technology-Supported Teaching and Research Methods for Educators* (pp. 128–148). IGI Global. doi:10.4018/978-1-5225-5915-3.ch007

Goosen, L. (2019b). Research on Technology-Supported Teaching and Learning for Autism. In L. Makewa, B. Ngussa, & J. Kuboja (Eds.), *Technology-Supported Teaching and Research Methods for Educators* (pp. 88–110). IGI Global. doi:10.4018/978-1-5225-5915-3.ch005

Goosen, L. (2019c). Information Systems and Technologies Opening New Worlds for Learning to Children with Autism Spectrum Disorders. Smart Innovation, Systems and Technologies, 111, 134 - 143. doi:10.1007/978-3-030-03577-8_16

Goosen, L. (2019d). *Innovative Technologies and Learning in a Massive Open Online Course*. In L. Rønningsbakk, T.-T. Wu, F. E. Sandnes, & Y.-M. Huang (Eds.), Lecture Notes in Computer Science (Vol. 11937, pp. 653–662). doi:10.1007/978-3-030-35343-8_69

Goosen, L. (2021). Organizational Knowledge and Administration Lessons from an ICT4D MOOC. In M. Khosrow-Pour (Ed.), *Encyclopedia of Organizational Knowledge, Administration, and Technologies* (pp. 245–261). IGI Global. doi:10.4018/978-1-7998-3473-1.ch020

Goosen, L., & Mukasa-Lwanga, T. (2017). Educational Technologies in Distance Education: Beyond the Horizon with Qualitative Perspectives. In U. I. Ogbonnaya, & S. Simelane-Mnisi (Ed.), *Proceedings of the South Africa International Conference on Educational Technologies* (pp. 41 - 54). Pretoria: African Academic Research Forum.

Goosen, L., & Van Heerden, D. (2017). Beyond the Horizon of Learning Programming with Educational Technologies. In U. I. Ogbonnaya, & S. Simelane-Mnisi (Ed.), *Proceedings of the South Africa International Conference on Educational Technologies* (pp. 78 - 90). Pretoria: African Academic Research Forum.

Gubbi, J., Buyya, R., Marusic, S., & Palaniswami, M. (2013). Internet of Things (IoT): A vision, architectural elements, and future directions. *Future Generation Computer Systems, 29*(7), 1645–1660. doi:10.1016/j.future.2013.01.010

Guimaraes, P., Ferraz, L., Torres, J. V., Mattos, D., Alvarenga, I., Rodrigues, C., & Duarte, O. (2013). Experimenting content-centric networks in the future internet testbed environment. *IEEE International Conference on Communications Workshops (ICC)*, 1383-1387. 10.1109/ICCW.2013.6649453

Guo, B., Zhang, D., Wang, Z., Yu, Z., & Zhou, X. (2013). Opportunistic IoT: Exploring the harmonious interactions between human and the internet of things. *Journal of Network and Computer Applications, 36*(6), 1531–1539. doi:10.1016/j.jnca.2012.12.028

Hey, A., & Pápay, G. (2014). *The Computing Universe: A Journey through a Revolution.* Cambridge University Press. doi:10.1017/CBO9781139032643

Igarashi, Y., Altman, T., Funada, M., & Kamiyama, B. (2014). *Computing: A Historical and Technical Perspective.* CRC Press. doi:10.1201/b17011

Kahn, R. (1972, Jan). *Communications Principles for Operating Systems.* Washington, DC: Bolt, Beranek and Newman (BBN).

Kanniappan, J., & Rajendrin, B. (2017). Privacy and the Internet of Things. In I. Lee (Ed.), *The Internet of Things in the Modern Business Environment* (pp. 94–106). IGI Global. doi:10.4018/978-1-5225-2104-4.ch005

Kaur, N., & Sood, S. (2015). Cognitive decision making in smart industry. *Computers in Industry, 74,* 151–161. doi:10.1016/j.compind.2015.06.006

Kleinrock, L. (1961, July). *Information Flow in Large Communication Nets.* RLE Quarterly Progress Report.

Kranz, M. (2016). *Building the Internet of Things: Implement new Business Models, Disrupt Competitors, Transform Your Industry.* John Wiley & Sons.

Lambert, L., Poole, H., & Woodford, C. (2005). *Internet: A Historical Encylopedia.* Moschovistis Group.

Landweber, L. H. (1992). Computer networking courses at the University of Wisconsin—Madison. *Computer Communication Review, 22*(1), 52–61. doi:10.1145/141790.141795

Laudon, K., & Traver, C. (2006). *E-commerce: business, technology, society.* Pearson Prentice Hall.

Licklider, J. C. (1963, April). *The Intergalactic Computer Network.* Retrieved from http://imiller.utsc.utoronto.ca/pub2/licklider_intergalactic_1963.pdf

Ligthart, L., & Prasad, R. (2016). Role of ICT for Multi-Disciplinary Applications in 2030. Gistru: River Publishers.

Lindsay, D. (2007). *International Domain Name Law: ICANN and the UDRP.* Bloomsbury Publishing.

Lueg, C., & Fisher, D. (2012). *From Usenet to CoWebs: Interacting with Social Information Spaces.* Springer.

Luttrell, R. (2016). *Social Media: How to Engage, Share, and Connect.* Rowman & Littlefield.

Madakam, S., Ramaswamy, R., & Tripathi, S. (2015). Internet of Things (IoT): A Literature Review. *Journal of Computer and Communications, 3*(5), 164–173. doi:10.4236/jcc.2015.35021

Margolis, M., & Resnick, D. (2000). *Politics as Usual: The Cyberspace Revolution.* SAGE Publications.

Mavromoustakis, C., Mastorakis, G., & Batalla, J. M. (2016). *Internet of Things (IoT) in 5G Mobile Technologies.* Springer. doi:10.1007/978-3-319-30913-2

Meinel, C., & Sack, H. (2016). *Internetworking: Technological Foundations and Applications.* Springer Science & Business Media.

Messier, R. (2014). *Collaboration with Cloud Computing: Security, Social Media and Unified Communication.* Elsevier.

Moin, A. (2015). Sense-Deliberate-Act Cognitive Agents for Sense-Compute-Control Applications in the Internet of Things and Services. In *Internet of Things. User-Centric IoT: First International Summit, IoT360 2014, Rome, Italy, October 27-28, 2014, Revised Selected Papers, Part 1* (pp. 21-28). New York: Springer. 10.1007/978-3-319-19656-5_4

Murray, A. (2016). *Information Technology Law: The Law and Society.* Oxford University Press.

Ngugi, J., & Goosen, L. (2018). Modelling Course-Design Characteristics, Self-Regulated Learning and the Mediating Effect of Knowledge-Sharing Behavior as Drivers of Individual Innovative Behavior. *Eurasia Journal of Mathematics, Science and Technology Education, 14*(8). doi:10.29333/ejmste/92087

O'Regan, G. (2013). *Giants of Computing: A Compendium of Select, Pivotal Pioneers.* Springer Science & Business Media. doi:10.1007/978-1-4471-5340-5

Pacheco-Torgal, F., Rasmussen, E. S., Granqvist, C., Ivanov, V., Kaklauskas, H. A., & Makonin, S. (2016). Start-Up Creation: The Smart Eco-efficient Built Environment. Sawton: Woodhead Publishing.

Perara, C., Zaslavsky, A., Christen, P., & Goergakopoulos, D. (2014). Context aware computing for the internet of things: A survey. *IEEE Communications Surveys and Tutorials, 16*(1), 414–454. doi:10.1109/SURV.2013.042313.00197

Rahman, H., Rahmani, R., Kanter, T., Persson, M., & Armundin, S. (2013). Reasoning Service Enabling SmartHome Automation at the Edge of Context Networks. In Á. Rocha, A. M. Correia, H. Adeli, L. P. Reis, & M. Teixeira (Eds.), *Advances in Information Systems and Technologies* (Vol. 1, pp. 777–795). Springer.

Rittinghouse, J., & Ransome, J. (2016). *Cloud Computing: Implementation, Management, and Security*. CRC Press.

Roberts, L. (1967, October). Multiple Computer Networks and Intercomputer Communication. *ACM Gatlinburg Conference*. Gatlinburg: ACM.

Russell, A. (2014). *Open Standards and the Digital Age: History, Ideology and Networks*. Cambridge University Press. doi:10.1017/CBO9781139856553

Salim, F., & Haque, U. (2015). Urban computing in the wild: A survey on large scale participation and citizen engagement with ubiquitous computing, cyber physical systems, and Internet of Things. *International Journal of Human-Computer Studies, 81*, 31–48. doi:10.1016/j.ijhcs.2015.03.003

Sathi, A. (2016). *Cognitive (Internet of) Things: Collaboration to Optimize Action*. Palgrave Macmillan. doi:10.1057/978-1-137-59466-2

Seel, P. (2012). *Digital Universe: The Global Telecommunication Revolution*. John Wiley & Sons.

Simon, H. A. (1963). *The heuristic compiler*. Rand Corporation.

Slama, D., Puhlmann, F., Morrish, J., & Bhatnagar, R. (2015). *Enterprise IoT: Strategies and Best Practices for Connected Products and Services*. O'Reilly Media.

Smart, P., Heersmink, R., & Clowes, R. (2016). The cognitive ecology of the internet. In S. J. Cowley & F. Vallée-Tourangeau (Eds.), *Cognition Beyond the Brain: Computation, Interactivity and Human Artifice* (2nd ed., pp. 251–282). Springer International Publishing.

Sturken, M., Thomas, D., & Ball-Rokeach, S. (2004). *Technological Visions: The Hopes and Fears that Shape New Technologies*. Temple University Press.

Sundmaeker, H., Guillemin, P., Friess, P., & Woelfflé, S. (2015). *Vision and challenges for realising the Internet of Things*. European Commission. Retrieved from http://www.internet-of-things-research.eu/pdf/IoT_Clusterbook_March_2010.pdf

Tomlinson, R. (2009). *The first network email.* Retrieved from Raytheon BBN Technologies: https://www.raytheon.com/sites/default/files/news/rtnwcm/groups/public/documents/content/rtn12_tomlinson_email.pdf

Tripathi, K. (2015). Optimizing Operational and Migration Cost in Cloud Paradigm (OOMCCP). In P. Sharma, P. Banerjee, J.-P. Dudeja, P. Singh, & R. K. Brajpuriya (Eds.), *Making Innovations Happen* (pp. 83–91). Allied Publishers.

United States Congress Committee on Commerce, Science and Transportation. (1991). *High-Performance Computing and Communications Act of 1991: hearing before the Subcommittee on Science, Technology, and Space of the Committee on Commerce, Science, and Transportation, United States Senate, One Hundred Second Congress, first session, on S.* Washington, DC: Congress of the U.S.

Varadharajan, V., & Bansal, S. (2016). Data Security and Privacy in the Internet of Things (IoT) Environment. In Z. Mahmood (Ed.), *Connectivity Frameworks for Smart Devices: The Internet of Things from a Distributed Computing Perspective* (pp. 261–280). Springer. doi:10.1007/978-3-319-33124-9_11

Vermesan, O., & Friess, P. (2015). Building the Hyperconnected Society: Internet of Things Research and Innovation Value Chains, Ecosystems and Markets. Gistrup: River Publishers. doi:10.13052/rp-9788793237988

Vincenti, G. (2010). *Teaching through Multi-User Virtual Environments: Applying Dynamic Elements to the Modern Classroom: Applying Dynamic Elements to the Modern Classroom.* IGI Global.

Vorster, J., & Goosen, L. (2017). A Framework for University Partnerships Promoting Continued Support of e-Schools. In J. Liebenberg (Ed.), *Proceedings of the 46th Annual Conference of the Southern African Computer Lecturers' Association (SACLA)* (pp. 118 - 126). Magaliesburg: North-West University.

Wieser, M. (1991). The computer for the 21st century. *Scientific American, 265*(3), 94–104. doi:10.1038cientificamerican0991-94 PMID:1675486

Wu, Q., Ding, G., Xu, Y., Feng, S., Du, Z., Wang, J., & Long, K. (2014). Cognitive internet of things: A new paradigm beyond connection. *IEEE Internet of Things Journal, 1*(2), 129–143. doi:10.1109/JIOT.2014.2311513

Zelnick, B., & Zelnick, E. (2013). *The illusion of Net Neutrality: Political Alarmism, Regulatory Creep and the Real Threat to Internet Freedom.* Hoover Press.

Zhang, G., Li, Y., & Lin, T. (2013). Caching in information centric networking: A survey. *Computer Networks, 57*(16), 3128–3141. doi:10.1016/j.comnet.2013.07.007

Zhang, Y., & Tao, F. (2016). *Optimization of Manufacturing Systems Using the Internet of Things*. Academic Press.

Zuckerman, E. (2013). *Digital Cosmopolitans: Why We Think the Internet Connects Us, Why It Doesn't, and How to Rewire It*. W.W. Norton & Company.

Chapter 6
Sustainability of Cloud-Based Smart Society

Dimpal Tomar
USICT, Gautam Buddha University, India

Pooja Singh
Shiv Nadar University, India

Jai Prakash Bhati
Noida International University, India

Pradeep Tomar
iD https://orcid.org/0000-0002-7565-0708
USICT, Gautam Buddha University, India

ABSTRACT

Today, everything is progressing to 'Smart' to enhance the environment via technological progress including IoT, big data, AI, ICT, and so on. But, in this whole process, the sustainability of being 'smart' is implemented by the cloud-based technology, which also acts as an engine. Smart society is another live example of this era that makes potential use of digital technology and sensor devices to improve people's lives through the internet. It also incorporates cloud computing, which significantly benefits them by offering a sustainable environment to access the computing power at large scale, which they could not previously access due to lack of resources. This chapter provide a broad overview of smart society that covers the scope and services, technological pillars, features necessities to be titled as 'smart', and a sustainable development. Also, it broadly covers the role of cloud computing, related technologies, and generic architecture for the sustainability of smart societies followed by applications with a case study and challenges.

DOI: 10.4018/978-1-7998-6981-8.ch006

INTRODUCTION TO SMART SOCIETY

Over a decade, the term 'Smart' revolves around every new innovation which is technology based and has been utilized with respect to everything from smart framework to a smart planet. Though, being 'Smart' is eventually all about the advantages that technology can contribute which means technology must be truly smart when it added value for public and society in terms of improving liveability and resource-efficiency. As the number of communities, cities and societies keep on increasing, they also required to employ smart technology in order to deal with many rising issues, such as; how will technology add value to construct energy efficient buildings and energy systems? How will technology reduce congestion and waste less resources ? How will technology play its role in making our cities or societies more liveable and sustainable? The only solution to all the issues is to implant a smart technological approach that cannot develop just a smart society, but a sustainable and smart society, as discussed by Bruun (2018).

A smart society was defined by Chakravorti and Chaturvedi (2017) as "A society where government thoughtfully deployed the digital technology in order to fulfil the three major goals; Citizens well-beingness, economically strong, and the productiveness of organizations". The society is making headway to be 'Smart' viz. Smart home, Smart parking, Smart car, Smart agriculture, Smart infrastructures, and Smart transportation. Cloud computing act as an engine for the development of 'smart' and have become chief component in the improvement of numerous aspects of life. Cloud is considered more than an Internet and an exemplar of green technology which support environmental sustainability directly or indirectly in organizations.

This section will try to address an overview on understanding the Scope and Services of Smart Society, technological pillars, Certain features or characteristic requirements to be titled as 'smart' followed by brief discussion on sustainable Development and Smart Society.

Review of Literature

Internet of Things and cloud computing together put a lot of efforts in the domain of making the societies smarter one with the more improved governances, education and lifestyle for citizens. For the same, number of researchers has gained the attention towards the designing and implementation of various application and services that enhance the environment of society.

Tan (2018) discussed in an article about the crucial role of cloud computing to the future of next level societies. Smart Society (2019) published a white paper on building the better future with smart technologies for citizens in which they tried to cover various case studies from different dimensions. Foresti, et al. (2020) discussed big data technology for smart maintenance by proposing an approach which is able to govern the data flow in man-machine interaction. Jiménez, Solanas and Falcone (2014) provided the manifold synopsis on interoperability of e-government, latest advances, also discussed opportunities followed by issues of operability in e-government. Mehmood, et al. (2017) introduced a framework for smart societies that provide teaching and learning services through the system known as UTiLearn and the framework was validated on 11 datasets.

Scope and Services of Smart Society

The buzzword 'Smart' is extensively used with home, cities, car, phone, buildings etc. which means that the mentioned things (i.e. cars, home phone) intended to perform their functions autonomously, without the intervention of the owner, through Artificial Intelligence (AI) or sensor technology. However, the sense of understanding the 'smart' term is different in various domain, for instance, smart mobility cannot be accomplished by just swapping manual cars with driverless automobiles. Smart mobility also include the reduction in vehicle dependency so that more space created for walking and cycling which in turn brings down the CO_2 emissions, minimizes the noise pollution and recovers the city making it a better place for people. Similarly, in 'Smart Learning', students performed learning all by itself by means of smart devices in the 'Smart school' environment. In contradiction of devices or services, 'Society' is comprised of various primary components which include 'Citizens', 'Governance', and 'Lifestyle', and so on. Hence, a society is supposed to be called 'Smart' when its primary components (Citizens, Governance and Lifestyle) should also be smart. In this context, smartness can be characterized through four traits, they are as follows

- Sensor technology employed to perform an autonomous operation.
- Machine learning approaches are adopted for the development of AI.
- Mobile technology is used to deliver the ubiquitous services without the regard of time and locations.
- A constant communication among consumers and providers enable users-centric services.

Among all the four above mentioned traits, the last element appears most critical for bestowing the society with the name of 'Smartness'.

These smartness elements incorporated into the environment of society to make it "Smart Society" which influences the capability of innovation to make individuals more gainful by permitting them to prioritize the resources for the activities and associations that is essential and eventually to upgrade the well-being, prosperity and the individual fulfilment.

Technological Pillars of Smart Society

The continuous advancement in technology directly or indirectly influences the lifestyle, work and play of an individual. People's virtual and physical spaces are gradually getting interconnected. Also, most of the communications are progressively facilitated via machines. The cloud computing, hyper-connectivity, Internet of Things (IoT), wearable technology, Machine-to-Machine (M2M) and intelligent living are the significantly growing areas. The fundamental outline is to establish novel connectivity approach, new sorts of advanced connections through digital technology, and anchor possibilities introduced by the more noteworthy amalgamation of related techniques and innovations into regular daily existences.

As a result, the world is sluggishly shifting towards 'Smart Society' which is being referred as "One that magnificently take the advantage of connected sensor devices and the digital technology and the utilization of digitally connected networks in order to enhance an individuals' lives", as mentioned by Levy and Wong (2014). The smart society can deliver their promises on the basis of three technological pillars which include network connectivity, smart equipment and software development, as shown in *figure 1*.

Figure 1. Smart society technological pillars

- **Connectivity**

Networks such as broadband, mobile, Virtual Private Network (VPN), Local Area Network (LAN), Metropolitan area network (MAN), Wide Area Network (WAN) together with modern technologies form connectivity. Nowadays, radio spectrum is most often used for connectivity. However, connectivity is a key element and essential requirement of communication technology and derived application services, for example, road safety, traffic management and e-government.

- **Smart Equipment's**

Everyday intelligent things intended to perform self-governing computation and able to connect with other intelligent objects. These smart objects play an important role in the development of smart societies. Meters (Electricity, water and gas), power grids, home appliances, health monitors, cars, water pumps, parking system, traffic lights, street lights and cameras are few things which essentially turn out to be smart, connected equipment's in order to deliver the sustainable advancements to improve the social and economic progresses, especially for developing countries.

- **Software Development**

Software development holds a principle responsibility to assure two main objectives firstly, the aforementioned pillars works together and secondly, a flawlessly connected platform will stimulate the entire process in order to reinforce the new facilities that would never happened previously.

Characteristics Requirements

Several components and their amalgamation forms a "Society". There are six major components of society with distinct peculiarities which include Citizens, Public Service and administration, Politics, Industrial & Fiscal Movement, Education, Attitude & life style (Culture). For smart society, each of the component must possess certain features to be titled as 'smart' as discussed in the table given below.

As per the aforementioned components and their respective characteristics; derive the new definition for smart society as "The smart society all about legislative issues, policy implementation and administration, industrial and financial exercises, education, attitude and lifestyle (culture) and citizens where all of them operate altogether with active participation, not only through the utilization of cutting edge ICT as well as encouraged by the new amendments and administration of society".

Table 1. Components and their related characteristic requirements

Component	Certain features or characteristic requirements to be titled as 'smart'
Citizen	• Developing the ability of the citizens to take an interest in knowledge creation and public services.
Public services and administration	• For smooth processing of Public administration and delivery of services require all citizens to participate actively. • Process of public administration and delivery of public services must be transparent. • Transform public administration and services from government official to citizen centred.
Politics	• Politics controls process of law and policy making; hence it must also include active involvement of citizens. • Processes for laws and policy making must be transparent.
Industrial & Fiscal Movement	• Adoption of sensing and AI technologies for products and its services development in order to perform an autonomous operation. • Understanding the interest and demands of all the citizens with respect to industrial and fiscal movement.
Education	• Information production processes require even a common man to participate actively, for example, collective intelligence. • At the school level, student driven-learning must be realized.
Attitude & life style (Culture)	• Improving the way of life to empower creative and resident driven lifestyles. • Understanding the harmonization of different ways of life and values towards all citizens with non-discriminating conduct irrespective of their status, for example, race, sex, age, pay, area and so forth

Sustainable Development and Smart Society

The smart society characteristics as discussed above empower the formation of a supportive circumstances for the accomplishment of goals in support of Sustainable Development at every fronts, confirmed by United Nations (n.d.).

Various goals with respect to sustainable development can be achieved with the society in which it employs smart approaches in order to develop itself, notably in other terms fond of giving rights to individuals and realization of an open government system which is capable enough to learn the citizens necessities and demands, precisely comprehensive and also, people appreciate the education system, in addition to that knowledge and wealth are not only consumed but also produced by the individuals. A society which shows matter of concern with respect to the environment and support emerging opportunities for the better improvement of various domain which include paperless work through virtualization, transportation, support digital making &marketing and energy efficiency to help the people so they can have a healthy, safe, and happier life.

The dream of achieving the smart society can be fulfilled through the integration of cloud computing technologies as a core element for the policies issued by the government, nationwide e-policies must be developed with respect to the goals of public development, enabling citizens to introduce new learning methodologies, promoting skills at large scale required for building new innovation and ensuring financial support for the innovation.

CLOUD COMPUTING FOR SUSTAINABLE DEVELOPMENT

Smart societies are those having an interconnected network of technologies for transmission, communication and analysing the crucial data in order to sustain and enhance the societal operations. Nowadays, every societal infrastructure require such technologies which covers environment, energy, health, traffic, transportation, financial and social development etc. Genuinely, if smart societies want to perform its intended function immaculately at the public as well as private sector, it is the principle requirement for the deployment of Cloud computing together with the Internet of Things (IoT). Indeed, it is being seen that smart societies adopting both the technologies together i.e. Cloud and IoT are achieving improved outcomes.

Basically, it is close to difficult to envision the smart societies without the amalgamation of Cloud that can encourage efficient power consumption, improve the safety of public, create firm society despite having the efficiency to follow anything from garbage management to congestion.

This section delve into the role of Cloud computing technology in smart society to support sustainable development and also, explore some of the technologies which are related with the of the Cloud-based technology; that are deployed in order to deliver the appropriate transformation.

Role of Cloud Computing in Smart Society

There are numerous reasons identified while exploring the cloud computing applications that will depict why should smart societies adopt cloud technology. At the point when societies build up an advanced foundation on digital technology, it not only helps in delivering massive amount of crucial information for private and public sectors, yet in addition establishes a more secure environment.

Though apart from this, smart societies also require improvement of operations, more openness and develop better ways for citizens to take an interest in businesses and society services. Cloud has its applications and advantages in the same direction while deploying in societies. Hence, some of its benefits are highlighted further (Smartcity 2018).

- **Efficient Data Management**

Smart societies is required to work out on one of the main aspects including data integration and data mining. However, the massive data need to be process, fusion, analyse and manage the flow is still critical, even for the smart societies that turn up. Hence, cloud is required in order to assure that these above mentioned changes occur in a consistent and efficient manner. The Cloud computing upgrade itself that endorse data consumption and fast delivery.

- **Sustainability Aspect**

Certainly, it is very clear that without the sustainability support, no smart societies is able to perform their intended operations. Hence, the role of cloud technology turns out to be considerably more applicable. Smart societies are using such assets that definitely affect the atmosphere. To deal with such difficulties, societies are investigating reliable and sustainable solutions which may include improved planning, resourcing, design, administration and better decision-making that work in accordance with the standards of sustainability. In respect to the same, the cloud based technology play the role of spine with sustainable infrastructure for societies. The development in Cloud computing is dramatically enhancing the Internet efficiency in order to deliver a broad spectrum of services and applications. Moving the smart society services over the cloud show the significant improvement of handling the information as well as shaping the citizens life simpler and smarter.

- **Economy Rise**

In order to endorse the development of smart societies, ground-breaking innovations and technologies are established which ultimately leads to the rise in economy. Mutually beneficial collaboration among societies and commerce can draw in colossal benefits.

- **Cost Reduction**

The entire thought of building up a smart society goes to huge success, when societies cannot minimize the functional costs. Hence, it is important that smart societies must designed in such a way that the operational costs must be reduced and delivered services to citizens with high improvement. In other words, Cloud-based platform provide the ability to the various applications and services to deliver the better service for citizens while reducing the operational costs.

Generic Architecture of Cloud Computing

From small scale organization to the idea of developing the smart infrastructures, cloud-based technology is deployed everywhere through which the information can be stored and accessed using Internet from any location regardless of any time.

A generic architecture of Cloud computing is a combination of two core architectures which include service-oriented and event-driven architectures. The entire architecture is decomposed into two major sections i.e. front end and back end, as shown in the *figure 2*. From the *figure 2,* front end depicts the infrastructure used by the client at its end, essential to access the platforms of cloud Computing. Frond end comprised of interfaces and applications, thin and fat clients, web server and devices at the client-side, whereas back end depicted the service provider through which all the resources are managed which is responsible for delivering the services of the cloud technology. However, for such high level services cloud technology comprised of massive data storage, virtual machines, security mechanism, deployment of models, traffic control mechanisms, servers, etc, as discussed by Jaiswal (n.d.). All they (front end and back end) need is Internet connection.

The generic architecture has many components that make it cloud computing platform, which include client infrastructure, application, services (i.e. Software as a Service (SaaS), Platform as a Service (PaaS), Infrastructure as a Service (IaaS)), runtime cloud, storage, infrastructure, management, security and Internet.

Technologies Associated With Sustainable Cloud Computing

Cloud computing offered sustainability in such a manner that small-scale organizations empowered by the specific technology and allow them to get the accessibility to computing power in a substantial amounts over very short period of time; consequently, the cloud based technology for large organizations turned out to be more competitive, as mentioned by Domdouzis (2015). There are several technologies that possess the similar properties as cloud based technology or associated to the cloud technology, they are highlighted below:

- **Grid computing**

Grid computing technology comprised of numerous nodes that are parallelly connected in order to create a large cluster of supercomputing resources. The cluster of computing resources are of distinct sizes and able to execute on any of the operating system. These resources are able to perform bulky and complex computing operations. This technology involve machines of three types, namely, Control Node, Provider and User, as deliberated by Dhivya and Sunitha, (2015).

Figure 2. Generic Architecture of Cloud Computing

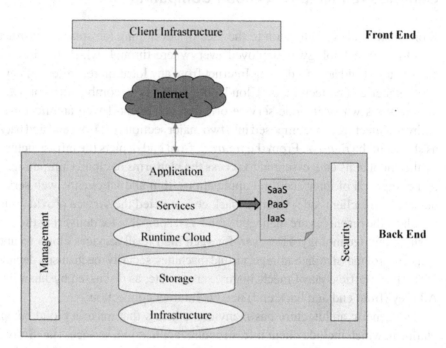

- **Virtualization**

Visualization is the substructure of cloud based technology. Several applications are consolidated and transformed into virtual containers which is located on a standalone or multiple servers, this entire process is handled by the virtualization, as weigh up by Padala et al. (2007). Visualization provide the accessibility of servers to the users, without learning the detailed information of those servers.

- **Utility computing**

This service model is one of the most trending technology. It provides computing resources and infrastructure on "pay-per-use" or "on-demand" approach. Due to which this model enhance the efficiency of computing resources by reducing the related costs. For computing services and storage, large organizations implemented their own services through utility computing, such as Amazon and Google, discussed by Kumar et al., (2015).

- **Autonomic computing**

In autonomic computing, the connected systems possess the self-managing properties through which automatically adapts unpredictable variations in the underlying infrastructure by covering the inherent complexity to the users, mentioned by Gibbs, (2002).

- **Web services**

The application-to-application communication simplified by the Web services through a structured and efficient framework drawn up on the basis of open XML and current Web protocols standards. There are three key elements involved in this framework, namely, service descriptions, communication protocols, and service discovery, provided by Curbera, et al. (2002).

APPLICATIONS OF CLOUD-BASED SMART SOCIETY WITH CASE STUDY

In this section, a detailed explanation is provided about the applications of cloud technology in various domains of society followed by various case studies concerning deployment of cloud technology that offers sustainability for the flawless functioning of smart society.

Applications of Cloud Computing in Different Domains of a Society

Benedict (2018) proposed very good quality advances, for example, Cloud, Edge, Fog processing, etc have significant ramifications on tending to the arising issues of social orders. A few driving cultural issues, for example, air contamination, water contamination, defilement, and destitution could be ideal told or tended to with the utilization of these very good quality advancements. In this section, we have talked about a couple of cultural applications and the significance of an IoT Cloud empowered advancements.

The recent advancements reported in cloud services and ICT domain majorly affect the developments of all the sectors of a society whether it is education, health, transport, agriculture, environment, business, etc. The role of cloud technology is crucial in managing, protecting, securing and developing all the sectors of a smart society. Cloud technology has potential to handle all the issues faced by rural and urban sectors.

The three important technical aspects of cloud technology including network connectivity, IoT devices and software development are committed to transform a society into a smart society. Apart from these, the principles of sustainable development are also responsible for developing a smart society. This section provides the detailed discussion on the categorization of Societal Applications.

Smart Living at Home

Individuals, generally living in metropolitan urban areas, foresees a savvy living. This implies that their wearable gadgets ought to be distantly associated and synchronized in a manner to such an extent that the arrangements ought to consistently help them to seek after their day by day schedules effortlessly. For occasions, the developing arrangements have dominatingly pulled in individuals to upgrade their home with security contraptions and fire/flood/wave alert machines; coolers do speak with the individual cell phones to remind them about shopping milk around evening time, as discussed by Hargreaves et al., (2017).

Smart Living at Society

Society ought to be robotized so the future may remain socially and financially serious. The recent concerns of finding a shopping centre, distinguishing the concerned official to report an issue, tackling condo complexities, etc. could be handily tended to with the assistance of these applications, as mentioned by Low et al., (2019).

Smart Environment

Climate ought to be perfect. What steps do we technocrats embrace for guaranteeing neatness? The Indian government, through its Swatch Bharath mission, has taken different steps to build up a Clean India. In spite of a few inceptions, Frontline (Feb.16 2018 issue) has detailed a situation where enterprises dump synthetic squanders to Noyyal stream of TamilNadu. Why careful steps are not being embraced? Can't advancements help the concerned administrative offices? These inquiries ought to be genuinely managed for the future Clean India. What's more, air contamination is likewise staying as a genuine worry in different pieces of India, which brings about wellbeing perils to the general public.

Smart Agriculture

Advancing watering at rural terrains could expand the economy of the general public – i.e., the ranchers on the loose. Climate helped cultivating with processing arrangements do an enormous part in boosting up the economy of the general public. Also, a couple of horticulture intriguing ICT or disturbing frameworks while demolishing agrarian fields could be created utilizing these advances, mentioned by Sciforce, (2019).

Smart Health

In the period of globalization and data age, medical services businesses are strongly elevating and embracing cloud technology to improve understanding consideration. At the point when an ever increasing number of patients as wellbeing purchasers look for and focus on quality in their lives through improved medical care therapies and administrations, it places extraordinary requests on the medical care industry's data dealing with capacities and foundation, as weigh up by Bodenheimer (1999). As right on time as 2006, the World Bank in its report perceived that solid data and viable correspondence are vital components in general wellbeing rehearses. The utilization of fitting advances can build the quality and the scope of both data and correspondence.

Over the age of 40, the majority of the south Indian residents are inclined to a few medical problems – most transcendently, the diabetes mellitus. A sound society is a gainful society. Understanding observing and wellbeing checking machines ought to be delivered in a practical way for the usage of any average person (Activeadvise, 2017)

Case Studies

This section will cover certain case studies that were initiated with the successes of the enforcement of cloud computing in various sectors like, smart learning, smart education system, smart environment and so on.

Smart Education in the Republic of Korea

The Korean Ministry of Education, Science and Technology set up in 2007 the "Advanced Textbooks Generalization Plan" which dispatched a pilot project pointed toward creating computerized reading material models for six subjects in thirteen rudimentary pilot schools.

In 2011, the government set the objective of building an incredible country with capable individuals and chose to seek after SMART training approaches for the 21st century. Brilliant Self-coordinated, Motivated, Adaptive, Resource free and Technology inserted (SMART) schooling is an, "Wise and redone instructing and learning framework". As the acronym SMART shows, understudies are required learning with fun, roused, and self-coordinated ways dependent on their stages and inclination in an asset improved climate, suggested by Anderson (2010).

The significant five mainstays of SMART instruction strategy comprise of consolidating advanced course books into the educational system by 2015; advancing on the web classes and evaluation; improving the legitimate structure and copyright laws; building up the limit of instructors; and developing a distributed computing based framework. Because of a cloud-based registering climate, computerized course book substance can be promptly downloaded with the goal that understudies can access forward-thinking data whenever and anyplace (Creating the smart society: Social and economic development through ICT applications 2017).

Smart Learning Program in United Arabs Emirates

The United Arab Emirates dispatched the Smart Learning Program in 2012. This is a significant segment of UAE's Vision 2021 – "to turn into an information based economy through the reconciliation of innovation in schooling". The activity was granted by ITU in 2014.

Through the Program, the UAE is contributing intensely to carry the most recent innovation to the schools, empowering the improvement of innovativeness, logical reasoning and development. Program means to shape another learning climate and culture in government schools through the dispatch of "brilliant classes" that will furnish each understudy with an electronic tablet and admittance to high velocity 4G organizations by 2019. The activity, subsidized through the Telecommunications Regulatory Authority's Information and Communication Technology (ICT) Fund, is under the direction of the Ministry of Education just as the Prime Minister's office. This is a testament to both the guarantee of the Program and the commitment of the UAE Government to schooling and ICT.

A Case Study on Plastic Free Environment

Plastic is a demon for the climate and no one can disagree to this fact. We all are very much aware about the disadvantages of plastic and the health hazards it causes to mankind. Even after knowing all these facts, we are so much dependent on the things made up of plastic that we cannot stop using them. In the past, it has also been seen that when government impose strict restrictions on plastic use, either people keeps on using them illegally or they stop using plastic and the plastic made up things for some time and again start using it at the same rate. So, to solve this problem of plastic, instead of banning we can think of recycling it. The plastic which has been thrown in the garbage as a waste can be recycled and can be reused again and again after recycling without letting it go to the nature and ill-effect it. Most of the plastic that is being used by the society is actually become dangerous only because it cannot be decomposed. So, instead of decomposing it, we can try to recycle it.

An AI model has been developed that can help in solving this problem by scanning the items and figuring out what kind of plastic it contains and then suggesting ways to recycle them. Even this model can also be used during the manufacturing of the plastic materials themselves. During the manufacturing itself, the items can be labelled with the kind of plastic it is made up of and where it should be recycled. This way, we can reduce the effect of plastic on nature without actually banning its use, as suggested by Narayani, (2014).

CHALLENGES AND FUTURE PROSPECTS OF SUSTAINABLE CLOUD-BASED SMART SOCIETY

Carroll (2017) notes that with the advancement in technologies and new innovations, it seem seems to be very easy to develop smart societies. But on the other hand we face various challenges in deployment of cloud -based smart societies that are sustainable too. In this section we are going to discuss a few of them (Creating the smart society: Social and economic development through ICT applications 2017).

Constraints in Designing and Engineering

- **Cooling management**

As the Cloud Data Centres (CDCs) generates a lot of heat; it results in degradation of the performance of electronic equipment and components. So it must be managed efficiently, keeping in mind not to increase the operational cost of maintenance. A lot of cooling techniques are available currently, but the most efficient, cost effective and beneficial one must be adopted. One of the economic ways is that CDCs must be established nearby a natural source of running water like rivers and canals. Water cooled systems can be implemented in which fresh and cold water from the water bodies can be channelized across the servers through ducting network, which absorbs the dissipated heat of servers and flow into the water bodies, keeping inside temperature of CDCs low.

- **Replacement of conventional energy resources with renewable ones**

There will be a great increase in demand of cloud –services to be deployed across the various CDCs over a large geographical region in order to establish the smart societies. These CDCs must be in demand of huge amount of energy to get them operational, which definitely raise the running cost as well as have an adverse impact on the environment in terms of carbon footprints. In order to overcome this challenge, for sustainable cloud computing services to reduce the carbon footprints up to a great extent, the conventional energy resources like fossil fuel based power grids must be replaced by some renewable source of energy.

- **Dissipated heat utilization**

The cloud servers dissipates enormous amount of heat when they are operational, that goes in vain. Normally the temperature of CDCs is recorded in between 80-115 degree F. Although this temperature is not significantly high, but can be recycled in many ways. Excess heat can be directed to nearby buildings through ducts in order to keep the buildings warm during winters. Waste heat can be utilized to maintain the temperature of swimming pools in nearby neighbourhood in colder regions.

ICT Policies and Regulations in Various Countries

New generation technologies are the foundation of smart societies that will foster the development of cloud computing services, in smart societies. Thus it is to be expected from the local governments that their policies will encourage and support the implementation of new technologies for the deployment of cloud computing infrastructure. And the policies must create an environment favourable for investors to male investments in developing robust and reliable networks in significant technology development. Policies must be drafted in such a way to support the global standards for cloud services, as it is the duty of policy makers and regulators to provide favourable environment to promote and encourage the development and deployment of new technologies necessary for cloud based smart societies along with ensuring the privacy and security of end user data, as mentioned by Palvia, (2015).

Demand of Skilled Human Resources

Skilled human resources are key role players in achieving the smart societies and will be in great demand. Lack of skilled people required for deployment of IoTs is a great challenge in most of the developing countries even in a few developed countries too. In order to tackle such problems, Governments must come forward to establish numerous skill development centres where newly graduates can acquire specialized skills that are necessary in running smart societies.

Reduction of Operational Cost

Budget plays a vital role in any operations of any system. Keeping budget in control remains the main focus of any project or an organization. And one way to optimise the budget to minimise the operational cost of smart societies. This can be achieved by emphasizing on the innovation of new, efficient and sustainable technologies, and adopting them in deployment of smart societies, as deliberated by Ture˘cková and Nevima, (2020).

Reliability

Another significant challenge in achieving sustainable cloud based smart societies is the reliability of the cloud computing infrastructure that serves as backbone for IoTs implemented in smart societies.it must be ensured to the service users that up to what extent the services are available with high reliability. How much is the fault tolerance capacity of the system provided to end users.

CONCLUSION

The society is making headway to be 'Smart' viz. Smart home, Smart parking, Smart car, Smart agriculture, Smart infrastructures, and Smart transportation. Cloud computing act as an engine for the development of 'smart' and have become chief component in the improvement of numerous aspects of life. This chapter provide all the necessary aspects and techniques used in smart societies useful for designing and development of better governance, citizens and lifestyles which will change the outlook towards societies.

REFERENCES

Activeadvise. (2017). *What is Smart Health and How do People Benefit?* Retrieved from https://www.activeadvice.eu/news/concept-projects/what-is-smart-health-and-how-do-people-benefit/

Anderson, J. (2010). *ICT transforming education: a regional guide.* https://unesdoc.unesco.org/ark:/48223/pf0000189216

Benedict, S. (2018). IoT-Cloud Applications for Societal Benefits – An Entrepreneurial Solution. *IEEE Web Hosting.* http://site.ieee.org/indiacouncil/files/2018/05/p59-p62.pdf

Bodenheimer, T. (1999). The American health care system: The movement for improved quality in health care. *England Journal of Medicine, 340*(6), 488–492. doi:10.1056/NEJM199902113400621 PMID:9971876

Bruun, H. P. (2018). *Building A Smart Sustainable Society*. Ramboll. https://de.ramboll.com/-/media/61247eef6e694d33886e9f54b20af51a.pdf

Carroll, A. (2017). *How The Heat Generated by Data Centres can be Recycled?* https://lifelinedatacenters.com/data-center/heat-generated-by-data-centers-can-be-recycled/

Chakravorti, B., & Chaturvedi, R. S. (2017). The "Smart Society" of the Future Doesn't Look Like Science Fiction. *Harvard Business Review*. https://hbr.org/2017/10/the-smart-society-of-the-future-doesnt-look-like-science-fiction

Curbera, F., Duftler, M., Khalaf, R., Nagy, W., Mukhi, N., & Weerawarana, S. (2002). Unraveling the web services web: An introduction to SOAP, WSDL, and UDDI. *Internet Computing, 6*, 86–93. doi:10.1109/4236.991449

Dhivya & Sunitha. (2015). Article on Grid Computing Architecture and Benefits. *International Research Journal of Engineering and Technology, 2*(9), 1070-1074.

Domdouzis, K. (2015). Sustainable Cloud Computing. In *Green Information Technology: A Sustainable Approach*. Elsevier. doi:10.1016/C2014-0-00029-9

Foresti, R., Rossi, S., Magnani, M., Bianco, C. G. L., & Delmonte, N. (2020). Smart Society and Artificial Intelligence: Big Data Scheduling and the Global Standard Method Applied to Smart Maintenance. *Engineering, 6*(7), 8835–8846. https://doi.org/10.1016/j.eng.2019.11.014

GibbsW. (2002). *Autonomic Computing*. Retrieved from https://www.scientificamerican.com/article/autonomic-computing/

Hargreaves, T., Wilson, C., & Hauxwell-Baldwin, R. (2018). Learning to live in a smart home. *Building Research and Information, 46*(1), 127–139. doi:10.1080/09613218.2017.1286882

Jaiswal, S. (n.d.). *Cloud Computing Architecture*. https://www.javatpoint.com/cloud-computing-architecture

Jiménez, C. E., Solanas, A., & Falcone, F. (2014). E-Government Interoperability: Linking Open and Smart Government. *Computer, 47*(10), 22–24. doi:10.1109/MC.2014.281

Levy, C., & Wong, D. (2014). *Towards a smart society*. Big Innovation Centre. https://www.biginnovationcentre.com/wp-content/uploads/2019/07/BIC_TOWARDS-A-SMART-SOCIETY_03.06.2014.pdf

Low, M. P., Chung, C., Ung, L., Tee, P., & Kuek, T.-Y. (2019). Smart Living Society Begins with A Holistic Digital Economy: A Multi-Level Insight. *7th International Conference on Information and Communication Technology (ICoICT)*, 1-7. 10.1109/ICoICT.2019.8835199

Mehmood, R., Alam, F., Albogami, N. N., Katib, I., Albeshri, A., & Altowaijri, S. M. (2017). UTiLearn: A Personalised Ubiquitous Teaching and Learning System for Smart Societies. *IEEE Access: Practical Innovations, Open Solutions*, *5*, 2615–2635. doi:10.1109/ACCESS.2017.2668840

Mondal, Kumar, R. & Sarddar, D. (2015). Utility Computing. *International Journal of Grid and Distributed Computing*, *8*, 115–122. doi:10.14257/ijgdc.2015.8.4.11

Narayani, N. (2014). *Protect the environment: Go plastic-free with these 11 easy everyday tips.* Retrieved from http://www.folomojo.com/protect-the-environment-go-plastic-free-with-these-11-easy-everyday-tips/

Padala, P., Zhu, X., Wang, Z., Singhal, S., & Sin, K. G. (2007). *Performance Evaluation of Virtualization Technologies for Server Consolidation.* http://137.204.107.78/tirocinio/site/tirocini/TirocinioZuluaga/Documents/virtualizzazione/Technologies%20for%20Server.pdf

Palvia, P., Baqir, N., & Nemati, H. (2015). ICT Policies in Developing Countries: An Evaluation with the Extended Design-Actuality Gaps Framework. *The Electronic Journal on Information Systems in Developing Countries*, *71*. Advance online publication. doi:10.1002/j.1681-4835.2015.tb00510.x

Sciforce. (2020). *Smart Farming: The Future of Agriculture.* Retrieved from https://www.iotforall.com/smart-farming-future-of-agriculture

Smart Society. (2019). [REMOVED HYPERLINK FIELD]https://www.azbil.com/top/pickup/whitepaper/pdf/Azbil_Smart_Society_WP_12022020.pdf

Smartcity. (2018). *Smart Cities Need To Be On The Cloud To Speed Up Sustainable Development.* https://www.smartcity.press/cloud-computing-benefits/

Tan, J. (2018). *Cloud Computing Is Crucial To The Future Of Our Societies.* https://www.forbes.com/sites/joytan/2018/02/25/cloud-computing-is-the-foundation-of-tomorrows-intelligent-world/?sh=483139c64073

The role of ICT in the proposed urban suatainable development goal. (2014). https://www.ericsson.com/assets/local/news/2014/9/the-role-of-ict-in-the-new-urban-agenda.pdf

Turečková, K., & Nevima, J. (2020). The Cost Benefit Analysis for the Concept of a Smart City: How to Measure the Efficiency of Smart Solutions? *Sustainability, 12*, 2663. doi:10.3390u12072663

United Nations, Department of Global Communications. (n.d.). *The 17 goals.* https://sdgs.un.org/goals

Chapter 7
Cloud–Based Smart City Using Internet of Things

Indu Malik
Gautam Buddha University, India

Sandhya Tarar
Gautam Buddha University, India

ABSTRACT

The cloud-based smart city is a way to provide resources and data on demand. Two technologies used to build cloud-based smart city, IoT, and cloud computing are explored. Using smart sensors can capture the movement of the environment, humans, and city infrastructure like building maintenance, traffic control, transportation, pollution monitoring. This is possible through IoT. Future movement could be predicted based on present and past data. Cloud computing is used for cloud storage. Using cloud, users can access resources in virtual mode at any time or anywhere. It can be accessed at different locations at the same time through high speed internet. Cloud is managed by a third party. Users don't have any knowledge regarding resource location and data, such as where user data is stored. Users use cloud service in virtual mode. Basically, cloud is a service provider platform that provides resources and data storage facility in a virtual way; users don't need to purchase resources.

INTRODUCTION OF CLOUD-BASED IOT

Cloud computing is a paradigm where all computing resources are available. These are providing to the user when needed, user-pay according to its use. For example: If a user needs 4 GB of storage on the cloud, but it has used only 2GB, then the

DOI: 10.4018/978-1-7998-6981-8.ch007

user pays only for 2GB which is used, the rest 2GB will be released by the user, the user will not pay for unused space. Users can access any resource on-demand from the cloud. Internet is an essential thing, which is required to access cloud service. Without the internet, users cannot get cloud service. "Cloud computing is a model for enabling convenient, on-demand network access to a shared pool of configurable computing resources (e.g., networks, servers, storage, applications, and services) that can be rapidly provisioned and released with minimal management effort or service provider interaction. This cloud model promotes availability and comprises five essential characteristics, three service models, and four deployment models."

The primary cloud computing model is shown below. Servers, storage, applications, and services are accessed via a shared network. They are shared between organizations and accessed by users or applications. The users may be members of the organizations working on-premise, remote workers, customers, or general public members.

Figure 1. Basic Cloud Computing Model

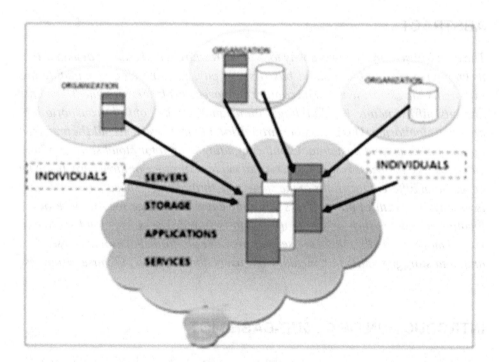

Cloud computing (Amoore, 2013) resources are rapidly provisioned and released with minimal management effort or service provider interaction. This means an organization can have more or fewer servers. It depends on the scale of organization stores, applications, or services and can configure the ones it uses to meet its requirements, as and when it wishes to do so, and without significant effort.

IoT stands for the Internet of Things (Angwin, 2013). IoT is a system referred to the interrelated and inter-connected devices or objects, which can transfer data. All IoT devices have one purpose: to collect data and share that data worldwide using wireless internet. Internet is essential for both cloud and IoT.

Standards and Protocol for Cloud-Based Smart City

The world has been becoming Smart (Antonopoulos, 2010) day by day. Every day has been introducing new technologies and Smart technologies with the higher growth of Science and Technology. People are automatically connected with Smart devices like mobile devices, computers, watches, wearable devices. The journey of communication from human to machine era is changing very rapidly. IoT comes as a backbone for the digital world, or you can say the Smart world and the Machine to Machine communication. The European Union adopted the IoT (Internet of Things) concept in the Commission Communication on RFID. (Radio Frequency ID) (Armbrust, 2010, Arts, 2015) It was published in March 2007 (Palattella et al., 2013). "It is an assumption by 2025 Internet will cover all everyday things, like food packages, paper, documents, toys, machine furniture, etc. For Smart City (De-ren, 2012), the main task of developments is future opportunities and risks when people can remotely control, locate, and monitor the devices. For Cloud-based Smart City using IoT, we get data, resources from the cloud, and real event data from sensors sent to the server. On-demand of Cloud-based Smart City (Duda, 2018), we need to combine digital devices with IoT and cloud. Technology advances could drive widespread diffusion of an Internet of Things (IoT) that could, like the present Internet, contribute invaluably to economic development and military capability". For example, To check the water level and quality, sensor have to use like: sensors mounted on a river or any water tank, data will be uploaded to a server, then it will process by the various department according to the requirement that is matched with a pre-decided data pattern that can be returned with a decision making quality of water up to human consumption, floods due to over floor of river boundaries, available water quantity. Smart City (Bastin, 2013, Belgaum 2017) is also contributing to the medical field; if A person has to wear Smart watch or another Smart device that automatically detects the persons abnormality in health conditions and send current data to a dedicated server/cloud and traces the conditions by GPS (Holte, 2017, Benson, 2015), and mapped this data with, which is stored in a data bank and send an emergency alert to the very nearest reachable hospital, dedicated consultant physician, and send GPS location of that person to the ambulance and family members also who is using its mobile, vehicle embedded Global Positioning System (GPS) transceiver. In the virtual concept, people's mental, social, physical, and all other aspects are interconnected through the virtual model. The cloud-based Smart City model also essential in analyzing previous infrastructure data (building, organization) and predict future scenarios most prominently. In the Internet of Things, each device can easily communicate with each other devices without any interception of humans. When the concept of the IoT was blended with Digital City (Bhosale, 2014), at the same time, human society and electronic devices are also integrated. In 2008, Smart City was introduced, and it is low consumption, low pollution, and low emission for supporting a low-carbon economy to some extent.

CLOUD-BASED SMART CITY

Cloud-based (Ji, Z, 2014) Smart City hubs provide a promising approach for developing an IoT-centric framework, which is used for smart cities. It works on two concepts. The first one is a consistent and easy-to-use interface for emerging IoT infrastructure within the city that systems integrators and application developers can use. The second one supports the system-of-systems approach to smart cities. A cloud-based hub can integrate several sub-systems that collectively make up the complete smart city software infrastructures.

Resources on cloud (Houze Jr, 2014) are swiftly provided and released with least service provider interaction and least management effort. That organization which is providing cloud services they do not have more server. They have limited number

Figure 2. An IoT hub acts as a portal for Smart City

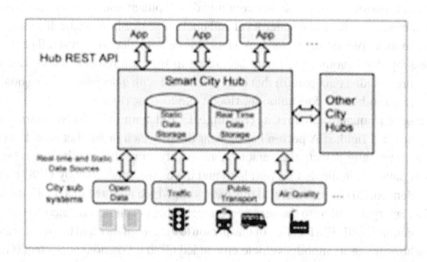

of server to process consumer request. Actually number of servers depends on the scale of organization. It also depends on some other factors like scale of organization stores, applications, or services.

What is Smart City?

The blending of digital City with the Internet of Things has created a new Smart City concept.

FROM DIGITAL CITY TO SMART CITY

Digital City is the heart of Smart City. The combination of digital City and the IoT is the advancement of Smart City.

INTERNET OF THINGS

IoT stands for the Internet of Things. IoT is a system referred to the interrelated and inter-connected devices or objects, which can transfer data. All IoT devices have one purpose: to collect data and share that data worldwide using wireless internet. Wireless (Biermann, 2012, Biermann, 2010) is a type of network. In the world, It has connected all the devices in a virtual model for data sharing. Data collection, data transfer, and data storage and communication become easy using IoT. Nowadays, anyone machine can communicate with another machine without required any human interaction because of IoT. Internet of Things used technology, and it is called RFID. RFID stands for Radio Frequency Identification. RFID is an automated technology and is used to aids machines or computers to identify any object. It also uses for recoding metadata (metadata is data about data). It can control any target using radio waves. RFID is also used for real-time data collection. IoT has RFID with infrared sensors, GPS (Shi, 2011), and laser scanner sensor (Fleming, 2001) equipment for object observation. It observes the location, all movement of the object; it can also exchange data and information. IoT is an intelligent system it is capable of the identification of intelligence, location-tracking, and monitoring.

1. Device connection

Figure 3. Field of IoT

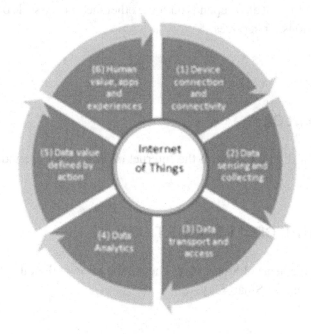

All IoT devices have to connect with other devices like, machine, and sensor (Husmann, 2002). Correct device connectivity is a very important for any IoT based system. IoT devices, IoT connectivity, embedded intelligence comes under the device connection.

2.   Data Sensing

Sensor is used to sense the event as well as capture it for further processing. Data sensing consider data capture, sensors, and tags storage.

3.   Communication

When data is sending from one location/machine to another or it may be send to the server (or on cloud server) it needs internet. Data is transfer from one Machine to another machine using internet. Data transfer process is also known as data communication process, and it focus on access networks, cloud, edge, data transport.

4.   Data analytics

Large data is processed using AI and ML. Data analytics includes extensive data analysis, AI and cognitive, and the analysis at the edge.

5. Data value

Data value is a task when action is taken on the data. It has to perform analysis to action, APIs and processes, and actionable intelligence also.

6. Human value

Human get smart application which does not require human interaction like Smart applications, Stakeholder benefits.

HISTORY OF IOT

The phrase Internet of Things is 16 years old. But the idea of connected devices had been much longer, at least since the 70s. The idea was often called "embedded internet" or "pervasive computing." The term "Internet of Things" was invented by Kevin Ashton in 1999 during his work at Procter & Gamble. Ashton, who worked in supply chain optimization, wanted to attract senior management's consideration to a new exciting technology called RFID. Because the internet was the most exciting recent trend in 1999 and because it somehow earned sense, he called his presentation "Internet of Things."

Smart City has merged both the digital City and the IoT with a single unit called Smart City. When the IoT and the digital City are comprehensively merged, almost every system in the City can contribute as a Smart system. Smart City is equal to digital City and content networking. Smart City is developed using lots of Smart devices. Smart devices collect massive data, which is transfer to the server, and this data is called cloud data, which is location independent. Authorized people can access this data anywhere in the world. Smart City uses data houses for data storage.

METHODOLOGY

The methodology section contains three parts. The first one is used for collecting data; the second one is used for sending it to the server, and the third one is used to provide data or resource to the user on its demand. This section contains the descriptions of IoT, sensor, communication, Hadoop (Borthakur, 2007), data, and data transfer. The methodology section describes the workflow of Smart City.

Figure 4. Block Diagram of Cloud-based Smart City

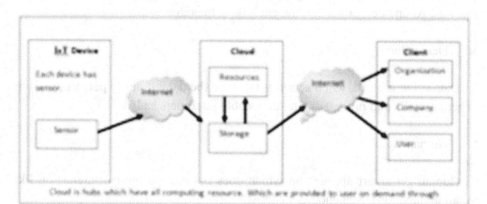

Step 1: Sensor sensing the movements and send it corresponding to the server using the internet.

Step 2: The data is stored on the server. All computer resources are available on the cloud.

Step 3: Provide the required resource to the client on-demand through the internet.

Internet of Things (IoT)

Internet of Things (IoT) has opened the doors for the Smart City, or we can say for the Smart world. Smart City's concept connects various devices and objects such as wearable devices, mobile phones, vehicles, electronic devices, and computers. The purpose of connecting all the devices is to interchange the information throughout the world. The critical factors in IoT can be classified as sensing, communication, Cloud-Based Capture & Consolidation, and information delivery. IoT uses sensors for sensing the object and the things.

Sensor

A sensor is a device or a subsystem used to detect events or changes in an environment and send information to the computer processor. Sensors (Fleming, 2001) are various types like biometric sensors, radiation sensors, temperature sensors, position sensors, etc. A particular sensor is used for an appropriate task. Through sensors, data is collected and send to the servers, or maybe in data centers, or maybe on a cloud.

Biometric sensors are fitted to sense biometric, environmental, biological, audible, or visual. The sensor data is further processed and analyzed for a specific purpose.

Communication

Communication is an act of conveying information from one source to another. Communication may be between two persons or person to machine (P2M) or a machine to machine (M2M). P2M and M2M are both examples of IoT. Alexa is an example of P2M communication. In communication, many IoT protocols are such as Near Field Communication (NFC), IEEE 802.15.4, Wi-Fi (IEEE 802.11).

Hadoop

Hadoop (Das, 2010) is an open-source Java framework. We are using Hadoop for storing and processing extensive data in Smart City technology. Basically, in Smart City (Khan, 2014), we are using a distributed file system to store extensive data. In a distributed file system (DFS), data is stored on a different node as a cluster, and we can process in both ways like independently and centrally. DFS is allowed fault tolerance. Hadoop uses HDFS (Hadoop Distributed File System) (Shvachko, 2010) for data storage. Hadoop uses the MapReduce model, and It is used fast data storage and data retrieval from each node.

Hadoop (White, 2012) is used for storing data and running applications on clusters of commodity hardware. It provides bulky storage for any type of data, enormous processing power, and the ability to handle virtually limitless concurrent tasks or jobs.

Why is Hadoop important?

Hadoop Storage: Hadoop can store and process vast amounts of data quickly. With data volumes and varieties constantly increasing, especially from social media and the Internet of Things (IoT), that's a key consideration.

Computing power: Hadoop distributed computing model processes big data fast. The more computing nodes can used, the more processing power we have.

Fault tolerance: Data and application processing are protected against hardware failure. If a node goes down, jobs are automatically redirected to other nodes to ensure the distributed computing does not fail. Multiple copies of all data are stored automatically.

Flexibility: Unlike traditional relational databases, you don't have to preprocess data before storing it. You can store as much data as you want and decide how to use it later. That includes unstructured data like text, images, and videos.

Low cost: The open-source framework is free and uses commodity hardware to store large quantities of data.

Scalability: You can quickly grow your system to handle additional data simply by adding nodes, for this only little administration is required.

IoT and Hadoop

Things in the IoT need to know what to communicate and when to act. At the core of the IoT is streaming, always on torrent of data. Hadoop is often used as the data store for millions or billions of transactions. Massive storage and processing capabilities also allow you to use Hadoop as a sandbox for the discovery and definition of patterns to be monitored for prescriptive instruction. You can then continuously improve these instructions because Hadoop (Kulwicki, 1991) is continuously updated with new data that doesn't match previously defined patterns.

Data

Smart City technology requires data architectures, and it provides computing resources or services such as data storage and data replication. Data growth is exponential in Smart City technology; it has to process real-time data also. The joint efforts between the different organization (may be private or government) such as physicists, biologists, environmental scientists, engineers, computer scientists, and meteorologists implemented an unprecedented array of sensors to produce 468 million depth measurements. Prior constraint for Smart City reverses is the data abundance. It will define challenge for effective environmental authority in the future.

Data Transfer

Data collected from the sensors have to be transferred on a cloud where data is processed and converted into information; it may be sent to other devices or stored for future use. The processed information should be sent to the end-user. Multiple device platforms across multiple operating systems can be used, such as android, iOS, Windows.

Our main task is achieving a Cloud-based Smart City model through IoT (TJB, 2017, Verma, 2018). It gives access to a large volume of valuable data in everyday things, for example, dynamic vehicular traffic conditions, real-time weather conditions, public transport schedules, plantations, literacy, infrastructure, etc.

CHARACTERISTICS OF CLOUD-BASED SMART CITY

Cloud computing has five characteristics. They all are:

1. On-demand self-service
2. Broad network access
3. Resource pooling
4. Rapid elasticity
5. Measured service.

Figure 5. The essential characteristics of Cloud Computing

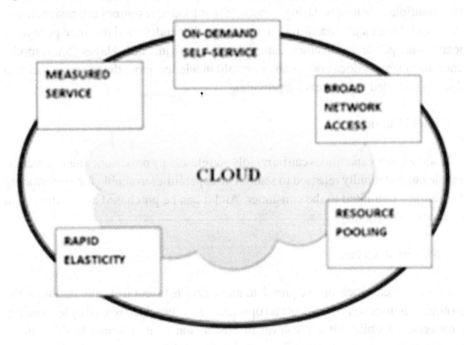

The features that distinguish it from other computing models.

1. On-Demand Self-Service

Cloud resource is access at any time with human interaction. Cloud service is an automatically provided to consumer according to demand. A consumer can unilaterally plan computing capabilities, such as server time and data storage, resources as needed automatically without any human interaction.

2. Broad Network Access

Resource capabilities are available over the network at any time and, it can access in any way like through standard mechanisms. Standard mechanisms promote heterogeneous thin or thick client platforms. Such as: mobile phones, laptops, and PDAs.

3. Resource Pooling

Resource pool is the group of resources together. At the same time, multiple consumers request for the same resource is processed by the service provider using resource pooling. The service provider's firstly pooled the computing resources to serve multiple consumers. Using a multi-tenant model, resources are assigned and reassigned dynamically according to consumer demand. Cloud resource pooling is location-independence. In cloud computing (Grossman, 2009, Hayes, 2008) model generally customer does not has any control/knowledge about the resource location which is provided by the service provider.

4. Rapid Elasticity

In some cases, capabilities can be rapidly and elastically provisioned automatically, to scale out and rapidly released to scale. The capabilities available for provisioning often appear unlimited to the consumer. And it can be purchased at any time or in any amount of quantity.

5. Measured Service

Cloud system does not required manual action to control and optimize the resource. It automatically control and optimize resource which is used by leveraging. A metering capability at some level of abstraction is appropriate to the type of service (such as storage, processing, bandwidth, and active user accounts). By use of transparency, resource usage can be monitored, controlled, and reported for both the provider and consumer of the utilized service.

Cloud-based Smart City is a digital technology; Cloud-based Smart City is the latest technology connected to the world in a single unit for sharing data and resources. To make a Cloud-based Smart City using IoT, electronic devices are connected through the internet for sharing data and resources. Sensors are embedded with these devices and convert into smart devices. All these devices are connected through the internet. Cloud-based Smart City is for human life and all, which is a part of the world. It is either living or non-living such as animals, agriculture, environment, infrastructure, pollution, etc. In Cloud-based Smart City, we use sensor-based devices to collect data, send it to the server, and resources or data on the cloud share with the user when needed. Even though, in Smart City, infrastructure is using sensor-based devices. The sensors are used in every field such as hospital, railway stations, City, tunnel, roads, bridge, etc. Nowadays, sensors are embedded in every field, such as water supply systems, Railways, Hospitals, Universities, Bridges, Power grids, Tunnels, Roads, Dams, Oil, and Gas pipelines. The data which is stored on the cloud, its spread all over the world using the internet; it makes make human life better.

The intelligence of the City refers to a system. That is known as an intelligence system. Here, intelligence does not refer to the collective intelligence of a human. We are talking about system intelligence, which means how a machine can automatically do its task without using human interaction. An intelligence system describes a reasonable organizational structure, flawless operation, structure of particles, and procedures. The cloud-based Smart City system considers natural systems and artificial systems to create the digital world, making the world run at a higher-level intelligence and forming an interactional system combined by individuals, businesses, organizations, governments, natural and artificial systems. The main reason behind this interaction is to create a perfect, efficient, and more productive use of resources and data.

Cloud-based Smart City gives a significant contribution to controlling manual work. Various special machines have been created to increase virtual output as well as reducing men's power.

Cloud-based (Zhou, 2017) Smart City provides the concept of reusing resources again and again. Users don't need to perchance any resource to access needed resources from the cloud and pay according to use.

Water-saving is also a part of Cloud-based (ZHU, 2014) Smart City. For water-saving, we are using lots of technologies like sensor-based tabs, water reusing concepts, etc.

City pollution monitoring is possible using IoT-based devices (Lea, 2010, 2014) and send that data to the cloud.

Smart City is also using in industries. It is prompting mutual in the aspect of the digital infrastructure and the physical infrastructure in the world. Industries are using sensor embedding devices to collect data and store it on the server.

APPLICATION OF CLOUD-BASED SMART CITY

Smart City has lots of applications, and some applications are explained in this section.

Smart Dynamic Vehicular Traffic Control System

People's daily routines face lots of problems due to traffic. Unpredictable traffic conditions create numerous various problems. The number of vehicles has been increasing on the roads in day-to-day life. It becomes the cause of congestion. Still, we are not able to get information about congestion in advance. Hence, we need to watch the traffic condition before entering that area to use alternative routes. In present-day vehicular traffic control systems depend on static vehicular traffic data, which is not a perfect clarification for the dynamic, complicated traffic conditions. Hence, we can implement traffic nodes and settle data according to a period and process vehicular traffic count and upload it to a server infrastructure, which will be controlled by a Programmable Logic Controller (PLC) (Biswas, 2014, Bridge, 2017). It is processing real-time data, and it changes the node timing according to the live traffic condition. At the same time, all the data is also be updated in a mobile application. The mobile application is easy to access by the users. According to the live vehicular traffic condition, this application serves the shortest root using the Global Positioning System (GPS) to identify the user.

Smart Health Care System

Health Care performance can be improved using embedded sensors and actuators in patient monitoring systems that can track the health conditions and upload the data patterns to a dedicated server or cloud, mapped with particular abnormal health conditions. Data can be collected by the hospital servers and personal wearable devices. The system can be correlated with ambulance services and personal consultant physicians.

Disaster Recovery Management System

Unpredictable weather conditions could be monitored using pre-placed sensors, such as using Smart weather stations; we can collect data and process it using Smart technology. We can get weather information through a Smart sensor (Liana, 2012) and the weather station. The weather station can be accessed to the worldwide weather link and compare the abnormality in weather (e.g., heavy rainfalls, floods, Tsunami, volcano eruption, earthquakes). A lot of life can be saved by the pre-assumption of natural disasters.

Smart Grid

Power can be offered proportional to population growth. Energy consumption can be enhanced using monitoring systems and enhance the Quality of Service (QoS). Meanwhile, using IoT power system protection, power shedding can be analyzed, and production failures can be reduced.

Smart Building

Smart City has made a massive contribution to creating a Smart building. Many technologies are using to monitor the building; these buildings are known as Smart buildings. Buildings can be monitor and operated according to the Smart City model data fed from the servers. (e.g., responsible persons can analyze the opened windows, control the illuminance inside the building eco-friendly, heating and air-conditioning systems, weather conditions around the building, etc.)

Closed-Circuit Television (CCTV)

CCTV is used for security. By addressing a particular node, CCTV feeds can be achievable. This implementation can be used for data recovery and forensic data analysis. Particular digital video footage can be gained using the Smart City model.

Transportation Schedules

Data regarding transportation schemes (e.g., Public Transport Systems) can be monitored and retrieve data using the Smart City model. (i.e., Tourists can access a particular country train schedule, and by submitting their start and destination, they can retrieve live video feeds, prises, and connect with other people who had experienced on particular transportation scheme and share ideas). Technologies applied to achieve Smart City model.

M2M (Machine to Machine)

Machine to Machine is a process where two machines can communicate. Meanwhile, where one machine can communicate with another machine without any human interaction, they can also share data; It became successful because of using IoT. These types of machines are called Smart machines. Smart machines are also a part of Smart City. 3GPP is a Machine to Machine communication. It could be carry over the mobile and computer network is known as Machine Type Communication (MTC). Mobile network is used as a transport network in M2M communication.

DC (Data Center)

Data Center is where all data has been stored; it is collected from various data nodes. Data Center is a centralized approach. All distributed data center is connected there. It provides facilities to centralize IT (Information Technology) operations and equipment, storing, managing, and disseminating data. We can perform asset discovery and asset tracking from there. Data Center follows the virtualization concept. It creates a virtualization environment where all data centers are connected for data sharing. Data Centers are capable of integrating real-time monitoring systems. Therefore it collects actual power usage/environmental data to optimize capacity management, allowing review of real-time data vs. assumptions around nameplate data.

CC (Cloud Computing)

Cloud computing is a service that provides IT resources on-demand to the internet user. Users use these resources according to their requirements and pay according to resource uses, and there is no need to purchase any resource. Cloud computing is a third-party service that provides IT resources over the internet. Users can access technology services, such as data storage [49, 50], database, etc. AWS (Amazon Web Service) is an example of it. Some other examples are online file storage, social networking sites, webmail, and online business applications.) It provides a shared pool of resources, including data storage space, networks, Computer processing power, specialized corporate and user applications, etc.

RFID (Radio-Frequency Identification)

RFID stands for Radio Frequency Identification. RFID is an automated technology and is used to aids machines or computers to identify any object. It also uses for recoding metadata (metadata is data about data); it can control any target using radio waves. RFID is also used for real-time data collection. IoT has RFID with infrared sensors, GPS, and laser scanner sensor equipment for object observation. It observes the location, all movement of the object; it can also exchange data and information. RFID systems can recognize separate tags, which are located in the common area without human assistance.

WSN (Wireless Sensor Network)

Wireless Sensor Network is an environmental sensor. It is a group of sensors used to monitor and record the environment's physical condition and send these data to the server, where it is processed for further use. It can measure environmental conditions such as temperature, sound, pollution, wind, etc. To monitor environmental and physical conditions, WSN uses autonomous sensors.

WBAN (Wireless Body Area Network)

A WBAN is a new technology for health monitoring. WBAN uses sensors and actuators. It connects all independent devices, like sensors, these sensors may be situated in the clothes or the human body, or they may be under the skin of a person. A WBAN is using in many areas such as remote health monitoring, medicine, and health care. The sensor nodes might be on the body, or they might be implanted in the body.

Sensor Clouds

Sensor-Cloud is playing a vital role in providing Sensors-as-a-Service (Se-aaS) platform while satisfying many applications' requirements by forming virtual sensors in a cloud platform. Sensor-Cloud is a new model, which is used for cloud computing. It uses physical sensors to gather data and transmit all that data into a cloud computing infrastructure. Sensor-Cloud is used to handles the sensor data efficiently; this data is used for monitoring lots of applications.

Data Market

Collected and processed data from servers and clouds can be processed in a proper client base method. Android, Windows, and iOS-based applications can be developed for user requirements. Furthermore, data pools can be created, which can be host by the user-based platform with easy access to the required information within no time. Processed data can be host via web portals such that data will be automatically processed using intelligent algorithms and share with necessary peer applications. The system should be able to self-correct using the current data available in the system.

Security

Security is a significant concern in this Smart City model. Smart City Model mainly depends on IoT applications, and security attacks can be problematic in this manner. All sensors and actuators can be accessed physically, and the system openness and accessibility for the system contains a vast risk arena. City model security concerns a high risk due to sensitive data (i.e., health conditions, personal documents, etc.) City Model should provide its services in random failure scenarios as well as attack situations. IoT applications should be able to recover effectively from security threats. After deploying the system, it should adapt to the recent attacks. The system should capable of strong attack detection capabilities. The system should be capable of self-healing from attacks and share the information with neighboring systems.

Privacy

Smart City Model gives access to valuable and useful data; these services can be useful as individuals but create more opportunities to violate privacy. Smart City model privacy policies should be specified to reduce privacy breaches. Privacy should be enforced with the users of the system. New privacy language should be implemented. One of the most challenging privacy problems is that systems interact and communicate with other systems. Separate systems have their privacy policies.

CONCLUSION

In this chapter, discussion have on Cloud-based Smart City's concept; creation of Cloud-based Smart City (Palmieri, 2016, Persson, 2015) using IoT and cloud. IoT is the combination of smart devices and the internet (when the sensor is embedded within an electronic device is known as Smart devices). The development of Cloud-based Smart City with IoT and cloud has faced many problems, various technologies, and IoT and cloud issues. Sensors are embedded within devices or machines to collect data automatically and send it to the server. Smart City, Smart devices, all these topics are part of Smart World. Cloud-based Smart City (Sharma 2019) has covered various sectors like infrastructure, organization, educational institute, pollution, traffic, transportation, and industry. Cloud-based Smart City is based on data and resources, so we can use Machine Learning here to process data speedily. But in this chapter, we are using Hadoop (Holmes, 2012, Polato, 2014) for data processing. Smart devices play the leading role in achieving the Smart City model. Mainly we have established the concepts based on the Smart City model using real-time scenarios, which can be performed using IoT. IoT is the backbone of Smart City. The technologies related to the Cloud-based Smart City model (e.g., RFID, Cloud Computing, M2M, Data Centers, Hadoop, etc.) have been introduced.

FUTURE SCOPE AND RESEARCH AREA

We feel that two areas require further for work: First one is integrated or federated cloud, and the second one is application development.

Federated Cloud: Federated cloud, it required to accept the present scenario of the existing infrastructure of the city, which is currently managed by the City's IT departments. For constrained this issue hybrid cloud is needed. A second constraint, which is not addressed, that is new cloud infrastructure. It will be necessary to ensure that our cloud-based smart city hub can accommodate several peer PaaS services and offer application developers a framework that allows them to exploit residents' services and functionality in other clouds.

IoT application development tools: The second area of work which is critical for the widespread adoption of cloud-based smart city hubs is the complex issue of IoT application development. In this constrained to typical web-based applications.

REFERENCES

Amoore, L. (2013). *The politics of possibility: Risk and security beyond probability.* Duke University Press. doi:10.1215/9780822377269

Angwin, J. (2013). NSA struggles to make sense of flood of surveillance data. *Wall Street Journal.*

Antonopoulos, N., & Gillam, L. (2010). *Cloud computing.* Springer. doi:10.1007/978-1-84996-241-4

Armbrust, M., Fox, A., Griffith, R., Joseph, A. D., Katz, R., Konwinski, A., Lee, G., Patterson, D., Rabkin, A., Stoica, I., & Zaharia, M. (2010). A view of cloud computing. *Communications of the ACM, 53*(4), 50–58. doi:10.1145/1721654.1721672

Arts, K., van der Wal, R., & Adams, W. M. (2015). Digital technology and the conservation of nature. *Ambio, 44*(4), 661–673. doi:10.100713280-015-0705-1 PMID:26508352

Bastin, L., Buchanan, G., Beresford, A., Pekel, J. F., & Dubois, G. (2013). Open-source mapping and services for Web-based land-cover validation. *Ecological Informatics, 14*, 9–16. doi:10.1016/j.ecoinf.2012.11.013

Belgaum, M. R., Soomro, S., Alansari, Z., Musa, S., Alam, M., & Su'ud, M. M. (2017, November). Challenges: Bridge between cloud and IoT. In *2017 4th IEEE International Conference on Engineering Technologies and Applied Sciences (ICETAS)* (pp. 1-5). IEEE.

Benson, E. (2012). One infrastructure, many global visions: The commercialization and diversification of Argos, a satellite-based environmental surveillance system. *Social Studies of Science, 42*(6), 843–868. doi:10.1177/0306312712457851

Benson, E. (2015). Generating Infrastructural invisibility: Insulation, interconnection, and avian excrement in the Southern California power grid. *Environmental Humanities, 6*(1), 103–130. doi:10.1215/22011919-3615916

Bhosale, H. S., & Gadekar, D. P. (2014). A review paper on big data and hadoop. *International Journal of Scientific and Research Publications, 4*(10), 1–7.

Biermann, F., Abbott, K., Andresen, S., Bäckstrand, K., Bernstein, S., Betsill, M. M., ...Gupta, A. (2012). Navigating the Anthropocene: Improving City system governance. *Science, 335*(6074), 1306–1307. doi:10.1126cience.1217255 PMID:22422966

Biermann, F., Betsill, M. M., Vieira, S. C., Gupta, J., Kanie, N., Lebel, L., Liverman, D., Schroeder, H., Siebenhüner, B., Yanda, P. Z., & Zondervan, R. (2010). Navigating the anthropocene: The City System Governance Project strategy paper. *Current Opinion in Environmental Sustainability, 2*(3), 202–208. doi:10.1016/j.cosust.2010.04.005

Biswas, A. R., & Giaffreda, R. (2014, March). IoT and cloud convergence: Opportunities and challenges. In *2014 IEEE World Forum on Internet of Things (WF-IoT)* (pp. 375-376). IEEE.

Borthakur, D. (2007). The hadoop distributed file system: Architecture and design. *Hadoop Project Website, 11*, 21.

Das, S., Sismanis, Y., Beyer, K. S., Gemulla, R., Haas, P. J., & McPherson, J. (2010, June). Ricardo: integrating R and Hadoop. In *Proceedings of the 2010 ACM SIGMOD International Conference on Management of data* (pp. 987-998). 10.1145/1807167.1807275

De-ren, L., Yuan, Y., & Zhen-feng, S. (2012). New mission for surveying, mapping and geomatics in Smart City era. *Science of Surveying and Mapping, 6*.

Duda, O., Kunanets, N., Matsiuk, O., & Pasichnyk, V. (2018). Cloud-based IT Infrastructure for "Smart City" Projects. In Dependable IoT for Human and Industry: Modeling, Architecting, Implementation. River Publishers.

Fleming, W. J. (2001). Overview of automotive sensors. *IEEE Sensors Journal, 1*(4), 296–308.

Gautschi, G. (2002). Piezoelectric sensors. In *Piezoelectric Sensorics* (pp. 73–91). Springer.

Grossman, R. L. (2009). The case for cloud computing. *IT Professional, 11*(2), 23–27.

Guo, H., Wang, L., Chen, F., & Liang, D. (2014). Scientific big data and digital City. *Chinese Science Bulletin, 59*(35), 5066–5073.

Hayes, B. (2008). *Cloud computing*. Academic Press.

Holmes, A. (2012). *Hadoop in practice*. Manning Publications Co.

Holte, J., Talley, L. D., Gilson, J., & Roemmich, D. (2017). An Argo mixed layer climatology and database. *Geophysical Research Letters*, *44*(11), 5618–5626.

Houze, R. A. Jr. (2014). *Cloud dynamics*. Academic press.

Husmann, A., Betts, J. B., Boebinger, G. S., Migliori, A., Rosenbaum, T. F., & Saboungi, M. L. (2002). Megagauss sensors. *Nature*, *417*(6887), 421–424.

Ji, Z., Ganchev, I., O'Droma, M., Zhao, L., & Zhang, X. (2014). A cloud-based car parking middleware for IoT-based smart cities: Design and implementation. *Sensors (Basel)*, *14*(12), 22372–22393.

Khan, Z., Pervez, Z., & Ghafoor, A. (2014, December). Towards cloud based smart cities data security and privacy management. In *2014 IEEE/ACM 7th International Conference on Utility and Cloud Computing* (pp. 806-811). IEEE.

Kulwicki, B. M. (1991). Humidity sensors. *Journal of the American Ceramic Society*, *74*(4), 697–708.

Lam, C. (2010). *Hadoop in action*. Manning Publications Co.

Lea, R., & Blackstock, M. (2014, December). City hub: A cloud-based iot platform for smart cities. In *2014 IEEE 6th international conference on cloud computing technology and science* (pp. 799-804). IEEE.

Li, X. X., & Bian, F. L. (2010). The Research of Dynamic GIS. *Geomatics World*, *6*.

Liana, D. D., Raguse, B., Gooding, J. J., & Chow, E. (2012). Recent advances in paper-based sensors. *Sensors*, *12*(9), 11505-11526.

Liu, J., Yu, X., Xu, Z., Choo, K. K. R., Hong, L., & Cui, X. (2017). A cloud-based taxi trace mining framework for smart city. *Software, Practice & Experience*, *47*(8), 1081–1094.

Palmieri, F., Ficco, M., Pardi, S., & Castiglione, A. (2016). A cloud-based architecture for emergency management and first responders localization in smart city environments. *Computers & Electrical Engineering*, *56*, 810–830.

Persson, P., & Angelsmark, O. (2015). Calvin–merging cloud and iot. *Procedia Computer Science*, *52*, 210–217.

Polato, I., Ré, R., Goldman, A., & Kon, F. (2014). A comprehensive view of Hadoop research—A systematic literature review. *Journal of Network and Computer Applications*, *46*, 1–25.

Sammer, E. (2012). *Hadoop operations*. O'Reilly Media, Inc.

Sharma, S., Chang, V., Tim, U. S., Wong, J., & Gadia, S. (2019). Cloud and IoT-based emerging services systems. *Cluster Computing*, *22*(1), 71–91.

Shi, Y. G., & Bian, F. (2011). The study of public service for remote sensing information based on cloud platform. *Geomatics World, 3*.

Shvachko, K., Kuang, H., Radia, S., & Chansler, R. (2010, May). The hadoop distributed file system. In *2010 IEEE 26th symposium on mass storage systems and technologies (MSST)* (pp. 1-10). IEEE.

TJB, D. D., Subramani, A., & Solanki, V. K. (2017). Smart City: IOT Based Prototype for Parking Monitoring and Management System Commanded by Mobile App. *Annals of Computer Science and Information Systems*, *10*, 341–343.

Verma, P., & Sood, S. K. (2018). Cloud-centric IoT based disease diagnosis healthcare framework. *Journal of Parallel and Distributed Computing*, *116*, 27–38.

Voss, A. (2010). *Cloud computing*. Academic Press.

Wang, Y., & Scott, S. (2007). *U.S. Patent Application No. 11/282,001*. US Patent Office.

White, T. (2012). *Hadoop: The definitive guide*. O'Reilly Media, Inc.

Witham, M. D., Argo, I. S., Johnston, D. W., Struthers, A. D., & McMurdo, M. E. (2006). Predictors of exercise capaCity and everyday activity in older heart failure patients. *European Journal of Heart Failure*, *8*(2), 203–207.

Zhou, J., Cao, Z., Dong, X., & Vasilakos, A. V. (2017). Security and privacy for cloud-based IoT: Challenges. *IEEE Communications Magazine*, *55*(1), 26–33.

Zhu, Y. J., Li, Q., & Feng, X. (2014). Study on technological framework of Smart City based on Big Data. *Science of Surveying and Mapping*, (8), 17.

Chapter 8
Internet of Things–Enabled Smart Entry System for Telecom Sites

Ruchi Garg
Gautam Buddha University, India

Harsh Garg
Delhi Technological University, India

ABSTRACT

Internet of things (IoT) is leading towards revolutionary applications with huge potential to improvise the efficiency multifold. IoT with the use of sensors has opened a huge window for applications in almost every area of life, and its penetration is endless with wireless connectivity. In this chapter, a wireless sensor-based solution for smart access control system for telecom sites is proposed and implemented. This project is initially implemented for 10 sites for a leading telecom operator, which will later on be scalable. This solution provides smart access to site engineers on the telecom site. Also, this system helps to remotely monitor multiple sites simultaneously, which protects the site from any forced entry and vandalism. The proposed solution and its implementation are given in detail in the chapter.

INTRODUCTION

During the recent digital transformation advancement, the Internet of Things (IoT) has a key role to play. Due to this remarkable presence of these upcoming computing technologies like IoT, we have entered a new era of digitization. This transformation

DOI: 10.4018/978-1-7998-6981-8.ch008

is all about managing the people, assets, methods, material and processes through the internet mode. Some years back, network technology consisted of communication between computers but now with the presence of IoT, all day-to-day items will not be in stand-alone mode. The things like home chores support gadgets to other industrial equipment, are all connected and communicate in their network domain. Use of IoT is giving way to new working models, applications, and solutions. In this 21st century most of the activities are carried out in this computing technological based ecosystem. For example, the government is managing its administration through e-governance digital platform services. Similarly, in commercial activities, various platforms have emerged such as E-commerce, E-transport booking systems etc. This has provided an ease of doing such activities and helped in improvement of quality of life for the human beings.

IoT and Industrial Internet of Things (IIoT) are sub-parts of the digital transformation ecosystem. Evolution of IoT is fundamentally based on connected devices commonly termed as sensor based smart devices (Feller, 2011). The IoT consists of smart devices interacting and communicating with other machines, objects, environment and infrastructures. As a result, huge volumes of data are being generated, and that data is being processed into useful actions that can "command and control" things to make our lives much easier and safer—and to reduce the adverse impact on the environment. Potential and coverage area of IoT is huge and constantly increasing. Every device in the network must have its own IP address to make it a smart device to enable Machine to Machine interaction (Hinden, 2003). To cater this need IPv6 addressing is considered best as it can provide up to 2^{128} unique addresses (Forouzan, 2002). Large address space of IPv6 plays a very important role in the rise of IoT (Paul, 2016). IoT is not only a buzz word but it is covering our lives with applications in all sectors. IoT concepts are now a day well accepted in various business domains like manufacturing, services, infrastructure, asset management etc. They are widely used to improve the efficiency, productivity and analysis purposes. It helps in taking predictive and preventive steps and efficiency enhancement is its natural byproduct.

IoT has various sub-modules which majorly includes data acquisition, data connectivity, data processing, data analytics, alerts and notifications. Digital transformation is quite visible in industry 4.0 strategy. It includes the evolution of steam engines to IIoT for the next generation manufacturing practices. This has significantly impacted the automation of smart factories. Automation has improved the productivity, efficiency and fast decision-making capabilities from real time basis with the help of IIoT implementation. This has resulted in a new concept of lean manufacturing practices. Similarly, IoT has created a wide range of applications in home automation, climate change monitoring, farming industries and different appliances used by society and industries. These technologies are all about the user experience, autonomous services, encouragement in collaborative efforts and improving the system based on data points, trends and charts and feedback mechanism to make robust and intelligent systems. One of the application areas is in telecom sites.

Telecom sites provide infrastructure support to the telecom equipment. Telecom sites are meant for giving last mile connectivity to the user. The infrastructure of telecom sites are widely used by the Global System for Mobile (GSM) (Heine, 1999), Wi-Fi, Internet Service Providers. Looking at the large demography in India there are approximately 2.5 lakhs of telecom sites in various locations. By 2020 it is expected to touch approximately 5 lakhs. These sites are equipped with various devices and infrastructure like tower, power supplies, air conditioners, telecom equipment, battery banks and different support copper accessories. Telecom cell sites are usually located in remote areas and geographically apart hence they are vulnerable for anti-social issues like theft and vandalism. As this infrastructure is very expensive and important in national interest so service providers do their best to protect these assets. The operator has two main challenges to control and monitor these assets. First challenge is to provide constant security to protect the sites from theft of copper cables and battery banks. Second challenge is to provide access to service men who visit sites for maintenance work of tools like air conditioners, batteries, power supply etc. which are equipped in the sites. These servicemen have to come to the client office to collect the door key of the site and then they reach the site for work. After completion of the task, they have to go back to the client office to return the key. Collecting and returning keys indulges in a lot of commuting and unnecessarily wastage of time. Hence wireless sensor based remote monitoring system is proposed to monitor the telecom sites to handle below written two major problems.

Various objectives were set for this research work. Objective one is to provide smart access to authorized persons. Second objective is to optimize the operational efficiency of complete man-power attached to the system. Third objective is to monitor the sites remotely using the concept of remote monitoring systems. Fourth objective is to monitor multiple sites on a simultaneous basis. Fifth objective is to secure the site from theft of copper cables, battery banks and other equipment.

This chapter proposes a smart way to handle the technicalities on telecom sites which are remotely located. Background work is explained which also covers the details of IoT, the basis of the proposed work of this chapter. After that the concept of a remote monitoring system is explained. This is followed by a problem statement of the telecom sites for which the solution is proposed. Technical specifications of the sensors and other technical devices which are used for implementation is given. Test scenarios, demonstration details and complete flow of the system is presented.

This is followed by future work of the topic covered in this chapter. Conclusion is well presented.

BACKGROUND WORK

The Internet of Things (IoT) is leading towards revolutionary applications with huge potential to improvise the efficiency multifold. Almost no area of day-to-day life is untouched without the presence of such IoT applications. They use low power sensor nodes with wireless connectivity. Various solutions and prototypes for entry systems and also for providing the security systems have been suggested from time to time by various researchers and authors. In this section, work done by other authors has been presented. Along with this, the building blocks of IoT is also explained, which is the basis of work presented in this chapter.

The authors (Saxena, 2018) have presented a digital solution to control the out system. Their solution is IoT based and uses RFID (Radio-Frequency Identification) technology. According to authors, the system can replace the traditional way entry of employees of an organization. The system uses hardware devices like Raspberry Pi, NodeMCU, MFRC552 Card Reader and software tools like Django, SQLite and Python script for the implementation.

The authors (Kaseem, 2016) have created a prototype for an innovative lock system. The solution uses the Wi-Fi security features. This system helps in smart entry for almost everywhere like in apartments, home gates or cars.

As mentioned by authors (Rajiv, 2016), now-a-days, people expect reliable home security and entry systems. Such systems could be created using the latest technologies. Present systems need a greater extent of authentication process. It also needs hardware and software in a customized way. The proposal by the authors gives remote access using the email service of the internet. It can also be used as a surveillance system. To design such a system generic hardware can be used.

Researchers (Bhattarai, 2018) have proposed a home security and entry system in the work. The solution is named as Authentic Gate Entry System (AuthGES). Concept of face recognition is the basis of this system. The system uses local binary pattern histograms (LBPH) face detection algorithms.

A user authentication system is suggested by the authors (Almadhoun, 2018). The basis of the solution is blockchain technology. In this proposed work, blockchain-enabled fog nodes are used. The fog nodes interface to smart contracts to authenticate users to access IoT devices. As IoT devices are resource constraint, hence fog computing provides the capability. It provides localized computing power, storage, and networking for a group of IoT devices.

Though various solutions have been provided by various researchers using the various technologies, the system proposed and implemented in this proposed work of the chapter is novel. It is completely based on IoT, cloud computing and GSM. The fundamental blocks of IoT architecture are Sensor layer, Connectivity layer, Device Management layer, Data Analytic layer and User Application layer (Garg, 2018). It is shown in figure 1. Each layer has its own challenges and limitations hence various technologies have evolved to overcome these limitations so that these devices can communicate seamlessly.

Figure 1. Building Blocks of IoT

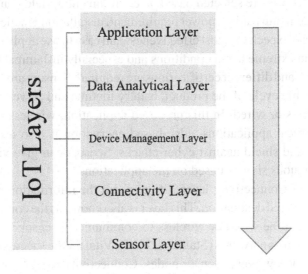

Sensor layer has sensor-based nodes which can connect, communicate, and share the real time information seamlessly (Hui, 2008). Sensor node is an electronic device which captures the real time information, converts it into electronic signals and transmits to the intended server where it could be processed by processing units. They are of various types like motion, heat, temperature, humidity, light, pressure, chemical, sound, RFID based sensors etc. Selection of sensors depends upon the applicability in the solution. Capacity and range of these sensors also varies depending upon the application. Node architecture typically has four parts including sensing subsystem for capturing the physical aspects, radio transceiver for communication, microprocessor and power supply which is usually battery operated (Garg, 2020). All sensor nodes have a unique ID (its IP address) using which they are connected in network. The sensor nodes not only transmit the captured information but can also be triggered and controlled remotely depending upon application. Sensors can be passive or active. In passive sensors, they only give predefined signals of fixed value as analog or digital output. In active sensors, they have limited computing capabilities and it can be defined as a different threshold based on the system requirements. They filter the unnecessary signals, alerts and notifications which do not fall in the threshold windows. They can be remotely configured, accessible and monitored remotely. They are intelligent and have a battery back up to support the system engineering. Both the sensors are widely used in various industries based on their applications, need, efficiency and cost effectiveness of the system. These sensors can be communicated in multiple protocols to their parent application. Some of the protocols are Modbus, TCP/IP, RS 485, UART interfaces (Gadre, 2018), (Nanda, 2016). The sensors are selected based on environmental, field condition, topology, bandwidth, miniaturization, power requirement, installation practices, operation and maintenance perspectives, cost effectiveness and easy to use applications. To protect the sensors in extreme harsh conditions and especially inflammable environments, special casing and different certifications are required. Sensors are also judged based on accuracy, life cycle of the product, battery lifetime and power backups. Sensors can be wireless or wired. In this proposed application, wireless sensors are used. In highly critical applications, edge-based encryption is also used to protect the information and shield against cyber-attacks. Sensors can give video, continuous or non-continuous signals based on the applications.

The role of Connectivity layer is to transmit the information sensed by sensor nodes to the desired destination. This layer is also known as the communication layer. This layer could be wired or wireless to communicate sensors with their various applications across networks (Stallings, 2002). Vital for the success of IoT is wireless connectivity of low power sensor nodes. Connectivity can be configured through multiple technologies. Nodes are connected in mesh technology so that there is no loss of information. Communication layer is selected based on robustness, cost and operation perspectives. Based on the field and various research documents, each communication has its own advantages and disadvantages. Wired connectivity is efficient, unlimited bandwidth, stable and low maintenance. It is highly secured and efficient. In this way of connectivity, there are three layers of network topologies which are selected based on the complexities of the project. The devices are connected to distributed edge switches, which are further connected to aggregated switches, and they are further connected to core switches. One can easily plan the redundancies in the communication layer based on hardware, or route topology. Normally at the core layer, hardware redundancies are planned and at aggregation and edge level. Route redundancies are planned. Fiber and CAT6 are commonly used cables in the wired network. Such networks can be easily planned for IPv4 and IPv6 configurations. One can implement firewalls and UTMs to protect the networks from cyber threat. It is observed that a highly dense sensor network is planned in a hybrid combination of wireless and wired topology. Wireless connectivity has an impact due to line of sight, environmental factors like rain, noise etc., drain of power and clean frequency availability. To plan a good wireless network, one should cleverly use the spot frequencies, control the interference and design a good signal-to-noise ratio. Majorly, it includes Wi-Fi, Bluetooth, and ZigBee, NFC (Coskun, 2013) and 3G/4G /LTE (Tjensvold, 2007). To plan a dense sensor network, a good planner should take care of all the above factors otherwise it will create delays, loss of data, jitters and fragile networks. The selection of wireless technologies also depends on the data rate, transmission range, frequency band, media of transmission like air, water. It is better to simulate the environmental conditions in appropriate planning tools so one can dimension the network based on suitability of above parameters. This will save the cost, efforts and resource optimization while executing on the field. In the proposed prototype of this chapter, a Wi-Fi technology is used with the end sensors.

The raw data from the sensors is communicated through the communication layer and reach to the computing resources i.e., servers. The captured data can be structured or unstructured based on the applications. The device management layer is hosted on the server to create a discipline and usable data formats. It has got multiple functions to create the log of data formats from various sensor interfaces. It plays an important role in protocol interfaces; packaging of the data frames and instruction sets to the sensors and communication layers. Based on the data streams, the various platforms are selected like SQL, Big-data etc. Device management transmits the information to the application layer via sockets etc. this layer is very important to maintain the sanctity and quality of the data.

Data analytical layer captures the real time data from the sensor layer through the communication layer. This layer is hosted in the cloud or in a private domain. It includes structured algorithms and decision-making tools. It helps to regroup, cascade to reach the conclusion and helps in decision making. Once the data is processed remotely, the trigger commands are sent to processing nodes through a connectivity layer.

Application layer is a GUI interface which supports the end user in interpreting the data to a logical end. This helps the user to understand the data flow, trend and interpretation in graphical formats. All components of layers working together provide various applicability and usability of IOT.

There are many major challenges (IEEE, 2003) which are acting as barriers for the deployment of IoT and its applications which slows down the development of it. The first of major issues is deployment of IPv6 (still IPv4 is in use). As discussed earlier, sensor nodes need unique IP addresses which will not be possible to provide through IPv4. In the coming years IPv4 address space will soon run out of addresses.

It will not be able to fulfill the requirement of providing unique IP addresses to billions of sensor devices.

Second issue is constant power supply for sensor nodes. Most of the IoT applications require deployment of sensor nodes in such terrains where direct power supply to nodes is not possible. Usually, sensor nodes work on batteries. But that may also pose problems. With use and span of time the batteries may also discharge. Although research is going on to generate electricity environmental components like air flow, light and even motion vibrations. This will make the sensor nodes self-sustaining.

Thirdly it is the agreement on standards to be used. IEEE is constantly working on the standards for privacy, routing across heterogeneous networks, architecture etc.

Looking at the benefits of IoT, the challenges it poses will soon get over with time.

Applications of IoT will have its presence in every aspect of our life with some examples as listed below. All such applications come under Remote Monitoring Systems.

- Health monitoring systems
- Parking management
- Lightning control systems
- Supply chain automation
- Vehicle congestion control systems
- Smart homes
- Air quality control
- Building automation
- Water quality monitoring
- Environment monitoring

REMOTE MONITORING SYSTEM (RMS)

RMS (Ghosh, 2016) is proactive and remote tracking of complex infrastructure like power plants, factories, telecom cell sites, buildings, airports etc. Installing sensing and communication devices and its support system on client domain and gathering information from there for the sake of taking some action remotely is the main task of it. The reports generated through the system are used to take further work decision steps related to the application. Using RMS, various sites and multiple clients can be managed easily and efficiently. Detecting troubles, generating alerts, alarming service providers and automated information to problem resolver to fix the problem is the prime purpose of RMS (Peijiang, 2008). In such an environment the corrective actions can be taken quickly before the customer gets affected. Nowadays RMS is a highly effective administration tool because it is economical, cuts the cost, and indulges less men power, full utilization of resources and most important quick fixation of problems (Malasinghe, 2019). These systems may even help to automate the scheduled maintenance tasks like auto-updating of operating systems, antivirus software, and defragmentation of hard disks and so on.

Besides advantages it also has various operational challenges. Next focus is on prime four challenges and their remedial. The first challenge with RMS is availability of constant internet connection and bandwidth, especially in the semi urban and rural areas. This issue gets multifold if the number of communicating devices are more and bandwidth is limited. This results in delay in sharing the real time information to the customer. To overcome this limitation, generally the system follows the principle of queue management. The technique of queue management uses store and forward approach. In this approach data is stored in SD cards or in secondary sources. Sequenced data is transmitted once the bandwidth is available. Second major limitation is to develop a high security network. For all sorts of communication usually public networks like the internet or mobile communication are used hence there is a high possibility that encryption of data can be breached. To strengthen the network use of hosted Virtual Private Network (VPN) services could be used (Zhang, 2004). Using VPN, information is made available in a restricted environment but this results in increased cost due to VPN set up. Third limitation is the protocol inter-portability. It becomes really challenging to interface the old devices with the new system architecture as the protocols do not support the latest technologies. Fourth challenge is communication break-up. In RMS information is transmitted from machine and devices hence sometimes it becomes difficult to know if there is any break up in the connectivity. This results in loss of information which is fully undesirable in real time scenarios. To overcome this limitation normally the communication is set up from device to cloud and cloud to device so they are in constant synchronization with each other.

The benefits of RMS are enormous as it saves a lot of operational cost, safety of the operation team and improves the reliability of the operations. It is highly scalable and the solution is reusable. Information can be further analyzed by using the various business analytical tools. Looking at enormous benefits a solution is suggested for remote monitoring of telecom sites and keyless access.

PROBLEM STATEMENT AND PROPOSED SOLUTION

Telecom sites provide infrastructure support to the telecom equipment. Telecom sites are meant for giving last mile connectivity to the user. The infrastructure of telecom sites are widely used by the Global System for Mobile (GSM), Wi-Fi, Internet Service Providers. Looking at the large demography in India there are approximately 2.5 lakhs of telecom sites in various locations. By 2030 it is expected to touch approximately 10 lakhs. These sites are equipped with various devices and infrastructure like tower, power supplies, air conditioners, telecom equipment, battery banks and different support copper accessories. Telecom cell sites are usually located in remote areas and geographically apart hence they are vulnerable for anti-social issues like theft and vandalism. As this infrastructure is very expensive and important in national interest so service providers do their best to protect these assets. The operator has two main challenges to control and monitor these assets. First challenge is to provide constant security to protect the sites from theft of copper cables and battery banks. Second challenge is to provide access to service men who visit sites for maintenance work of tools like air conditioners, batteries, power supply etc. which are equipped in the sites. These servicemen have to come to the client office to collect the door key of the site and then they reach the site for work. After completion of the task, they have to go back to the client office to return the key. Collecting and returning keys indulges in a lot of commuting and unnecessarily wastage of time. Hence wireless sensor based remote monitoring system is proposed to monitor the telecom sites to handle below written two major problems.

- Provide smart access to authorized people with the aim to optimize the man power operational efficiency.
- Secure the site from theft of copper cables, battery banks and other equipment.

Wireless sensor-based technology is used in proposed solutions. The sensors are connected to the control panel via Wi-Fi connectivity. They are distributed and connected to control panels in various zones. Each zone means one device dedicately connected to one individual Input-Output port of the control panel. This control panel can maximum accommodate eight various sensors. Technical details are explained in the next section. The proposed solution is divided into six process flows.

Process Flow #1: Communication From Site Engineer to Network Operations Center (NOC)

The site engineer will reach the site. From there he will call NOC. A network operations center (NOC) is a centralized location used by network administrators to manage, control and monitor multiple telecom networks simultaneously. To optimize network operations across a variety of platforms, mediums and communications channels is the main function and purpose of NOC. Site engineer will be asked to provide details like his name, company name, mobile number, Aadhar number and purpose of visit. The purpose of seeking all these details is to authenticate the site engineer.

Process Flow #2: Communication From NOC to Site Engineer

Once the NOC authenticates the site engineer, the system will generate two One Time Passwords (OTP). These OTPs are received simultaneously by the site panel and site engineer's authenticated mobile phone.

Process Flow #3: Site Engineer Inside the Site

Site engineers will use the first OTP to open the door using the electronic keyboard fitted on the telecom site's entry door. Once the door is open, he will use a second OTP to disarm the intrusion control panel. In 3 minutes, the person has to disarm the intrusion panel using a second OTP otherwise the entrant will be treated as unauthorized visitor. The panel is disarmed so that no alarms, hooters and alerts are generated and the person can finish his task. Depending upon the type of work, a time limit is set, during which the panel will remain disarmed.

Process Flow #4: Sensors Activation

Once OTP is entered and authenticated by the control panel, the hydraulic lock is triggered. Main access door is open. As the person steps inside, the motion sensor-based camera senses the motion and gets triggered. It captures the snapshots and sends on the File Transfer Protocol (FTP) server hosted on cloud. Door sensor sends the status to the NOC. Motion sensor senses the motion and updates the status on the server. This will not generate any alarms as this is a case of authenticated entry.

Process Flow #5: After Completion of Task

When the site engineer finishes the task, he has to arm the intrusion panel by pressing a number through the keyboard of the intrusion panel. If he forgets to arm the intrusion panel and leaves the site then door sensor will trigger the intrusion panel. The intrusion panel will be armed again within 3 minutes.

Process Flow #6: Case of Forced Entry

In case of unauthenticated and forced entry inside the telecom site, the motion sensor will trigger the intrusion panel. Hooter system will be triggered by the intrusion panel. Motion sensors will trigger the camera & pictures will be captured. Alerts will be sent to the control room & to the site staff. These alerts are sent through email, SMS, mobile Apps or pop-up on the screen. Corrective action can soon be taken. Figure 2 depicts the complete proposed solution and its process flow.

Figure 2. Process Flow of the Complete System

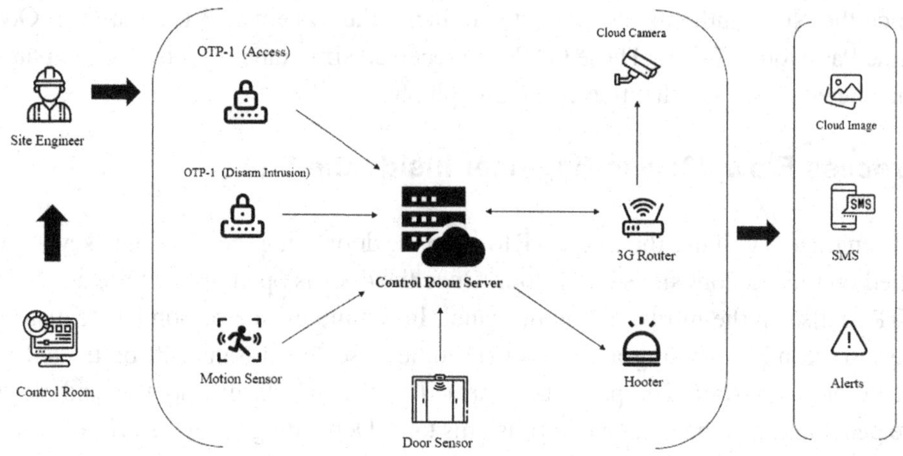

TECHNICAL SPECIFICATIONS AND IMPLEMENTATION

Various technical elements are used in the implementation of the work which is presented in this chapter. They are all explained in detail for more clarity.

Control Panel

Control panel is an embedded setup which includes the chip set of intrusion and access control in a customized way. For I/O ports various relays are used to interface the sensors and output devices. This control panel has an emergency reset button which on pressing, the hooter could be stopped. It also contains an embedded key pad for its configuration. It also has a charging mechanism for a 7Ah for battery backup which is used when mains power is switched off. It can serve the battery backup for 7-8 hours. It has a 32-bit processor with inbuilt RAM and one TCP/IP port for IP connectivity. The data from the control panel goes to cloud via SIM based router. This router is used to provide the internet interface to the control panel. The limitation is that there should be mobile coverage of 2G /3G network (Patel, 2018). The advantage of this router is, dedicated bandwidth is not required from mobile operators and normal SIM cards are used for IP connectivity. This improves the flexibility, mobility and secure connectivity.

Router

A device which forwards the packets in the networks is called a router (Macfarlane, 2007). A router is connected to at least two networks. Usually, it is two LANs or WANs or a LAN and its ISP's network. Routers are located at gateways, the places where two or more networks connect.

Routers use headers and forwarding tables to determine the best path for forwarding the packets, and they use protocols such as ICMP to communicate with each other and configure the best route between any two hosts. Routers take information that arrives through a broadband signal via a modem, decipher it, and deliver it to the computer. The router will also choose the best route for the data packet so that receives the information quickly. Many different types of routers have been developed so that the information coming over from broadband connection can be sent to a variety of different receivers including computer, phone, and others.

As the sites are located in remote areas it is very difficult to give the reliable dedicated leased lines. Lease lines are also very expensive to implement. To overcome this problem, we have incorporated the connectivity while using the 2G/3G router. This is an industrial grade router which can sustain the harsh environment and can work in up to 70-degree temperature. It can operate with a 2G /3G network. It has four Local Area Network (LAN) ports and one Wide Area Network (WAN) port for device interface. The basic purpose of this router is to convert the mobility i.e., cellular network into the TCP/IP LAN network. The purpose of this router is to sink the inbound and outbound data streams from CCTV (Velastin, 2009) (Van, 2005) and control panel to the respective software and application part. To secure the network against infiltration we can create a VPN network so that our data is protected.

Multiple sensors will be required to provide the solution.

- Motion Sensor
- Inbuilt Motion Sensor in Camera
- Door Sensor

Motion sensor is also called a motion detector. It is an electronic device. It is used to sense any sort of movements (Yong, 2011). It also measures the degree of movement. They can be used in various applications. Applications can be for home utility or for business security systems. In this proposed solution a motion sensor is used. They are not only used in security system applications but can also be used in gaming consoles, phone applications, virtual reality systems etc. The Motion Detector is used to measure position, velocity, and acceleration of moving objects. Mainly four types of motion sensors are there which are like Microwave sensors, Vibration motion sensors, Ultrasonic motion sensors, and Reflective motion sensors.

Active ultrasonic sensors emit ultrasonic sound waves that reflect off objects and bounce back to the original emission point. Motion detection cameras, lights, and sensors used in home security systems generally rely on PIR sensors (Urfaliglu, 2008). These detect infrared energy, which humans and animals release as heat. Motion sensor used in the implementation is of TYCO made under the DSC brand with model number LC-100-PI. This sensor uses Digital signal analysis for reliable detection. Quad Linear Imaging Technology for sharp analysis of body dimensions and differentiation from backgrounds and pets. It has Passive Infrared (PIR) sensitivity adjustment. A PIR sensor is a motion detector which detects the heat (infrared) emitted naturally by humans and animals (Sahoo, 2017). When a person in the field of vision of the sensor moves, the sensor detects a sudden change in infrared energy and the sensor is triggered (activated). This is meant to calibrate the motion sensor coverage so that the sensing area can be adjusted based on room size. It can cover approximately 10 meters from its installed location. This motion sensor is pet immune up to 25 kg. This means it will not generate any false alarm due to motion or entry of a pet animal on the site.

When the camera is armed, rather than recording 24 hours, worth of video footage, the camera is triggered by a motion sensor. Motion sensors use PIR detection— passive infrared motion sensor technology. The motion sensor is able to detect infrared radiation in the form of body heat. The way it works is to compare sequential images from your video and if enough of the pixels have changed between those frames, the camera software determines something moved and sends you an alert. And motion detection is basically the process of comparing sequential images and determining whether the differences between them represent motion. If there are significant differences between two consecutive images, the cameras "conclude" that there has been motion within the camera view.

The CCTV is of 2-megapixel resolution which has capability to store the images directly on the camera mounted SD card. Based on the site requirement the resolution, frame rate (18 fps) is set for optimum resolution and storage requirement. This camera has TCP/IP port which can interface to the outside world via 3G router. It sends the images based on the connectivity on the cell site. It also sends the heart beat images (default images after every 1 minute) so that we come to know the camera is active. This feature can also be disabled. Camera is IP 66 and can be used in multiple applications. This means the camera is robust so that it is not damaged by low intensity rains, high winds and hence it is an all-weather camera.

Mounting of CCTV for Best Coverage

The camera is mounted on the wall opposite to the gate and covers the maximum area in site. It should be installed in such a manner that the face of the intruder is clear and visible even in dark so that it can be used as evidence in case of theft for FIR purposes. Picture of the user is to be mapped with the access control database also. This is only possible if the outside camera is mounted and integrates the camera with the access control on the main gate. It is to be implemented otherwise it is not possible. Once a user enters the site "light" will automatically be lit inside the shelter. 8W LED light is installed inside the cage to ensure the night intruder's face clearly. Camera will be taking pictures/ video – Out of 10 trial sites- 5 sites in photo mode and 05 sites cameras in Video mode. Camera inside the cage will take the snapshot/ video only on motion. Transmit pictures or video to the cloud for storage and it will also store the images inside the SD card (64 GB). For trial 32 GB should be used 64 GB not available in the technology of camera. IP camera 3.2/ 4 MP of reputed make is used. Cameras to be viewed remotely on laptop or Mobile applications. Storage for 30 days in the cloud can be done but it can be a very costly affair.

Door Sensor

A sensor and a magnet is used in the alarm sensors of doors and windows (Assaf, 2012). These sensors are either placed on the door and windows but they can be placed inside their frames as well. Whenever there is any intrusion, the magnet will separate from the sensor. A switch which is present inside the sensor gets tripped. In reaction to this, the sensor will send a signal to the alarm system. Door alarms can be very effective home security devices (Singh, 2009). They help in stopping the unwanted intrusion. The door gets opened automatically when the door controller receives an activation signal. This signal is sent by the sensor. It activates the gear motor to drive the belt and pulley. When no one is detected inside the activation area, the door starts closing after a designated period of time. One piece is attached on the door frame, and the other is attached parallel to the first piece on the door itself. The two parts create a closed circuit when the door is shut. As the door opens, the magnet and switch separate, breaking the circuit. When the circuit breaks, the sensor signals the central control panel.

TEST RESULTS AND DEMONSTRATION SCENARIOS

The smart access system is implemented as a pilot project for a leading telecom company. The trial tests have been made to get the correct functionality results from it.

When the field engineer, technician or any company representative (user/ visitor) approach near the site, he calls TOC/Operator (at IME office) and gets OTP (6-digit dynamic) (through SMS) is generated after giving registration details. The details are entered first time by giving one-time registration details (by email or telephonic) like name, company, purpose of visit, Aadhar card number, mobile number etc. Application Visual basic front end and database for records purpose. The registration details shall be valid for 06 months from the date of registration. One additional camera is integrated with the access control so once he punches his PIN the image will also be mapped with timing. This is one of the important features of our access control. Very important feature as we can compare with the snapshot sent by the CCTV. Next time onwards the user calls operator and he get OTP to unlock the electronic lock installed at site. The OTP shall be valid for 30 to 60 minutes for first time access. The operator shall also allot time for site access for completion of work say 2 hours, 3 hours etc. basis assessment. In case the work goes beyond initial allotment, the entire process repeats as above. Scenario of 2 or more users asking permission at same time shall also be built in. Database reports shall be generated. Figure 3 depicts the steps while entering in the telecom site. Figure 4 shows the steps to be followed while leaving the site. The complete process flow is depicted in Figure 5.

Figure 3. Steps while entering the site

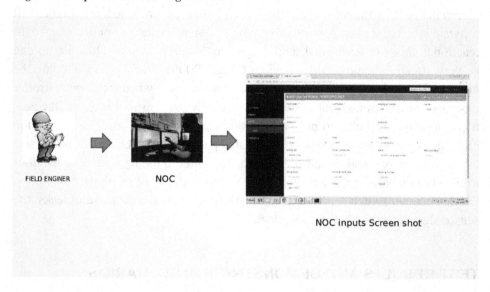

FIELD ENGINER   NOC

NOC inputs Screen shot

Intrusion alarm keyboards shall be installed near the entry gate inside the site. Once a user enters a password, it will disarm the intrusion panel. The 4-digit password will come in the same SMS as OTP to the user. Users will get an initial 60 seconds or 90 seconds to punch the password after entering the cage of the site. Users entering the right code shall be treated as Good visitors and incorrect one shall

Figure 4. Steps during leaving the site

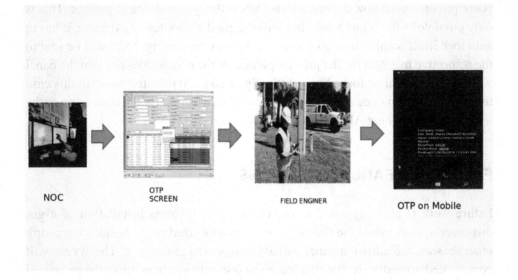

be considered as Bad visitors. Not entering a password shall also lead to defining a person as a bad visitor. SMS will be sent to the mapped people for alert – 3 people in case of a bad visitor. IVR recorded voice – Voice Text shall shout (for example "Go away you are photographed") in case of a bad visitor. Pop up operator screen

Figure 5. Complete system process

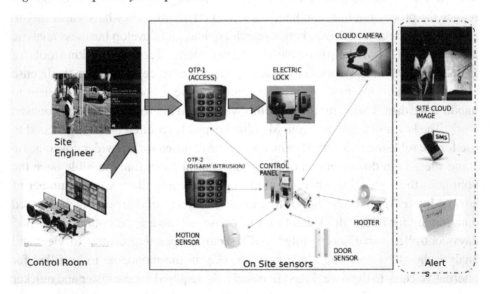

171

could be done too intimate regarding the entry of a bad visitor. Pop on the screen is not possible as of now as sending an SMS is the only solution at present. This is only possible in the future work. In case of a good visitor leaving the site, it has to auto lock itself within 10 or 20 minutes of the person leaving. SMS will be sent to the respective manager for the job completion. If the person does not arm the panel while going, it will be locked automatically in 10 to 20 minutes' time. In this case to avoid confusion once the person presses the exit button on the door to open the lock the panel will get ARM by itself.

FUTURE RESEARCH DIRECTIONS

Future work is also suggested to the company. It involves installation of a gas dispenser system inside the site. In case of unauthorized entry, besides triggering other sensors, the intrusion panel will also trigger the gas system. The system will be activated immediately. It will release gas instantly and in no time, the room will be filled with gas. This will make the unauthorized person unconscious for about half an hour. By that time, corrective action could be taken by the security team. To make the solution scalable we need to relook the strategies on the selection of hardware as well as software. In hardware the devices should be more agile, integrated and low powered. So that the maintenance and uptime of the system availability can be improved. As the site grows the data will increase to manifold. Hence the existing database and application software will not be able to cater the data processing demand. We need to re-plan our backend to a big data platform where the latest technologies are used. By using these technologies like Zoom, Hadoop will reduce the processing time and handle the data efficiently. They have capability to manage the queue and design better search engines and develop business analytic applications. This will help to create better deterrence and decision-making tools for maintaining the sites. As these tools are open source hence will reduce the license cost dramatically and make our future solution more economical and efficient to handle huge data. There are various points which need improvement in the proposed work. The key points are as given. Metallic keypad is required and will be good to use for the robustness. Multiple cameras will be required for the wider coverage on some sites. Trim down version of the smart control panel (only feasible once the volume is there meaning when solution to be implemented on a large number of sites). Mobile App to be developed for more convenience of the user. Big data-based data mining for future alerts and faster response will be a good option. 24*7*365 days-controlled surveillance called SOC (security operating centre) to view and analyse the alerts and deterrence purpose. Gap in the monopole to be filled for alternative entry to the cage. Fixed IP based SIM required for the faster and quicker connectivity. CMS (central monitoring system) to be implemented. Cloud location to be fixed for future transactions.

CONCLUSION

In this chapter, a solution is presented to handle two major problems faced by owner companies of telecom sites. The solution is based on wireless sensors using remote monitoring systems. The strategically mounted sensors push constant monitoring reports in the control room. This minimizes the time in taking any corrective action. To make the solution scalable it is required to relook the strategies on the selection of hardware as well as software. In hardware the devices should be more agile, integrated and low powered. So that the maintenance and uptime of the system availability can be improved. The solution offered multifold advantages like controlling the theft, constant monitoring of the multiple sites, and immediate alerts in various forms (SMS, hooters, and alarms). It increases the efficiency by saving a lot of commuting time of the site engineer by providing a smart access to the site.

REFERENCES

Almadhoun, R., Kadadha, M., Alhemeiri, M., Alshehhi, M., & Salah, K. (2018, October). A user authentication scheme of IoT devices using blockchain-enabled fog nodes. In *2018 IEEE/ACS 15th international conference on computer systems and applications (AICCSA)* (pp. 1-8). IEEE. 10.1109/AICCSA.2018.8612856

Assaf, M. H., Mootoo, R., Das, S. R., Petriu, E. M., Groza, V., & Biswas, S. (2012, May). Sensor based home automation and security system. In *2012 IEEE International Instrumentation and Measurement Technology Conference Proceedings* (pp. 722-727). IEEE. 10.1109/I2MTC.2012.6229153

Bhattarai, K. P., Gautam, B. P., & Sato, K. (2018, October). Authentic Gate Entry System (AuthGES) by Using LBPH for Smart Home Security. In *2018 International Conference on Networking and Network Applications (NaNA)* (pp. 191-196). IEEE. 10.1109/NANA.2018.8648705

Coskun, V., Ozdenizci, B., & Ok, K. (2013). A survey on near field communication (NFC) technology. *Wireless Personal Communications*, *71*(3), 2259–2294. doi:10.100711277-012-0935-5

Feller, G. (2011). The internet of things: In a connected world of smart objects. *Accenture & Bankinter Foundation of Innovation*, 24-29.

Forouzan, B. A. (2002). *TCP/IP protocol suite*. McGraw-Hill Higher Education.

Gadre, D. V., & Gupta, S. (2018). Universal Asynchronous Receiver and Transmitter (UART). In *Getting Started with Tiva ARM Cortex M4 Microcontrollers* (pp. 151–167). Springer. doi:10.1007/978-81-322-3766-2_12

Garg, R., & Sharma, S. (2018). Modified and improved IPv6 header compression (MIHC) scheme for 6LoWPAN. *Wireless Personal Communications, 103*(3), 2019–2033. doi:10.100711277-018-5894-z

Garg, R., & Sharma, S. (2020). Cooja Based Approach for Estimation and Enhancement of Lifetime of 6LoWPAN Environment. *International Journal of Sensors, Wireless Communications and Control, 10*(2), 207–216. doi:10.2174/221 03279096661 90409124604

Ghosh, A. M., Halder, D., & Hossain, S. A. (2016, May). Remote health monitoring system through IoT. In *2016 5th International Conference on Informatics, Electronics and Vision (ICIEV)* (pp. 921-926). IEEE. 10.1109/ICIEV.2016.7760135

Heine, G., & Horror, M. (1999). *GSM networks: protocols, terminology, and implementation*. Artech House, Inc.

Hinden, R., & Deering, S. (2003). *Internet protocol version 6 (IPv6) addressing architecture*. RFC 3513. http://tools.ietf.org/ html/rfc3513

Hui, J. W., & Culler, D. E. (2008, November). IP is dead, long live IP for wireless sensor networks. In *Proceedings of the 6th ACM conference on Embedded network sensor systems* (pp. 15-28). 10.1145/1460412.1460415

IEEE Standards Committee. (2003). Part 15.3: Wireless Medium Access Control (MAC) and Physical Layer (PHY) Specifications for High Rate Wireless Personal Area Networks (WPANs). *IEEE Std, 802*(3).

Kassem, A., El Murr, S., Jamous, G., Saad, E., & Geagea, M. (2016, July). A smart lock system using Wi-Fi security. In *2016 3rd International Conference on Advances in Computational Tools for Engineering Applications (ACTEA)* (pp. 222-225). IEEE. 10.1109/ACTEA.2016.7560143

Macfarlane, J. (2007). *Network routing basics: Understanding IP routing in Cisco systems*. John Wiley & Sons.

Malasinghe, L. P., Ramzan, N., & Dahal, K. (2019). Remote patient monitoring: A comprehensive study. *Journal of Ambient Intelligence and Humanized Computing, 10*(1), 57–76. doi:10.100712652-017-0598-x

Nanda, U., & Pattnaik, S. K. (2016, January). Universal asynchronous receiver and transmitter (uart). In *2016 3rd international conference on advanced computing and communication systems (ICACCS)* (Vol. 1, pp. 1-5). IEEE.

Patel, S., Shah, V., & Kansara, M. (2018). Comparative Study of 2G, 3G and 4G. *International Journal of Scientific Research in Computer Science. Engineering and Information Technology*, *3*(3), 1962–1964.

Paul, H. C., & Bacon, K. A. (2016). A study on IPv4 and IPv6: The importance of their coexistence. *International Journal of Information System and Engineering*, *4*(2).

Peijiang, C., & Xuehua, J. (2008, December). *Design and Implementation of Remote monitoring system based on GSM. In 2008 IEEE Pacific-Asia workshop on computational intelligence and industrial application* (Vol. 1). IEEE.

Rajiv, P., Raj, R., & Chandra, M. (2016). Email based remote access and surveillance system for smart home infrastructure. *Perspectives in Science*, *8*, 459–461. doi:10.1016/j.pisc.2016.04.104

Sahoo, K. C., & Pati, U. C. (2017, May). IoT based intrusion detection system using PIR sensor. In *2017 2nd IEEE International Conference on Recent Trends in Electronics, Information & Communication Technology (RTEICT)* (pp. 1641-1645). IEEE. 10.1109/RTEICT.2017.8256877

Saxena, A., Tyagi, M., & Singh, P. (2018, February). Digital Outing System Using RFID And Raspberry Pi With MQTT Protocol. In *2018 3rd International Conference On Internet of Things: Smart Innovation and Usages (IoT-SIU)* (pp. 1-4). IEEE. 10.1109/IoT-SIU.2018.8519923

Singh, R. S. S., Ibrahim, A. F. T., Salim, S. I. M., & Chiew, W. Y. (2009, November). Door sensors for automatic light switching system. In *2009 Third UKSim European Symposium on Computer Modeling and Simulation* (pp. 574-578). IEEE.

Stallings, W., & Prentice, P. (2002). *Communications and Networks*. doi:10.1109/ PACIIA.2008.195

Tjensvold, J. M. (2007, September). Comparison of the IEEE 802.11, 802.15. 1, 802.15. 4 and 802.15. 6 wireless standards. IEEE, 18.

Urfalıoğlu, O., Soyer, E. B., Toreyin, B. U., & Cetin, A. E. (2008, April). PIR-sensor based human motion event classification. In *2008 IEEE 16th Signal Processing, Communication and Applications Conference* (pp. 1-4). IEEE.

Van Voorthuijsen, G., van Hoof, H. A. J. M., Klima, M., Roubik, K., Bernas, M., & Pata, P. (2005, October). CCTV effectiveness study. In *Proceedings 39th Annual 2005 International Carnahan Conference on Security Technology* (pp. 105-108). IEEE. 10.1109/CCST.2005.1594815

Velastin, S. A. (2009, November). CCTV video analytics: Recent advances and limitations. In *International Visual Informatics Conference* (pp. 22-34). Springer. 10.1007/978-3-642-05036-7_3

Yong, C. Y., Sudirman, R., & Chew, K. M. (2011, September). Motion detection and analysis with four different detectors. In *2011 Third International Conference on Computational Intelligence, Modelling & Simulation* (pp. 46-50). IEEE. 10.1109/CIMSim.2011.18

Zhang, Z., Zhang, Y. Q., Chu, X., & Li, B. (2004). An overview of virtual private network (VPN): IP VPN and optical VPN. *Photonic Network Communications*, 7(3), 213–225. doi:10.1023/B:PNET.0000026887.35638.ce

ADDITIONAL READING

Areny, R. P., & Webster, J. G. (2001). *Sensors and signal conditioning*. Wiley.

Garg, R., & Sharma, S. (2017). A study on the need for an adaptation layer in the 6LoWPAN protocol stack. *International Journal of Wireless and Microwave Technologies*, 7(3), 49–57. doi:10.5815/ijwmt.2017.03.05

Maheepala, M., Joordens, M. A., & Kouzani, A. Z. (2020). Low Power Processors and Image Sensors for Vision-Based IoT Devices: A Review. *IEEE Sensors Journal*, 21(2), 1172–1186. doi:10.1109/JSEN.2020.3015932

Shelby, Z., & Bormann, C. (2011). *6LoWPAN: The wireless embedded Internet* (Vol. 43). John Wiley & Sons.

Slama, D., Puhlmann, F., Morrish, J., & Bhatnagar, R. M. (2015). *Enterprise IoT: Strategies and Best practices for connected products and services*. O'Reilly Media, Inc. http://www.gsma.com/aboutus/gsm-technology/gsm

KEY TERMS AND DEFINITIONS

CCTV: It stands for Closed-Circuit Television. A CCTV system consists of a camera, lens, monitor and recorder.

Cloud Computing: Cloud computing is the online support of computing services which usually includes servers, storage, databases, networking, software, analytics, and intelligence, over the Internet.

GSM: The Global System for Mobile Communications (GSM) is a standard developed by the European Telecommunications Standards Institute (ETSI) to describe the protocols used by mobile devices.

Industrial Internet of Things: It is defined as machines, computers and people enabling intelligent industrial operations.

Internet of Things: IoT is a system in which devices are connected to the internet to send data or receive instructions.

Router: It is a device designed to receive, analyze, and forward data packets between computer networks.

Sensor: It is a device that senses the physical environment and captures the value for which that sensor has dedicated work.

Sim Card: It is an electronic chip that stores identification information that pinpoints a smartphone to a specific mobile network.

Wireless Sensor Network: It's a wireless networking technology that allows devices to interface with the internet.

Chapter 9
Internet of Things–Based Water Quality Control and Monitoring System for Urban Society

Prerna Sharma
Jagan Institute of Management Studies, Guru Gobind Singh Indraprastha University, India

Piyush Jain
Jagan Institute of Management Studies, Guru Gobind Singh Indraprastha University, India

Latika Kharb
(iD) https://orcid.org/0000-0002-8549-0920
Jagan Institute of Management Studies, Guru Gobind Singh Indraprastha University, India

ABSTRACT

In this chapter, an attempt has been made to develop a hardware-based remote water quality monitoring system using a single-chip microcontroller, Atmega328P, in synchrony with some sensor technology and GSM/GPRS module for long-distance data transmission. The proposed system is able to perform a qualitative test on the water, taking into consideration both the chemical behavior as well as physical properties exhibited by the latter. The fluid will be analyzed in terms of its ph value (i.e., the molar concentration of hydrogen ions, the haziness caused by the major

DOI: 10.4018/978-1-7998-6981-8.ch009

suspension of minute particles). The device aims to transmit all the deliberated parameters of the wastewater along with the longitude and latitude information to the concerned authorities for real-time monitoring of that data. The subject aims to devise a robust solution that can be used to analyze the quality of large water bodies and send the analysis report to the authorities of pollution control for further implication.

INTRODUCTION

Wastewater is simply the water that humans have used. It results from the ordinary daily life usage of water, marking its origin from industries, residential and domestic sources. Human beings intentionally or unintentionally pollute/consume water, contributing to the water's degradation, making it physically or chemically unfit to use again. Standard practices like animal bathing, agricultural runoff, domestic chores, sewer infiltration, untreated effluent discharge from commercial establishments and industries, and recklessly mixing litter and non-biodegradable constituents in water deteriorate the quality of the latter to a great extent.

Wastewater treatment before it flows back into the environment, i.e., natural water bodies, is essential. A recent report from WHO says "Insufficient treatment of wastewater and faecal sludge spread disease and is a driver of antimicrobial resistance". Therefore, Advanced separation methods and comprehensive techniques to treat the water rather than turning a blind eye to this cause are mandatory.

It is evident with the hype graph that the convergence of Information technology with significant innovations in the embedded technology, IoT, and cybernetics results in advancements and optimization in algorithms and strategies, yielding optimal results w.r.t traditional systems. Unfortunately, this intersection of powerful technologies has not been explored and utilized to the fullest potential for developing solutions to control and manage pollution sustainably and optimally. One of the major concerns in the timeline of the treatment of the water is analyzing the pollutants. Wastewater also varies chemically; some wastewater may contain hazardous dissolved toxins and chemicals, while others have particles, sediments, and suspended matter of all sizes. It is essential to know what pollutants constitute the water and their concentration in the same. After the analysis, it is easy to predict and design a water treatment solution specifically for that wastewater.

This chapter postulates a strategy and a device to monitor the quality of water remotely and in real-time. The device will run a quality check on the fluid in terms of ph and turbidity. The system is not just developed for monitoring the parameters but also for devising a water treatment mechanism. The system will constantly measure the parameters and will transmit the data to the destination for further improvisations. Since the device is placed on the floating shafts at different levels of the water body, it is very uncertain to predict whether internet communication will be possible or not. A more reliable approach would be to use a text message service (GSM). As per Kharb L. et al. (2021), Need of the hour today is the portable devices and tools which can be combined with different platforms like android and able to transmit data.

The system will be equipped with the GPS module, which will output current longitude and latitude parameters. Thus the subject will also help to investigate the source of a particular pollutant by sending the location information piggy bagged with the parameter value in real-time. The detailed information about the system design and architecture is disclosed in the following divisions of the paper.

LITERATURE REVIEW

Developers, researchers, and environmentalists are continually making progress and proposing progressing solutions for designing and developing cost-effective, sustainable, and efficient algorithms, separation mechanisms, and techniques to manage wastewater treatment without further damage to the environment. Xin Wang et al. (2011) featured a hierarchical structure to minimize the cost and dependency upon network infrastructure while monitoring the water quality in real-time. The prime consideration points to the optimization of wireless networking in remote monitoring. Haqva H. et al. (2015) proposed a prototype for monitoring seawater quality against pH, ORP, conductivity and, temperature employing IoT and Remote sensing procedures. Meghana Kiran Urs et al. (2018) developed a model for remote sensing of vitals of water. The system runs on solar power and is backed with a GUI to access that data. Shannon MA et al. (2008) outlines some of the techniques and methodologies being developed to improve the disinfection and decontamination of water, as well as efforts to increase water supplies through the safe reuse of wastewater and efficient desalination of sea and brackish water. Beate Escher et al. (2012) summarized the science and techniques of bioanalytical tools in water quality assessment in the book. Animesh Agarwal et al. (2015) carried out water analysis using regression and correlation and predicted contamination level of Gagan river water, India. This method comes out to be cost-effective as well as time-saving. Holger R. Maier et al. (2004) used artificial neural networks to forecast water quality parameters. Samreen Jahan et al. (2019) featured an IoT-based solution for water quality assessment using a Raspberry Pi. In the development of the model, Raspberry Pi is used as a central controller. Moreover, a flood alert system is also deduced from the existing approach. Sharma P. et al. (2020) developed a robust hardware-software security system incorporating the constituent hardware to continually sample the environment parameters for any unauthorized or malicious activity in physical space, local intelligence for decision-making capabilities, network capabilities, and software aspects to notify the concerned authorities. Kharb L. et al. (2020) proposed a prototype to manage health care in real-time which can be utilized both by hospitals and ambulance in critical times.

SYSTEM ARCHITECTURE

ATMEGA328P & Arduino

ATMEGA328P is a widely employed microcontroller from the MegaAVR microcontroller series. The bit width is 8 bits, with the frequency of the clock as 16 megahertz and the flash size of 32 KB memory. It is substantially used to provide local intelligence and define the operativeness of the proposed system. This chip adds to the intellectual capacity of the device by giving decision-making abilities. All the sensors and actuating apparatus are integrated as a submodule with this chip to meet the system's desired requirements.

Atmega328P also comes soldered in a prototyping plug-in-play board such as Arduinos which makes dealing with microcontrollers easy for developers and beginners. Sharma P. et al.(2019) stated that Arduinos are an apt, cost-effective, quick, and simple solution to microcontrollers, and the latter is embedded in the Arduino. The sketches (C++ programs written in Arduino IDE) defining the iterative functionality and predicates of the system, written in C++, are deployed on a prototyping board using the Integrated Development Environment. As per Sharma P. et al. (2019), using the chip individually could be cumbersome for beginners but in Arduino Platform, instructions can be uploaded through USB very easily and no prerequisite knowledge and expertise with microcontrollers are really required.

SKU: SENO189

Turbidity is referred to as the measure of the solid suspended particles present in the fluid. As a result of the higher concentration of suspended particulates present in the water, the water becomes hazy and has high turbidity. The clear water thus has very low turbidity. The suspended particles absorb the heat and raise the temperature of the water. The water with relatively higher temperatures has a relatively low concentration of dissolved oxygen, making it difficult for aquatic animals to survive. Thus, making turbid water less suitable for marine life. To measure the turbidity, we

181

Figure 1. ATMEGA328P Pin Mapping

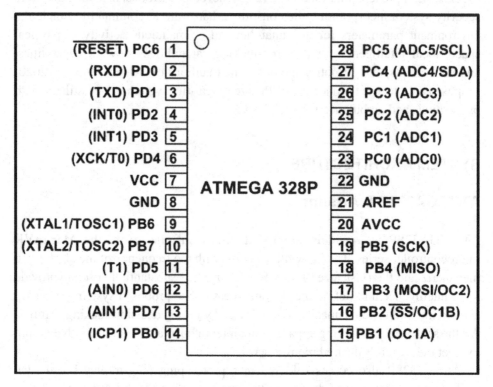

will be using a turbidity sensor SKU: SENO 189. It is a sensor with an operating voltage of 5V and a working phenomenon based on the Tyndall effect principle. It functions as an optical sensor by emitting a beam of light directed in the water. It then detects the amount of light returning to it after being scattered by the suspended particles. The intensity of light detected is directly proportional to the concentration of suspended particles. This unit provides both digital and analog output modes. The sensor's sensitivity or threshold gets easily adjusted in the digital o/p manner via the potentiometer soldered on the sensor board. This sensor is widely employed in washing machines, dishwashers, and water tanks to monitor water's turbidity level. As stated by Kharb L. (2018), the process of building applications has been a journey and it varies depending on one's application requirements and purpose. In future, applications can be designed for this.

SKU: SEN0161

The ph value of a fluid refers to the concentration of hydrogen ions. The scale of pH widens from 1 to 14, 7 considered neutral. Since pH can be affected by chemicals in the water, pH is an important indicator of water that is changing chemically. Since there's a requirement to monitor real-time value at regular intervals, the pH meter sensor is an apt choice. The pH sensor working phenomenon is based on the difference in the electric potential of the two fluids generated. The fluid whose ph is known, such as NaCl (ph -7) is compared chemically with the liquid whose ph is unknown.

NEO -6M GPS MODULE

Neo-6m is a cost-effective, highly efficient four-pin GPS module. The module is widely used to retrieve location parameters and is highly compatible with microcontrollers—the module is equipped with an antenna, rechargeable button battery, and serial communication capabilities. As an output, the GSM module returns NMEA Strings. NMEA (National Marine Electronics Association) is a standard that permits marine electronics to send information to computers and to other marine equipment and GPS receiver communication is defined within this specification. Microcontrollers can parse these NMEA strings to obtain longitude and latitude information. Apart from longitude and latitude parameters, various other aspects such as velocity, time, date, altitude, etc can also be retrieved.

SIM 900A

SIM 900A is a widely employed wireless Quad-Band GSM/GPRS module with 68 SMT pads with an operating voltage is 3.2V ~ 4.8V. This module extends great support for long-distance data transmission. The unit can be configured according to the requirements of the system with the help of AT Commands. The module can be configured to transmit/receive data, send/receive text messages, and making voice calls. It has a port for inserting sim cards, and then the module can be recognized with the registered number of the former. Serial communication is provided through USART communication.

WORKING STRATEGY

When the system with operating voltage, SIM900A will tend to establish a connection with the stated private network or destination with the required payload to post data when it's available. It's a one-time process and takes at least a minute for the same. Once the connection gets established, it is ready to post data. Likewise, the neo -6m module will prepare for setup but take a little time for that. Once the setup mentioned above is done, the system's sensing aspect will initiate and instruct the sensors to start the sampling process or create any pre-required phenomenon. Turbidity & pH modules will immediately begin sampling procedures once initialized. They are programmed to sample the ph and turbidity every two seconds continuously. Both the sensors are instructed to function to average every successive sample throughout a minute before processing it further. In the digital output mode, the threshold value of the turbidity sensor can be adjusted using a built-in potentiometer on the sensor board. We calculate a threshold value based on the subject's environmental parameters in which we experiment. These values are specific to the sensor and can be slightly different for each module, and are highly customizable according to the needs.

The sensory aspect of the system will generate analog values proportional to the concentration of the target pollutant. The microcontroller will constantly be monitoring all the sensor values. Neo-6m is programmed to yield the current longitudinal and latitudinal coordinates at a regular interval of a single minute. The GPS module will produce NMEA Strings. The microcontroller will then parse those strings. The microcontroller will then instruct the sim 900A to post the obtained location parameters and averaged turbidity and pH values. Once we post data, a response gets generated from the destination, which will be beneficial during the hardware testing and debugging phase. This type of response mechanism, however, is not at all required currently. The proposed device will check on the parameters in the loop and post once in a minute. Time and post request destination is programmable thus customizable. These activities will keep on repeating in a loop, provided the system has operating voltage.

FUTURE SCOPE & APPLICATIONS

Through this chapter, we proposed an optimal and robust wastewater monitoring system development. The developed system is capable of posting data in real-time and has built-in location tracking functionality. This sort of development procedure and algorithm is a fundamental step towards an extensive aim. Because the need for pure water is ubiquitous, this system is installed anywhere: it may be an organization, wastewater treatment plants, institutes, hospitals, military camps, chemical industries, conveyor belts, fish tanks, or as small as one's home for water quality assessment. This hardware provides an uninterrupted and scalable solution to remote and real-time water assessment.

With minor modifications, the system gets turned into an alert system that checks the water quality if it goes beyond a certain level surpassing the pre-adjusted threshold value. As an extension of the proposal, developing a subsystem with customizations like a typical valve-like enclosing on it with some gets possible. The valves can

Figure 2. Flowchart for wastewater management

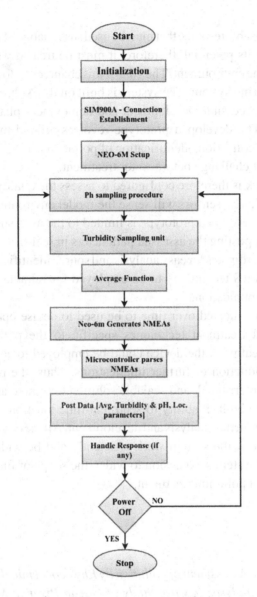

be opened and shut via some servos as instructed by microcontrollers. Once some specific type of pollutant is found, the right amount of absorbents can be released into the water to treat it.

Since the system is posting data related to water every other minute, the huge data collected over time can be used to devise optimized separation methodologies and treatment techniques specific to the pollutants.

CONCLUSION

Water is an indispensable resource that must be used sustainably. Moreover, wastewater must be valued for its potential, therefore, it must be treated without causing any further damage to the environment. The goal of this chapter was to develop a powerful wastewater monitoring system. The system is built on the Arduino platform, which offers a relatively accessible development and deployment platform compared to microcontrollers. The developed prototype revolves around the areas of remote sensing (RS). Data collection, identification of pollutants, and source analysis have always been a great challenge before water treatment.

A sensor network is therefore configured to assess the quality of water in terms of turbidity and pH. The sensors will sense the model environment and collect the required data. The developed prototype is limited to the assessment of the fluid. It extends support for posting the assessed parameters in real-time and the latitudinal and longitudinal coordinates for easy analysis and source identification. High-quality quadband GSM/GPRS technology to be employed for reliable and uninterrupted long-distance communication.

Hence, the data collected over time to be used to devise optimized separation methodologies and treatment techniques specific to the pollutants. Moreover, after subsequent treatment, the device could be employed to analyze the former's aftereffect and conduction of further implications. Thus, the proposed hardware offers a robust, uninterrupted, and scalable solution to remote and real-time water assessment with the built-in ability to send real-time location piggy bagged with other parameters for further analysis and development. All the components employed in the development of the system work efficiently and be widely available. It is expected from this system's expansion to widen the scope of future improvements in sustainability and pollution treatment.

REFERENCES

Animesh, A. (2015). *Assessment of pollution by Physicochemical Water Parameters Using Regression Analysis: A Case Study of Gagan River at Moradabad- India.* Pelagia Research Library Advances in Applied Science Research.

Escher. (2012). Bioanalytical Tools in water Quality Assessment. IWA Publishing Alliance.

Haqva, H. (2015). Smart water quality monitoring system. *2nd, Asia-Pacific World Congress on Computer Science and Engineering (APWC on CSE),* 1-6. 10.1109/APWCCSE.2015.7476234

Jahan. (2019). Raspberry Pi Based Water Quality Monitoring and Flood Alerting System Using IoT. *International Journal of Recent Technology and Engineering, 7*(6S4), 640-643.

Kharb, L. (2018). A Perspective View on Commercialization of Cognitive Computing. *2018 8th International Conference on Cloud Computing, Data Science & Engineering (Confluence).* 10.1109/CONFLUENCE.2018.8442728

Kharb, L. (2020). Proposing Real-Time Smart Healthcare Model Using IoT. In P. Raj, J. Chatterjee, A. Kumar, & B. Balamurugan (Eds.), *Internet of Things Use Cases for the Healthcare Industry.* Springer. doi:10.1007/978-3-030-37526-3_2

Kharb, L. (2021). "VISIO": An IoT Device for Assistance of Visually Challenged. In V. C. Pandey, P. M. Pandey, & S. K. Garg (Eds.), *Advances in Electromechanical Technologies. Lecture Notes in Mechanical Engineering.* Springer. doi:10.1007/978-981-15-5463-6_84

Kiran Urs. (2018). Real-time Water Quality Monitoring using WSN. *3rd IEEE International Conference on Recent Trends in Electronics, Information & Communication Technology (RTEICT-2018),* 1152-1156.

Maier, H. R. (2004). Use of artificial neural networks for predicting optimal alum doses and treated water quality parameters. *Environmental Modelling & Software, 19*(5), 485–494. doi:10.1016/S1364-8152(03)00163-4

Shannon, M. A., Bohn, P. W., Elimelech, M., Georgiadis, J. G., Mariñas, B. J., & Mayes, A. M. (2008). Science and technology for water purification in the coming decades. *Nature, 452*(7185), 301–310. doi:10.1038/nature06599 PMID:18354474

Sharma, P. (2020). Intrusion Detection and Security System. In Big Data Analytics and Intelligence: A Perspective for Health Care. Emerald Publishing Limited. doi:10.1108/978-1-83909-099-820201011

Sharma, P., & Kamthania, D. (2019). Intelligent object detection and avoidance system. In *International Conference on Transforming IDEAS (Inter-Disciplinary Exchanges, Analysis, and Search) into Viable Solutions* (pp. 342-351). Macmillan Education.

Wang. (2011). Online Water Monitoring System Based on ZigBee and GPRS. Key Laboratory of Advanced Process Control for Light Industry (Ministry of Education). *Procedia Engineering, 15,* 2680-2684.

APPENDIX

Figure 3.

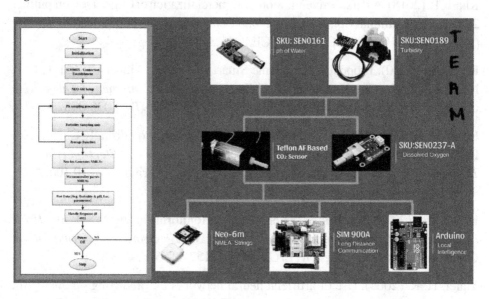

Figure 4.

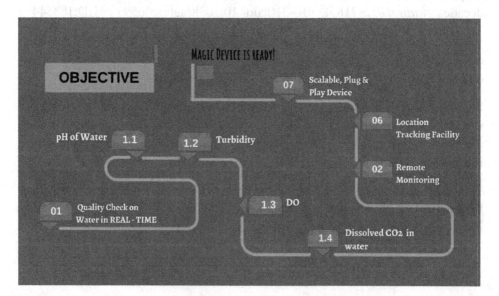

Figure 5.

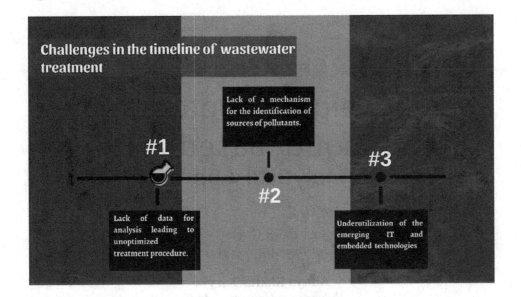

Chapter 10
Lightweight Cryptography in Cloud–Based IoT:
An Analytical Approach

Payel Guria
Vidyasagar University, India

Aditya Bhattacharyya
Vidyasagar University, India

ABSTRACT

IoT and cloud computing are the novel fields that are rapidly progressing in the world of internet technology. A huge and massive amount of data are communicating via IoT and cloud devices. Along with the highly configured devices, IoT and cloud also empowered many resource-constrained devices to communicate and compute information through network. But the major problem that they face is how to provide data security through conventional cryptographic algorithms in such resource-constrained devices having smaller size, limited memory spaces, low computation capabilities, and limited power. In this scenario, the biggest driver towards the problem is lightweight cryptography (LWC). This chapter discusses thoroughly the LWC, different schemes of LWC, and cryptanalysis of different LWC schemes.

INTRODUCTION

Internet of Things (IoT) are widely rambling day by day, in which cloud computing is providing an additional essence. Cloud in IoT act as a catalyst for the growth of future Internet Technologies. Everyday IoT devices deal with huge volume of

DOI: 10.4018/978-1-7998-6981-8.ch010

data that need to be stored and processed. But due to its limited storage, resource constrained and shortage in communication, it always requires cloud for outsource storage and computation. This collaboration of cloud and IoT though provides a new dimension in the field of Internet technologies but give rise to a new series of challenges in the field of security and privacy.

Although many encryption schemes have already been encompassing to provide security and privacy to the data but the major problems that the cloud-IoT faces are with its resource constrained devices having smaller size, limited memory space, low computational capability and limited power. As per its requirement the cryptographic algorithms need to be lightweight in respect to storage, power consumption and computational capability. This leads to a new evolution in the field of cryptography and Lightweight Cryptography (LWC) arises as the solution. This chapter talks about this new trend of cryptography comprising the following sections.

- In the first section of the chapter is all about LWC and its need or more precisely its usefulness in Cloud based IoT.
- In the next section of the chapter several LWC Schemes that are currently in use for data encryption like LWC Stream Cipher, Block Cipher, Hash function, ECC have been discussed.
- The third section will describe the cryptanalysis of the above mentioned LWC Schemes.
- Lastly, the chapter focus towards the future aspects of LWC in Cloud based IoT.

LIGHTWEIGHT CRYPTOGRAPHY

Many encryption algorithms or cryptographic algorithms have been used so far to provide network security and privacy of data. The urge for new design criteria of cryptographic algorithm has arises due to the resource constrained Cloud-IoT devices. The most of these devices may have any one or more of the below mention requirements.

- Low computational power
- Limited storage capability
- Minimum size for hardware implementation.
- Low cost.
- High Security.

The conventional cryptographic algorithms found to be well suited for servers, computers and mobile devices but in case of low-end devices used in Cloud-IoT like RFID tags, Sensor nodes, embedded system, etc. they failed to fulfil their requirements. Thus, a new branch of cryptography has introduced, and termed as "Lightweight Cryptography (LWC)" that act as a solution for the resource constrained devices. There is no specified requirement in LWC but it tries to provide modest key size, smaller block size, lesser code, minimal clock cycle and a smaller number of iterations for encryption or decryption. Keeping in mind the trade-off between cost, security and performance in cryptographic algorithm, it has been attempted by the researchers to optimize the design goals while designing different LWC schemes.

LIGHTWEIGHT CRYPTOGRAPHIC SCHEMES

Lightweight cryptographic schemes are designed to optimize the cryptographic primitives such as cost, key size, block size, cycle rate and number of iterations. It is generally divided into three categories namely:

- Lightweight Symmetric Key Cryptography.
- Lightweight Asymmetric Key Cryptography.
- Lightweight Hash Function.

The Figure 1 represents the different division and sub-division of Lightweight cryptographic schemes.

Figure 1. Lightweight Cryptographic Schemes

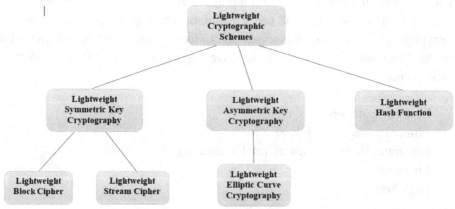

LIGHTWEIGHT SYMMETRIC KEY CRYPTOGRAPHY

Lightweight symmetric key cryptography is a secret key or shared key cryptography where a sender and a receiver share a common key for both encryption and decryption through a secret communication channel. There are two methods of encryption that belongs to the family of lightweight symmetric key cipher, namely, Block cipher and Stream cipher.

LIGHTWEIGHT BLOCK CIPHER

In block cipher an entire block of plain text is processed at once for both encryption and decryption. Here a common key is used for both the operation (encryption and decryption). There are several modes of operations of block cipher, but this chapter is focussing only on the design structure which is based on two types: SPN and Feistel network structure.

SPN stands for Substitution- Permutation Network. This network takes a block of plain text as input along with the key and produce the cipher text as output by applying several rounds or levels or layers or more precisely iterations of substitutions (S-boxes) and permutation (P-boxes). The decryption is done by performing the same procedure but in reverse form. As this structure require less execution rounds or iterations, therefore it is suitable for low power expenditure.

Feistel structure network or only Feistel network is named after a German cryptographer "Horst Feistel". This network uses round function that takes a data block and a subkey as inputs and produce an output of same size as the input block. The round function is applied to one half of the data that is to be encrypted and the output of the function is XORed with the other half of the data. This process is repeated for a fixed number of iterations and at the end, the final output is produced that is the encrypted data or cipher text. The decryption procedure is similar to that of encryption but the only thing one should keep in mind is the reversal of key schedule or subkeys. Since the cipher that it produce is more or less halved, this network results in low memory usage and minimal block size or code size or circuit size.

Utilizing the advantages of any one or both of these networks (SPN & Feistel), several lightweight block ciphers has been designed by the researchers to meet the basic three challenges of minimal memory usage, less power consumption and passable security level. In this chapter, only the notable lightweight block ciphers are discussed mentioning their basic parameters of evaluation like key size, block size, number of iteration and design structure.

RC5

RC5 is the simplest symmetric key cipher, designed by Ronald Rives in 1994 (Rives,1994) having the following properties

- It is suitable for both hardware and software implementation.
- Same variable-length key is used for both encryption and decryption where plaintext and cipher text are of fixed length blocks.
- It is word oriented which means the operators used to perform the computational operations can work on full words of data at once.
- It provides high security and low memory usage.
- The structure of the algorithm is Feistel like network and use 0 to 2040 bits for key size and 32/64/128 bits for block size.
- Number of round or iteration it required is from 1 to 255.

TEA

TEA, a symmetric block cipher stands for Tiny Encryption Algorithm, was designed by David Wheeler and Roger Needham in 1994 (Wheeler et al, 1994). It holds all the properties of lightweight block cipher. It encrypts 64 bits of data by utilizing 128 bits key. To provide non-linearity, it uses two operation – ADD and XOR. It is quite secure and has Feistel structure. The most notable weakness of TEA is Key Equivalence which means that the effective key size is 126 bits only rather 128 bits as key is equivalent to other three key.

XTEA

The weakness of TEA has overcome by a new lightweight block cipher, XTEA (Extended TEA) which was proposed by the designer of TEA in 1997. Here by including a complex key schedule and by adjusting and rearranging the shift, XORs and addition operations the weakness of TEA has been removed.

AES

In 1998 two Belgian Cryptographers Vincent Rijmen and Joan Daeman developed a symmetric cipher called AES – Advanced Encryption Standard (Rijmen and Daeman,1998). It is based onto the design structure of SPN. Like other block cipher, it encrypts or decrypts a block of plaintext of size 128 bits with key size of 128, 192 or 256 bits. The number of rounds required to convert a plaintext into cipher text can be determined from the key size i.e. if the key sizes are 128, 192 and 256 bits then 10, 12 and 14 rounds are required to get cipher text. This block cipher is efficient for both hardware and software implementation.

DESL

DESL was introduced by Gregor Leander along with his fellow researchers Christof Paar, Axel Poschmann and Kai Schramn in 2007 (Leander et al., 2007). It is a lightweight version of DES (Data Encryption Standard) based on Feistel structure. It required 56 key bits and 16 rounds to generate 64-bit cipher. It provides security against several linear and differential cryptographic attack and also well suited for low cost platform in respect of implementation.

PRESENT

Bogdanov along with his co researcher has introduced an ultra-lightweight block cipher in 2007 and named it as PRESENT (Bogdanov et al 2007). It is a new hardware optimized block cipher that has been designed for area and power constrained devices of Cloud-IoT. It is an instance of SPN and supports two key length of 80 and 128 bits, block length of 64 bits and required 31 rounds to convert a plaintext to cipher text. It is highly efficient for hardware implementation but not for software implementation.

KATAN and KTANTAN

KATAN and KTANTAN belongs to the family of hardware-oriented block cipher. It was designed by Christophe De Canniere, Orr Dunkelman and Miroslav Knezevic in the year of 2009 (Canniere et al., 2009). The family is divided into two sets of six block ciphers. The first set is KATAN consist of three block ciphers of block sizes 32,48 or 64 bits and the second set is KTANTAN consist of the rest three block ciphers with the block size same as KATAN. As the key is completely burnt into the device and cannot be altered in KTANTAN, it is more compact to the hardware than KATAN.

Hummingbird

Daniel Engels et al. in the year 2010 introduced an ultra-lightweight cryptography algorithm called Hummingbird, inspired from the design of Enigma machine (D. Engels et al., 2010). It is designed to meet the requirements of resource constrained devices of Cloud-IoT such as RFID tags, smart card, wireless sensor nodes, etc. It provides security and resistant against the Linear and Differential attacks with smaller block size. In respect to the size and speed optimized implementation Hummingbird can provide faster throughput compare to the other ultra-lightweight block cipher such as PRESENT.

TWINE

TWINE (T. Suzaki et al., 2011) is a 64-bit block cipher that support two key length of 80 and 128 bits. It uses GFN Feistel structure. TWINE is basically designed to achieve hardware efficiency but it is also effective on software implementation.

KLEIN

KLEIN belongs to the family of lightweight block cipher, having a fixed block size of 64 bits and a variable-length key of size 64,80 or 96 bits (Zheng Gong et al., 2012). The structure of KLEIN is SPN. The input and output of KLEIN are one-dimension arrays of bytes where byte-oriented algorithms are used to optimized all the operations during round transformations. It is designed as a software efficient block cipher but also efficient for hardware implementation.

PRINCE

PRINCE is a block cipher that provide a new way to lightweight cryptography by accomplishing low latency and unrolled hardware implementation (Borghoff et at., 2012). The 'alpha reflection' is the most remarkable feature in PRINCE where the encryption with a related key is used for decryption thus provides a very low computational cost. It also holds the other properties of lightweight cipher like minimum number of rounds, low logic depth, etc. SPN structure is used along with 64 bits block size and 128 bits key size.

RECTANGLE

RECTANGLE, introduced in 2014 by Wentao Zhang et al., is a block cipher that uses bit-slice techniques to provide lightweight and fastest implementation (Wentao Zhang et al., 2014). It uses SPN and is extremely hardware friendly. Due to the use of bit-slice technique, not only it is beneficial for hardware but also achieved a very impressive performance in software. It is an iterative block cipher that uses SPN structure with 64 bits block size, 80- or 128-bits key size and required 25 number of rounds to produce cipher text.

Midori

The urge for optimal energy consumption gave rise to a new block cipher named Midori (S. Banik et al., 2015). The main aim behind the cipher is to provide a circuit that will function both encryption and decryption by reducing the overhead in respect to area and energy consumption. There are two block cipher in the family of Midori – Midori64 and Midori128 that accepts block size of 64 and 128 respectively but uses same key size of 128 bits. It is based on SPN structure. These ciphers are used for low energy budget devices like RFID tags, battery based portable devices and sensor nodes.

ANU

ANU is a Feistel based ultra-lightweight block cipher, designed by Gaurav Bansod et al. in 2016 (Bansod et al., 2016). The main goal behind ANU is to provide high security to the resource constrained devices of IoT and Cloud against various cryptographic attacks like Linear and Differential attack, Zero-coorelation attack, Biclique attack, Algebraic attack, etc. It has 25 number of rounds and supports key length of 128 bits with 64 bits block-length. It needs less gate equivalents thus minimizes memory size along with power consumption. It is well suited for cloud, IoT based application.

SFN

SFN is a new lightweight block cipher proposed by Lang Li et al. in the year 2018 (Li et al. 2018). It is a cipher that utilizes the advantages of both SPN and Feistel structure. It supports 64 bits block size and 96 bits key length where the round function uses both Feistel and SPN structure for encryption or decryption. In SFN encryption or decryption is performed using SPN and key expansion is conducted by Feistel structure. Thus, it achieves a strong immunity against attacks. It is well suited for both hardware and software implementation.

The Table 1 shows the tabularized form of the notable lightweight block ciphers.

Table 1. Lightweight block ciphers

Name	Year	Structure	Key size (bits)	Block size (bits)	No. of iteration
RC5	1994	Feistel	0-2040	32,64,128	1 - 255
TEA	1994	Feistel	128	64	-
XTEA	1997	Feistel	128	64	64
AES	1998	SPN	128,192,256	128	10,12,14
DESL	2007	Feistel	56	64	16
PRESENT	2007	SPN	80/128	64	31
KATAN & KTANTAN	2009	NLFSR	80	32/48/64	254
Hummingbird	2010	Hybrid	256	16	4
TWINE	2011	GFN Feistel	80/128	64	32
KLEIN	2012	SPN	64/80/96	64	12/16/20
PRINCE	2012	SPN	128	64	11
RECTANGLE	2014	SPN	80/128	64	25
Midori	2015	SPN	128	64/128	16/20
ANU	2016	Feistel	80/128	64	25
SFN	2018	Feistel + SPN	96	64	32

LIGHTWEIGHT STREAM CIPHER

A Stream cipher is another type of Symmetric key cipher where plaintext is converted into cipher text by encrypting each digit of plain text one at a time with the corresponding digit of key stream by applying XOR operation. Different types of digital registers are used to generate a random value of key stream from the main key (seed key) and that key stream value is used as cryptographic key for both encryption and decryption. Several types of stream ciphers have been proposed so far by the researchers, here only the famous and notable ciphers are discussed along with their key size and register used for key stream generation.

A5/1

A5/1 is a stream cipher that uses GSM standards to provide privacy over the air communication (Biryukov et al. 2001). It uses 114 bits sequences of key stream for each burst sequence which was XORed with 114 bits data before the modulation. A5/1 is based on three Linear Feedback Shift Registers (LFSR).

Rabbit

Rabbit was first proposed in 2003 (Boesgaard et al., 2003) and later get public in the year 2008 (E. Zenner, 2008). It is a stream cipher that uses 64 bit IV (Initialization Vector) and 128 bits secret key. A bit stream generator acts as its main component to encrypts 128 message bits in each iteration. Encryption and decryption are performed by XORing the keystream data with the plaintext or cipher text. The main aim behind the designing of Rabbit is to provide high performance in software, however it is also found to be very fast and efficient in hardware implementation.

Grain

Grain was designed by Martin Hell et al. in 2005, especially for those hardware environments having limited power, memory and gate count (M.Hell et al., 2005). It is a synchronous stream cipher based on two shift register- Linear Feedback Shift Registers (LFSR) and Non-Linear Feedback Shift Registers (NLFSR). A minimum period of key stream to provide balanced output is obtained by LFSR and nonlinearity to the cipher is achieved by the use of NLFSR together with a nonlinear output function. It provides higher security in hardware environment compare to the other stream cipher designed prior to Grain.

Trivium

Trivium is another synchronous stream cipher designed by Christophe De Canniere and Bart Preneel in 2005. It uses 80 bits Initialisation Vector (IV) and 288 bits secret state consisting three interconnected NLFSR of length 93, 84 and 111 respectively. It was designed for hardware constrained devices to achieve high throughput (Canniere et al., 2005).

MICKEY

Mickey stands for Mutual Irregular Clocking KEYstream generator was developed by Steve Babbage and Matthew Dodd in 2008 (Babbage et al., 2008). MICKEY was designed to achieve low complexity and high security. It has two variants – MICKEY and MICKEY 128. Both the variants take two inputs as parameter – 80/128-bit secret key and Initialisation vector of length between 0 to 80/128 bit. Two registers R and S are used for keystream generator that works in a non-linear fashion with the control variables (input bit R, input bit S, control bit R and control bit S). The keystream generated by the registers are used to produce cipher text by performing bitwise XOR operation with plaintext. By the use of non-linear loading mechanism MICKEY provides protection against the resynchronisation attacks.

Salsa20 and Chacha

Salsa20 and Chacha are the stream ciphers introduced by Daniel J. Bernstein in the year 2005 and 2008 respectively (Bernstein, 2005, 2008). Chacha is designed as a modified version of Salsa20 to achieve better performance by increasing diffusion in each round. Both the ciphers use pseudorandom function to perform ARX (Add-Rotate-XOR) operations. The function in both the ciphers can map 256 bit key, 64 bit counter and 64 bit nonce to a 512 bit block of key stream which provide an additional advantages to the user to opt for any position in the key stream at constant time.

Snow3G

SNOW 3G is a stream cipher that acts as a core part of the 3GPP system's security architecture (Orhanou et al., 2010). The standardised algorithms (UEA2 & UIA2) of the system is based on SNOW 3G stream cipher. This stream cipher is word oriented where a 32-bit word sequence is generated with 128-bit key and 128-bit IV (Initialisation Vector) which is used to mask plaintext. It consists of both FSM (Finite State Machine) and LFSR. LFSR is used to fetch the next state of the FSM. It is used for UMTS (Universal Mobile Telecommunication System).

Plantlet

Plantlet is a ultra-lightweight stream cipher introduced by Mikhalev, Armknecht and Müller in 2017 (Mikhaley et al. 2017). Like Grain it uses two registers- LFSR and NLFSR of size 40-bit and 61-bit respectively. The secret key and Initialization vector used by the cipher is of length 80-bit and 90-bit. Due to its novelty in design this cipher can provide security against the Time-Memory-Data trade-off attacks.

Espresso

The aim behind the designing of Espresso stream cipher (E. Dubrova et al., 2017) is to achieve both the optimal hardware size and speed to provide an enriched security level. This class of stream cipher utilizes the advantages of both the Galois Configured NLFSR and Fibonacci Configured NLFSR along with the short propagation delay. It is the fastest cipher among the other like Grain and Trivium and is designed especially for 5G wireless communication system.

Lizard

Lizard, a lightweight stream cipher is designed for the devices having limited power like RFID tags (Hamann et al. 2017). Lizards uses 120-bits key with 64-bit IVs and have 121 bit of inner state length. It provides 80-bit security against key recovery attacks and can generate 218 bits of keystream for each pair of IV which can be sufficient for many communication networks like WLAN, HTTPS, Bluetooth, etc.

Table 2. Lightweight stream ciphers

Name	Year	Key size (bits)	Gate Equivalents (GE)	Type of Register
A5/1	1987	64	923	LFSR
Rabbit	2003	128	3800,4100	LFSR+NLFSR
Grain	2005	80,128	1294,3239	LFSR+NLFSR
Trivium	2005	80	2580,4921	3-NLFSR
Salsa20	2005	128,256	12126	ARX
MICKEY	2008	80,128	3188,5039	LFSR+NLFSR
Chacha	2008	256	750	ARX
SNOW 3G	2010	128	-	LFSR+FSM
Plantlet	2016	80	928	LFSR+NLFSR
Espresso	2017	128	1500	Galois structure NLFSR
Lizard	2017	120	1161	NLFSR

LIGHTWEIGHT ASYMMETRIC KEY CRYPTOGRAPHY

Lightweight Asymmetric key cryptography, also known as public key cryptography is a cryptographic system where a pair of keys - public key and private key are used for encryption and decryption respectively. In a cryptographic system, some fundamental aspects are to provide like Confidentiality, Data Integrity, Data Authentication, Non-repudiation. Many cryptographic schemes were proposed and used for securing data - Public Key Cryptography (PKC) is one among them. The common public-key cryptosystems are RSA, Discrete Logarithm (DL) and Elliptic Curve Cryptography (ECC). In 1985, Victor Miller & Neal Koblitz proposed independently the concept of ECC (Miller,1985) (Koblitz,1985). The security level of a public-key cryptographic system lies to the hardness of the mathematical problem underlying the cryptographic algorithm. The commonly used public-key crypto-schemes provide their security using mathematical theories like Integer factorization problem (IFP), Discrete logarithm problem (DLP), Elliptic curve Diffie-Hellman (ECDH), Elliptic curve discrete logarithm problem (ECDLP), Elliptic curve digital signature algorithm (ECDSA) etc. The hardness of the integer factorization problem is essential for the security of RSA public-key encryption and signature schemes. Again, the security of ElGamal public-key encryption and signature schemes and their variants depends on the hardness of DLP. Elliptic curve cryptography security depends on the intractability of ECDLP which is another form of classic DLP. When selecting a family of public-key cryptosystem for an application we have to take some criteria in consideration. The basic ones are security and efficiency. It is known that the fastest algorithms known for solving integer factorization problem of RSA have sub-exponential expected running time. Again, in order to solve ECDLP, the known fastest algorithms have exponential expected running time. This advantage allows ECC to achieve the same level of security with smaller key sizes and higher computational efficiency. Again, the performance of the arithmetic operations of the public-key crypto algorithms directly depends upon the size of the keys. When typical RSA implementations employ 1024- or 2048-bit keys, for attaining same security by using ECC, it can be done by 160- and 224-bit keys successively. Thus, there are several public key algorithms has developed still date but the main aim is to use such type of cryptographic algorithm which will be lightweight for the resource constrained devices of Cloud-IoT and ECC prove to be one of them.

ELLIPTIC CURVE CRYPTOGRAPHY

An elliptic curve E over Fp (with prime characteristic p > 3) is the set of solutions (x, y) which satisfy the simplified form known as Short Weierstrass equation:

$$E : y2 = x3 + ax + b \, mod \, p$$

where a, b $\in$ Fp and $4a^3 + 27b^2 \neq 0$, The rational affine points on the curve and the point at infinity O form an abelian group. The point O is used as an identity element of the group. Thus, for every point P $\in$ E, P+O = O +P = P.

The ECDLP can be defined as:

Given an elliptic curve E defined over a finite field Fq, a point P $\in$ E(Fq) of order n, and a second point Q $\in$ $\langle$ P$\rangle$, determine the integer d such that Q = dP. The operation dP represents the addition (P+P+$\cdots$ (d −1) times). It is a one-way function, where forward computation, i.e., given d and P, the computation of Q = dP is easy. But the reverse problem is computationally hard. The ECDLP is the heart of elliptic curve cryptography. The security of an elliptic curve scheme is based on the difficulty to solve this problem.

For its shorter key size and faster field arithmetic operation ECC can be the ideal choice for implementing security in resource constrained device. There are huge works in Elliptic Curve Lightweight Cryptography (ECLC). Among several schemes, NANO ECC, Tiny ECC and MoTE ECC has been considered in this chapter for their efficiency.

NANO ECC

The scheme was proposed by Piotr Szczechowiak et.al in the year 2008. The design of the scheme has been made in such a manner that it becomes reasonably fast in ATmega328P at 16MHz (AVR, 2-cycle 8x8 bit multiply) with a very small key size. The Nano ECC has been designed for 8-bit microcontroller with ECDH and ECDSA in built in it (Szczechowiak et.al, 2008). There are more NIST certified elliptic curves. The NANO ECC are compatible with 4 types of elliptic curve, namely, secp128r1, secp192r1, secp256r1, and secp384r1. It has a large number of library functions in build in it. So, writing of ECC based program becomes very flexible. The main advantages are that it has no dynamic memory allocation and it resists side channel attack. Also, the speed is optimized in it.

Tiny ECC

A flexible, publicly available, configurable ECC based packaged namely Tiny ECC was introduced in 2008 (An Liu et. al., 2008). Speeding up the wireless sensor network, they have chosen Tiny OS as platform and the code has been written in nesC. The optimization process is done by using some conventional ECC process like Barrett Reduction, Hybrid Multiplication and Hybrid Squaring, using Projective Coordinates and finally introducing Sliding Window for Scalar Multiplication in Non-Adjacent Form(NAF). The algorithm is used in different WSNs like MICAz, TelosB, Tmote Sky and Imote2 .

MoTE ECC

ECC proves its efficiency in respect of its speed and its shorter key size. To standardized ECC, NIST recommends 15 elliptic curves in FIPS 186-4. Researchers have tried a lot to introduce many operations like scalar multiplication, point addition etc on different elliptic curves. Zhe Liu et al has considered Montgomery and Twisted Edward elliptic curve and has performed successive two scalar multiplications- first one on fixed base point to get key pair and second one to get input as arbitrary point to develop MoTE ECC (Zhe Liu et al.,2014) It is a scalable, efficient, Simple Power Analysis attack (SPA) resistant lightweight protocol that performs on ATmega 128. Considering the lower key size like 160,192,224 bits in Prime Field of Montgomery and Twisted Edward elliptic curve, MoTE ECC maintains security and lower execution time i.e., time, memory, power consumption.

LIGHTWEIGHT HASH FUNCTION

Lightweight Hash function is a new branch of lightweight cryptography that converts a message of arbitrary length into a fixed length message. The output message is called message digest. The computation associated with hash function includes MAC (Message Authentication Code), digital signature and data integrity. There are two parts of Hash function, one is Construction and other is Compression. To iterate compression, construction is designed. Several constructions like Sponge construction, Merkle Damgård, Davies-Mayer, and Haifa are designed and used in different hash function. The most common and notable hash functions are Quark, Keccak, PHOTON, SPONGENT, L-Hash, Hash-One, Neeva and ERNEST.

Quark

Quark, the first lightweight hash function (Aumasson, 2010) is based on sponge construction and is designed to minimize the memory using a single security level. There are three members in the family of Quark – U-Quark, D-Quark and T-Quark. The security provided by the three Quark are of 64-bit, 80-bit and 112-bit respectively. Quark is basically based on the stream cipher Grain and block cipher KATAN.

Keccak

Keccak is the best-known hash function that uses an innovative cryptographic permutation named Keccak-f permutation (Kavun et al., 2010). Keccak-f is the variant of SHA-3 hash function. Keccak is based on Sponge construction and is designed to achieve authentication as well as for pseudorandom number generation. Keccak was standardized for mobile communication (3GPP) and NIST standards (SP 800-185 & FIPS 202).

PHOTON

PHOTON is the smallest and compact lightweight hash function (Jian Guo et al., 2011). It uses sponge construction and AES as internal unkeyed permutation.

It is used for 64-bit to 128-bit collision resistance security and characterized as PHOTON- n/r/r`. The internal state size depends on the size of the hash output ranges between 64-bit to 256 bits. It covers a wide range of applications with its different flavours: PHOTON-80/20/16, PHOTON-128/16/16, PHOTON-160/36/36, PHOTON-224/32/32.

SPONGENT

A new member to the family of lightweight hash functions is the Spongent (Bogdanov et al., 2011). Following the strategy of Hermetic sponge strategy, Spongent is based on Sponge construction with PRESENT-type permutation. It required smallest GE (Gate Equivalent) implementation (738,1060,1329,1728 & 1950 GE) in ASCI and also produce smallest hash footprints in hardware compare to SHA-2, SHA-3, PRESENT and Quark. In terms of serialization and speed, Spongent provides lots of flexibility. It also proves to achieve high security levels against several dedicated attacks.

LHash

LHash is a new hash function (Wenling Wu et al., 2013) that supports three different sizes of message digest - 80 bits, 96 bits and 128 bits. To improve the diffusion speed, it uses Feistel- PG structure and required 989 GE and 1200 GE with 54 and 72 block cycles respectively. By adjusting its parameters, it provides a remarkable trade-off between cost, speed, security and energy consumption. It achieves a high margin of security against several well-known attacks.

Hash-One

Hash-One (Meghna Mukundan et al., 2016) was proposed to reduce hardware complexity and to achieve high standard security. It is based on sponge construction with permutation function that provides 80-bit security against generic attacks. The sponge construction produces 160 bits message digest and uses two NLFSRs to update its state.

Neeva

Neeva is the newest lightweight hash function, (Bussi et al., 2016), designed especially for RFID technology to provide effective cost and security. It is based on sponge construction and PRESENT block cipher. It also provides 112 bits collision resistance and faster than SPONGLET.

Ernest

Ernest was suggested in 2017 by Ernest Worthman, especially for IoE (Internet of Everything) devices. It is a new technology for next generation lightweight cryptography. It used binary code size, memory metrics and execution time as IoE primitives' driver (Ernest, 2017).

CRYPTANALYSIS

Different lightweight cryptographic algorithms have been discussed earlier. The main challenges in lightweight schemes is to maintain balance between the performance of low constrained devices and its security. In the next section, different cryptographic attacks have been discussed in short and have considered how the attacks are performed on different lightweight cryptographic systems.

Side-Channel Attack

When the information is retrieved from the encryption device in the form of power consumption statistics, electromagnetic radiation, sound wave even in the form of timing information, the attacks are named as Side-Channel attack. The attacker can reveal the information using those data used in the cryptographic devices.

Linear and Differential Key Attack

Linear key attack is a type of theoretical attack where the approximation of result is done by the action of a block cipher. (Matsui,1993). By this approach, the attacker finds a linear approximation between the elements used in plaintext and ciphertext. Let, the ciphertext and plaintext be denoted as C and P, if C=f(P), the intruder performs a linear approximation of the function f by doing a chain of binary XOR operation over bits used in plaintext and ciphertext and get the result.

The Differential key attack is nothing but a type of chosen-plaintext attack (Biham and Shamir,1990), i.e., The cipher text and its corresponding plaintext can be accessible by the attacker.It is similar to linear cryptanalysis: at first it maps bitwise difference in inputs to difference in outputs in order to reverse engineer the action. Finally, it predicts the high probability of certain occurrences of differences in plaintext and consequently the differences into the cipher. Let a cryptosystem having input $X=[X_1,X_2,.....X_n]$ and output $Y=[Y_1,Y_2,.....Y_n]$. Also let 2 inputs to the system be X' and X'' having corresponding output Y' and Y'' respectively. Now, finding out the input difference (say ΔX) and output difference (say ΔY) by doing

XOR operation over system input and system output, the pair $(\Delta X, \Delta Y)$ bring out the probability of occurrence of key structure. For a particular input difference ΔX, the particular output difference ΔY occurs with a probability $1/2^n$, where n is the no. of bits in X.

Meet –in-the-Middle (MITM) Attack

MITM is a type of passive known plaintext attack (Diffie & Hellman, 1977) performed on block cipher. The intruder applies some kind of space or time tradeoff during this attack. At first, the introducer applies brute force process over both ciphertext and plaintext. The attacker then performs encryption on plaintext to get an intermediate ciphertext. Simultaneously, he applies decryption algorithm over the ciphertext. Comparing the intermediate ciphertext with the plaintext getting from encryption and matching, there is a high probability to gain access to the data.

Two algorithms used in the MITM attack can be constructed using two simpler encryption and decryption algorithms:

Let C be the ciphertext, P be the plaintext, E and D represents Encryption and Decryption algorithm, Kx,Ky be two secret keys,

C=Ey(Ky,Ex(Kx,P)) and P=Dx(Kx,Dy(Ky,C)) and equation for the cipher be Dy(Ky,C)=Ex(Kx,P). At first, calculate Ex(Kx,P) & keep in a table in a sorted manner for easier searching.

Later, calculate Dy(Ky,P) & compare the result with earlier value kept in the table. Attacker find the value of Kx & Ky when Ex(Kx,P) and Dy(Ky,P) is same.

Biclique Attack

A Biclique attack is atype of MITM attack performed on full AES (Bogdanov, 2011). At first, all sorts of possible secret keys are separated into a set of groups of keys. Then, a bipartile graph for each group of keys is formed. Performing partial matching for eliminating the wrong key from the graph, get the candidate keys for the corresponding correct keys. Finally, atrue pair of (plaintext, ciphertext) is applied to find out the original key.

Related Key Attack & Rectangle Attack

The Related key model was proposed by Biham in 1994. The attacker is given access to encrypt for finding out the relation between the multiple unknown keys. This model seems to be very strong to attack. It is a type of differential attack. Later treating two short differentials instead of one long differentials, the attack was renamed as amplified boomerang or Rectangle attack (Bihan, Dunkelman and Nathan Keller, 2001)

Denial of Service (DoS) Attack

By damaging or shutting down the network connection and making unavoidable to the user, DoS attack cause a serious problem to the sensor-based network. In this attack, the intruder sends a huge request. As a result, the target network has flooded with traffic or crash the service.

Davies-Murphy Attack

Davies –Murphy attack is a type of linear attack performed on DES (Davies, Murphy,1993). For a known set of possible distribution over a key k and performing odd/even round XOR-operation over S-boxes, may reveal the key bits.

Cube Attack

In some stream cipher, it is not an easy task to attend the cipher by using low degree maxterm. Generally, the cryptographic polynomial can be expressed as tweakable polynomial over GF (2) having plaintext and ciphertext as variable. The Cube attack was proposed over the tweakable polynomial by considering some arbitrary values of the secret variables (Dinur & Shamir, 2009). By changing the value of these tweakable variables, the intruder can get different closely related polynomial equations. Considering the random master polynomial and eliminating the provable high probability based non-linear terms, the n linear equations can be solved by n^2 bit operations for n variables.

Saturation Attack

It is a type of chosen-plaintext attack and it can be extended to known-plaintext attack (Hwang, 2002). In this cryptanalysis, the attacker considers the whole group of plaintexts and applies the algorithm to break the cipher. As a result, the intruder gets information from the cipher (S-boxes).

Black-Hole Attack

In wireless mobile ad-hoc network (MANET), there are numerous routing protocols like proactive, reactive and hybrid routing protocols. In a MANET, the source node finds and sends message to the destination node through the shortest path. During this finding process, let the attacker placed as misbehaviour node (suspected) on the transmission path and makes a false response that the node has the shortest path to the destination node. Thus, considering the shortest path erroneously, the source node sends data packet to the destination node through the suspected node. As a result, the malicious node drops the packets. This type of attack is called black hole attack in MANET.

Flood Rushing Attack

In this attack, the intruder uses a fake node in the network and make realise the target node as a genuine node. The attacker then sends a flood of packet through this fake node. Thus, discarding the legitimate security link and adopting the adversarial route, the attackers flood the network.

Sybil Attack

The sybil attack is seen in peer to peer network (Douceur,2002). Considering the many identifies and using them in routing algorithm as original nodes with other nodes, the attacker disrupts the network. The intruder's aim is to make influence over the network and to perform some illegal operations related to the rules of the networking system by creating multiple fake identities (like user accounts, IP address-based accounts etc,). The other original node considers these fake identities as real unique identities. Thus, creating additional entity with misbehaving node, the network system gets collapsed.

TMDTO Attack

Time-Memory Data Trade-off attack was performed on stream cipher (Hellman,1980). The idea of the attack can be stated as: consider a stream cipher having search space $N=2^n$ (n is the size of the bits), now the internal state of cipher can be recovered using TMDTO attack by using the condition satisfies $TM^2D^2=N^2$, where T be the time complexity, M be the required memory, D be the amount of data available online. To avoid this attack, stream cipher should be designed in such a manner that the size of the state is more than twice of the size of the secret key.

Though there are many cryptanalysis processes on different lightweight schemes, very few has been considered for this chapter. The attack operations performed on different lightweight schemes (already discussed earlier) will be analysed in this section:

Though there are some attacks on cryptographic hash function like Collision attack, Birthday attack but still, hash function is more secured. Again, Differential

Table 3. Different attacks on block ciphers

Name of the Block cipher	Name of the attacks
RC5	Differential attack
TEA	Related Key attack
XTEA	Cube attack
AES	Man-in-the-Middle attack
DESL	Davies-Murphy attack
PRESENT	Differential attack
KATAN & KTANTAN	Meet-in-the Middle attack
Hummingbird	Differential attack
TWINE	Differential attack
KLEIN	Biclique attack
PRINCE	Related Key attack
RECTANGLE	Rectangle attack
Midori	Biclique attack
ANU	No attack till date
SFN	Related key attack

Table 4. Different attacks on stream ciphers

Name of the Block cipher	Name of the attacks
A 5/1	TMDTO attack
Rabbit	Saturation attack
Grain	Linear attack, Cube attack
Trivium	Differential attack
MICKEY	Differential attack
Chacha	Differential attack
Snow3G	Multiset
Plantlet	TMDTO attack
Espresso	Related key attack
Lizard	TMDTO attack
Fruit	Secured

Power analysis attack or Fault tolerance attack effect ECC, but for lightweight schemes ECC could be the better choice for its lower key size and faster operation.

Apart from these cryptographic attack on lightweight schemes, there are some attacks on different layers of network like physical layer, data link layer, network layer of a lightweight device. The attacks like Flood Rushing attack, Sybil attack, Blackhole attack, Denial of Service etc. affects a lot for a constrained device.

FUTURE DIRECTIONS AND CONCLUSION

Lightweight cryptographic algorithms have been developed for resource constrained IoT devices. Not only the description of different schemes, their analysis in respect of round, key-size and cryptanalytic attacks on different schemes have been analysed in this chapter. There is a scope of significant improvement in terms of optimizing computational cost, memory space & reducing power consumption. The act of reducing the chip area and block size, minimizing the key size and simplifying the construction of cipher may be the future challenge of stream and block cipher. In case of ECC, the researcher should concentrate on improvement of key execution time by optimizing field operation. The needs of designing new lightweight schemes in respect of latency and chip area, has opened a new dimension in the field. After solving basic shortcomings of different lightweight schemes in constrained devices, the researchers will start to go deeper into the cloud based IoT Lightweight cryptographic schemes and will provide a highly secure cloud based IoT framework.

REFERENCES

Aumasson, J.-P., Henzen, L., Meier, W., & Naya-Plasencia, M. (2010). Quark: A lightweight hash. In *International Workshop on Cryptographic Hardware and Embedded Systems* (pp. 1–15). Springer.

Babbage, S., & Dodd, M. (2008). The MICKEY stream ciphers. In *Proceeding of New Stream Cipher Designs* (pp. 191–209). Springer. doi:10.1007/978-3-540-68351-3_15

Banik, S., Bogdanov, A., Isobe, T., Shibutani, K., Hiwatari, H., & Akishita, T. (2015). *Midori: A block cipher for low energy*. Springer.

Bansod, G., Patil, A., Sutar, S., & Pisharoty, N. (2016). ANU: An ultra-lightweight cipher design for security in IoT. *Security and Communication Networks*, *9*(18), 5238–5251. doi:10.1002ec.1692

Barkan, E. (2006). *Eli Biham, Adi Shamir, Rigorous Bounds on Cryptanalytic Time/ Memory Tradeoffs, Advances in Cryptology, proceedings of Crypto 2006* (Vol. 4117). Lecture Notes in Computer Science. Springer-Verlag.

Bernstein, D. J. (2005). The Salsa20 stream cipher, slides of talk. In *ECRYPT STVL Workshop on Symmetric Key Encryption*. http://cr.yp.to/talks .html#2005.05.26

Bernstein, D. J. (2008). *ChaCha, a variant of Salsa20*. http://cr.yp.to/paper s.html#chach

Biham, E. (1994). New types of cryptanalytic attacks using related keys. *Journal of Cryptology*, 7(4), 229–246. doi:10.1007/BF00203965

Biham, E., Dunkelman, O., & Keller, N. (2001). The Rectangle Attack – Rectangling the Serpent. In *Advances in Cryptology, Proceedings of EUROCRYPT 2001*. Innsbruck: Springer-Verlag. 10.1007/3-540-44987-6_21

Biryukov, A. (2006). *Improved Time-Memory Tradeoffs with Multiple Data. In* Lecture Notes in Computer Science: Vol. 3897. *Proceedings of Selected Areas in Cryptography 2005*. Springer-Verlag.

Biryukov, A., Shamir, A., & Wagner, D. (2001). *Real time cryptanalysis of A5, 1 on a PC, Fast Software Encryption (FSE), LNCS* (Vol. 1978). Springer.

Boesgaard, M., Vesterager, M., Pedersen, T., Christiansenm, J., & Scavenius, O. (2003). *Rabbit: A new high-performance stream cipher, FSE, LNCS* (Vol. 2887). Springer.

Bogdanov, A., Knudsen, L. R., Leander, G., Paar, C., Poschmann, A., Robshaw, M. J. B., Seurin, Y., & Vikkelsoe, C. (2007). PRESENT: An ultra-lightweight block cipher. In Proceeding of Cryptographic Hardware and Embedded Systems—CHES 2007 (pp. 450–466). Springer.

Borghoff, J., Canteaut, A., Güneysu, T., Kavun, E. B., Knezevic, M., Knudsen, L. R., Leander, G., Nikov, V., Paar, C., Rechberger, C., Rombouts, P., Thomsen, S. S., & Yalçın, T. (2012). PRINCE—A low-latency block cipher for pervasive computing applications. In *Proceeding of ASIACRYPT 2012* (pp. 208–225). Springer. 10.1007/978-3-642-34961-4_14

Bussi, K., Dey, D., Kumar, M., & Dass, B. K. (2016). Neeva: A Lightweight Hash Function. *IACR Cryptology ePrint Archive*, (42). https://eprin t.iacr.org/2016/042

Davies, D., & Murphy, S. (1993). Pairs and Triplets of DES S-boxes. *Journal of Cryptology*, 8(1), 1–25.

De Cannie're, C., & Preneel, B. (2005). Trivium—A stream cipher construction inspired by block cipher design principles. *ECRYPT Stream Cipher*. http://www. ecrypt.eu.org/strea m/paper sdir/2006/021.pdf

De Canniere, C., Dunkelman, O., & Kneževi'c, M. (2009). KATAN and KTANTAN—a family of small and efficient hardware-oriented block ciphers. In *International Workshop on Cryptographic Hardware and Embedded Systems* (pp. 272–288). Springer. 10.1007/978-3-642-04138-9_20

Diffie, W., & Hellman, M. E. (1977, June). Exhaustive Cryptanalysis of the NBS Data Encryption Standard. *Computer, 10*(6), 74–84. doi:10.1109/C-M.1977.217750

Dinur, I., & Shamir, A. (2009). *Cube Attacks on Tweakable Black Box Polynomials*. Cryptology ePrint Archive. ePrint 20090126:174453.

Douceur, J. R. (2002). The Sybil Attack. In P. Druschel, F. Kaashoek, & A. Rowstron (Eds.), Lecture Notes in Computer Science: Vol. 2429. *Peer-to-Peer Systems. IPTPS 2002*. Springer. doi:10.1007/3-540-45748-8_24

Dubrova, E., & Hell, M. (2017). Espresso: A stream cipher for 5G wireless communication systems. *Journal of Cryptography and Communication, 9*(2), 273–289. doi:10.100712095-015-0173-2

Engels, D., Fan, X., Gong, G., Hu, H., & Smith, E. M. (2010). Hummingbird: ultra-lightweight cryptography for resource-constrained devices. In Financial Cryptography and Data Security—FC 2010, LNCS, 6054 (pp. 3–18). Springer. doi:10.1007/978-3-642-14992-4_2

Ernest, W. (2017). *Light primitives and new technologies are driving the next generation of lightweight cryptography*. https://semiengineering.com/lightweight-cryptography-for-the-ioe/

Gong, Z., Nikova, S., & Law, Y. W. (2012). *KLEIN: A new family of lightweight block ciphers*. doi:10.1007/978-3-642-25286-0_1

Guo, J., Peyrin, T., & Poschmann, A. (2011). *The PHOTON family of lightweight hash functions, CRYPTO 2011, LNCS 6841*. International Association for Cryptologic Research.

Hamann, M., Krause, M., & Meier, W. (2017). LIZARD—A lightweight stream cipher for power constrained devices. *IACR Transmission Symmetric Cryptology, 1*, 45–79. doi:10.46586/tosc.v2017.i1.45-79

Hell, M., Johansson, T., & Meier, W. (2005). *Grain—A stream cipher for constrained environments*. In Workshop on RFID and Light-Weight Crypto: Workshop Record, Graz, Austria.

Hwang, K. (2002). Saturation Attacks on Reduced Round Skipjack. In J. Daemen & V. Rijmen (Eds.), *FSE 2002. LNCS* (Vol. 2365, pp. 100–111). Springer.

Kavun, E. B., & Yalcin, T. (2010). A lightweight implementation of keccak hash function for radiofrequency identification applications. In *International Workshop on Radio Frequency Identification: Security and Privacy Issues* (pp. 258–269). Springer.

Koblitz, N. (1985). Elliptic Curve Cryptosystem. *Mathematics of Computation*, *48*, 203–209.

Leander, G., Paar, C., Poschmann, A., & Schramm, K. (2007). New lightweight DES variants. In A. Biryukov (Ed.), *The 14th Annual Fast Software Encryption Workshop—FSE 2007, LNCS 4593* (pp. 196–210). Berlin: Springer-Verlag.

Li, L., Liu, B., Zhou, Y., & Zou, Y. (2018). SFN: A new lightweight block cipher. *Microprocessors and Microsystems*, *60*, 138–150.

Liu, Z., Wenger, E., & Großschädl, J. (2014). MoTE-ECC: Energy-Scalable Elliptic Curve Cryptography for Wireless Sensor Networks. In *Applied Cryptography and Network Security - 12th International Conference, ACNS 2014, Lausanne, Switzerland, June 10-13, 2014. Proceedings* (pp. 361-379). Springer.

Liu & Ning. (2008). Tinyecc: A configurable library for elliptic curve cryptography in wireless sensor networks. In *Information Processing in Sensor Networks, 2008. IPSN'08. International Conference on*. IEEE.

Martin, E. (1980). Hellman, A Cryptanalytic Time-Memory Tradeoff. *IEEE Transactions on Information Theory*, *26*(4), 401–406.

Mikhalev, V., Armknecht, F., & Muller, C. (2017). On ciphers that continuously access the non-volatile key. *IACR Transmission Symmetric Cryptology, 2*, 52–79. doi:10.13154 /tosc.v2016.i2.52-79

Miller. (1986). Use of elliptic curves in cryptography. In *Advances in Cryptology, Proceedings of Crypto'85, LNCS, 218*. Springer Verlag.

Mukundan, P. M., Manayankath, S., Srinivasan, C., & Sethumadhavan, M. (2016). Hash-One: A lightweight cryptographic hash function. *IET Information Security*, *10*(5), 225–231.

Orhanou, G., Hajji, S. E., & Bentalab, Y. (2010). SNOW 3G stream Cipher operation and complexity study. *Contemporary Engineering Sciences*, *3*(3), 97–111.

Proceeding of RFIDSec. (2011). Springer.

Rivest, R. L. (1994). The RC5 Encryption Algorithm. *Proceedings of the Second International Workshop on Fast Software Encryption (FSE)*, 86–96.

SPONGENT. (2011). *A lightweight hash function, CHES*. International Association for Cryptologic Research.

Suzaki, T., Minematsu, K., Morioka, S., & Kobayashi, E. (2011). TWINE: A lightweight, versatile block cipher. In *Proceeding of ECRYPT Workshop on Lightweight Cryptography 2011* (pp. 146–169). Academic Press.

Wenling, W., Shuang, W., Zhang, L., Zou, J., & Dong, L. (2013). *LHash: A lightweight hash function (full version)*. https://eprin t.iacr.org/2013/867

Wheeler, D. J., & Needham, R. M. (1994). TEA, a tiny encryption algorithm. In *Proceeding of international workshop on fast software encryption* (pp. 363–366). Berlin: Springer.

Zenner, E. (2008). *The eSTREAM Project - eSTREAM Phase 3 "Intellectual Property: Rabbit has been released into the public domain and may be used freely for any purpose"*. Academic Press.

Zhang, W., Bao, Z., Lin, D., Rijmen, V., Yang, B., & Verbauwhede, I. (2014). RECTANGLE: A bit-slice ultra-lightweight block cipher suitable for multiple platform. *Science China. Information Sciences*, *58*(12), 1–15.

ADDITIONAL READING

National Institute of Standards and Technology (NIST). (2001). Advanced Encryption Standard (AES). Federal information processing standards publication 197, November 26. http://csrc.nist. gov/publicatio ns/fips/fips1 97/fips-197.pdf

KEY TERMS AND DEFINITIONS

Cryptanalysis: Is the study of investigating a cryptosystem to find out the weakness of the system through mathematical approach. The process is done by without knowing the structure of key.

Gate Equivalent (GE): A unit of measure that specify manufacturing-technology-independent complexity of digital circuits. In lightweight cryptography GE means physical area of a single NAND gate used in different CMOS technologies.

Initialization Vector (IV): A random number used to encrypt data along with a secret key. It is also called nonce – "number occurring once" that can be used only once in an encryption process.

Key Length: The key size or key length represents the number of bits used in a cryptographic algorithm. It is an important factor to both symmetric and asymmetric algorithm.

Message Digest: A unique value generated by cryptographic hash function from data and unique symmetric key.

Prime Factorization: The process for finding the prime number multiply together to get the given (original) number. As for example, let the given number be 21, then the prime factors of 21 are 3 & 7, as 3 & 7 are prime numbers.

Chapter 11
Monitoring and Detecting Plant Diseases Using Cloud–Based Internet of Things

Taranjeet Singh
IFTM University, India

Devendra Singh
IFTM University, India

S. S. Bedi
Mahatma Jyotiba Phule Rohilkhand University, India

ABSTRACT

A device composed of actuators is the internet of things. The internet of things (IoT) should be used for enhancing agricultural efficiency in precision agriculture. The bedrock of the Indian economy, agriculture, is adding to the country's total economic performance. Nevertheless, the efficiency contrasts with world norms. Regardless of the usage of minimum agricultural advancements and farmers from villages today for other productive enterprises, regions move to a metropolitan region, and they cannot rely on agriculture. Farming creativity is not new, but smart farming is expected to be pushed to the following internet level by IoT, a unit made up of actuators or sensors. This chapter demonstrates IoT's role in agriculture and its use in identifying plant diseases through leaf images. Several researchers' works in the domain are also outlined, and future perspectives of IoT in recognizing plant diseases are discussed briefly.

DOI: 10.4018/978-1-7998-6981-8.ch011

INTRODUCTION

India is predominantly a nation of agriculture. More than 60% of the Land area in India is used for agriculture in terms of overall agricultural space, and it is the second-most populous country. Farmers adopt conventional methods such as manual field inspection, which requires regular irrigation of crops and applying pesticides with or without knowledge of the volume of pesticides to be added to combat pests, Ferentinos (2018). There are risks of these conventional methods, such as waterlogging in fields, improper pesticide use, fungicides, lack of knowledge about the variety of crops cultivated for a specific type of land. Low-quality Production, lack of soil fertility, and predicted output from agricultural land are the consequences of these disadvantages.

In comparison, a recently created service such as Cloud-IoT allows a free online service that helps the remotely installed sensors to be plugged and played. As farmers have begun to implement innovative farming strategies that have resulted in increased crop yields, developments in agricultural methods have rendered it relatively straightforward. Previous processes were time-consuming, expensive, and needed more labor, but it is clear to execute multiple activities now in no time, Singh et al.(2021). Earlier diagnosis of the disease was entirely based on conventional techniques as farmers used their expertise and employed a professional to diagnose signs to locate the condition and take some required preventive steps. The traditional approach has various disadvantages as it relies on the expert's eyesight, has been very time-consuming, slow, labor-intensive, and loses accuracy Singh et al.(2020). Therefore, it is necessary to substitute manual techniques for detecting diseases with automatic techniques since one of the critical issues is the consistency and protection of agricultural products. Seeing conditions at their earlier stages is very significant since their spread can be easily managed without hindering crop quality and productivity, Singh et al.(2020). This chapter introduces diverse methods for the identification of diseases suggested by scholars from all around the world.

Background

IoT blueprints demonstrated the potential to blast the mind in certain headways in farm spaces and the continuous illustration of plant precision. Air sensors, earth sensors, radiation sensors, atmosphere stations stress that data sources are almost sensors and sensors protected and used for inspection, data excavation, and monitoring. The IoT advancement community offers all the necessary resources for building and sustaining those foundations and administrations specifically designed to assist supply chains in the agricultural sectors. In recent decades, sensors have been widely used in horticulture, such as wired and remote sensors, Baranwal et al.(2019), Jogin et al.

(2018), Abdullahi et al. (2017), and Alfarisy et al. (2018). It is urgent to detect the soil in which processing occurs and the crops' chemical reactions to the environment to make the correct and progressively specific choices to streamline farmers' viability and nature. Gadgets with solid computing capabilities, an extraordinarily beneficial structural aspect, and ease will now be used on batteries and operate with large batches with the aid assistance of strength selection units. What is more, today's embedded gadgets have sufficient resources for serving multiple varieties of sensors and the service of increasingly modern computer management protocols to extend traditional system administration functionality, Singh et al.(2019); Mohan et al. (2016), Shin et al. (2016) and Hershey et al. (2017).

The most extreme requirement for farmers and farming specialists is to identify diseases in the plant. With the assistance of IoT, the goal of the system will be to identify plant diseases. The illness on plant leaves starts in the more significant portion of the plants. Researchers also consequently considered plant diseases, especially on plates, in the proposed work Shrivastava et al. (2019). Depending on the Variation of temperature, humidity, and shading, the differentiation of healthy and diseased plant leaves could be calculated. The pigments in the leaves are responsible for the striking variations in shading in the autumn. In the autumn, temperature, sunshine, and soil humidity expect a job in how the leaves would appear. Rich sunshine and low temperatures allow the chlorophyll to be demolished more quickly after the abscission layer frameworks. Some researchers used a temperature sensor named DHT11, Usman et al. (2020).

The DHT11 sensors were used for the detection of the temperature of the leaf. Sensors obtained from the sensor are transmitted via the Arduino board's Wi-Fi connection to the cloud level. Initially, we record the temperature of a plate. After that, the leaf is unsafe if the leaf's temperature does not drop to that level.

A common sign of plant disease is variations in the shade of plant tissue. The yellowing or browning of green cells and tissue attributable to chlorophyll's loss is routinely realized through these shading shifts. It is possible to total or halfway through such leaf shading suppression. Another parameter used to assess if the leaf is either diseased or stable is the shading sensor, which detects the leaf's shade under consideration, Rao et al.(2020).

The sensor is a practical knowledge acquisition invention, mainly used to capture, relate and synchronize any portion of current information, analyze them, and eventually render a responsive movement without consumer mediation. The (remote) detection center parts contain the following: Detection and citation of equipment (single component or exhibit), preparation device, communications unit, monitoring unit and other equipment -subordinate schemes as essential point components, sensors may be multi-point location clusters and have the potential to

Figure 1. Process of plant disease identification

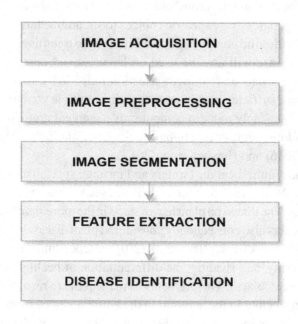

coordinate enormous sizes, low assistance, flexibility for scale, mobility for different environments. Figure 1 displays the process of disease identification.

MAIN FOCUS OF THE CHAPTER

Issues, Controversies, Problems, Solutions, and Recommendations

Farmers' problems are accessibility of labor, their standards, their expertise, and expenditure in the capital (seeds, fertilizers, chemicals, machinery, etc.) are some of the problems that farmers face while employed in the fields. Several researchers highlighted the challenges faced by farmers, Pavel et al. (2019); Memberg et al. (1999); and Kimiti et al.(, 2009). The challenges experienced by practitioners are discussed below:

- **Inadequate knowledge** - Farmers in India do not know today to change the way they cultivate. The methods and techniques used to grow crops successfully and commercially are not up-to-date.

- **Inadequate infrastructure** - Almost 70% of the property does not have irrigation. The accessibility of roads to agricultural industries and markets is weak. Farmers, therefore, have to struggle to reach markets to offer their products through other routes (like rivers). There are fewer agro-processing units, so without adding value, large amounts of crops have to be sold, and farmers won't wait for decent offers to sell their produce. It is challenging to locate the land study's specifics, fertilizer usefulness, bad insecticide results, etc., and often not necessary.
- **Lack of financial options-** like liability control or solutions for insurers. A productive yet minimal phase in this path is the establishment of minimum rates.
- **Adopting modern mechanisms** - Owing to lower availability, most farmers will not embrace mechanization. Most producers hold a relatively limited agricultural holding. Thus, for guiding the machines in the fields, the land scale is a restriction. In the case of machinery failure, help points are far off the field, and they must transport their vehicles for the operation to distant areas. This helps them to borrow enormous capital from unorganized businesses. Further adding to their dilemma is the absence of self-sustainable business model insurance cover.

Pavel et al. (2019) suggest IoT allows devices that submit Real-time atmosphere details to the servers and the plant picture Leaf for disease classification using image analysis and multiclass processing Vector machine help. The proposed model is defined in Figure2. A. Module and Structure of Device We also built a methodology for constructing this framework. Compact device storing the planned framework in a compact system Way Composed. The DHT22 biological air sensor, Parameters such as air temperature and dampness are measured. Also, for soil conditions, the basic pH meter of gravity is used to extract the topsoil's pH. Apart from that, the Grove dampness has been composed. In specific, this gadget provides steady parameters to the Arduino in a particular period. Along with these, Data, the parameters also provide image details as we have Set up a camera with a Raspberry Pi on the computer. Handling Photo A system has been introduced to identify the leaf of the plant An disease by taking an image and analyzing it. All the details in a packet form were assembled. Correspondence with computers The Wi-Fi module worked was finished using the Framboise pi. All the sensor parameters are submitted using methods. Recalling that, the sum of the overall system was reduced to such a whole; to pull it up, it ended up being particularly wise. Even the computer, the primary interface, has been organized to be included in General to install and be conveniently introduced by everyone. The Raspberry Pi 3 wireless system is designed based on The IoT definition.

- **Detection and assessment of Plant Disease** Camera detection have been introduced to predict and preprocess images. In this phase, four activities are performed: the acquisition of photographs and Preprocessing, impacted area segmentation, feature Extraction, and grouping utilizing a vector of multiclass help algorithm for the computer.
- **Data Acquisition and Preprocessing Image:** Authors have collected multiple images available online. Images consisted of Bacterial blight, Anthracnose, Cercospora Leaf disease, Alternaria alternata, and leaf diseases from Tomatoes, cucumbers, and eggplants. There are 50 photos here. Twenty-five photos are for training for each dataset, and among those and 25 of them are for study. Those images would be preprocessed to Decreases difficulty in segmentation and Extraction of functionality. The mean filter in which each pixel value has substituted A picture with its neighbors' median value, including It, is used to minimize noise. The 5x5 kernel used here Delete noise and light-smooth image, which does both. The picture is then resized, and the contrast is 256x256. They are improved to sharpen it.
- **Segmentation:** For performing segmentation of leaves' diseased regions, color-based k-mean clustering segmentation algorithm is implemented, which Returns to three clusters designed based on Variation of tone. Firstly, the RGB image of the source is translated. Into the color space of L*a*b* where L is luminosity, a* and a* and B* are chromaticity-layers that refer to the color decrease together with the red-green axes, and the axes are blue, yellow. Accurately allocates n experiences to one of the k clusters of centroids characterized to execute the This algorithm partitions the data and segmentation. It tests the average per cluster and sets each collection of points to the nearest one Computing Euclidean interval squared. The algorithm Classifies the*b* colors and marks each pixel from the pixel A k-mean result. Therefore, the development of clustered photos

Segmented from the main picture, which distinguishes the Sections of the leaf are influenced and unchanged.

- **Extraction of Features:** After segmentation of the features based on color, texture and shape are then removed from the affected section.
- **Grouping using Vector Multi-Class Help Computer:** Supports a kernel-based vector machine (SVM) algorithm for supervised learning constructs a hyper A high- or infinite-dimensional plane or group of hyperplanes Space and can be used to distinguish. SVMs, the kernel trick is applied to create a transformation by which The optimal boundaries can be established between the potential exits. Outputs. The multiclass SVM is used in our situation. We

are classifying the pathogens of plants. From a finite range, it draws labels of multiple components. "Here, the "one against the other" solution "One" is used to translate binary classification into multiclass classification. It produces n*(n-1)/2 times if There are n classes for a multiclass problem. Of these is he was educated in two schools. The primary aim of SVM is to Indicate the class by drawing of each plant disease belonging to between data sets, hyperplanes. Based on the extracted details, Features, we are educated in the dataset. Applied and introduced the dataset checking for grouping. Getting sensors operated by the IoT and Raspberry Pi help one examine the disease and well-being of plants. Besides, regardless of the adequate knowledge, we can get, we can assemble and process effectively and observe the classification with a 97.33 percent precision.

The article by Thorat et al. (2017) introduces IoT techniques to incorporate technology in Cultivation. The paper contains various features, such as leaf disease identification, Remote management device focused on servers, humidity and Temperature detection, moisture detecting, soil, etc. It makes use of the Networks of sensors for the calculation of humidity, temperature, Instead of manual inspection and humidity. The various sensors monitor all these sensors, installed in different locations of farms. A single controller named Raspberry PI was used (RPI). Leaf Camera interfaces with RPI may diagnose illness. Instantaneous A farm's standing as a leaf disease and other environmental concerns Factors that control crops, such as humidity, temperature, and humidity, are Send the farmers using WIFI Server via RPI. Information obtained from sensors and Submit via wired or wireless devices to Raspberry Pi.

Data on the server-side is tested and balanced with data's ideal values, such as the importance of temperature, humidity, and soil moisture. If there were a variance concerning the predefined, the threshold value would then be submitted to the Farmer on his notice—mobile phones or blogs. Sensor performance is produced in the Farmer and webpage. Get accurate details regarding his crop and his environment from everywhere on a farm. By utilizing image recognition, crop disease identification is carried out. The camera is located next to the crop to take a shot of a weed from the camera. The recorded picture is submitted to and used by the cloud. Leaf disease image processing techniques are observed; status of on a web page & smartphone, a leaf is sent back to the Farmer on the app's phone.

- **Raspberry Pi-**One of the most common controllers in the industry is the Raspberry Pi. It is like a micro machine composed of a USB port and data output. Sticks, USB, HDMI, SD card scanner, and many more Increased accessibility. The Raspberry PI has a BCM2835 Broadcom on a chip (SoC),

Including an ARM1176JZFS processor with 700 MHz, Video. The core IV GPU and 256 megabytes of RAM were delivered, Upgraded later to 512 MB. It does not have a complicated built-in Disk or solid-state drive, except for booting and using an SDcard, Persistent warehousing. The Base supports Debian and Arch. Linux ARM Download Distributions. Available resources areas the strong programming language in Raspberry Pi for Python Panel. You may link various types of sensors together, input via entry; sensors are saved in raspberry pi from sensors. In this prototype, sensors using Python or Java programming requires python code for Raspberry Pi Installation:

(a)   Running the OS (Raspbian OS for Raspberry PI)

(b)   Installation of OpenCV for Editing Photographs

(c)   Installation of all the necessary camera drivers Raspberry pi Interfacing Sensors

(d)   Moisture of soil

(e)   Humidity and Temperature

(f)   USB port Video camera image

- Sensors-

1)   **Temperature & Moisture:** The DHT11 sensor in this device is used to determine temperature, including precipitation and temperature. This sensor is low-cost; it displays digital Production at the temperature and humidity terminals. It demonstrates success. The findings are about 20-80 percent humidity with 5 percent precision. 0-50 ° C temperature of $\pm$ 2 ° C specificity. Outcomes may become on in 2 seconds. DHT11 is connected to the Raspberry PI in this framework using the Connectors, and output is sent to the server on the server-side. The performance is saved in the database file and shown simultaneously on Mobile growers. Here are the DHT11 sensor and its Raspberry PI interface. The design of the circuit is given in figure 2 below.

2)   **Soil Humidity:** The soil's water content is determined by capacitance. This sensor has both analog and digital outputs. This works on the open circuit theory; if the surface is warm, then the current is wet. Pass to another terminal from one terminal, and the circuit Completes, thus showing low voltage benefit. When soil the present is a dry current that would not travel through the circuit, and The performance is then optimum and can operate as an open circuit. The Soil Moisture Sensor is platinum-coated, it's corrosion-prone, and the sensor has a long existence. The Soil Moisture sensor's performance is seen in this device on Mobile farmers by tapping on the Soil Status Bar. The soil humidity sensor is connected to the Raspberry PI utilizing a soil moisture sensor. Input

Performance pins for connectors and utilizing python programming Access is from raspberry PI. Whether the performance is vital or low, this output, shown on the terminal, is submitted to the server and processed. This results in a computer file and is also shown on farmers.

• Cellphone:

User Applications

1. The Method of Service: Raspbian is a free Raspberry operating system used by Huh. Pi. The installation guide for raspberry pi is available on the official webpage. The explanation why Raspbian was selected is Installing and running OpenCV is relatively straightforward in this regard. From the OS.
2. SERVER: To receive data and submit it, an Apache server is used to the page.
3. LANGUAGES USED: Python is a foundational language for programmers and processors. Arduino, Raspberry PI, etc. controls such as Both the photos Sensor-related encryption will be performed in this Tongue, language. It is simple to adapt this vocabulary Since it seems like simple C language coding.
    1) 3 Variants of the Python IDE were used on the framework.
4. OpenCV: It is a C++ library for editing images and Vision for machines.
5. PROCESSING Picture: The processing of photographs is the technique that processes the picture and the opportunity to search for something we like. Usage of different approaches included in OpenCV Masking, segmentation, and libraries, for example, Extraction of functions, etc.

The model proposed by Kajol et al. (2018) provides farmers with knowledge on the crop rotation method to promote multi-crop-based agriculture, increasing soil productivity and decreasing pests' impact on crops. This has encouraged us to prepare the Automated Agricultural Field Analysis and Monitoring System (AAFAMS) for growth, which tracks fields in an automated, cost-effective, and more innovative way to help farmers. AAFAMS is an idea for an agricultural robot to be built. It is a Line Follower robot that intelligently watches the ground. This will help track farmers' agricultural fields by identifying pests (if any), the amount of humidity in the soil, showing the appropriate pesticide relevant to the detected problems, and transmitting this information to the cloud for storage. It also uses an algorithm for image recognition to identify the existence of pests. The data is stored in the cloud, and the appropriate pesticides would be present if the pests are present. In the form of a report from an Android program, the processed details will be submitted to the Farmer. The images found in dropbox are later taken to find chemicals that need to be applied to avoid the crops' pests. Using android software, the Farmer is shown details on the condition of soil moisture, pests contained in crops, and the kind of pesticide to be used to prevent harm to crops caused by problems. A complete report of the information listed above will be included in the application. The circuit relationship in AAFAMS, as seen in Figure 2, is an array of IR sensors used to feel a black line for the robot to move along that line. The IC PCF8591P is used in the form of digital signals to take analog data from the soil moisture sensor and to provide the raspberry pi with input. Two ICs of the L293D are used for auto racing. For the power source, there is a battery in the robot. But encouraging natural resources to be used would be a better option.

So, the solar panels that store the sun's energy and sustain the work of AAFAMS are to be installed. The report created by an android application for five crops is manly. They are corn, eggplants, okra, onions, and soybeans. Details about using

Figure 2. Model Proposed by Thorat et al. (2017)

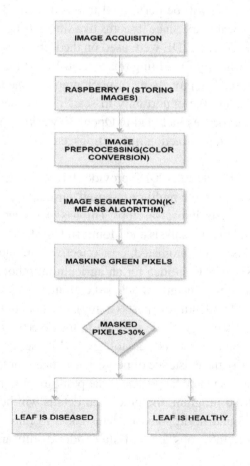

the software are given in the option called How to Use, and information regarding the AAFAMS device is provided in AAFAMS.

The month of the scheme is retrieved to get information about the varieties of best crops for the season. When the Fetch report alternative is selected for a particular crop, this information is acquired. After the report has been received, the pest images are downloaded from the dropbox cloud and stored in the android phone's internal storage in a folder labeled pests. The pictures of crops that are retrieved from the dropbox cloud may also be easily viewed. In the Previous Report substitute, the previously retrieved report is available—implementation Stage. Figure 2 outlines the model Proposed by Thorat et al. (2017)

There are four steps in the implementation phase:

Step 1: The IR proximity sensor array comprises five sensors, three of which are used for line detection and two at the end of the unit for barrier detection. In all three sensors, Raspberry Pi receives 0. If it senses a line, it receives 1. If all three sensor values are 0 if the left side sensor receives one and two other sensors receive 0, the robot goes forward if the left side sensor receives 0, so only the left wheels shift such that the system turns slightly left and changes itself to the line and continues in the same direction when the right-side sensor receives 1. Finally, if all three sensors obtain 1, it indicates no more rows, and the Robotic Arm goes forward for 3 seconds and tests the soil's moisture content.

Step 2: Soil Moisture sensor is the sensor that takes soil moisture material and generates analog format output. This information is supplied to transform it to digital format as an input to 8bit AD/DA converter. This knowledge is submitted to the cloud for storage.

Step 3: Pest Identification where we need to identify the pest in crops. We need to record the camera footage to extract a picture frame from the video every 10 seconds on the 5th second. This image is uploaded and analyzed on a cloud.

Step 4: In the Android application for the Farmer, if a detailed report with average moisture content is accessible in the cloud, pests attacking the crop, the pesticide for that crop, seasonal produce, the date, and period of the generated report would be available. Using this information, farmers may learn about the field's conditions and other details to manage the field effectively. AAFAMS is an easy and more innovative way for farmers to track the fields. Automating the analysis process eliminates the work for farmers. It allows them to diagnose pests in the fields and forecasts pesticides used for these pests, improving the fields' production potential, and preserving the soil's productivity through the logging of water and stops other chemicals from being added. Via the solar panels that accumulate the energy to provide power supply, AAFAMS uses natural energy from the sun. A simple report produced from the sensors and camera is displayed to farmers through the android application.

Figure 3. Workflow of the model proposed by Kajol et al. (2018)

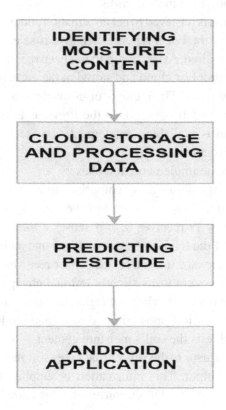

Usman et al. (2020) proposed a device that includes humidity, temperature, and shading sensors to collect details dependent on the temperature, mugginess, and shade spectrum from plant leaves. The variations that a plant experiences are documented and dissected with Arduino programming by the Moisture and Shading temperature sensors. For the Arduino. UNO devise, the data obtained with. Temperature, moisture, and shading sensor are defined after the data remains transmitted to the ranchers. The application uses the Wi-Fi shield to transfer the host framework details for review to the cloud level. In the cloud process, the information obtained is then compared with the dataset to decide if the leaf under consideration is normal or affected. Figure 4 displays the work proposed by Usman et al. (2020).

1) Obtaining information: We recognize tests of multiple leaves as the data here. The sensors then sense these leaves to establish various parameters based on the sound or infection is interpreted.

2) Temperature sensors: Modernized temperature sensors such as DHT11, which is fundamental and ultra-simple. A capacitive moisture indicator is used, and a propelled symbol discharges (no essential information pins required) on the data stick.

3) Humidity sensor: The DHT11 is a central sensor of suddenness propelled by ultra-simplicity. It employs a capacitive moisture sensor and even a thermistor to monitor the built-in climate and discharges an electronic sign on the data stick.

4) Color Sensor: The TCS3200, is a programmable light-to-recurrence shading converter/sensor. The sensor is a CMOS integrated solitary solid circuit that consolidates a calibratable silicon photodiode and a current-to-recurrence converter.

5) Aurdino: The United Nation Corporation is an open standard control board that depends on the Arduino. Cc-prepared ATmega330P microcontroller for extensive use.

6) Stage of Cloud: Here, we use the "ThingSpeak" cloud stage to pass the cloud's practical information. This information is illustrated against the diagram to see the difference in the temperature, mugginess, and shading. We verify if the characteristics fall into a standard set based on the plotted data against the diagram. On the unlikely chance they do as well, the leaf is sound at that stage, or else it's ill.

In this work, a system is established to determine the existence of the leaves. The suggested method uses sensor gadgets to identify the leaves' parameters, such as temperature, stickiness, and shadow, compared with the information index by testing if the characteristics obtained fall within the range determined in the information set. In different countries, ranchers, industrialists, botanists, food designers, and doctors will use the proposed model. In addition to the suggested system, the roads for more work here utilize the picture handling methods to render it increasingly competent and specific to determine the qualities and characterize whether the leaves are unsafe or sound. We may use the picture preparation method to assemble an all-encompassing form of the structure that defines the type of sickness influenced by the leaf and classes the various infections within the leaves. Here we will build a mechanized system with the objective that it is useful for producing enormous scales and allows to discover the diseases early, allowing customers to execute and increase the yield of the crop properly.

Figure 4. Architecture of Device proposed by Usman et al. (2020)

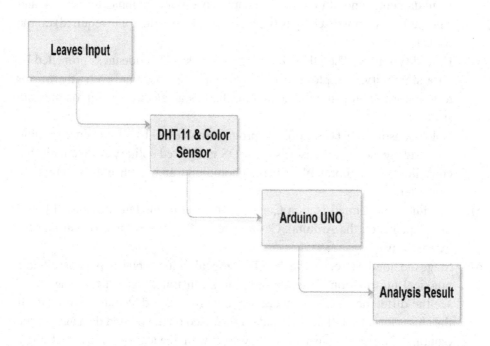

FUTURE RESEARCH DIRECTIONS

The identification of plant diseases is one of the main factors for agricultural applications to improve yield. Mobile Apps could be built to warn farmers and provide them with real-time solutions. Several approaches such as Genetic Algorithms Bhardwaj et al. (2016,2013a,2013b,2014 and 2021), Autonomic Computing Singh et al. (2016), Deep Learning, Singh et al. (2019a and 2019b), and Machine Learning, Daniya and Vingeshwari (2019), could be applied to the domain for efficient detection of plant diseases along with IoT. Future work will be using IoT in plant disease detection to achieve a high-performance system using field images of plant leaves.

CONCLUSIONS

The main goal of the research was fulfilled; the goal was to survey the integration of "Internet of Things" and "Artificial Intelligence Techniques" in the detection of plant diseases.

– It needs an hour to substitute manual techniques for detecting diseases with automatic techniques since one of the critical issues is the consistency and protection of agricultural products. Detecting diseases at their earlier stages is very significant since their distribution can be easily managed without hindering crop quality and productivity.

– This article demonstrates the role of IoT in agriculture. The use of IoT in identifying plant diseases through leaf images is outlined.

– Works of several researchers in the domain are also mentioned, and future perspectives of IoT in recognizing plant diseases are discussed briefly.

– Future work will be using IoT in plant disease detection to achieve a high-performance system using field images of plant leaves.

REFERENCES

Abdullahi, H. S., Sheriff, R., & Mahieddine, F. (2017, August). Convolution neural network in precision agriculture for plant image recognition and classification. In *2017 Seventh International Conference on Innovative Computing Technology (INTECH)* (Vol. 10). IEEE. 10.1109/INTECH.2017.8102436

Acharya, D., Goel, S., Asthana, R., & Bhardwaj, A. (2020). A novel fitness function in genetic programming to handle unbalanced emotion recognition data. *Pattern Recognition Letters, 133*, 272–279. doi:10.1016/j.patrec.2020.03.005

Alfarisy, A. A., Chen, Q., & Guo, M. (2018, April). Deep learning based classification for paddy pests & diseases recognition. In *Proceedings of 2018 International Conference on Mathematics and Artificial Intelligence* (pp. 21-25). 10.1145/3208788.3208795

Baranwal, S., Khandelwal, S., & Arora, A. (2019, February). Deep learning convolutional neural network for apple leaves disease detection. In *Proceedings of International Conference on Sustainable Computing in Science, Technology and Management (SUSCOM)*. Amity University Rajasthan. 10.2139srn.3351641

Barbedo, J. G. A. (2013). Digital image processing techniques for detecting, quantifying and classifying plant diseases. *SpringerPlus, 2*(1), 1–12. doi:10.1186/2193-1801-2-660 PMID:23419944

Bharathi, R. J. (2020). *Paddy Plant Disease Identification and Classification of Image Using AlexNet Model*. Academic Press.

Bhardwaj, A., & Tiwari, A. (2013, July). A novel genetic programming based classifier design using a new constructive crossover operator with a local search technique. In *International Conference on Intelligent Computing* (pp. 86-95). Springer. 10.1007/978-3-642-39479-9_11

Bhardwaj, A., & Tiwari, A. (2013, July). Performance improvement in genetic programming using modified crossover and node mutation. In *Proceedings of the 15th annual conference companion on Genetic and evolutionary computation* (pp. 1721-1722). 10.1145/2464576.2480787

Bhardwaj, A., Tiwari, A., Bhardwaj, H., & Bhardwaj, A. (2016). A genetically optimized neural network model for multiclass classification. *Expert Systems with Applications, 60,* 211–221. doi:10.1016/j.eswa.2016.04.036

Bhardwaj, A., Tiwari, A., Varma, M. V., & Krishna, M. R. (2014, July). Classification of EEG signals using a novel genetic programming approach. In *Proceedings of the Companion Publication of the 2014 Annual Conference on Genetic and Evolutionary Computation* (pp. 1297-1304). 10.1145/2598394.2609851

Bhardwaj, H., Tomar, P., Sakalle, A., & Sharma, U. (2021). Artificial Intelligence and Its Applications in Agriculture With the Future of Smart Agriculture Techniques. In Artificial Intelligence and IoT-Based Technologies for Sustainable Farming and Smart Agriculture (pp. 25-39). IGI Global.

Chandra, A. L., Desai, S. V., Guo, W., & Balasubramanian, V. N. (2020). *Computer vision with deep learning for plant phenotyping in agriculture: A survey.* arXiv preprint arXiv:2006.11391.

Daniya & Vigneshwari. (2019). A review on machine learning techniques for rice plant disease detection in agricultural research. *System, 28*(13), 49-62.

Ferentinos, K. P. (2018). Deep learning models for plant disease detection and diagnosis. *Computers and Electronics in Agriculture, 145,* 311–318. doi:10.1016/j.compag.2018.01.009

Gavhale, K. R., & Gawande, U. (2014). An overview of the research on plant leaves disease detection using image processing techniques. *IOSR Journal of Computer Engineering (IOSR-JCE), 16*(1), 10-16.

Hershey, S., Chaudhuri, S., Ellis, D. P., Gemmeke, J. F., Jansen, A., Moore, R. C., ... Wilson, K. (2017, March). CNN architectures for large-scale audio classification. In *2017 IEEE international conference on acoustics, speech and signal processing (icassp)* (pp. 131-135). IEEE.

Jogin, M., Madhulika, M. S., Divya, G. D., Meghana, R. K., & Apoorva, S. (2018, May). Feature extraction using convolution neural networks (CNN) and deep learning. In *2018 3rd IEEE International Conference on Recent Trends in Electronics, Information & Communication Technology (RTEICT)* (pp. 2319-2323). IEEE.

Kajol, R., & Akshay, K. K. (2018). Automated agricultural field analysis and monitoring system using IoT. *International Journal of Information Engineering and Electronic Business, 11*(2), 17.

Kimiti, J. M., Odee, D. W., & Vanlauwe, B. (2009). *Area under grain legumes cultivation and problems faced by smallholder farmers in legume production in the semi-arid eastern Kenya*. Academic Press.

Muthukannan, K., Latha, P., Selvi, R. P., & Nisha, P. (2015). Classification of diseased plant leaves using neural network algorithms. *Journal of Engineering and Applied Sciences (Asian Research Publishing Network), 10*(4), 1913–1919.

Pavel, M. I., Kamruzzaman, S. M., Hasan, S. S., & Sabuj, S. R. (2019, February). An IoT Based Plant Health Monitoring System Implementing Image Processing. In *2019 IEEE 4th International Conference on Computer and Communication Systems (ICCCS)* (pp. 299-303). IEEE. 10.1109/CCOMS.2019.8821782

Pilli, S. K., Nallathambi, B., George, S. J., & Diwanji, V. (2015, February). eAGROBOT—A robot for early crop disease detection using image processing. In *2015 2nd International Conference on Electronics and Communication Systems (ICECS)* (pp. 1684-1689). IEEE.

Pothen, M. E., & Pai, M. L. (2020, March). Detection of Rice Leaf Diseases Using Image Processing. In *2020 Fourth International Conference on Computing Methodologies and Communication (ICCMC)* (pp. 424-430). IEEE. 10.1109/ICCMC48092.2020.ICCMC-00080

Purohit, A., Bhardwaj, A., Tiwari, A., & Choudhari, N. S. (2011, June). Removing code bloating in crossover operation in genetic programming. In *2011 International Conference on Recent Trends in Information Technology (ICRTIT)* (pp. 1126-1130). IEEE. 10.1109/ICRTIT.2011.5972430

Sakalle, A., Tomar, P., Bhardwaj, H., & Sharma, U. (2021). Impact and Latest Trends of Intelligent Learning With Artificial Intelligence. In Impact of AI Technologies on Teaching, Learning, and Research in Higher Education (pp. 172-189). IGI Global.

Shin, H. C., Roth, H. R., Gao, M., Lu, L., Xu, Z., Nogues, I., Yao, J., Mollura, D., & Summers, R. M. (2016). Deep convolutional neural networks for computer-aided detection: CNN architectures, dataset characteristics and transfer learning. *IEEE Transactions on Medical Imaging, 35*(5), 1285–1298. doi:10.1109/TMI.2016.2528162 PMID:26886976

Shrivastava, V. K., Pradhan, M. K., Minz, S., & Thakur, M. P. (2019). Rice plant disease classification using transfer learning of deep convolution neural network. *International Archives of the Photogrammetry, Remote Sensing & Spatial Information Sciences*.

Singh, Kumar, & Chandana, (2020). A Review on PDIS (Plant Disease Identification Systems). *International Journal of Engineering Research & Technology, 8*(10).

Singh, P. P., Kaushik, R., Singh, H., Kumar, N., & Rana, P. S. (2019, December). Convolutional Neural Networks Based Plant Leaf Diseases Detection Scheme. In *2019 IEEE Globecom Workshops (GC Wkshps)* (pp. 1-7). IEEE.

SinghT. (2020). *A Survey on Intelligent Techniques for Disease Recognition in Agricultural Crops*. Available at SSRN 3616700.

Singh, T., & Kumar, A. (n.d.). Survey on Characteristics Of Autonomous System. *International Journal of Computer Science and Information Technologies, 8*.

Singh, T., Kumar, K., & Bedi, S. S. (2021). A Review on Artificial Intelligence Techniques for Disease Recognition in Plants. *IOP Conference Series. Materials Science and Engineering, 1022*(1), 012032. doi:10.1088/1757-899X/1022/1/012032

Singh, U. P., Chouhan, S. S., Jain, S., & Jain, S. (2019). Multilayer convolution neural network for the classification of mango leaves infected by anthracnose disease. *IEEE Access: Practical Innovations, Open Solutions, 7*, 43721–43729. doi:10.1109/ACCESS.2019.2907383

Thanh, N. C., & Singh, B. (2006). Constraints faced by the farmers in rice production and export. *Omonrice, 14*, 97–110.

Thorat, A., Kumari, S., & Valakunde, N. D. (2017). An IoT-based smart solution for leaf disease detection. In *2017 International Conference on Big Data, IoT and Data Science (BID)*, (pp. 193-198). IEEE. 10.1109/BID.2017.8336597

Usman, A., Bukht, T. F. N., Ahmad, R., & Ahmad, J. (2020). Plant Disease Detection using Internet of Things (IoT). *Plant Disease, 11*(1).

Venkataramanan, A., Honakeri, D. K. P., & Agarwal, P. (2019). Plant disease detection and classification using deep neural networks. *International Journal on Computer Science and Engineering*, *11*(08), 40–46.

ADDITIONAL READING

Campbell, C. L., & Madden, L. V. (1990). *Introduction to plant disease epidemiology*. John Wiley & Sons.

KEY TERMS AND DEFINITIONS

Cloud Computing: Cloud computing is the on-demand availability of computer system resources, especially data storage and computing power, without direct active management by the user. The term is generally used to describe data centers available to many users over the Internet.

Image Processing: Digital image processing is the use of a digital computer to process digital images through an algorithm. As a subcategory or field of digital signal processing, digital image processing has many advantages over analog image processing.

Internet of Things: Is the interconnection via the Internet of computing devices embedded in everyday objects, enabling them to send and receive data.

Smart Agriculture: Smart farming is a big leap from traditional farming as it brings certainty and predictability to table. Robotics, automation, and cloud software systems are tools for smart farming.

Chapter 12
Smart Farming Using Internet of Things:
A Solution for Optimal Monitoring

Rishabh Verma
Jagan Institute of Management Studies, Guru Gobind Singh Indraprastha University, India

Latika Kharb
iD https://orcid.org/0000-0002-8549-0920
Jagan Institute of Management Studies, Guru Gobind Singh Indraprastha University, India

ABSTRACT

Smart farming through IoT technology could empower farmers to upgrade profitability going from the amount of manure to be used to the quantity of water for irrigating their fields and also help them to decrease waste. Through IoT, sensors could be used for assisting farmers in the harvest field to check for light, moistness, temperature, soil dampness, etc., and robotizing the water system framework. Moreover, the farmers can screen the field conditions from anyplace and overcome the burden and fatigue to visit farms to confront problems in the fields. For example, farmers are confronting inconvenience while utilizing right quantity and time to use manures and pesticides in their fields as per the crop types. In this chapter, the authors have introduced a model where farmers can classify damaged crops and healthy crops with the help of different sensors and deep learning models. (i.e., The idea of implementing IoT concepts for the benefit of farmers and moving the world towards smart agriculture is presented.)

DOI: 10.4018/978-1-7998-6981-8.ch012

INTRODUCTION

Climate variability is a significant cause of hazard to small landholder farmers and pastoralists, particularly in dryland regions. Nourishment lack is an important issue confronting globally all over the world. The shortage of nourishment is affected by financial, natural, and social factors. For example, crop disappointment, overpopulation, and inadequate government arrangements are the fundamental driver of nourishment shortage in many nations. Climate change and its impacts are well recognized today, affecting both the physical and biological systems.

Regardless of high technology advancements and industrialization, approximately 70 percent of the Indian population is connected with agriculture and its related activities as discussed by Agale, R. et al. (2017). Natural elements decide the harvests deliver in a given spot; financial aspects decide the purchasing and generation limit, and socio-political factors determine the dispersion of sustenance to the majority. Sustenance lack has extensive long and transient adverse effects, incorporating starvation, hunger, expanded mortality, and political agitation. The art and science of harvesting crops, rearing livestock for the economy and humanity is Agriculture. It plays a vital role in the life of every species by declining the agony of starvation. It is the backbone and oldest activity of the country. However, authors are still inadequate in this field as agronomists are not well aware of utilizing the correct quantity and time to use manures and pesticides in their areas as per the crop types. Agriculture gives the 50% of employment to the country and 17-18% of G.D.P. growth, but this development is depleting day by day. Since insufficient knowledge about crops and agriculturalists are not able to grow healthier crops for the country. Bugs are in charge of two noteworthy sorts of harm to developing yields. First is the plant's immediate damage by the nourishing creepy-crawly, which eats leaves or tunnels in stems, organic products, or roots. Maharjan, K.L. et al. (2013) stated that average crop yields increase at a decreasing rate with the quantity of inputs used and decrease with the area planted to the crop.

The chapter's organization starts with presenting the objective, the need for the proposed idea, its components for implementation, the model architecture followed a brief introduction to various IoT sensors used, and the opening of the proposed model viz. IoT devices that will help in achieving the objective of optimal monitoring the farming.

OBJECTIVE OF CHAPTER

Through this project, the author is determined to remove all the barriers to increasing the country's healthier crops. Our main intention is to truncate (minimize) the workload of the farmers. Intellect harvesting through IoT sensors makes farmers' lives easier by automating most of the work and diminishing manual labor on farms. The usable amount of manure and the quantity of water for irrigating their fields also decrease wastage. Sensors check for light, moistness, temperature, soil dampness, etc., and robotizing the water system framework. The results will demonstrate how we can save most of the spoilt harvests as farmers are not getting the correct knowledge/reminder about when to utilize fertilizers.

PROPOSED MODEL: NEED AND IMPLEMENTATION

A standout amongst the most mind-boggling issues on the planet today concerns the human populace. The quantity of individuals living off the world's assets and focusing on its environment has multiplied in only forty years. There is no clue what the most extreme number of individuals the earth will bolster. Expansion of population concurrently increases the farmer's load, but the author tries to decrease the farmers' load from agriculture in this chapter. By examining the farmers' inconvenience, we realize that farmers face trouble while using fertilizers and pesticides. Chen, C. C. et al. (2004) stated that one of the issues with respect to climate change involves its influence on the distribution of future crop yields.

Crop responses to global climate change can vary depending upon the crop, location, and climate change scenario. Results show that most of the crops are spoilt because farmers are not getting the right image of when to use fertilizers. Using this compelling idea of the project author will gather all the data regarding the damaged crops. Gradually, the author will use that data to identify the future need whenever the crops are about to hurt or slowly get spoiled. Through IoT devices (raspberry pi or Arduino) and sensors author will indicate the farmers and let them know which part of the crop has a blemish. As per Kharb L. et al. (2021), Arduino board along with software developing kit (SDK)-based programming used for interacting and commanding different sensors. After implementing this idea, the agriculturist is free from visiting the farm/crops every time. They will give command through a web interface on receiving the damaged crop status, and our sensors will automatically throw pesticides on the crops. Authors at this moment innovate the design and implementation of robotic farming with less usage of manual load.

PROPOSED MODEL: COMPONENTS & HIGHLIGHTS OF MODEL

As per Ayaz M. et al. (2019), the rapid emergence of the Internet-of-Things (IoT) based technologies redesigned almost every industry including "smart agriculture" which moved the industry from statistical to quantitative approaches. The main components of our implementation are:

Web Interface

The primary and foremost step in our project implementation and design through which farmers will operate their crops. Figure 1 displays the proposed user interface, which contains different options and modules.

Figure 1. Screenshot of proposed web interface

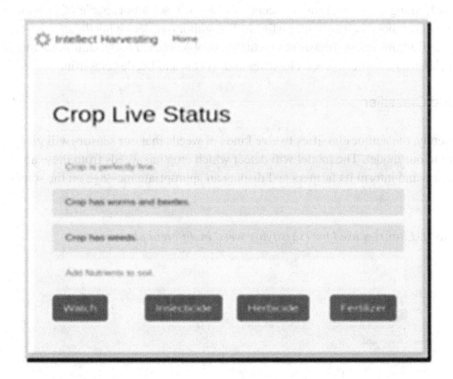

This User Interface is fully dynamic where farmers get the message highlight based on the sensors input and our classifier output. According to the highlighted message, its corresponding option will be pop up, and others will remain hidden. There are three diverse classes of pesticides, namely herbicides, insecticides, and fungicides. All three of these pesticides kill different types of pests found on a farm. Whenever the message "crops have worms and beetles" pop up and highlights, then only the insecticide option will be displayed and selecting that option. After this, the sensors will get a signal, and based on that signal, machines will sprinkle an adequate amount of chemicals on crops. Similarly, depending upon the other messages highlighted, the corresponding options will appear on the screen, and by selecting those respective tasks will be performed. Lastly, the watch option will always display on the web portal for the farmers to watch the crops' live stream whenever they want to by just clicking on that WATCH option.

Deep Learning: Model Architecture

Based on farmers' observations, we can understand their course of adaption to diverse climatical situations across India. Prathibha S. R. et al. (2017) stated that smart farming is an emerging concept, because IoT sensors capable of providing information about their agriculture fields. The authors are deploying the state-of-the-art Deep Learning neural network to achieve our objectives. This module implements two classifiers, namely, weed classifier and worms and beetles classifier.

Weed Classifier

Currently, the author classifies twelve kinds of weeds that our sensors will give as input to our model. The model will detect which crop has weeds from these above data sets and inform its farmers and display an appropriate message on the screen.

Figure 2. Libraries used for classifying weed in different plants

```
[74] import torch
     import numpy as np
     import torch.nn as nn
     import matplotlib
     import matplotlib.pyplot as plt
     import seaborn as sns
     from torch import optim
     from copy import deepcopy
     from torchvision import datasets, transforms, models
     from PIL import Image
     import os
```

Import Statement

Figure 2 shows the various libraries used for classifying weeds in different plants.

Data Transformation

Dataset transformed in training data according to various shapes, heights, and rotations.

Figure 3. Dataset transformed in training data

```
# Train data augmentation
train_transforms = transforms.Compose([
        transforms.Resize(255),
        transforms.CenterCrop(224),
        transforms.RandomHorizontalFlip(),
        transforms.RandomRotation(10),
        transforms.ToTensor(),
        transforms.Normalize((0.485, 0.456, 0.406), (0.229, 0.224, 0.225))
])
# Test data augmentation
test_transforms = transforms.Compose([
        transforms.Resize(255),
        transforms.CenterCrop(224),
        transforms.ToTensor(),
        transforms.Normalize((0.485, 0.456, 0.406), (0.229, 0.224, 0.225))
])
```

Training Classifier

The training weeds classifier will help us determine the goldilocks-spot (i.e., at which author should stop training our model).

Validation Pass

The train-approve test process helps distinguish when model overfitting begins to happen, with the goal that ceases preparation. It saves the classifier's best state dict and computes the validation loss at each pass.

Figure 4. Training the weed classifier

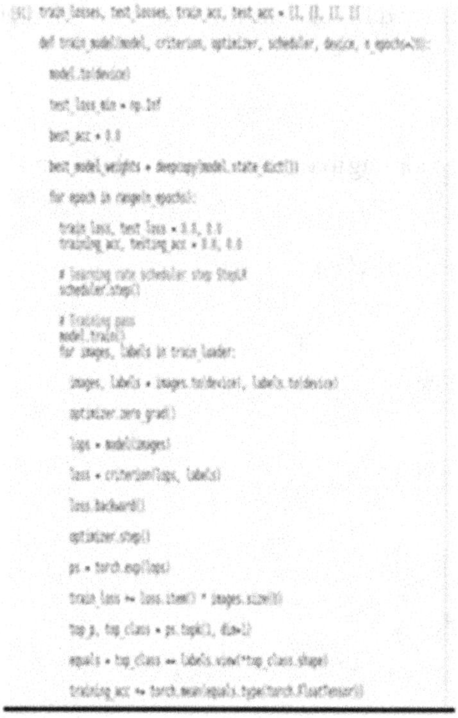

```
[6] train_losses, test_losses, train_acc, test_acc = [], [], [], []

    def train_model(model, criterion, optimizer, scheduler, device, n_epochs=25):
        model.to(device)
        test_loss_min = np.Inf
        best_acc = 0.0
        best_model_weights = deepcopy(model.state_dict())
        for epoch in range(n_epochs):
            train_loss, test_loss = 0.0, 0.0
            training_acc, testing_acc = 0.0, 0.0
            # learning rate scheduler step StepLR
            scheduler.step()

            # Training pass
            model.train()
            for images, labels in train_loader:

                images, labels = images.to(device), labels.to(device)

                optimizer.zero_grad()

                logs = model(images)

                loss = criterion(logs, labels)

                loss.backward()

                optimizer.step()

                ps = torch.exp(logs)

                train_loss += loss.item() * images.size(0)

                top_p, top_class = ps.topk(1, dim=1)

                equals = top_class == labels.view(*top_class.shape)

                training_acc += torch.mean(equals.type(torch.FloatTensor))
```

Model Accuracy

For evaluation of our model author has computed the absolute accuracy of the model.
Our model is depicting 93% accuracy by predicting the right weed of the crops.

Results: Model Evaluation

Figure 7 and Figure 8 show the Visualizations/graphs of the model accuracy and validation losses to check for the Overfitting of the training data.

Worms and Beetles Classifier

The following image displays classification into 38 different groups of Worms and beetles. The above data set is used for worm and beetle classifier (neural network) training. The author is currently only classifying 38 kinds of worms and beetle that our sensors will give as input to our model. The model will detect which crop has

Figure 5. Test process

```
# Validation Pass
model.eval()
with torch.no_grad():

    for images, labels in test_loader:

        images, labels = images.to(device), labels.to(device)

        lops = model(images)

        loss = criterion(lops, labels)

        test_loss += loss.item() * images.size(0)

        ps = torch.exp(lops)

        top_p, top_class = ps.topk(1, dim=1)

        equals = top_class == labels.view(*top_class.shape)

        testing_acc += torch.mean(equals.type(torch.FloatTensor))
    #losses
    train_losses.append(train_loss/len(train_loader.dataset))
    test_losses.append(test_loss/len(test_loader.dataset))
    #accuracy
    train_acc.append(training_acc/len(train_loader))
    test_acc.append(testing_acc/len(test_loader))

    print('Epoch {}/{}\tTrain loss: {:.6f}\t Validation loss: {:.6f}'.format(
        epoch+1,
        n_epochs,
        train_loss,
        test_loss
    ))

    if test_loss <= test_loss_min:
        print('Validation loss decreaesd from {:.6f} ---> {:.6f}'.format(
            test_loss_min,
            test_loss
        ))
        test_loss_min = test_loss
        best_model_weights = deepcopy(model.state_dict())

model.load_state_dict(best_model_weights)
return model
```

worm and beetle from these above data set and inform it to farmers and display an appropriate message on the screen.

Import Statement

It is used for importing the libraries in the weed classifier script.

Data Transformation

It is used for transforming the training data into various shapes, heights and rotations.

Training the Classifier

It is used for training the weed classifier. It will help us to determine the goldilocks-spot.

Figure 6. Final Accuracy of the system

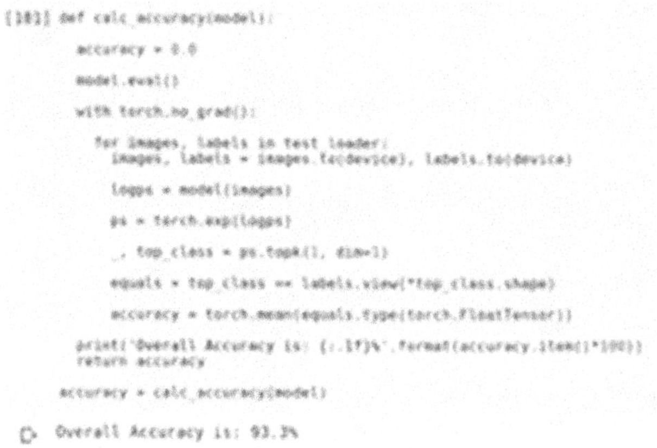

```
[10] def calc_accuracy(model):
        accuracy = 0.0
        model.eval()
        with torch.no_grad():
            for images, labels in test_loader:
                images, labels = images.to(device), labels.to(device)
                logps = model(images)
                ps = torch.exp(logps)
                _, top_class = ps.topk(1, dim=1)
                equals = top_class == labels.view(*top_class.shape)
                accuracy = torch.mean(equals.type(torch.FloatTensor))
            print('Overall Accuracy is: {:.1f}%'.format(accuracy.item()*100))
            return accuracy
        accuracy = calc_accuracy(model)

    Overall Accuracy is: 93.3%
```

Validation Pass

It helps in saving the best state_dict of the classifier and also to compute the validation loss at each pass.

Model Accuracy

It's for computing the absolute accuracy of the model.

Our model is depicting 90% accuracy by predicting the right weed of the crops.

IoT SENSORS

In this project, the author uses different kinds of sensors to detect the spoilt crops for the ease of farmers as there are various kinds of sensors that can deploy here in this project, which classify which crop has weeds, worms, and beetles. According to the crop's image (healthier/spoilt), the sensor input passes to the model classifier, and the action acts as output.

Sensors used in this model are image sensors, electrochemical sensors.

Image sensors (Optical sensors), used for providing images to the model. It will classify the images into weeds, worms, and beetles.

Some of the optical sensors to be used are:-

Figure 7. Validation losses

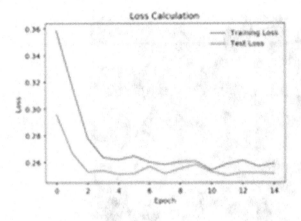

- Green seeker
- Crop circle

Both of the above sensors will send the captured image as a signal.

Electrochemical sensors are used to detect the proper nutrients in the soil. These sensors provide information regarding the ph and soil nutrients level; It detects ions in the ground.

Some of the electrochemical sensors include:

Figure 8. Accuracy visualization

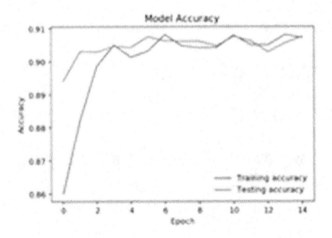

Figure 9. Different groups of worms and beetles

Figure 10. Importing the libraries

```
[74] import torch
     import numpy as np
     import torch.nn as nn
     import matplotlib
     import matplotlib.pyplot as plt
     import seaborn as sns
     from torch import optim
     from copy import deepcopy
     from torchvision import datasets, transforms, models
     from PIL import Image
     import os
```

Figure 11. Transforming the training data

```
# Train data augmentation
train transforms = transforms.Compose([
    transforms.Resize(255),
    transforms.CenterCrop(224),
    transforms.RandomHorizontalFlip(),
    transforms.RandomRotation(10),
    transforms.ToTensor(),
    transforms.Normalize((0.485, 0.456, 0.406), (0.229, 0.224, 0.225))
])
# Test data augmentation
test transforms = transforms.Compose([
    transforms.Resize(255),
    transforms.CenterCrop(224),
    transforms.ToTensor(),
    transforms.Normalize((0.485, 0.456, 0.406), (0.229, 0.224, 0.225))
])
```

Figure 12. Training the worms and beetles classifier

```
□ CODE  □ TEXT    ♦ CELL  ♦ CELL

def train_model(model, criterion, optimizer, scheduler, device, n_epochs=20):
    model.to(device)

    test_loss_min = np.Inf

    best_acc = 0.0

    best_model_weights = deepcopy(model.state_dict())

    for epoch in range(n_epochs):

        train_loss, test_loss = 0.0, 0.0

        # learning rate scheduler step StepLR
        scheduler.step()

        # Training pass
        model.train()
        for images, labels in train_loader:

            images, labels = images.to(device), labels.to(device)

            optimizer.zero_grad()

            logps = model(images)

            loss = criterion(logps, labels)

            loss.backward()

            optimizer.step()

            train_loss += loss.item() * images.size(0)

        # Validation Pass
        model.eval()
        with torch.no_grad():

            for images, labels in test_loader:

                images, labels = images.to(device), labels.to(device)
```

Figure 13. Compute the validation loss at each pass

```
□ CODE  □ TEXT    ♦ CELL  ♦ CELL

  ○     # Validation Pass
        model.eval()
        with torch.no_grad():

            for images, labels in test_loader:

                images, labels = images.to(device), labels.to(device)

                lops = model(images)

                loss = criterion(lops, labels)

                test_loss += loss.item() * images.size(0)

            train_loss /= len(train_loader.dataset)
            test_loss /= len(test_loader.dataset)

            print('Epoch {}/{}\tTrain loss: {:.6f}\t Validation loss: {:.6f}'.format(
                epoch+1,
                n_epochs,
                train_loss,
                test_loss
            ))

            if test_loss <= test_loss_min:
                print('Validation loss decreaesd from {:.6f} ---> {:.6f}'.format(
                    test_loss_min,
                    test_loss
                ))
                test_loss_min = test_loss
                best_model_weights = deepcopy(model.state_dict())

        model.load_state_dict(best_model_weights)
        return model
```

- Cropx
- Sigfox

Both of the above electrochemical sensors were well-thought-out for soil fertility, nutrients, and chemical properties.

FUTURE RESEARCH DIRECTIONS

As per Ray P. P. (2017), the advent of Internet of Things (IoT) has shown a new direction of innovative research in agricultural domain. Authors will be using the raspberry pi as the central hub device through which our Intellect Farming (web app) and all of the required sensors to be connected. Through raspberry pi, the author will use sensor data as input and pass it to our weed classifier and worm and beetle classifier. Based on the classifier output, our web app will change itself accordingly, and it will display only those options to the farmer that need to execute at that particular moment for the crops. Once the agronomist selects the required option as shown in the web app, A signal to be sent to the machines that would implant

Figure 14. Computing the final accuracy of the model

```
def calc_accuracy(model):

    accuracy = 0.0

    model.eval()

    with torch.no_grad():

        for images, labels in test_loader:
            images, labels = images.to(device), labels.to(device)

            logps = model(images)

            ps = torch.exp(logps)

            _, top_class = ps.topk(1, dim=1)

            equals = top_class == labels.view(*top_class.shape)

            accuracy = torch.mean(equals.type(torch.FloatTensor))

        print('Overall Accuracy is: {:.1f}%'.format(accuracy.item()*100))
        return accuracy

    accuracy = calc_accuracy(model)

Overall Accuracy is: 90.0%
```

in the agronomist farm. Nowadays, IoT is widely used for connecting device and collecting data information as discussed by Muhammad, Z. et al. (2020). Machines will automatically sprinkle an adequate number of pesticides to the crops. After that, the crops' final status will get updated, and the web app will show an appropriate message to the agronomist. So, the research work by Kharb L. et al. (2020), focuses on incorporating technology into people's life without disturbing their daily routine and does not require separate time to use.

CONCLUSION

Expansion of population concurrently increases the farmer load, but the author tries to decrease the farmer load from agriculture in this chapter. By examining the farmer's inconvenience, we realize that farmers face trouble while using fertilizers and pesticides. In this chapter, the author has focused on crops health to help the farmers save their crops from damages. Climatic changes are the most challenging issue as it is unpredictable at times. Farmers face huge loss due to crops are damaged due to worms and beetles. This chapter has introduced a model where farmers can classify damaged crops and healthy crops with different sensors and deep learning models. Farmer can check damaged crops done by weed, worms, and beetles. The authors have trained our models and achieved an accuracy score of 90%.

REFERENCES

Agale, R. (2017) Automated Irrigation and Crop Security System in Agriculture Using Internet of Things. *2017 International Conference on Computing, Communication, Control and Automation (ICCUBEA)*, 1-5. 10.1109/ICCUBEA.2017.8463726

Ayaz, A., Ammad-Uddin, M., Sharif, Z., Mansour, A., & Aggoune, E.-H. M. (2019). Internet-of-Things (IoT)-Based Smart Agriculture: Toward Making the Fields Talk. *IEEE Access: Practical Innovations, Open Solutions, 7*, 129551–129583. doi:10.1109/ACCESS.2019.2932609

Chen, C. C., McCarl, B. A., & Schimmelpfennig, D. E. (2004). Yield variability as influenced by climate: A statistical investigation. *Climatic Change, 66*(1–2), 239–261. doi:10.1023/B:CLIM.0000043159.33816.e5

Kharb, L. (2020). Proposing Real-Time Smart Healthcare Model Using IoT. In P. Raj, J. Chatterjee, A. Kumar, & B. Balamurugan (Eds.), *Internet of Things Use Cases for the Healthcare Industry*. Springer. doi:10.1007/978-3-030-37526-3_2

Kharb, L. (2021). 'VISIO': An IoT Device for Assistance of Visually Challenged. In V. C. Pandey, P. M. Pandey, & S. K. Garg (Eds.), *Advances in Electromechanical Technologies. Lecture Notes in Mechanical Engineering*. Springer. doi:10.1007/978-981-15-5463-6_84

Maharjan, K. L. (2013). Effect of climate variables on yield of major food-crops in Nepal: A time-series analysis. In *Climate Change, Agriculture and Rural Livelihoods in Developing Countries* (pp. 127–137). Springer. doi:10.1007/978-4-431-54343-5_9

Muhammad, Z. (2020) Smart Agriculture Using Internet of Things with Raspberry Pi. *2020 10th IEEE International Conference on Control System, Computing and Engineering (ICCSCE)*, 85-90. 10.1109/ICCSCE50387.2020.9204927

Prathibha, S. R. (2017). IoT Based Monitoring System in Smart Agriculture. *2017 International Conference on Recent Advances in Electronics and Communication Technology (ICRAECT)*, 81-84. 10.1109/ICRAECT.2017.52

Ray, P. P. (2017). Internet of Things for Smart Agriculture: Technologies. *Practices and Future Direction, 1*(Jan), 395–420.

Chapter 13
Smart Grid Using
Internet of Things

Kuldeep Singh Kaswan
Galgotias University, India

Jagjit Singh Dhatterwal
PDM University, India

Nitin Kumar Gaur
Galgotias University, India

ABSTRACT

The IoT (internet of things) is a network of people and stuff at any moment, anytime, for anyone, with any network or service. IoT is therefore a major complex worldwide network backbone for online service providers. The smart grid (SG) is one of IoT's main applications. SG is an interconnected data exchange network that gathers and analyzes data obtained from transmission lines, generation stations, and customers through the power grid. The internet of things has risen as the basis of creativity for energy grids. The chapter is based on the idea that, if one grid station transmitting electricity to customers is cut off due to some defects of IoT-based systems, all grid station loads can be connected to another system so that power is not disrupted. The authors discuss the IoT and SG and their relationship in this chapter. The best advantages for SG and specifications can be addressed in the SG works, creative innovations using IoT in SG, IoT software, and facilities in SG.

DOI: 10.4018/978-1-7998-6981-8.ch013

INTRODUCTION

The "grid" is the power supply network supplying all city residents, businesses and facilities. The Smart grid is the current iteration of energy grids that have been upgraded to allow intelligent use of services through communication technologies and networking.

Wireless networks, such as sensors, radio devices, passes and routers are among those which make today's modern IoT-capable power grid "smart." These systems have advanced networking and collaboration to enable customers to make smarter energy use decisions, to conserve resources and costs in urban areas and to encourage electricity authorities to restore power quicker after a breakdown. The increasing trend for communities currently is for a multitude of considerations to go to smart grid technology (Crezil, 2015). This includes the need for energy conservation, improved customer service to their people, emergency preparedness and the costly updating of outdated technology. Moreover, the advances in technologies have made it inexpensive and convenient to operate in smart grid systems, both cellular as well as the RF (radio frequency) (Andrew, 2014).

According to New Scientist, the U.S. has 200,000 miles of high voltage wires and over 1 million gigawatt hours of power combined. In the US, all of these infrastructures were created in the twentieth century in the course of a multi-million dollar undertaking that was primarily designed and carried out before the Network was created and, definitely, cellular (and RF) innovation was established as a feasible substitute for costly cables (Akaber *et al*, 2019).

With the existing grid infrastructure ageing, policymakers around the world are focused on implementing and incorporating smart grid technologies.

In the European Union, it's a "self-sustaining, financial and political supply of energy" scheme that has been in sight for years. A century since the nation initiated its first policies in this direction, attempts to move towards smart and renewable energy in the USA have begun. The United States government apparently funded funding, technological testing and smart grid growth.

In this section we will learn how smart grid operates and how smart grid technology and implementations are rising on a national and international level (Castanier, 2014).

INTERNET OF THINGS

The Internet of Things (IOT) is an internetworking of physical objects that are used to communicate and share data, such as cars, home appliances and other products integrated with electronics, applications, sensors, controls and networking. Growing thing is special to its built-in computer framework but can communicate with the communications infrastructure. The IOT makes it possible to monitor or manipulate devices remotely across current network infrastructures to provide possibilities for more direct incorporation of the real environment into virtual networks, and in addition to a reduction in human interference, to increase performance, accuracy and cost-effectiveness. Increased IOTs by embedded systems make the technology a simplified example of cyber-physical networks that can incorporate innovations such as smart grids, virtual power generating systems and intelligent homes. Smart transportation and innovative towns (Campbell, 2014).

ARDUINO Uno: Arduino is a tools, software, and project open-source enterprise that develops and produces single-board microcontrollers, digital sensors and virtual objects that are capable of sensing and controlling objects, physically and digitally. GSM MODULE: Initially, the global framework for mobile communication was established as an ETSI norm to clarify protocols used for smart phones such as the notebook for the second generation in Finland, first introduced in December 1991. As of 2014, mobile communications became the world standard with over 90 percent market share in more than 193 countries and regions.

Mode of WiFi:

Wi-Fi is a local wireless networking technology for IEEE 802.11-based applications. Wi-Fi is a Wi-Fi Alliance trademark which restricts the use of products of the word Wi-Fi Certified interoperability certification tests were recently performed.

In 2005, the book Mattern and Fleisch (Campbell P, 2013) was written in the field of IoT. The RFID technology in the names of some of the RFID lectures, for example, 'From RFID to IoT' (2006) and 'RFID: towards IoT) was originally used by European leaders in IoT. European policy makers have been involved in this field (2007). The first science conference (Denair, 2016) took place in IoT in March 2008. The Internet Protocol for Smart Objects (IPSO) Alliance was initiated by a consortium of high-tech corporations in 2008 with the following aims (Evans, 2017).

1. Interoperability: arrange compatibility checks to prove that goods and utilities for smart objects using IP are able to work together and to comply with business communication requirements.
2. Investment in innovation: helps inventors to gain industry exposure in small businesses which produce IP devices and Internet items.
3. Promoting IP: Promoting IP as the first approach for Smart Objects connectivity and connectivity – in print, internet, media.
4. Uphold standard: endorse the IETF and other guidelines implementation agencies for developing standards on smart artifacts. 4. Uphold standards: support the IETF.

The U.S. Intelligence Community Council classified the Internet of Things in April 2008 as a top six "Disruptive Civil Technologies," with possible implications for U.S. priorities (Biogeotech, Energy Storage Material, Biofuels and Bio-based chemicals, Clean Coal Technologies, Service Robotics, and the Internet of Things) (Fleisch et al. 2005).

President Obama introduced the concept of a cleverer world as a national agenda in January 2009 and thereby addressed global questions. A devoted European Union committee released a European Implementation Plan to develop a modern and wide-ranging framework: Transformation from an integrated computing network and humans to an embedded people's choices network of objects or things (IoT) in 2009 (Gershenfeld,1999). In the Frost and Sullivan region, Andrew Milroy (Gershenfeld, 2004) anticipated that 2014 would be the network year and that IT purchasers and sellers would be focusing on IoT. Furthermore, in 2014 more data will be provided by machines ('things') than by people.

Today, the IoT is used to identify an integrated connectivity of computers, services and software, which goes beyond conventional machines. Connectedness will be totally different and future worldwide networks will consist not only of individuals and computers but of all types of things as well. Real objects can link to the virtual universe, be remotely managed and serve as Internet service physical points of entry. IoT can now be used as a network of networks.

IoT's 3 dreams are available (Ghasempour, 2016a): Internet-oriented: it is important to render smart objects with an internet-oriented view. The artifacts shall use the IP protocol specification. Semantic: The amount of sensing devices is high in semantic vision and the data obtained would be immense. The original data must then be analyzed and handled for greater interpretation and representation.

- Topical: we detect objects using sensors and all-round technology in the object-oriented view. Any item can only be defined by an electronic component code (EPC).

Using sensors, the EPC is expanded.
Three main features of the IoT (Ghasempour, 2017):

1. Intelligent meaning: Use sensors to collect data every time and anywhere on anything. 2. Intelligent processing: the use of analysis of large volumes of data in order to monitor objects using methods such as cloud technology.
2. Reliable transfer: accurate delivery of data in real time through the network of telecommunications and the Internet.

In order to monitor the expected amount of connectivity between December 2012 and July 2020, Cisco has generated complex connections (Ghasempour, 2016b). There were 8.7 billion related items in December 2012, compared to over 12.3 billion in May 2014. Cisco has analyzed the possible inflationary impact of the Internet of All and the research reveals that there is a potential economic benefit of 14,4 trillion dollars. The advent of the Internet of things (Ghasempour., 2016c) for multinational private-sector companies during the coming decade. In the future, Cisco Internet Business Solutions Group (IBSG) expects that by 2015 there will be 25 billion Internet-based computers and by 2020 there will be 50 billion Internet-based ones (Ghasempour, A. *et al.* 2016d). A separate report by Morgan Stanley estimates that a total of 75 billion can be made, and says that two hundred specific user products or appliances may still not be connected to the Internet (Kaswan *et al*, 2021). Michael Mandel (Jarvis *et al*, 2019) explains how technical innovation, especially in the context of the Internet of All (IoE), could drive the American economy from a 'slow-growth rut,' in his study at the Progressive Policy Institute. By 2020, 50 billion to 100 billion smartphones are expected by the European Council (Information Society and Media DG). Future technical advances in IoT and its scientific requirements are highlighted for the next twenty years (Kaswan *et al*, 2021). Because IoT technologies are increasingly used, there is a rapid increase in the number of IoT manufacturing ventures and IoT articles.

SMART GRID

The intelligent grid is designed to resolve problems relating to the power grid (for example, poor stability, high outages, and high carbon emissions, high emissions of pollution, economy, protection and energy) (Meng *et al.* 2014). One of the concepts of a smart grid is that the smart grid is a network above the energy grids for gathering and analyzing electricity supply-demand data from various components of a power grid (Miao *et al*, 2010). Readers should read (Morgan Stanley, 2020) for extensive details and knowledge of the properties and advantages of the SG, the contrast of a power grid with SG and the general specifications of the SG network infrastructure. In a government proposed framework and technical institute smart grid model, the 7 domains are specified in the smart grid and the functions of those domains are decided in order to share the knowledge needed and to make necessary decisions (Kaswan *et al*, 2021). Any of the features and functionality needed for using the intelligent grid are:

Networks of connectivity: public, residential, Wired, and Wireless Networks that can be utilized as a global information and communication infrastructure (Mouftah, H.T. *et al*, 2019).

Cyber security: evaluating steps to ensure that the connectivity and control technology needed for the management, operation and protection of smart grid transportation systems is accessible, integral and confidential (Nathan S, 2019).

Energy supplies for distribution: use of various generation types (e.g., renewables) and / or warehouse networks (batteries) attached to distributed systems of two-way electric cars (Qi, F.; Yu, P, *et al*, 2018).

Grid distribution management: to optimize the efficiency and integration of components into the transmission of distribution system networks, such as feeders and transformers, to improve reliability; Boost the performance of the distribution grid and control clean energy distributions (Rafiei, S, et al, 2012).

Electric transport: integration of large-scale electric plug-in vehicles (Refaat *et al*, 2018).

Electricity: Mechanisms for various types of consumers to adapt to energy consumption at peak hours and to maximize the power supply-demand balance (Mohamed *et al*, 2018).

Store energy: Use of hydroelectric pumped storage methods, direct or indirect, (Sarma *et al*, 2000).

Wide-range tracking: monitoring components of the power system over a vast geographical area to maximize output and avoid issues until they occur (Schoenberger, 2002). Advanced Metering infrastructure (AMI): AMI is a core component of SG which provides a bilateral exchange network for collecting, sending and analyzing customer energy usage data between Smart Meter (SMS) and distribution system (Singh, D et al, 2014).

The AMI edition for automated smart meters is upgraded and updated. Data was gathered immediately in an automated meter reading and transmitted through some kind of one-way transmission network to a central system for future analysis and payment. AMI was adopted because the automated measurement did not provide bidirectional communications. AMI carries out a range of activities, such as self-healing, intelligent resource pricing, infrastructure development, energy performance improvements, enhancing SG stability, interoperability with other networks, power quality tracking and management, outages governance, communications between both the central system and SMs, energy conservation and SM device upgrading (Santos M., *et al*, 2017).

AMI elements include the central system, bidirectional networking networks, data concentrations and intelligent meters. SMs are deployed at customer premises or at other smart grid places in order to monitor and forward data to the centralized computer through means of billing contact networks, information to customers about their use, etc. In automatic process management, SMs will provide overviews of electricity usage and scheduled periods to enable and disable devices to change the load in SG. In the event that the power grid generates additional electricity, a direct load controller can add distributed energy resources to SG for greater load (Sherki Y., N, *et al*, 2015).

Smart computers, SMs and power usage control systems can communicate with each other through a home automation network, including decentralized energy resources, electric cars, gateways, home energy displays. The home region network can be used with Bluetooth, IEEE 802.11b, IEEE 802.-2010, power line and ZigBee technology (Suzuki et al., 2007) Numerous SMs are sending their information through a Neighborhood Area Network (NAN) to the appropriate data concentrator (Sherki *et al*, 2015). Numerous homes given by a transformer build, for example, a NAN. NAN should also hold a significant amount of data and meet its criteria for quality of operation.

NAN applicants include IEEE 802.11 family standard, the third and fourth generation of cellular wireless networks (for example, long term development (LTE), global interoperability with microwave access (WiMAX), wideband multi-access, and optical networks: (e.g., passive optical networks or Ethernet passive optical networks). In addition, field facilities can be operated across a network of field areas (FAN). A FAN is geographically similar to NAN. Related networks and techniques of connectivity can also be used for the FAN.

The data concentrator attaches and penetrates uplink data from SMs and passes downlink data to SM. The data concentrator improves SG scalability, eliminates SM energy consumption, and eliminates data collision between the data transmission of SMs. However, it somewhat enhances the latency in sending SMs data. A large area network connects several data storage systems to the central infrastructure (WAN). In WAN it is possible to use long-term and high-bandwidth communications technologies (e.g., advanced WiMAX, LTe, or LTE).

SM data are collected and analyzed by the central machine. It may have multiple elements, such as a meter data system (Thibaut, 2018), a Geographic Information Systems, a malfunction management system, a customer information system, a power quality management system, and demand prediction systems, linked by a network in the local areas. For example, a data management system meter captures, stores and processes SMs' data in databases (Santos *et al*, 2017).

DEFINITION OF SMART GRID

Such a thing would be the shortest smart grid definition (Takeshi *et al*, 2013):

The power grid is comprised of an infrastructural, hardware and software infrastructure that provides two-way connectivity between all systems elements and participants and delivers effective energy generation and delivery through the supply chain (Weiser, 1991).

The intelligent grid is often defined as an independent distributed infrastructure. It can supply electricity, including renewables and storage, from various energy sources. Furthermore, the application of this method helps manufacturers and customers to regulate and handle without precedent.

HOW SMART GRID WORKS

A dynamic network that involves many connections between appliances and supply chain partners is a smart grid that does not like a conventional grid of Single lane Communications. This arrangement allows multiple possibilities for transferring and controlling the electricity generated. This is the most important step-by-step situation.

Creating

Switching to the intelligent grid enables electricity from diverse and sometimes dispersed sources to be used. It comprises conventional power stations, green wind and solar power as well as electric plug-ins and storage of electricity.

Transmitted

The power transforms to the appropriate voltage spectrum if desired (for solar power or wind) and is delivered through the end users through a network of power stations, transmission lines and integrated delivery systems.

Using End-user's energy storage applications such as Smart meters, Sensor-enabled devices, Smart Sockets or connectors can have broad exposure and capacity control. Using these technologies, users become active partners in the management of energy supply—used smartphones or online applications for the monitoring and remote control of energy consumption.

Monitoring

People, utilities and other energy sector experts are expanding their monitoring and management skills in the power grid. Linked households, municipalities and cities both use electricity and generate usage and load data. Any approved individual in the supply chain can use these details. Computer analysis and visualization applications transform data on energy consumption into information on which to base future decisions. Energy providers, for example, can control grid infrastructure and forecast repairs, utilities can develop request response systems, people can react accordingly to the gap in demands and reduce energy consumption when it is most costly.

Superstore

Household members do not only use electricity with greater prudence, they often store power enough to supply a house off-grid. Houses conserve additional energy with space, select the loading they will need to back it up or use this power, for example, in the event of an interruption. In addition to the maintenance advantages, storage is one of the groundbreaking smart grid systems that are vital to autonomous residential grids that are entirely based on sustainability and produce significant surpluses.

WHY DO WE NEED A SMART GRID?

Initially, conventional grids are ageing and are no longer accurate in the face of increasing demand for electricity. The picture reveals that a typical smart grid shows the underlying variations and advantages. Besides these benefits, we require smart grid technologies and solutions for four primary reasons.

To Reduce Costs and Risks

The main challenges with intelligent grid solutions are pollution and insecurity. The implementation by residences and cities of smarter grid technologies aims to track and automate energy use in real time and maximize it in the best interest of the people and the community.

Simultaneously, the increased monitoring of all grid elements - loads, facilities, transmission lines, appliances-helps management to identify, fix, and avoid any problem in a timely or even advanced manner, and costly and risky interruptions such as downtime or downtime (Wang et al, 2012).

The U.S. costs USD 150 billion annually, according to the Department of Energy.

Reducing Pollution and High-Carbon Power

Smart grids not only have energy usage information, awareness, control and connectivity, but also allow for renewable electricity.

First of all, lowered pollution comes along with decreased waste of electricity. Second, the topology of intelligent grids enables the integration of renewables into the network, making clean energy sources easier for people (Yin-Min et al, 2008).

To Make Democracy and Durability Possible

Currently, smart grid technology is used to track and automate electricity demand at the market level. It makes an occupant of a household a willing member and a policy maker in the life cycle of the grid.

The household will momentarily exit the grid using technology such as energy storage or photovoltaic systems in the event of repairs or injuries. The tenants will then disperse their resources in a complex way in the home. Or they can focus entirely on their electricity generation and thus be completely independent of their regional grid (Yin- Min et al., 1999).

INNOVATIVE SMART GRID TECHNOLOGIES

Smart grid service is powered by a wide array of infrastructure and technological solutions. The IoT and information technologies-based intelligent grid dominates and consists of many key components (Youssef et al, 2007).

- **Intelligent devices and meters**. These are the very fundamental components of an intelligent grid which allow the customer to monitor power usage. In order to allow tracking and regulation, sensors in smart devices constantly produce and document status information. Smart meters collect information on energy usage and provide a full view, featuring loads and average costs, of energy use in the home (Zhao et al. 2018).
- **Delivery automatically.** Sophisticated manufacturing processes use real-time information to react automatically to demand shifts, to detect blackouts, and to ensure proper power distribution for both security and environmental benefits. This section incorporates automation and personality through the smart grid using IoT.
- **Intelligent recycling and connecting points**. Power storage and charge stations have a major role to play in the introduction of the smart grid. These innovations not only enable residences to retire comfortably in the event of breakdowns or crashes. The requirement for autonomous solar residential applications has also risen.

BEST THREE BENEFITS OF SMART GRID

The three following examples illustrate how beneficial an upgraded power system can be, even if there are many advantages to the intelligent grid (Zambrano *et al*, 2014).

Enable the Generation of Renewable Energy

The conventional energy grids are built to provide power to a wide network of households and enterprises in the region from a massive, centralized power plant. At this time, the electricity grid cannot accept input from households and companies that generate electricity through photovoltaic arrays or wind turbines. An intelligent grid is planned to embrace renewable energy.

In combination with wirelessly connected smart meters, the intelligent grid will monitor how much electricity is generated and reimbursed by a net positive institution. The intelligent grid also requires solar panels and devices to be monitored. We said before that the intelligent grid will minimize the impact of a catastrophe, such as a terrorist incident and a natural catastrophe, on a power plant. A limited number of power stations operated in a town under the standard paradigm. These facilities were also susceptible to risks due to large-scale outages and electricity shortages. Since the main plant is taken offline, a decentralized model requires several renewable outlets, including renewable energy, to supplement the grid's energy. It is even tougher to disconnect this decentralized structure, which provides robustness that cannot be achieved if one plant runs a whole community.

Smarter Accounting, Smarter Forecasts

Two advantages are offered by smart meters. Second, they can capture an immense amount of data from wireless IoT devices, which service providers have never before accessed. Providers may use this knowledge to help predict when energy supply increases and in which places the requirement is greatest. Secondly, the smart grid ensures easier payment for customers. Earlier energy prices were standardized between municipalities and suburbs at peak periods. Now you're going to be fined if you use power at elevated prices. And you can lower the bill accordingly if you switch off equipment and conserve energy. This makes everyone increasingly accountable for the use of energy (Zambrano et al. 2017).

Intelligent Grid is Better

A survey from the US Department of Energy (DDEE) shows that US power outages cost companies about 150 billion dollars annually. This is merely an approximation, as these power failures have lost only $50 billion a year, a crisis that needs to be resolved.

Energy will be rapidly redirected with intelligent grid technology if a blackout takes place, mitigating the consequences for families and companies. IoT sensors may also report current certification to allow for improvements before malfunction.

Utilities should inform their clients when a failure occurs rather than reacting reactively to consumer calls and disclosing failures (via e-mail/social media).

USING INTERNET OF THINGS IN SMART GRID

The role of IoT in intelligent girding is, you can see, important. The internet of things is in large part the enabler of the intelligent gird as its IoT modules are largely focused on hardware and infrastructure.

Connected Equipment, Equipment, Hubs

Energy consumption data is provided by sensing IoT devices, devices and jacks that power an intelligent house or any interconnected area. This knowledge is often used for the study of energy consumption, cost estimation, remote control systems, decision-making on load delivery, system identification, fault detection, risk of failure, etc.

Data and Visualization in Real Time

As already stated, sensor data is the center of intelligent grid activity. Synchronous IoT data collection, sorting, washing, evaluating and visualizing give insight into the manufacturing process from the time the energy is generated to the degree that an end-user uses it. Data work allows for automation, control, maintenance, problem analysis and smart grid forecasting.

Innovative Algorithms

Machine learning is now popular on the Internet of Things, such that big data is best understood and used, and a smart grid is no different. We know that machine learning works well for large datasets, identifies patterns, and predicts. Consequently, the use of sophisticated algorithms in the smart grid supply chain to process IoT data is another way to make it easier.

REQUIREMENTS FOR USING IOT IN SG

In order to be able to use IoT in SG, we must have certain technology and meet certain criteria as follows:

- **Communication technology**: communications technology may be used for the reception and dissemination of acquired SG system status information. We provide long- and short technology requirements for connectivity. Exemplary examples of short-range networking systems include ZigBee, Bluetooth and ultra-wideband technologies. The long-range networking system may be used for power line communications, optical fiber, cellular broadband networks such as 3G and 4G, as well as satellite communications.
- **Technologies for data fusion**: As IoT terminal services (like power, storage and frequency band) are minimal, no knowledge is sent to the target. Thus, data fusion methods may be used to capture and merge data and enhance the performance of knowledge collecting.
- The optical switching mechanism is very important for IoT implementations, e.g., using the various cameras and sensors to track different sections of a Smart Grid, as most IoT-devices use the battery as a primary power source.
- **Working in tough environments**: IoT systems built in power lines and substations of high voltage would operate in tough environments. In such environments, we could have sensors immune to high or low temperatures, anti-electromagnetic or water proof to prolong the service life of their sensors.
- **Stability**: Existing technologies in different settings involve consistency, self-organization or self-healing to meet different requirements. Therefore, the appropriate IoT system must be chosen to deal with overwhelming environmental problems depending on the current climate.
- For example, where certain systems cannot transmit data due to energy deficiency, a new data routes have to be sought for the network to stay at the desired degree of consistency.
- **Authentication**: Security procedures for transmitting, preserving and handling data, avoiding leakages and breaches of information and preservation of data must be incorporated into all IoT layers.
- **Sensors**: Sensors calculate amounts such as current, voltages, frequencies, temperatures, energy, light and other signals, and provide the relevant data for delivery, analysis and processing. Genetic engineering has recently been employed to include high performance content covering various detail analysis and enhancing the development of the detection probability.

IoT SENSORS IN SMART GRID

For IOT-based schemes or frameworks, sensors play a very diverse role.

Sensors are current equipment used mostly to detect electric or optical signals and respond to them. A sensor essentially conveys the moisture, humidity, body temperature and the velocity physicochemical characteristics to a signal that can be electro-measured. The mercury on the glass thermometer, for example, increases and pacts the liquid to adjust the reading temperature of an individual on the balanced glass tube.

Various types of devices are accessible and play a prominent part in allowing creative applications. Innovative technology building blocks are vital to intelligent technologies such as all-round cameras, information procurement systems and huge information research. Efficiencies, flexibility and expense are properly integrated. The survey also serves as an intelligent basis for sustainable structures that allow substantive citizen involvement. The ability of these mechanisms will continue to increase, particularly as technology increases and mergers. An embedded control is called a microcontroller. We have a range of microcontrollers of varying duration lengths on the market, including 4-bit, 8-bit, 64-bit and 128-bit. A Microcontroller is a condensed mini or personal computer programmed to monitor and handle embedded systems functions in bureau computers, robots, household appliances, engines and some other gadgets. A microcontroller has various components such as memory, peripheral devices and a central processing unit.

In many new commercial processes, sensors play an integral role, such as grinding foods and regular tracking of events such as travel, air quality, medical therapy and more. The sophisticated sensors with Embedded Information Technologies (ICT) capability have been with us for more than a century. In other words, for a minimum of three decades, smart sensors have always been around. The computing capacities, storage, energy efficiency, and a number of form factors, network alternatives, and programming developments have been amazingly advanced. These developments emerged in conjunction with major sensing changes. We have seen bio sensors in a number of consumer goods, such as pregnancy checks, cholesterol, allergy and fertility, arise. Developing and promptly selling reasonable price EMS (MEMS) sensors, such as 3D accelerometers, has LCD to be integrated in a number of products ranging from iPhone and vehicles. According to inexpensive sensors, new fields of sensing platforms have been catalyzed, such as those for home tracking. The variety of low-cost sensors stimulated the development of overwhelming sensing.

In our living environments or even in our clothes, sensors and control systems can be incorporated with minimum impact on our everyday lives. These sensors offer modern preventive health frameworks for early identification of possible complications, such as cardiovascular risk (high cholesterol), liver disorder (higher urinary bilirubin levels), anemia (blood ferritin) etc., and so on. Sensors are being used progressively to track everyday tasks such as exercising on smartphones with immediate access to our results. There is a major shift in the interaction between our well-being and the climate. Sensor technology also enables everyday people to provide knowledge about the condition of air and water and other environmental matters, such as noise emissions. The distribution and socialization of this information online thus supports the emerging principles of citizen-LCD sensing. When people provide their information online, crowd-driven maps can be created and exchanged of criteria such as pollution levels over wide areas.

Early sensors were basic devices that calculated the number of interest and produced a certain type of mechanical, power or optical signal output. In the last generation, the capacities of a sensor have increased greatly with computers, comprehensive networking, web access, handheld smart devices and cloud convergence. Technology basic components are smart devices like Smart Meters, data collection systems, pervasive data access and Advanced Analytics. Performance, interoperability and cost savings are sufficiently incorporated. They may also serve as a long-term solution creativity forum. The ability of these systems will therefore continue to grow, specifically as technology progression and fusion increases. You can also see how tablets and smartphones are one of the breakthrough catalysts through combining technology. The use of sensors is also integral to the everyday routine of health centers, both to diagnose and to regular wellbeing surveillance. Intelligent facets of our lives will involve a larger pull than the de-facto method to date. Intelligent sensors and networks should be additional perspective, prototyped and forward-looking, particularly in the areas explored in this book, since they are directly and tangibly connected to end users. The equilibrium between the artistic and empirical processes is necessary to preserve. We need to ensure that needs are recognized and relevant knowledge gained, in order to realize potential from consumer, scientific, technology and economic perspectives in a manner that makes sense.

There are rising chip manufacturing stages in the continuing technological development of sensors. Increasing convergence with the ICT capacity will continue to lead to smarter sensors. This will serve as an innovative forum for future products and services for creativity. ATmega32P is the sensor for the smart girds. The increased, reduced AVR Microcontroller AVR incorporates 32KB ISP flash storage, 1KB EEPROM, 2KB SRAM, 54/69 I/O line, 32 Field marshal registers, a JTAG on-chipped debugging/programmer interface, optional step comparison mode timers, internally and externally kept interrupting; serial PR for demarcation line and on-chip input validation; This device has been designed to track distribution transformer parameters online, which will provide valuable transformer information. For mentorship, all sensors are linked to the transformer. The voltage sensor is linked to the voltage sensor, the current sensor is used in the converter, the oil sensor is used to detect a petroleum level, and the pressure sensor is used to sense the temperature of the transformer.

IoT APPLICATIONS IN SMART GRID

IoT is able to support SG technology. IoT may enhance its extensive sensory and transmitting capacity, such as processing, alert, self-healing, incident response and performance. In combining IoT and SG, the construction of intelligent terminals, meters and detectors, structural systems, and communication devices can be promoted significantly. In different areas of SG (electricity production, transmission lines, and distribution/use), IoT can be used to carry out efficient data transmission in wired and wireless communication infrastructures as follows:

- IoT can be used for monitoring the production of electricity of various types of plants, including coal, wind, nuclear, biomass, carbon emissions, power storage, energy demand, and predicting the power required to serve customers.
- IoT is ideal for the procurement, dispatchment, tracking, security, maintenance and control of transmission lines, stations and towers.
- In consumer smart meters, IoT can be used in order to calculate various categories of metrics, smart energy usage, network interoperability, charging and unloading of electric cars, energy efficiency and management.

Application for control. The key scenarios of the IoT program are:

- Highly reliable AMI: in SG, AMI is a vital element. IoT can be used in AMI for data acquisition, measurement of anomaly in SG, data sharing between smart meters, electrical efficiency monitoring and distributed energy, and device usage trend analysis.
- Intelligent house: an intelligent home can be used to communicate with consumers and SG, optimize SG services, fulfill marketing demands, boost QoS, manage intelligent machines, read information on smart meter use, and track green energy.
- Transmission line surveillance: The transmission lines will be tracked to discover and eradicate problems with faults by using cellular internet networking systems.
- Assistant Control Scheme for Electric Vehicles (EV): EV Control Assistant services include charging points, power service systems and tracking centers. Users will inspect their parking details and charging stations in close proximity via GPS. The GPS directs drivers to the most convenient charging station immediately. The indicated for the management controls vehicle batteries, chargers, charging points and service optimization.
- Here are a few prominent models of IoT usage in smart grids ranging from global to residential beginning approaches.

- In order to introduce a smart grid scheme in Mannheim, France has incorporated IoT infrastructure and technological solutions. This project has encouraged broad green energy adoption and enabled energy use and development in the city to be organized.
- The light-energy platform is an excellent example of an IoT smart grid application which simultaneously allows cost savings, lower pollution and easier use of green energy.
- In order to maximize stockpiling and energy use as well as to make the incorporation of PV systems in the buildings, the firm provides an intelligent panel and data analysis instruments.
- Schneider Electric provides a range of wired technologies for solar household energy implementation. In order to totally disconnect or produce and transform solar energy to cover household demand, a company may outfit a household with PV systems, control and management instruments.

CONCLUSION

IoT provides many options that can increase intelligent grid efficiency due to real-time data collection, through analysis and the automation of some functions. However, IoT needs to overcome various technological, legal and economic issues, as well as many innovative materials, to become a fully prepared technology. IoT technology as a support for smart grid implementation was the aim of this chapter. There have been some potential implementations and key problems. To illustrate the difficulty of data estimation, a research analysis has been undertaken to approximate the possible volume and frequency of data transmitted from a local intelligent grid through the operator and from the device operator to the intelligent grid. To date, smart grid growth seems imminent and IoT may be a beneficial option.

REFERENCES

Akaber, P., Moussa, B., Debbabi, M., & Assi, C. (2019). Automated Post-Failure Service Restoration in Smart Grid through Network Reconfiguration in the Presence of Energy Storage Systems. *IEEE Systems Journal*, *13*(3), 1–10. doi:10.1109/JSYST.2019.2892581

Andrew. (2014). *Connectivity and the Internet of Things*. Available online: https://www.frost.com/reg/blog-display.do?id=3161648.

Campbell, P. (2013). *Connections Counter: The Internet of Everything in Motion.* Available online: https://newsroom.cisco.com/feature-content?articleId=1208342.

Castanier, F. (2014). Reduce Cost and Complexity of M2M and IoT Solutions via Embedded IP and Application Layer Interoperability for Smart Objects. *Proceedings of the M2M Forum.*

Crezil, P. (2015*). Can the Internet of Everything Bring Back the High-Growth Economy?* Available online: https://www.progressivepolicy.org/issues/economy/can-the-internet-of-everything-bring-backthe-high-growth-economy

Denair, G. (2016). *Disruptive Civil Technologies: Six Technologies with Potential Impacts on US Interests out to 2025.* Available online: https://fas.org/irp/nic/disruptive.pdf

Evans, D. (2017). *The Internet of Things: How the Next Evolution of the Internet is Changing Everything.* Available online: https://www.cisco.com/c/dam/en_us/about/ac79/docs/innov/IoT_IBSG_0411FINAL. pdf

Fleisch, E., & Mattern, F. (Eds.). (2005). *Das Internet der Dinge—Ubiquitous Computing und RFID in der Praxis* (1st ed.). Springer. doi:10.1007/3-540-28299-8

Gershenfeld, N. (1999). *When Things Start to Think* (1st ed.). Henry Holt and Company.

Gershenfeld, N., Krikorian, R., & Cohen, D. (2004). The Internet of things. *Am. 2004, 291,* 76–81.

Ghasempour, A. (2016a). Optimum Number of Aggregators based on Power Consumption, Cost, and Network Lifetime in Advanced Metering Infrastructure Architecture for Smart Grid Internet of Things. *Proceedings of the IEEE Consumer Communications and Networking Conference (IEEE CCNC 2016),* Las 9–12.

Ghasempour, A. (2016b). Optimized Advanced Metering Infrastructure Architecture of Smart Grid based on Total Cost, Energy, and Delay. *Proceedings of the 2016 IEEE Conference on Innovative Smart Grid Technologies (IEEE ISGT 2016),* 1–6.

Ghasempour, A. (2016c) Optimum Packet Service and Arrival Rates in Advanced Metering Infrastructure Architecture of Smart Grid. *Proceedings of the 2016 IEEE Green Technologies Conference (IEEE GreenTech 2016),* 1–5. 10.1109/GreenTech.2016.8

Ghasempour, A. (2017). Advanced Metering Infrastructure in Smart Grid: Requirements, Challenges, Architectures, technologies, and Optimizations. In J. Lou (Ed.), *Smart Grids: Emerging Technologies, Challenges and Future Directions* (1st ed.). Nova Science Publishers.

Ghasempour, A., & Gunther, J. H. (2016d). Finding the Optimal Number of Aggregators in Machine-to-Machine Advanced Metering Infrastructure Architecture of Smart Grid based on Cost, Delay, and Energy. *Proceedings of the 2016 13th IEEE Annual Consumer Communications & Networking Conference (IEEE CCNC 2016)*, 960–963.

Jarvis, R., & Moses, P. (2019) Smart Grid Congestion Caused by Plug-in Electric Vehicle Charging. *Proceedings of the 2019 IEEE Texas Power and Energy Conference (TPEC)*, 1–5. 10.1109/TPEC.2019.8662152

Kaswan, K. S., & Dhatterwal, J. S. (2021a). *Machine Learning and Deep Learning Algorithm IoD. The Internet of Drones: AI Application for Smart Solutions*. CRC Press.

Kaswan, K. S., & Dhatterwal, J. S. (2021b). *Implementation and Deployment of 5-G Drone Setups. The Internet of Drones: AI Application for Smart Solutions*. CRC Press.

Kaswan & Dhatterwal. (2021c). *The use of Machine Learning for Sustainable and Resilient Building. Digital Cities Roadmap: IoT-Based Architecture and Sustainable Buildings*. Scrivener Publishing Press.

Meng, X., & Feng, L. (2014). Research on application of internet of things technology to earthquake prevention and disaster reduction. *World Information on Earthquake Engineering*, *30*(2), 129–133.

Miao, Y., & Bu, Y. (2010). Research on the architecture and key technology of Internet of Things (IoT) applied on smart grid. *Proceedings of the International Conference on Advances in Energy Engineering (ICAEE)*, 69–72. 10.1109/ICAEE.2010.5557611

Mouftah, H. T., Erol-Kantarci, M., & Rehmani, M. H. (2019). Communication Architectures and Technologies for Advanced Smart Grid Services. In Transportation and Power Grid in Smart Cities: Communication Networks and Services. Wiley.

Nathan, S. (2019). *NIST Releases Final Version of Smart Grid Framework*. Available online: https://www.nist.gov/smartgrid/ upload/NIST-SP-1108r3.pdf

Qi, F., Yu, P., Chen, B., Li, W., Zhang, Q., Jin, D., Zhang, G., & Wang, Y. (2018). Optimal Planning of Smart Grid Communication Network for Interregional Wide-Area Monitoring Protection and Control System. *Proceedings of the 2018 IEEE International Conference on Energy Internet (ICEI)*, 190–195.

Rafiei, S., & Bakhshai, A. (2012). A review on energy efficiency optimization in Smart Grid. *Proceedings of 38th Annual Conference on IEEE Industrial Electronics Society*, 5916–5919. 10.1109/IECON.2012.6389115

Refaat, S. S., Abu-Rub, H., Trabelsi, M., & Mohamed, A. (2018). Reliability evaluation of smart grid system with large penetration of distributed energy resources. *Proceedings of the 2018 IEEE International Conference on Industrial Technology (ICIT)*, 1279–1284. 10.1109/ICIT.2018.8352362

Santos, M., & Oliveira, J. (2017). A big data system supporting bosch braga industry 4.0 strategy. *International Journal of Information Management*, *37*(6), 750–760. doi:10.1016/j.ijinfomgt.2017.07.012

Sarma, S., Brock, D. L., & Ashton, K. (2000). *The Networked Physical World*. Auto-ID Center White Paper MIT-AUTOID-WH-001.

Schoenberger, C. R. (2002). The Internet of things. *Forbes*, 155-160.

Sherki, Y., Gaikwad, N., Chandle, J., & Kulkarni, A. (2015). Design of real time sensor system for detection and processing of seismic waves for earthquake early warning system. *Conference: 2015 International Conference on Power and Advanced Control Engineering (ICPACE)*, 285–289. 10.1109/ICPACE.2015.7274959

Singh, D., Tripathi, G., & Jara, A. J. (2014). A survey of Internet-of-Things: Future Vision, Architecture, Challenges and Services. *Proceedings of the 2014 IEEE World Forum on Internet of Things (WF-IoT)*, 287–292. 10.1109/WF-IoT.2014.6803174

Stanley, M. (2020). *75 Billion Devices Will Be Connected to The Internet of Things By 2020*. Available online: https://www.businessinsider.com/75-billion-devices-will-be-connected-to-the-internet-by-20202013-10

Suzuki, Saruwatari, Kurata, & Morikawa. (2007). *Demo abstract: A high-density earthquake monitoring system using wireless sensor networks*. Academic Press.

Takeshi, Makot, & Yutaka. (2013). *Tweet Analysis for Real-Time Event Detection and Earthquake Reporting System Development*. Academic Press.

Thibaut, M. (2018). Convolutional network for earthquake detection and location. *Science Advances*, *4*(2), 2. doi:10.1126ciadv.1700578 PMID:29487899

Wang & Ni. (2012). Wireless sensor networks for earthquake early warning systems of railway lines. *Lecture Notes in Electrical Engineering, 148*, 417–426.

Weiser, M. (1991). The Computer for the 21st Century. *Am. 1991, 265*, 66–75.

Wu, Y.-M., & Kanamori, H. (2008). Development of an earthquake early warning system using Real-Time Strong Motion Signals. *PMC Article, 8*(1), 1–9. doi:10.33908010001 PMID:27879692

Yin-Min. (1999). *Development of an integrated Earthquake Early Warning System Case for the Hualien Area Earthquakes*. Academic Press.

Youssef, Y. El-Sheimy, & Noureldin. (2007). A novel earthquake warning system based on virtual mimo-wireless sensor networks. Academic Press.

Zambrano, P. Palau, & Esteve. (2014). Quake detection system using smartphone-based wireless sensor network for early warning. Academic Press.

Zambrano, Perez, Palau, & Esteve. (2017). Technologies of internet of things applied to an earthquake early warning system. *Future Generation Computer Systems, 75*, 206–215.

Zhao, Z., & Chen, G. (2018). An Overview of Cyber Security for Smart Grid. *Proceedings of the 2018 IEEE*.

Chapter 14
Blockchain of Internet of Things–Based Earthquake Alarming System in Smart Cities

Kuldeep Singh Kaswan
Galgotias University, India

Jagjit Singh Dhatterwal
PDM University, India

Krishan Kumar
KCC Institute of Technology and Management, India

ABSTRACT

The worst natural catastrophes occurring in well-settled intelligent cities are earthquakes. A framework of earthquake warning minimizes destruction and protects countless lives. A system built on IoT to identify the earthquake in the S waves and then to warn people by showing them an alert and where the earthquake happened is proposed. An early warning system is generated by a seismic wave survey. The larger the earthquake, the heavier the tremor. The waves are also breaking down the driveway. So the earthquake in the S wave is safer to find. Therefore, determining the extent of the early warning system is essential for creating an earthquake. The chapter addresses the detection of the frequency of earthquakes by identifying the size of earthquakes. In this chapter, we will discuss the elevated processors and IoT (internet of things) that can efficiently deploy an early warning device that can capture and transmit data over networks without manual interference. The early earthquake warning system (EEW) can be used to support smart urban planning, making earthquake areas less sensitive to disasters.

DOI: 10.4018/978-1-7998-6981-8.ch014

INTRODUCTION

An earthquake is also called a natural catastrophe, often called tremor or convulsion. The unexpected shaking on the world, shutting down the buildings and killing thousands of people. By predicting the surfaces, detectors that can alert the public earlier shake earlier. The hypothesis that S waves are the first wave of the attacks from the ground, followed by P waves that attack the surface of the S wave. So, in a few seconds or minutes, the public is alerted earlier. The Wi-Fi network is the network in which sensors are scattered spatially to usually detect the physical and environmental conditions. The low cost, simple maintenance, and reproducibility of WSN are used in many fields. The network of the wireless sensors is linked to multiple sensors which are linked to each other to track the atmosphere scenario with the same features. The term 'IOT' is generally called 'INTERNET OF THINGS.' The IoT is a digital conception that predicts a world in which real objects are connected to the internet every day and anywhere and can identify with other devices. In this chapter, IoT is the methodology or network used to transmit the accurate warning message more precisely to the public. IoT is the Internet network connecting the internet objects through a network, and the warning message is then sent more precisely to the public by IoT. To avoid geographical threats, the IoT applies a modern wave of information technology. Sensors are mounted and geo-hazard characteristic equipment installed at the appropriate sites, and IoT is then integrated into the current Internet. This interconnected network contains an extremely efficient central computing cluster capable of integrating and managing and controlling humans, machinery, facilities, and resources in real-time system. On just this principle, people have interpreted and treat information about geological-risks as more intelligent and complex, reach a state of understanding, and deepen the communication between people and the ecosystem.

Some Countries Have Cautions About Geo Disasters

In recent years geo-hazard tracking and IoT-based early warning are a research hub. For example, for real-time surveillance of landslides, the ground tilt, extensometer, underwater pressure sensor, geo-acoustic monitoring, and rainfall gauge are integrated (Reid et al., 1998).

Effective land surveillance systems focused on IoT, such as Winsock and Slews (Arnhardt et al., 2009), have been introduced by the European Union (EU). Also, the geo-safety monitoring and early alerting networks in geo-risk areas have been developed by Australia and Switzerland (Metternicht G. et al., 2005). A mudslide early-warning system in 1985 was developed jointly by the United States Geological Survey (USGS) and the National Wetter Service (Qin et al., 2018). In Japan, the landfill and refuse flow monitoring system includes a rain gage network, cameras, and photographs for ground and submerged, crucial precipitation requirements, an early warning model and a data transmitting system that tracks and alerts about waste and landfill. Multi-channels of contact is used for the system of real time slide surveillance in Hong Kong. Also, Taiwan established an experimental early alert and early warning system based on IoT (Hong Y.-M., H.-C. Lin, and Y.-C. Kan, 2011) the report was released.

LITERATURE SURVEY

Qingkai et al. (2005) Tweet Review for a long time Detection of events and coverage of earthquakes Development of systems: This paper uses the measuring unit widely used for localization estimates to detect the earthquake. To estimate the locations of target events, this particle filter operates through completely different forms. It combines tweets and the quest for target incidents with a nursing algorithm and develops another format to distinguish between earthquakes and human activity. The space-time model helps to locate the location of the incident later. The author examined how long a person has dealt with incidents such as a Twitter earthquake. The case is teetered and the news is distributed through all social platforms to warn people. The event is established. This detector measures earthquakes and notifications are sent much quicker than the JM unit's updates.

Dell et.al. (2012), Earthquake detection networks focused on smartphones: The only aim of this paper is to develop an alternative form of unstable network smartphones practice to improve the old unstable networks. We appear In this document, smartphones will be evaluated as alert devices; the smartphones have obtained both human- and simulated earthquake data practice, Their findings reveal that our algorithms can be used only as a recording device, a smartphone can even be used as an extremely correct earthquake prediction method. This will increase the safety of the world's earthquake-prone populations through networks of smartphones supported by seismic sensors. Richard Nursing has created an earthquake algorithm.

Andrew et al. (2013), Evaluation of distant sensations and earthquakes: impressions, limitations and prospects: Remote sensing is also a method that has been extensively used in the last decades for the discovery of earthquakes. This article uses a method in earth observation. The technique of earthquake surveillance (EO) is used to track all the earthquake damage in recent years and to locate the earthquake in the following days. It's an earthquake naturally occurring. This can occur in a fast phase that is more likely than mentioned. Awareness of ongoing events is also possible with the Earth Observation (EO). The catastrophe is closely regulated in the form of human and economic destruction, then the outcome is foreseen and earthquake warning.

Fabio Dell'Acqua et. al. (2009), Damages quickly Earthquake Remote data mapping by satellite: In an emergency context, the writers have been addressed entirely with the attention-grabbing. SAR and optical knowledge are combined, and this is an alternate knowledge. The optical is to distinguish between harm and no other damage types, while the SAR allows the various hazards to be included in texture choices. This technique identifies the damage to the region by satellite, which highly affects the area. Even if the damage to the area has not been deeply impacted by the satellite. The places that identify the damage are mostly poignant. In comparison to five, the number of detections is smaller.

Thibaut et. al. (2018), Earthquake: Distributed equipment Twitter System: System: The social media in this paper contribute and spread often geographic knowledge. The items contain references to incidents at or at poignant places. The data gathered from various sources support our knowledge of situations and enhance our comprehension and reaction to those incidents. In a single sensor, the earthquake is observed. When this earthquake has been detected, the distributed device alerts people every 10 seconds as an "earthquake." As a result of people starting trembling, USGS inquiry into shaking cases is possible. In five years, USGS claims it's not true. Nevertheless, the prediction of earthquakes by Twitter would not appear beneficial.

Takeshi et al. (2013), Earthquake tracking network: This is the most coevolutionary method for earthquake detection and is one of the most complex ways for scanning and retrieving unstable records from repeated signals. In Great Britain, in the USA, this technology has been used to date for 17 earthquakes. They forecast the natural science survey using the previous catalog. The formula is faster than the agreed methods. This is the most inviting network with a highly uplifting neural network. In the past few decades, the number of seismic data has exponentially increased, demanding economic algorithms to truly imagine and locate earthquakes. The most complicated techniques today evaluate over more seismic records and sort seismic signals repeatedly.

Christian et. al. (2004), SAR and optical data comparison and combining of earthquake risk capacity in urban areas: In this article, SAR data and electronic data are used to detect the earthquake. Optimized data is an effective and promising solution. They were able to look at and identify urban improvements. Also, a field relation based on completely based data is seen to boot. The photographs are promising and suitable. The algorithmic rule is extremely cost-effective, with the entire process complex O (N log) for the nursing N pixel image with medium length k choices. Also, a field relation, based mostly on experience, is seen. In the rural areas or where it seems that infrastructure is not well designed to ensure compulsory information transfers or where operability is greatly reduced due to equality the timely identification, estimation, and analysis of urban losses resulting from earthquakes.

Yin-Min and Kanamori (2008), Implementation of the early warning system in Taiwan for earthquakes in the Hualien region: All in all, the dependability of earthquake information and the time of the news are unavoidable tradeoffs. To grasp a shortened news duration (and thus an extended notice time), one must be obliged to use other original waveforms in an extremely short segment. If this is possible, it may be less accurate and alert. For example, in news, the generated method is faster, but the results are weak. On the other hand, through mercantilism, a long-term knowledge acquisition, and technology, the originated Hualien sub-network supplies additional trustworthy information. Thus the corresponding optimization goal is essential to occur.

Marco et. al. (2013), EARS: a real-time call network for earthquake crisis management: EARS (Earthquake alert report system): In this article, the sensed earthquake is transmitted by this method mechanically. Via INGV networks the trembling levels are determined. The e-mail and Twitter account send the post. Only the extensive tweet sets were used to pick very relevant sets. We are therefore committed to visualizing our findings with the official information provided by the INGV – the authority accused of dysfunctional analysis. Detection of earthquakes occurs often in seconds of the occurrence and much before, as INGV or alternate official networks exchange alerts. We are also inclined to squarely warn stakeholders promptly.

Yin-Min et. al. (1999), Early earthquake production system utilization of related early warning systems is robust Motion Signals: In this article, the associate EEW system alerts the regional area of the incoming long-lasting warning, generally a few seconds to a couple of tens of seconds, that is, the proximity of sustainable soil mobility before the entry of the dangerous S wave. Even a few seconds of adequate warning periods are useful in preventing the possibility of the derailment, to prevent the orderly interruption of gas pipelines to clean backfire, for the orderly closing of high tech production operations, and pre-programmed emergency measures for various crucial installations, such as rapid transit vehicles and high-speed trains.

INTERNET OF THINGS (IOT)

The IoT is a network of radio frequency identification (RFID), infrared sensors, a global positioning system (GPS, ultrasonic sensors, and other data sensor data that are intelligently detected, found, tracked, and controlled according to specified arrangements(Nord J., Koohang A., and Paliszkiewicz J., 2019).

The IoT's basic architecture (Martino et al., 2018) contains the preception layer in IoT, the transport layer in IoT, and the application layer in IoT in shown Figure 1.

Perception layer in IoT: The perception layer mainly gathers data from the outside physical world using cameras, sensors, and other appliances to overcome data collection physical environment problems and achieve the objective of detailed interpretation of knowledge. Sensor networks, RFID, etc. (Ray P., 2018) are the main technologies of the perception layer.

Transport layer: Data collected are exchanged through the Telephone, the communications Radio, TV, and various access networks and transport-level special networks (Montori et al., 2018). The major transport layer innovations involve wired long-distance and wireless protocols, network convergence, and smart mass information processing technology.

Application layer: It integrates IoT technologies with industry-specific implementations for a variety of intelligent applications such as Smart City (Jin et al., 2014) and Intelligent Transport (Lu et al., 2014).

These IoT Layers are very useful in collecting information on the immediate transmission to the central terminal for earthquakes. The newspapers, smartphones, and Syrian are then circulated.

Figure 1. IoT Sensing of earthquake

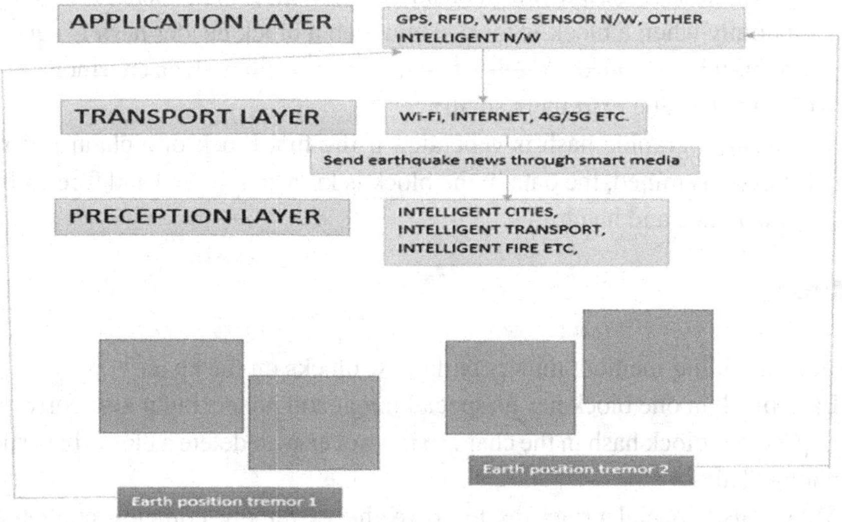

BLOCKCHAIN

Through using decentralization and crypto-hashing, Blockchain also referred to as distributed ledger technology (DLT), allows a history of all intangible assets unchangeable and clear.

A Google Doc is a basic analogy for blockchain technology comprehension. The text is circulated instead of copied or transmitted as we construct a report and exchange it with several people. This provides a dynamic supply chain that allows all people to view the paper simultaneously. Nobody should wait for updates from another party, as all doc changes are registered and made fully clear in real-time.

How Does Blockchain Work?

There are three main principles for Blockchain: miners, blocks, and nodes.

• Blocks

There are several blocks for each chain, and there are three basic elements for any block:

- Block info. Data.
- An all-number 32-bit was considered a nonce. The nonce is generated randomly when a block is formed and then a block header hash is generated.
- The hash is a wedded 256-bit integer. It must begin with an enormous number of zeros (i.e., be extremely small).
- The cryptographic hash is generated if the first block of a chain is formed. Unless it is mined, the data in the block is known assigned and forever bound to the nonce and hatch.

• Miners

Through a mining method, miners build new blocks on the chain.

Each block in one block has its special threat and nonce, but it also corresponds to the previous block hash in the chain so it is not easy to delete a block, in particular with long chains.

Miners use special programs to solve the extremely complex mathematical difficulty of determining a nonce that produces a hash. Since the nonce is just 32 bits and the hash is 256, approximately four billion nonce-hash variations have to be mined before the correct one. Once they have discovered the "golden nuncio," the miners are said to have attached their block to the chain. To make a transition into some block later in the sequence, not just the block needs to be re-mined, but all the blocks that follow. That is why manipulating blockchain technologies is incredibly difficult. Think of it as "safety in mathematics," because it takes an immense time and computational capacity to locate golden nuncios.

When a block is mined effectively, all of the nodes within the network support the update and the miner receives a financial payout.

• Nodes

Decentralization is one of the main principles of blockchain technology. The chain cannot be owned by any machine or company. It is instead a spread directory through the chain-linked nodes. Nodes can be an electrical component of some type that preserves blockchain copies and retains the network.

The network must algorithmically authorize each newly mined block for upgrading, confidence, and verification of the chain, each node has its copy of the blockchain. Any behavior in the ledger can be easily reviewed and interpreted since blockchains are transparent. A unique alphanumeric identification number showing their purchases is given to each participant. Integrating publicly available information with a control-and-balance structure lets blockchain preserve completeness and builds user confidence. In essence, blockchains can be considered as technologically scalable confidence.

BLOCKCHAIN IN EARTHQUAKE ALARMING SYSTEM

When the activity of earthquake whole information about it handle blockchain technology. Any data send through Wireless network whole message secure not to be changed in intermediate path complete information delivers adequately in figure 2.

Figure 2. BlockChain Alarming System

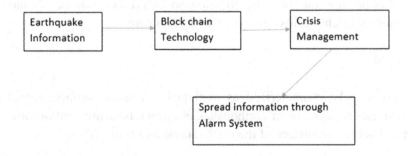

SMART CITIES

To improve community operations and facilities and communicate to people, the smart town concept incorporates information and communication technology (ICTs), and multiple physical devices linked to the IoT (Internet of Things) network. City leaders will communicate with the population and local facilities actively by using smart city technologies and track what happens in the town and how the city grows (Geller R.J. et al., 1997). It is used to improve the efficiency, productivity, and interactive elements of municipal facilities, to decrease Costs and use of services and increased contacts with the public. Smart urban technology is developed to track urban flows and have actual reactions. Therefore, a clever city will face its people's problems rather than just a transactional relationship. However, the word itself is vague and therefore subject to many meanings.

Features of Smart Cities

- Ensure optimal use of physical resources by artificial and data analysis (roads, developed environments, and other physical assets) to promote good and sound economic, cultural and social growth.
- Increasing the mutual wisdom of city institutions, using open innovation mechanisms and e-participation by e-governance and emphasizing citizenship participation and co-design, successfully engage municipal government authorities.
- Understand, adjust, improve, and adapt to evolving situations more efficiently and promptly by developing city intelligence.

EARTHQUAKE IN SMART CITIES

To protect smart cities from earthquakes (a type of geological hazard), the government spends funds on cities to protects nature eruptions and saves countless life (Santos et al., 2017). For pre-information about disasters so government and people take corrective action and fight against terrible changes in nature.

- The Hazards

Earthquakes may be characterized as earthquakes causing surface impact, movement of vibrations, dynamism, earthquakes, eruptions, tsunamis, and/or waves traveling on and below the surface of the earth (Hayakawa et al., 2010).

The period and the amount and seriousness of the aftermath of the earthquake are infuriating factors. Tsunami, fire, and landslide are compound threats.

- Factors of Vulnerability in Intelligent cities
  - Village sites and population size in earthquake zones.
  - Construction standards and laws are insufficient.
  - High occupancy dense construction concentration.
  - The shortage of earthquake-related alarm services and lack of public information.
- Public health impact of earthquakes

The key risks to public health differ in the size of the earthquake, its atmosphere, and its indirect effects (e.g. tsunamis, landslides, and fires) (Crampin et al., 1984) . In terms of their relation to risk factors, the results can be summarized as follows:

- Immediate health impact
  - Casualties and deaths associated with trauma from the fall of the house.
  - Deaths and indirect Impact of earthquakes and wave trauma, avalanche trauma, burns, and inhalation of smoke due to explosions.
- Medium-term health impact
  - Secondary illness with untreated injury.
  - Enhanced mortality rates and risk of conception, childbirth, and infant defects as a consequence of interrupted obstetrical and neonatal care.
  - A possible benefit of transmissible diseases, in particular in overcrowded environments.
  - Enhanced morbidity and risk of chronic illness complications from care interruption.
  - Increased mental fitness concerns.
  - Potential pollution of chemical/radiological agents after company infrastructure degradation.
- Earthquakes influence on the health system
  - Harm to health and transport facilities, resulted in interruptions to the delivery of care, resulting in limited access to all tiers of health services and reduced accessibility.
  - The lack of health staff whose houses and households were directly impacted by the earthquake, who could not access the already functioning healthcare facilities.
  - Lowered capacity to pay for health care when the families in question lose their land and livelihoods.

     ◦   Loss in materials and disrupted supply chains, including a large number of inventories.
- Mitigation and preparedness for earthquakes
  - Strengthen patient crisis control programs for emergencies.
  - Limit the likelihood of earthquake vulnerability by increasing the efficiency of the constructed environment, improved monitoring of land use, particularly construction regulation.
  - Guarantee the health facilities are hazard-resilient and will stay functional and responsive to expanded and modified health requirements following earthquakes with proper personnel training.
  - Be willing to deploy teams for emergency care including Field hospitals and temporary health facilities.
  - Investing in emergency preparedness – the first response is also groups.

BLOCKCHAIN IOT IN THE PREVENTION OF EARTHQUAKE DISASTERS

The terrible natural disasters affecting human civilization are earthquakes. The catastrophic damages resulting from repeated earthquakes are growing. As one of the new technology IoT is a current resource point in chapter (Lin et al., 2013, Guo et al., 2014, Botta et al., 2016, Chang et al. 2016) to use in the reduction of earthquake catastrophe and recovery operations to promote smart earthquake control and emergency relief.

- **Earthquake Prediction:** The central goal of the prediction of an earthquake is to predict when, where, and the magnitude of an earthquake(Keilis-Borok V., 2002, Gabrielov et al., 1994). During the earthquake incubation phase, abnormal values, including pressure, strain, severity, magnetoelectricity, and groundwater are observed. These irregular values are mostly captured and analyzed in the earthquake forecast. Therefore the intelligent IoT-based earthquake model is predicated must be created (Meng et al., 2014).
- **Earthquake Early-warning:** We need to anticipate earthquakes before they occur to mitigate the destruction caused by an earthquake. There would then be ample time to evacuate people from the earthquake region and cope with the secondary cause of catastrophe adequately at the same time 9 (Zambrano et al., 2017). IoT-based early warning technology has an important role; see Figure 3. Early warning technologies. Substantial work has been carried out in this region, using emerging IoT technologies, to establish an early warning system for earthquakes. Meng implemented IoT technology applications

focused on three aspects: early warning earthquake, restoration, and day-to-day relief material management. Alphonsa et al., (2016) proposed the IoT-based WSN early warning system which delivers early warning signals to alert people and automated electronic systems to prevent them from taking preventive action. Zambrano et al. (2017) has suggested an early-warning earthquake system with a communications IoT protocol. Suzuki et al., (2007) suggested a WSN seismic surveillance device focused on a high density calculating Lower cost and node density structural vibrations than before earthquake systems. The multiantenna WSN was developed by Youssef et al., (2007) based on the collaboration between the one-antenna wireless sensors, called a multi-input MIMO-WSN (virtual multiple input multi-input wireless sensor network). Wang D. et al., (2012) first introduced a modular early warning WSN system. Nachtigall et al., (2011) proposed a revised protocol on alert and routing, which meant that the early warning system needed to be extremely stable was able to face the difficulties. Early Alert Earthquake Device was presented with sensor systems (Picozzi et al., 2014, Sherki et al., 2015), and smartphone-based WSN.

- **Geohazards Induced by Earthquakes**: Trembling, scrambling, falling rocks, and other geo-hazards may cause landslides. To avoid further casualties, it is necessary to further track these earthquake-induced geohazards (Zambrano et al., 2014).

Figure 3. Blockchain of IoT based earthquake alarming system in smart cities

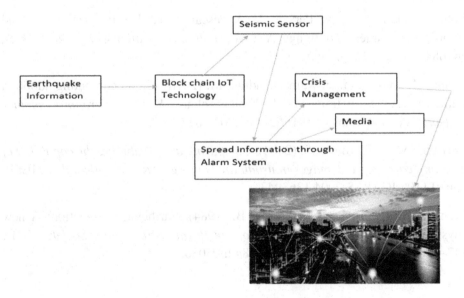

CONCLUSION

Several primary developments have also been addressed in this chapter in early earthquake prevention and IoT tracking systems. IoT-based equipment is more reliable, quicker, simpler, time-efficient, and smarter compared with traditional human-based earliest warning systems for earthquake protection. Yet several obstacles remain to be tackled. Firstly, unified standards and safety should be assured seriously. Secondly, the power usage and sensor stability should be improved in light of the dynamic and harsh geo-hazard climate. In Internet - of - things early warning and tracking systems geological-hazard avoidance, the use of new technologies like deep learning, edge computing, and 5G should also be encouraged.

REFERENCES

Alphonsa, A., & Ravi, G. (2016). *Earthquake early warning system by iot using wireless sensor networks*. Academic Press.

Andrew, A. Anthony and Jacek, (2013). Earthquake: Twitter as a Distributed Sensor-. *Transactions in GIS*. Advance online publication. doi:10.1111/j.1467-9671.2012.01359.x

Arnhardt. (2009). *Monitoring of slope-instabilities and deformations with micro-electro-mechanicalsystems (mems) in wireless ad-hoc sensor networks*. EGU General Assembly in Vienna.

Botta, A., De Donato, W., Persico, V., & Pescap, A. (2016). Integration of cloud computing and internet of things: A survey. *Future Generation Computer Systems*, *56*, 684–700. doi:10.1016/j.future.2015.09.021

Chang, V., Kuo, Y.-H., & Ramachandran, M. (2016). Cloud computing adoption framework: A security framework for business clouds. *Future Generation Computer Systems*, *57*, 24–41. doi:10.1016/j.future.2015.09.031

Christian, M., & Pierdicca, S. (2004). *Comparing and combining the capability of detecting earthquake damages in urban areas using SAR and optical data*. IEEE. doi:10.1109/IGARSS.2004.1368943

Crampin, S., Evans, R., & Atkinson, B. (1984). Earthquake prediction: A new physical basis. *Geophysical Journal of the Royal Astronomical Society*, *76*(1), 147–156. doi:10.1111/j.1365-246X.1984.tb05030.x

Dell'Acqua & Gamba. (2012). Remote sensing and earthquake assessment: experiences and perspectives. IEEE.

Dell'Acqua, F., Christian, M. Gianni, D., & Salvatore. (2009). Earthquake damages mapping by satellite remote sensing data. IEEE.

Gabrielov, A., & Newman, W. I. (1994). Seismicity modeling and earthquake prediction: A review. *Nonlinear Dynamics and Predictability of Geophysical Phenomena, 83*, 7–13. doi:10.1029/GM083p0007

Geller, R. J. (1997). Earthquake prediction: A critical review. *Geophysical Journal International, 131*(3), 425–450. doi:10.1111/j.1365-246X.1997.tb06588.x

Guo, H., Wang, L., Chen, F., & Liang, D. (2014). Scientific big data and digital earth. *Chinese Science Bulletin, 59*(35), 5066–5073. doi:10.100711434-014-0645-3

Hayakawa, M., & Hobara, Y. (2010). Current status of seismoelectromagnetics for short-term earthquake prediction. *Geomatics, Natural Hazards & Risk, 1*(2), 115–155. doi:10.1080/19475705.2010.486933

Hong, Y.-M., Lin, H.-C., & Kan, Y.-C. (2011). Using wireless sensor network on real-time remote monitoring of the load cell for landslide. *Sensor Letters, 9*(5), 1911–1915. doi:10.11661.2011.1522

Jin, J., Gubbi, J., Marusic, S., & Palaniswami, M. (2014). An information framework for creating a smart city through internet of things. *IEEE Internet of Things Journal, 1*(2), 112–121. doi:10.1109/JIOT.2013.2296516

Keilis-Borok, V. (2002). Earthquake prediction: State-of-the-art and emerging possibilities. *Annual Review of Earth and Planetary Sciences, 30*(1), 1–33. doi:10.1146/annurev.earth.30.100301.083856

Lin, J., & Ryaboy, D. (2013). Scaling big data mining infrastructure: The twitter experience. *SIGKDD Explorations, 14*(2), 2, 6–19. doi:10.1145/2481244.2481247

Lu, N., Cheng, N., Zhang, N., Shen, X., & Mark, J. (2014). Connected vehicles: Solutions and challenges. *IEEE Internet of Things Journal, 1*(4), 289–299. doi:10.1109/JIOT.2014.2327587

Marco. (2013). EARS (Earthquake Alert and Report System): Real Time Decision Support System for Earthquake Management. *KDD '14: Proceedings of the 20th ACM SIGKDD international conference on Knowledge discovery and data mining*, 1749–1758.

Martino, & ... . (2018). Internet of things reference architectures, security and interoperability: A survey. *Internet of Things, 1*, 99–112. doi:10.1016/j.iot.2018.08.008

Meng, X., & Feng, L. (2014). Research on application of internet of things technology to earthquake prevention and disaster reduction. *World Information on Earthquake Engineering, 30*(2), 129–133.

Metternicht, G., Hurni, L., & Gogu, R. (2005). Remote sensing of landslides: An analysis of the potential contribution to geo-spatial systems for hazard assessment in mountainous environments. *Remote Sensing of Environment, 98*(2), 284–303. doi:10.1016/j.rse.2005.08.004

Montori, Bedogni, L., Di Felice, M., & Bononi, L. (2018). Machine to-machine wireless communication Technologies for the internet of things: Taxonomy, comparison and open issues. *Pervasive and Mobile Computing, 50*, 56–81. doi:10.1016/j.pmcj.2018.08.002

Nachtigall, J., & Redlich, J.-P. (2011). Wireless alarming and routing protocol for earthquake early warning systems. In *4th IFIP International Conference on New Technologies, Mobility and Security*. IEEE. 10.1109/NTMS.2011.5720630

Nord, J., Koohang, A., & Paliszkiewicz, J. (2019). The internet of things: Review and theoretical framework. *Expert Systems with Applications, 133*, 97–108. doi:10.1016/j. eswa.2019.05.014

Picozzi, M., Milkereit, C., Fleming, K., Fischer, J., Jaeckel, K., Bindi, D., Parolai, S., & Zschau, J. (2014). Applications of a low-cost, wireless, selforganising system (sosewin) to earthquake early warning and structural health monitoring. Early Warning for Geological Disasters, 263–288.

Qin, L., Feng, S., & Zhu, H. (2018). Research on the technological architectural design of geological hazard monitoring and rescue-after-disaster system based on cloud computing and internet of things. *International Journal of Systems Assurance Engineering and Management, 9*(3), 684–695. doi:10.100713198-017-0638-0

Qingkai, Schreier, Allen, & Strauss. (2015). *Smartphone-based Networks for Earthquake Detection*. IEEE.

Ray P., (2018). A survey on internet of things architectures. *Journal of King Saud University - Computer and Information Sciences, 30*(3), 291–319.

Reid, M. E., & Lahusen, R. G. (1998). Real-time monitoring of active landslides along highway 50, el dorado county. *California Geology, 51*(3), 17–20.

Santos, M., & Oliveira, J. (2017). A big data system supporting bosch braga industry 4.0 strategy. *International Journal of Information Management, 37*(6), 750–760. doi:10.1016/j.ijinfomgt.2017.07.012

Sherki, Y., Gaikwad, N., Chandle, J., & Kulkarni, A. (2015). Design of real time sensor system for detection and processing of seismic waves for earthquake early warning system. *Conference: 2015 International Conference on Power and Advanced Control Engineering (ICPACE)*, 285–289. 10.1109/ICPACE.2015.7274959

Suzuki, Saruwatari, Kurata, & Morikawa. (2007). *Demo abstract: A high-density earthquake monitoring system using wireless sensor networks.* Academic Press.

Takeshi, Makot, & Yutaka. (2013). *Tweet Analysis for Real- Time Event Detection and Earthquake Reporting System Development.* Academic Press.

Thibaut, M. (2018). Convolutional network for earthquake detection and location. *Science Advances, 4*(2), 2. doi:10.1126ciadv.1700578 PMID:29487899

Wang & Ni. (2012). Wireless sensor networks for earthquake early warning systems of railway lines. *Lecture Notes in Electrical Engineering, 148*, 417–426.

Wu, Y.-M., & Kanamori, H. (2008). Development of an earthquake early warning system using Real-Time Strong Motion Signals. *PMC Article, 8*(1), 1–9. doi:10.33908010001 PMID:27879692

Yin-Min. (1999). *Development of an integrated Earthquake Early Warning System Case for the Hualien Area Earthquakes.* Academic Press.

Youssef, Y. El-Sheimy, & Noureldin. (2007). A novel earthquake warning system based on virtual mimo-wireless sensor networks. Academic Press.

Zambrano, P. Palau, & Esteve. (2014). Quake detection system using smartphone-based wireless sensor network for early warning. Academic Press.

Zambrano, Perez, Palau, & Esteve. (2017). Technologies of internet of things applied to an earthquake early warning system. *Future Generation Computer Systems, 75*, 206–215.

Chapter 15
Shifting Legacy Robotic Manufacturing Towards Industry 4.0:
Using Cloud IoT

Hadi Alasti
Purdue University Fort Wayne, USA

ABSTRACT

The mission of this chapter is to review and investigate the requirements and applications of using cloud-based internet of things (CIoT) for shifting the legacy robotic manufacturing towards Industry 4.0. Sensing and communications are two requirements of Industry 4.0. In the chapter, the legacy robotic manufacturing equipment collaborate with the environment, where it supports sustainable manufacturing. An implementation example of the proposed scenario will be discussed in this chapter.

INTRODUCTION

The advancement in information and communication technology (ICT) and Internet of things (IoT) and their rapid influence in industrial applications has been the foundation for a new revolution in industry (Li, 2017; Santos, et al., 2017). The fourth industrial revolution (industry 4.0) started around 2011, after the third industrial revolution with the presence of industrial computers and information technology in manufacturing sites (Atkeson & Kehoe, 2001). With the assistance of ICT and IoT, industry 4.0 can meet its objectives, such as improvement in production efficiency in

DOI: 10.4018/978-1-7998-6981-8.ch015

manufacturing sites, production speed enhancement, production reliability and quality improvement for better customer experience, reliable production automation, and integration of manufacturing and supply-chain management, with minimum human intervention (Tay, et.al, 2018; Qin, et.al. 2016). In an industry 4.0 ecosystem, the machine-to-machine (M2M) communication and machine-to-environment (M2E) communication improves the reliability, productivity and safety. In this ecosystem, IoT (Alasti, 2021), or in a more generalized concept, network of things (NoT) (Voas, 2016) provides the requirements of M2M and M2E.

Cloud computing with its continuously increasing importance in ICT and IoT services has an essential role in implementation of industry 4.0 services and development of its successor generations. The specific industrial ecosystem of the manufacturing sites, demands computing machinery with rugged attributes, where it may not be necessarily possible. Using cloud computing allows to shift the computing power over the cloud, where it drastically saves in the required special space and expenses. It is important to mention that cloud security is a major concern yet. As a solution to this issue, dynamical security enhancement has been proposed in literatures to overcome the tentative security breaches (Hamilton & Alasti, 2017; Li, et. al 2019; Sanislav, 2017; Tian & Jing, 2019). Some of these solutions are proprietary and need special permission over the data and service domain of cloud or the cloud broker service provider premises (Hamilton & Alasti, 2017).

Regardless of its security concern, cloud environment is one of the popular instances for data storage and processing, that can be used in implementation of ICT and IoT services. The collected data from the robotic and production machinery is transferred over the cloud for storage, online data visualization, data processing and filtering for better next step "on-site decisioning", and sending notification e-mail or text messages to the relevant identities such as the working machines, or technical and managing personnel, once it is required. Transmission of massive volume of the collected data from variety of the sensor observations for storage over the cloud can be considered as a big data problem. The advantages and weakness of using cloud-based IoT (CIoT) service for industry 4.0 application is discussed in the body of this chapter, in brief.

Collaboration with the other machines and the environment is one essential requirement in industry 4.0 (Alasti, 2021), and for this purpose the industry 4.0 machinery need to have a correct sense of their work environment to track changes. Thus, embedding different types of sensors in machinery and in the environment is of prime importance. Collection of the sensor observations over the cloud happens via communication that is usually wireless. Variety of wireless communication technologies, such as WiFi, cellular technologies, narrow-band IoT wireless communication categories, etc. can be used for collection of the sensor data to the CIoT site. One of the important requirements of the communication technologies that are used for industrial applications is short delay. However, communication is not the only reason for delay in industrial IoT (IIoT) and the other latencies due to coding nature, hardware interfaces, CIoT site bandwidth, etc. needs to be considered in a well-developed CIoT application.

Even though the penetration of industry 4.0 in manufacturing is increasing, however there are a considerable number of factories that have a large number of working legacy robotic machinery and replacement of them with expensive industry 4.0 machinery is not affordable in short term. This chapter proposes a transitional model for shifting towards industry 4.0 requirements by employing CIoT and embedding wireless sensors in the environment.

The rest of this chapter is organized as follows. In the next section, the motivation for proposing the transitional model will be reviewed. Next, the related technologies and their requirements will be given along with sufficient review of the related literature. The proposed transitional model will be introduced next, and finally a real-life implementation of the proposed model will be presented.

Motivation

The low-cost of wireless sensor platforms, the easily available wireless communication technologies, the relatively low-cost cloud services, and the available industrial computers with networking capability are the promising means for development of a transitional model to shift the application of the legacy robotic machinery towards industry 4.0. One major difference between the industry 4.0 machinery and their legacy robotic equipment are awareness and access to data. Low-cost CIoT services and flexible wireless sensor platforms with their small form factors, have made it possible to add the sensor observations for collection of work environment and the other machines' data and gather them over the cloud for processing purpose.

Most of the legacy robotic machines are controlled by proprietary robot controller units, and at times even the connection ports are proprietary standards of the same robot manufacturer. Several replacement options have been thought of for the robot controller units, such as programmable logic controllers (PLC). PLCs have been the workhorse of the manufacturing industries for decades (Chivilikhin, 2020). Unfortunately, PLCs usually have insufficient networking capabilities and cannot control variety of the robots due to their limited programming options. Luckily, there are programmable automation controllers (PAC) with extensive networking capability and possibility of being used instead of robot controllers. Pricewise, there are brands of PAC that are affordable and have lots of networking and communication features.

The affordable technology expenses, their powerful capability, flexibility and scalability are the main motivations for this transitional model to shift the application of the legacy robotic machinery towards industry 4.0.

Related Technologies

The proposed transitional model for shifting the legacy robotic equipment towards the requirements of industry 4.0 is based on employing a number of recent advancements in technology and science. Among them are IoT and IIoT, cloud computing, artificial intelligence (AI) and machine learning (ML), wireless sensing, and industrial computing. In this section, each and every of these branches of technology are reviewed, in brief and their connection to the proposed model are discussed.

As it was previously mentioned, one major difference between industry 4.0 and its predecessors is tethering data to the robotic and automation equipment that are used in manufacturing technology. By incorporating data to this technology, the equipment can collaborate with each other in order to improve the productivity, efficiency, quality of products, increase of safety, etc. In big picture, the presence of data with the help of sensing, wireless communications, cloud computing, IoT, AI techniques; industrial computation, increases the system's awareness and knowledge of inter-element, and as results they improve the production outcomes and reduce the risks and losses.

Cloud Computing

As an emerging technology, cloud computing provides means such as infrastructure for transferred data, space for storage of data, processing power for required computation and in short it provides customizable resources for Internet-based computations (Birjie, et. al, 2017). With its three main basic services of infrastructure as a service (IaaS), platform as a service (PaaS), and software as a service (SaaS) (Senyo, et. al, 2018), cloud computing provides access to virtual computing infrastructure, access to specific operating system, and access to specific applications via Internet. This virtualized computing allows scalable access to the above services for a large number of users, that are distributed over a wide geographical area. These services provide real-time access to data, which is one of the principal requirements of industry 4.0. This data is the sensor observation that are generated by the sensors, and cloud acts as intermediary access to data with processing capability. Figure 1, shows access to the stored and processed data and storing the generated data over the cloud. The sensor's data is sent over the cloud, where this data is retrieved, whenever it is needed.

Even though cloud computing provides fabulous services for storage and access to data, access latency due to remote or distributed nature of the service needs to be considered, as well. The emerging wireless communication systems such as 5G considers around 10 ms end-to-end latency, and 6G is expected to consider 1 ms or smaller. With these short end-to-end delays, the access to data for proper action in actuators is guaranteed. However, the latency is not just limited to the communication

Figure 1. Shows access to the stored and processed data and storing the generated data over the cloud

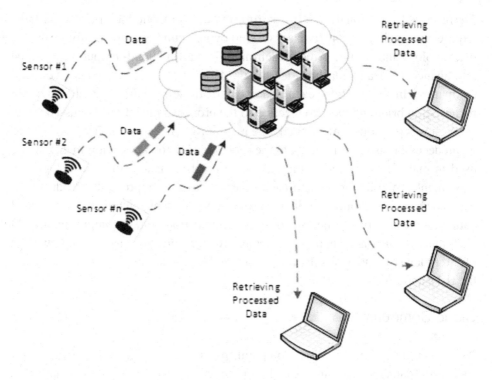

system's delay. Among the other instance of latency are the delay generated by running code on industrial computer, queueing delay on CIoT service site, delay caused by packet contention in WiFi network, etc.

Wireless Sensor Networks

Wireless sensor networks have been used for industrial application, military application, aerospace application, etc. The embedded technology along with the flexible programming language of the wireless sensor platforms allows to reshape their application based on needs. WSN used to have battery-life limitation, however in the course of time and after the built of low power microcontrollers and by using energy efficient wireless protocols and of course with the design of more durable batteries, battery-life is not a major issue in many applications. Moreover, in indoor manufacturing sites, the sensor platforms are often within the access range to local power outlets.

As mentioned in the introduced standard by NIST (Voas, 2016), sensors are one of the key elements of IoT, where they are responsible for collection of sensor data. This data that is used for industry 4.0 applications have to be shared with other machines. In CIoT model, all sensor observation data are stored over the cloud and the industrial computing systems retrieve the most recent data to respond properly to the changes by adjusting the reaction of the robotic machines (Alasti, 2021).

The most common short-range wireless protocols in wireless sensor applications are WiFi, ZigBee, Bluetooth, Near-field communication (NFC), ZigBee, etc. Amon these protocols, WiFi is the most common one due to its available bandwidth and supporting data rate, flexible coverage range in more recent WiFi protocols, and of course the most recent available security options after ratification of WPA3 security standard. WPA3, allows customizable security options that is very ideal for IoT-based devices. The most recent Bluetooth standards such as BT-5 is low power, however it has shorter coverage range and supports smaller data rate. NFC, similar to Bluetooth suffers from low data rate and short coverage range. ZigBee, similar to WiFi has a good coverage, however its options are not as flexible as WiFi.

A wireless sensor platform may support one or more than one wireless protocol. For instance, in comparison to MicaZ that used to support only ZigBee wireless protocol, there are variants of wireless platforms, such as ESP32 that support WiFi (802.11b/g/n), Bluetooth (IEEE 802.15.1) and LoRa (low power wide area network). This flexibility allows to have connectivity via different types of wireless protocols.

ZigBee:

ZigBee technology of ZigBee Alliance, is an inexpensive technology that meets the requirements of IEEE 802.15.4 in physical (PHY) and media access control (MAC) layers. The low duty cycle of this standard makes it suitable for battery-life maximization. Also, this technology has low latency, which is good for M2M applications. The protocol has limited encryption under advance encryption standard (AES). Connecting multiple ZigBee wireless nodes together using mesh networking option, is possible. This feature allows to connect multiple application nodes together, where it is suitable in M2M, smart homes, etc.

WiFi:

WiFi technologies that meet the requirements of IEEE 802.11 (a/b/g/n/ac/ad/ax/ ay) and WiFi Alliance allows the machines to communicate to each other directly in ad-hoc way, or in an infrastructure and via WiFi access-point. With their high data rate, the recent WiFi technologies are capable to convey variety of data and live high-definition video. WiFi technologies mostly use unlicensed bands, such as industrial-scientific-medical (ISM) in 2.4 GHz, 5 GHz and recently 60 GHz.

Bluetooth:

Bluetooth is a short-range standard for wireless personal area networks and its PHY and MAC meets the requirements of IEEE 802.15.1 standard. BLE, or smart Bluetooth is the low energy consumption release of this technology that was ratified in 2010. Bluetooth has application in wearable devices such as smart watches, wireless headphones, car audio, etc. Similar to ZigBee and WiFi, Bluetooth also work on unlicensed bands.

Figure 2. Wireless sensors collect the environment data and send them over the communication channel

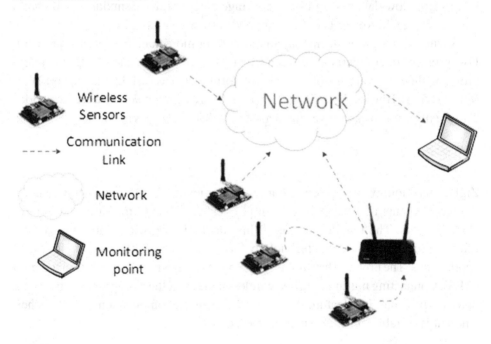

Internet of Things

Internet of things (IoT) is formed by combination of sensing, computation, communication, and actuation (Voas, 2016). The concept of IoT is that everything in different spots of our planet can be interconnected in the global dynamics of an expandable network (Farash, et.al, 2016), where in this network variety of devices are sharing data. This technology encompasses embedded technology, embedded software, communications, and "things". IoT with its trillion-dollar technology and market, is at high security risk (Lund, et.al, 2014), which is one of its challenges. Industrial internet of things or IIoT, is a collection of smart sensors that enables precise control and monitoring of complex processors over arbitrary distance (Huberman, 2016).

It is important to introduce network of things (NoT) as a more general concept than NoT, where the difference with IoT is subtle (Voas, 2016). In fact, IoT is an instance of NoT. Other instances of NoT are social media networks, sensor networks and industrial Internet of things (Voas, 2016). The elements of NoT, according to National Institute of Standards and Technology (NIST) are sensors, aggregators, communications, external utility, and decision trigger. The reliability and security of the aforementioned elements are also important. Figure 3, illustrates the elements of NoT.

Adding access to cloud computing for IoT relieves the computation and storage limitation of IoT. With this integration, IoT can enjoy the scalable, virtual computing resources of cloud computing (You, Feng, 2020).

Application of Industrial IoT (IIoT) are in variety of fields, such as performance optimization of motor drives and prediction of machine failure (Pye, 2016; Miskvitch, 2017), industrial energy systems (Robison, 2015), healthcare applications (Al-Turjman & Alturjman, 2018), asset management (Gandhewar, 2019), smart grid (Chaudhary, 2018), monitoring power substations (Zhao, 2019), agriculture and agro-industries (Almadani & Mostafa, 2021), etc.

Industrial Computing

Industrial computing machines, such as PLCs and programmable automation controllers have been used in forming the control systems in industry 3.0, for years. In this section a brief review for the capabilities of these two industrial computers is provided.

PLCs and PACs with their analogue and digital input/output (I/O) ports are used to control the functionality and process of systems in automation applications. PACs, unlike PLCs, can be used for controlling processes and multiple PLCs in lower level in architecture. For instance, PACs may handle large number of proportional differentiator-Integrator (PID) control loops, unlike PLCs. Moreover, the open architecture and modular design of PACs, allows them to support variety of communication and networking protocols. Accordingly, PACs can be used for control and monitoring of process, systems and sites based on the required communication and networking protocol.

Figure 3. IoT elements (This figure has been reproduced from (Voas, 2016))

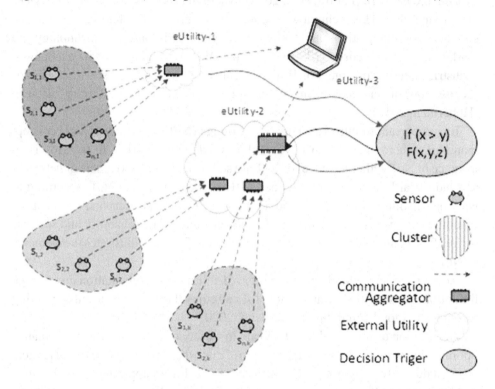

PACs normally support database and database languages, such as SQL and usually variety of programming languages can be executed over these machines. Accordingly, a PAC might be used like an industrial personal computer (iPC), which is a great advantage for the engineering project to implement an application that has been tested on regular PCs, on these industrial computers.

In shifting the legacy robotic machinery towards industry 4 application, a PAC can be used instead of the regular robot controller unit. Additional hardware such as port interface and driver might be required between the PAC and the legacy robotic equipment. The low cost of some brands of PAC makes them suitable choices for the proposed transitional model of this chapter, in shifting the legacy robotic machinery towards industry 4. Figure 4, illustrates the AMAX 5580 PAC that is used in implementation of the proposed transitional model in this chapter.

Artificial Intelligence

Artificial intelligence (AI), or the science of machine intelligent algorithms for machines to do the same work with better quality than human being, goes back

Figure 4. AMAX 5580, programmable automation controller (PAC) that is used in experimental implementation of the proposed transitional model

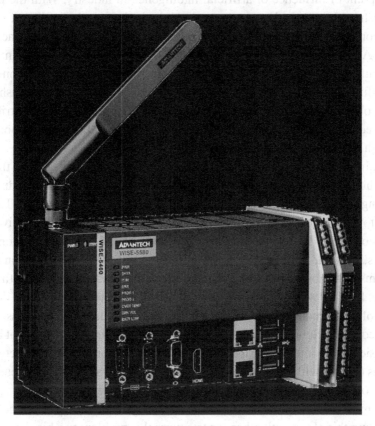

to the middle of the twentieth century. It happened by demonstration of the first running AI algorithm in Carnegie Mellon University. However, development of neural networks' algorithms based on human being's brain was laid in 1943. In 1965, ELIZA, the robotic system that could carry on dialogues in English was build.

AI has been used in different fields such as computer science, psychology, biology, mathematics, sociology, engineering and technology, etc. Nowadays, there are several real-life application fields that AI is heavily involved in, such as gaming, natural language processing, expert systems, vision systems, speech recognition, handwriting recognition, pattern recognition, intelligent robots, resource allocation optimization in wireless communication systems, patience monitoring in healthcare, industry 4.0, etc.

Patterns of industry operation has drastically affected by artificial AI and machine learning algorithms. The effect of these algorithms has replaced man by machine and has affected the man and machine interactions. Industry 4.0 is the turning point of influence of artificial intelligence in industry. With the power of AI, industry 4 improves the system productivity, enhances the quality of products, etc. Accordingly, it is true to say that industry 4's objectives are not achievable without AI and machine learning algorithms. The application of AI in robotics and manufacturing has been reported in literature. This application becomes more meaningful when robots are collaborating with each other in accomplishment of a bigger objective, where a number of robots are involved in. Either distributed or centralized decisioning about the role of each of these collaborating robots can be done with the help of AI algorithms.

ML algorithms, as a subset of AI allow the machines to learn on their own without human being intervention, which is one of the objectives of industry 4.0. Accordingly, industry 4.0 needs ML algorithms more than AI, in general. The added sensors to the robotic system allow the algorithms to exploit the massive sensor observations in order to optimize the final outcome of the collaboration among machines. Fast and efficient algorithms are required for implementation of these algorithms to be able to manage a number of robotic machines for an optimal final outcome. In other words, powerful computational systems are in need to do a large number of mathematical processing in a short time. Today, large processing loads are shifted to the cloud as it has integrated supercomputing capabilities at bearable cost. Besides computational capability, a low latency communication between the machines (M2M) with reliable resources is required to transfer the collected sensor observation data to the remote site with an acceptable delay.

Placement of variety of sensors in the field, results in variety of collected data. Considering this along with other aspects turns this problem to a big data problem. In other words, industry 4.0 demands the accumulation of different branches of science and technology and help of massive computing capability of supercomputing platforms.

The Proposed Transitional Model

A transitional model is proposed for using legacy non-collaborative robotic machinery in industry 4.0 environment. This model adds awareness to the legacy robotic machines by embedding wireless sensing devices in the work environment for collection of data, to allow the programable machines to react properly with the changes in the work environment and in accordance with the other working machines. Figure 5, shows a basic layout for sharing the environment data with a robot arm via CIoT. The wireless sensors track changes in the environment or the other machines' status and send the sensor observations to the cloud. The data is stored on CIoT storage and processed based on algorithms, such as nearest neighbours, which is a kind of

ML algorithm. The robot arm controller is replaced with the PAC and tentatively a proper hardware interface that comes between the PAC and the robot. The PAC frequently checks the CIoT storage for the most recent received data from the work environment. The PAC updates the motion of the robot according to the most recent updates from the environment.

A program code that runs on PAC is responsible for getting the most recent data from the cloud and controlling the arm's motion. The program code must be even-driven so that any sudden changes in the work environment can be tracked and its results be reflected on robotic machine's motion or behaviour.

As mentioned before, the communication must be with the least latency so that the proposed system can track the required changes in proper time. Luckily, the emerging wireless communication systems such as 5G and the upcoming 6G have short end-to-end delay (less than 1 ms), which is proper for M2M communications.

Figure 5. Elements of the proposed transitional model for shifting the application of e legacy robotic arm towards industry 4.0

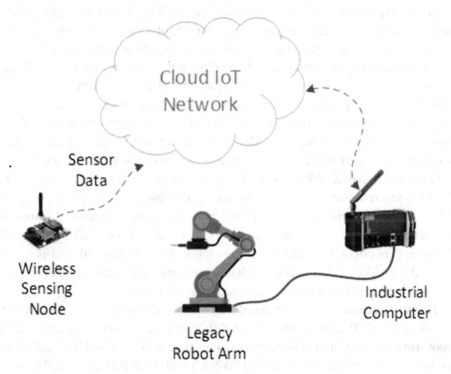

Experimental Work

In this section an implementation instance of the proposed transitional model to shift the legacy robotic towards industry 4.0, is reviewed and discussed. The elements of the experimental work and the employed communications are illustrated in figure 6. In this implementation, MECA 500-III is used as a non-collaborative robot arm and AMAX 5580 is used as an industrial computing unit and replacement for the legacy robot controller.

In this experiment, ESP8266 microcontroller unit is used as wireless computing platform. A directly attached ultrasonic proximity sensor to the ESP8266 provides data for the computing unit to specify the zones of the approaching object. This data can be used to manage the motion speed of the robot arm. For instance, if the approaching object is another robot or a human-being, the sensor data can be used for safety purpose, or collaboration with the other machines. The collected and processed data of the wireless sensor platform are sent over the cloud via a secure, private WiFi to the CIoT site. In this experiment, the sensor data are sent over the CIoT site every second.

In this experiment, the MathWorks affiliated CIoT service by Thingspeak is used for CIoT service. The free educational service of Thingspeak allows to upload data every 15 seconds. In this experiment, the academic service with data upload rate of one data per second is used. Even though this upload rate is not sufficient for practical work, however the same approach can be used with CIoT services with shorter latency. One attractive feature of the CIoT service of Thingspeak is the possibility of online writing of MATLAB codes for processing of the collected data. Specifically, using the solid ML algorithms of MATLAB that are useful in processing of data of multiple sensors makes the decisioning more accurate.

One unit of AMAX 5580, which is a PAC is used as robot controller unit. AMAX 5580, has several communication ports, such as Gigabit Ethernet port; RS-232, RS-485, and USB as serial data ports; HDMI port, that in this experiment is used for connection to monitor; etc. One featured characteristic of this PAC is its modular attribute. It is possible to add several modules of the aforementioned ports and EtherCAT to AMAX 5580. The unit has an optional WiFi network interface card that in this experiment is used for connection to the CIoT.

The network connectivity setting of the Gigabit Ethernet ports on AMAX 5580 are set on fixed IP address (instead of DHCP) for permanent connection of the robot arm to the PAC unit. The network connection of the PAC to CIoT site is setup via its wireless network interface card (WNIC) with DHCP IP address. The wired and wireless network interface cards allow to make two independent networks on AMAX 5580. One network is formed for the connected robotic machine and one

Figure 6. Experimental Implementation of the proposed transitional algorithm

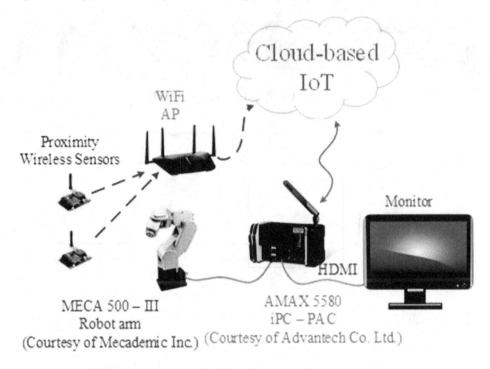

is used for retrieving data from the remote site. The modular feature of this PAC allows to manage several machines at the same time on different fixed IP addresses.

MECA 500 robot arm is used in this experiment as the non-collaborative arm. This robot arm, in its usual form is controlled by a personal computer in two possible forms. Either the robot arm is controlled using the web browser, or using script coding. In this experiment, Python code is used due to its strength in network coding, and simplicity of working with hardware. The Python code frequently checks the Thingspeak CIoT site for the most recent changes in sensor observation data. In this experiment, MECA 500 is connected to the PAC unit via Gigabit Ethernet port.

Figure 7, illustrates the distance data in inches from the proximity sensor that is placed in vicinity of the robot arm. The distance of the moving object from time to time is presented in this figure.

CONCLUSION

A transitional model is proposed and discussed in this chapter for using the legacy robotic machines in industry 4. The proposed model is based on using cloud-based

Figure 7. The distance of a moving object to the proximity sensor in inch

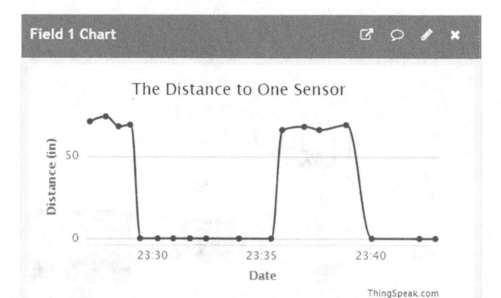

Internet of things (CIoT), as an intermediary service to store, process and visualize the sensor observation data. The related technologies for the proposed model are briefly reviewed.

An experimental implementation of the proposed model is presented based on using CIoT, on-site wireless sensing and replacement of the legacy robot controller unit with a programmable automation controller as an industrial computer. In this experiment, Thingspeak, a MathWorks affiliated CIoT is used for data storage, data processing and data visualization. Ultrasonic proximity sensor, that is directly attached to ESP8266 as wireless platform, is used for observation of the approaching objects to the robot arm. MECA 500, a product of Mecademic Inc. is used as a non-collaborative robot for this experiment. The common robot controller to this robot is a personal computer, which is replaced with AMAX 5580, a programmable automation controller (PAC) with communication and networking capability.

In this experiment, an academic service account with one sensor observation data per second is used, which results in latency more than one second. This latency is too much for real-life industrial automation application. However, the proposed solution is a valid solution in general. Therefore, in next step using services with lower latency will be implemented. Using low latency communication systems such as 5G, with its maximum end-to-end 10 ms delay is one candidate for communication system to use.

REFERENCES

Al-Turjman, F., & Alturjman, S. (2018). Context-sensitive access in industrial internet of things (IIoT) healthcare applications. *IEEE Transactions on Industrial Informatics*, *14*(6), 2736–2744. doi:10.1109/TII.2018.2808190

Alasti, H. (2021). Adapting legacy robotic machinery to industry 4: a CIoT experiment. *Technology Interface International Journal*.

Alasti, H. (2021). Turning A Legacy Robot to Collaborate To Fit in Industry 4.0 Demands. *Proceedings of the ASEE Conference*.

Almadani, B., & Mostafa, S. M. (2021). IIoT Based Multimodal Communication Model for Agriculture and Agro-Industries. *IEEE Access: Practical Innovations, Open Solutions*, *9*, 10070–10088. doi:10.1109/ACCESS.2021.3050391

Atkeson, A., & Kehoe, P. J. (2001). *The transition to a new economy after the second industrial revolution (No. w8676)*. National Bureau of Economic Research. doi:10.3386/w8676

Birje, M. N., Challagidad, P. S., Goudar, R. H., & Tapale, M. T. (2017). Cloud computing review: Concepts, technology, challenges and security. *International Journal of Cloud Computing*, *6*(1), 32–57. doi:10.1504/IJCC.2017.083905

Chaudhary, R., Aujla, G. S., Garg, S., Kumar, N., & Rodrigues, J. J. (2018). SDN-enabled multi-attribute-based secure communication for smart grid in IIoT environment. *IEEE Transactions on Industrial Informatics*, *14*(6), 2629–2640. doi:10.1109/TII.2018.2789442

Chivilikhin, D., Patil, S., Cordonnier, A., & Vyatkin, V. (2019, July). Towards automatic state machine reconstruction from legacy PLC using data collection. In *2019 IEEE 17th International Conference on Industrial Informatics (INDIN)* (Vol. 1, pp. 147-151). IEEE. 10.1109/INDIN41052.2019.8972143

Farash, M. S., Turkanović, M., Kumari, S., & Hölbl, M. (2016). An efficient user authentication and key agreement scheme for heterogeneous wireless sensor network tailored for the Internet of Things environment. *Ad Hoc Networks*, *36*, 152–176. doi:10.1016/j.adhoc.2015.05.014

Gandhewar, R., Gaurav, A., Kokate, K., Khetan, H., & Kamat, H. (2019, June). Cloud Based Framework for IIOT Application with Asset Management. In *2019 3rd International Conference on Electronics, Communication and Aerospace Technology (ICECA)* (pp. 920-925). IEEE. 10.1109/ICECA.2019.8821897

Hamilton, H., & Alasti, H. (2017). Controlled Intelligent Agents' Security Model for Multi-Tenant Cloud Computing Infrastructures. *International Journal of Grid and High Performance Computing*, *9*(1), 1–13. doi:10.4018/IJGHPC.2017010101

Huberman, B. A. (2016). Ensuring trust and security in the industrial IoT: The internet of things (ubiquity symposium). *Ubiquity*, *2016*(January), 1–7. doi:10.1145/2822883

Li, L. (2018). China's manufacturing locus in 2025: With a comparison of "Made-in-China 2025" and "Industry 4.0". *Technological Forecasting and Social Change*, *135*, 66–74. doi:10.1016/j.techfore.2017.05.028

Li, W., Cao, J., Hu, K., Xu, J., & Buyya, R. (2019). A trust-based agent learning model for service composition in mobile cloud computing environments. *IEEE Access: Practical Innovations, Open Solutions*, *7*, 34207–34226. doi:10.1109/ACCESS.2019.2904081

Lund, D., MacGillivray, C., Turner, V., & Morales, M. (2014). Worldwide and regional internet of things (iot) 2014–2020 forecast: A virtuous circle of proven value and demand. International Data Corporation (IDC). *Tech. Rep*, *1*(1), 9.

Moskvitch, K. (2017). When machinery chats. *Engineering & Technology*, *12*(2), 68–70. doi:10.1049/et.2017.0209

Pye, A. (2016). Drives in the Internet of Things. *Engineering & Technology*, *11*(3), 72–74. doi:10.1049/et.2016.0332

Qin, J., Liu, Y., & Grosvenor, R. (2016). A categorical framework of manufacturing for industry 4.0 and beyond. *Procedia CIRP*, *52*, 173–178. doi:10.1016/j.procir.2016.08.005

Robison, P., Sengupta, M., & Rauch, D. (2015). Intelligent energy industrial systems 4.0. *IT Professional*, *17*(3), 17–24. doi:10.1109/MITP.2015.48

Sanislav, T., Zeadally, S., & Mois, G. D. (2017). A cloud-integrated, multilayered, agent-based cyber-physical system architecture. *Computer*, *50*(4), 27–37. doi:10.1109/MC.2017.113

Santos, C., Mehrsai, A., Barros, A. C., Araújo, M., & Ares, E. (2017). Towards Industry 4.0: An overview of European strategic roadmaps. *Procedia Manufacturing*, *13*, 972–979. doi:10.1016/j.promfg.2017.09.093

Senyo, P. K., Addae, E., & Boateng, R. (2018). Cloud computing research: A review of research themes, frameworks, methods and future research directions. *International Journal of Information Management, 38*(1), 128–139. doi:10.1016/j.ijinfomgt.2017.07.007

Tay, S. I., Lee, T. C., Hamid, N. Z. A., & Ahmad, A. N. A. (2018). An overview of industry 4.0: Definition, components, and government initiatives. *Journal of Advanced Research in Dynamical and Control Systems, 10*(14), 1379–1387.

Tian, J., & Jing, X. (2019). A lightweight secure auditing scheme for shared data in cloud storage. *IEEE Access: Practical Innovations, Open Solutions, 7,* 68071–68082. doi:10.1109/ACCESS.2019.2916889

Voas, J. (2016). Demystifying the internet of things. *Computer, 49*(6), 80–83. doi:10.1109/MC.2016.162

Voas, J. (2016). Networks of 'things'. *NIST Special Publication, 800*(183), 800–183.

You, Z., & Feng, L. (2020). Integration of industry 4.0 related technologies in construction industry: A framework of cyber-physical system. *IEEE Access: Practical Innovations, Open Solutions, 8,* 122908–122922. doi:10.1109/ACCESS.2020.3007206

Zhao, L., Matsuo, I. B. M., Zhou, Y., & Lee, W. J. (2019). Design of an industrial IoT-based monitoring system for power substations. *IEEE Transactions on Industry Applications, 55*(6), 5666–5674. doi:10.1109/TIA.2019.2940668

Compilation of References

Aazam, M., Zeadally, S., & Harras, K. A. (2018). Offloading in fog computing for IoT: Review, enabling technologies, and research opportunities. *Future Generation Computer Systems*, *87*, 278–289. doi:10.1016/j.future.2018.04.057

Abdullahi, H. S., Sheriff, R., & Mahieddine, F. (2017, August). Convolution neural network in precision agriculture for plant image recognition and classification. In *2017 Seventh International Conference on Innovative Computing Technology (INTECH)* (Vol. 10). IEEE. 10.1109/INTECH.2017.8102436

Abrar, I., Ayub, Z., Masoodi, F., & Bamhdi, A. M. (2020). A Machine Learning Approach for Intrusion Detection System on NSL-KDD Dataset. *Proceedings - International Conference on Smart Electronics and Communication, ICOSEC 2020*, 919–924. 10.1109/ICOSEC49089.2020.9215232

Acharya, D., Goel, S., Asthana, R., & Bhardwaj, A. (2020). A novel fitness function in genetic programming to handle unbalanced emotion recognition data. *Pattern Recognition Letters*, *133*, 272–279. doi:10.1016/j.patrec.2020.03.005

Activeadvise. (2017). *What is Smart Health and How do People Benefit?* Retrieved from https://www.activeadvice.eu/news/concept-projects/what-is-smart-health-and-how-do-people-benefit/

Agale, R. (2017) Automated Irrigation and Crop Security System in Agriculture Using Internet of Things. *2017 International Conference on Computing, Communication, Control and Automation (ICCUBEA)*, 1-5. 10.1109/ICCUBEA.2017.8463726

Aguayo-Torres, M. C., Gómez, G., & Poncela, J. (2015). *Wired/Wireless Internet Communications (WWIC): 13th International Conference, May 25-27, Revised Selected Papers*. Malaga, Spain: Springer.

Ahmed Teli, T., & Masoodi, F. (2021). Security Concerns and Privacy Preservation in Blockchain based IoT Systems: Opportunities and Challenges. *ICICNIS 2020*.

Ajibola, S., & Goosen, L. (2017). Development of Heuristics for Usability Evaluation of M-Commerce Applications. In P. Blignaut, & T. Stott (Ed.), *Proceedings of the South African Institute of Computer Scientists and Information Technologists (SAICSIT)* (pp. 19 - 28). Thaba 'Nchu, South Africa: Association for Computing Machinery (ACM). 10.1145/3129416.3129428

Akaber, P., Moussa, B., Debbabi, M., & Assi, C. (2019). Automated Post-Failure Service Restoration in Smart Grid through Network Reconfiguration in the Presence of Energy Storage Systems. *IEEE Systems Journal, 13*(3), 1–10. doi:10.1109/JSYST.2019.2892581

Alamri, A., Ansari, W. S., Hassan, M. M., Hossain, M. S., Alelaiwi, A., & Hossain, M. A. (2013). A survey on sensor-cloud: Architecture, applications, and approaches. *International Journal of Distributed Sensor Networks, 9*(2), 917923. doi:10.1155/2013/917923

Alansari, Z., Anuar, N. B., Kamsin, A., & Soomro, S. (2018). Challenges of Internet of Things and Big Data Integration. *International Conference on International Conference on Emerging Technologies in Computing 2018 (ICETiC '18)*, 1–9. 10.1007/978-3-319-95450-9_4

Alansari, Z., Soomro, S., Belgaum, M. R., & Shamshirband, S. (2018). The rise of Internet of Things (IoT) in big healthcare data: Review and open research issues. *Progess in Advances in Intelligent Systems and Computing, 564*, 675–685. doi:10.1007/978-981-10-6875-1_66

Alao, A., & Brink, R. (2020). Impact of ICTs for Sustainable Development of Youth Employability. In *Promoting Inclusive Growth in the Fourth Industrial Revolution* (pp. 148–180). IGI Global. doi:10.4018/978-1-7998-4882-0.ch006

Alasti, H. (2021). Adapting legacy robotic machinery to industry 4: a CIoT experiment. *Technology Interface International Journal.*

Alasti, H. (2021). Turning A Legacy Robot to Collaborate To Fit in Industry 4.0 Demands. *Proceedings of the ASEE Conference.*

Alberti, A. M., dos Reis, E. S., Rosa Righi, R. D., Muñoz, V. M., & Chang, V. (2016). *Converging Future Internet, "Things", and Big Data: An Specification Following NovaGenesis Model.* Academic Press.

Alessio, B., De Donato, W., Persico, V., & Pescapé, A. (2014, August). On the integration of cloud computing and internet of things. In Proc. Future Internet of Things and Cloud (FiCloud) (pp. 23-30). Academic Press.

Alfarisy, A. A., Chen, Q., & Guo, M. (2018, April). Deep learning based classification for paddy pests & diseases recognition. In *Proceedings of 2018 International Conference on Mathematics and Artificial Intelligence* (pp. 21-25). 10.1145/3208788.3208795

Al-Fuqaha, A., Khreishah, A., Guizani, M., Rayes, A., & Mohammad, M. (2015). *Towards better horozontal integration among IoT services.* Academic Press.

Alhakbani, N., Hassan, M. M., Hossain, M. A., & Alnuem, M. (2014). A framework of adaptive interaction support in cloud-based internet of things (IoT) environment. In Lecture Notes in Computer Science (Vol. 8729, pp. 136–146). Springer Verlag., doi:10.1007/978-3-319-11692-1_12

Almadani, B., & Mostafa, S. M. (2021). IIoT Based Multimodal Communication Model for Agriculture and Agro-Industries. *IEEE Access: Practical Innovations, Open Solutions, 9*, 10070–10088. doi:10.1109/ACCESS.2021.3050391

Almadhoun, R., Kadadha, M., Alhemeiri, M., Alshehhi, M., & Salah, K. (2018, October). A user authentication scheme of IoT devices using blockchain-enabled fog nodes. In *2018 IEEE/ ACS 15th international conference on computer systems and applications (AICCSA)* (pp. 1-8). IEEE. 10.1109/AICCSA.2018.8612856

Alotaibi, K. H. (2015). *Threat in Cloud-denial of service (DoS) and distributed denial of service (DDoS) attack, and security measures*. Academic Press.

Alphonsa, A., & Ravi, G. (2016). *Earthquake early warning system by iot using wireless sensor networks*. Academic Press.

Al-Turjman, F., & Alturjman, S. (2018). Context-sensitive access in industrial internet of things (IIoT) healthcare applications. *IEEE Transactions on Industrial Informatics*, *14*(6), 2736–2744. doi:10.1109/TII.2018.2808190

Amadeo, M., Ruggeri, G., Campolo, C., Molinaro, A., Loscrí, V., & Calafate, C. T. (2019). Fog Computing in IoT Smart Environments via Named Data Networking : A Study on Service Orchestration Mechanisms. *Future Internet*, *11*(11), 222. doi:10.3390/fi11110222

Amoore, L. (2013). *The politics of possibility: Risk and security beyond probability*. Duke University Press. doi:10.1215/9780822377269

Anderson, J. (2010). *ICT transforming education: a regional guide*. https://unesdoc.unesco.org/ ark:/48223/pf0000189216

Anderson, R. (2001). *Security engineering : a guide to building dependable distributed systems*. Wiley.

Andrew. (2014). *Connectivity and the Internet of Things*. Available online: https://www.frost. com/reg/blog-display.do?id=3161648.

Andrew, A. Anthony and Jacek, (2013). Earthquake: Twitter as a Distributed Sensor-. *Transactions in GIS*. Advance online publication. doi:10.1111/j.1467-9671.2012.01359.x

Angwin, J. (2013). NSA struggles to make sense of flood of surveillance data. *Wall Street Journal*.

Animesh, A. (2015). *Assessment of pollution by Physicochemical Water Parameters Using Regression Analysis: A Case Study of Gagan River at Moradabad- India*. Pelagia Research Library Advances in Applied Science Research.

Antonopoulos, N., & Gillam, L. (2010). *Cloud computing*. Springer. doi:10.1007/978-1-84996-241-4

Aoki, H., Shikano, H., Okuno, M., Ogata, Y., Miyamoto, H., Tsushima, Y., . . . Nishimura, S. (2010, September). Cloud architecture for tight interaction with the real world and deep sensor-data aggregation mechanism. In *SoftCOM 2010, 18th International Conference on Software, Telecommunications and Computer Networks* (pp. 280-284). IEEE.

Armbrust, M., Fox, A., Griffith, R., Joseph, A. D., Katz, R., Konwinski, A., Lee, G., Patterson, D., Rabkin, A., Stoica, I., & Zaharia, M. (2010). A view of cloud computing. *Communications of the ACM*, *53*(4), 50–58. doi:10.1145/1721654.1721672

Arnhardt. (2009). *Monitoring of slope-instabilities and deformations with micro-electro-mechanicalsystems (mems) in wireless ad-hoc sensor networks.* EGU General Assembly in Vienna.

Arts, K., van der Wal, R., & Adams, W. M. (2015). Digital technology and the conservation of nature. *Ambio*, *44*(4), 661–673. doi:10.100713280-015-0705-1 PMID:26508352

Ashton, K. (2009). That 'internet of things' thing. *RFID Journal*, *22*(7), 97-114.

Ashton, K. (2011). *That "Internet of Things" thing.* RFID Journal.

Assaf, M. H., Mootoo, R., Das, S. R., Petriu, E. M., Groza, V., & Biswas, S. (2012, May). Sensor based home automation and security system. In *2012 IEEE International Instrumentation and Measurement Technology Conference Proceedings* (pp. 722-727). IEEE. 10.1109/I2MTC.2012.6229153

Atkeson, A., & Kehoe, P. J. (2001). *The transition to a new economy after the second industrial revolution (No. w8676).* National Bureau of Economic Research. doi:10.3386/w8676

Atlam, H. F., Alenezi, A., Alharthi, A., Walters, R. J., & Wills, G. B. (2017). Integration of Cloud Computing with Internet of Things. *Challenges and Open*, (October), 670–675. Advance online publication. doi:10.1109/iThings-GreenCom-CPSCom-SmartData.2017.105

Atlam, H. F., Walters, R. J., & Wills, G. B. (2018). Fog computing and the Internet of things: A review. Big data and cognitive. *Computing*, *2*(2), 10.

Atzori, L., Iera, A., & Morabito, G. (2010). The Internet of Things: A survey. *Computer Networks*, *54*(15), 2787–2805. doi:10.1016/j.comnet.2010.05.010

Ayaz, A., Ammad-Uddin, M., Sharif, Z., Mansour, A., & Aggoune, E.-H. M. (2019). Internet-of-Things (IoT)-Based Smart Agriculture: Toward Making the Fields Talk. *IEEE Access: Practical Innovations, Open Solutions*, *7*, 129551–129583. doi:10.1109/ACCESS.2019.2932609

Aziz, F., Chalup, S. K., & Juniper, J. (2019). Big data in IoT systems. In M. Y. & J. Khan (Eds.), Internet of Things (IoT): Systems and Applications. doi:10.1201/9780429399084-2

Baker, T., Aldawsari, B., & England, D. (2015). Trusted energy-efficient cloud-based services brokerage platform. *International Journal of Intelligent Computing Research*, *6*(4), 630–639. doi:10.20533/ijicr.2042.4655.2015.0078

Baktayan, A. (2018). *EAI Endorsed Transactions A Review on Cloud and Fog Computing Integration for IoT : Platforms Perspective.* 10.4108/eai.20-12-2018.156084

Bamhdi, A. M., Abrar, I., & Masoodi, F. (2021). An ensemble based approach for effective intrusion detection using majority voting. *Telkomnika Telecommunication Computing Electronics and Control*, *19*(2), 664–671. doi:10.12928/telkomnika.v19i2.18325

Bank, A. G. (2006). *TCP/IP Foundations* (2nd ed.). John Wiley & Sons.

Banks, M. (2012). *On the Way to the Web: The Secret History of the Internet and Its Founders.* Apress.

Bao, F., & Chen, I.-R. (2012). Dynamic trust management for internet of things applications. *Proceedings of the 2012 International Workshop on Self-Aware Internet of Things - Self-IoT '12,* 1. 10.1145/2378023.2378025

Bao, F., Chen, I.-R., & Guo, J. (2013). Scalable, adaptive and survivable trust management for community of interest based Internet of Things systems. *2013 IEEE Eleventh International Symposium on Autonomous Decentralized Systems (ISADS),* 1–7. 10.1109/ISADS.2013.6513398

Baranwal, S., Khandelwal, S., & Arora, A. (2019, February). Deep learning convolutional neural network for apple leaves disease detection. In *Proceedings of International Conference on Sustainable Computing in Science, Technology and Management (SUSCOM).* Amity University Rajasthan. 10.2139srn.3351641

Barbedo, J. G. A. (2013). Digital image processing techniques for detecting, quantifying and classifying plant diseases. *SpringerPlus, 2*(1), 1–12. doi:10.1186/2193-1801-2-660 PMID:23419944

Barnaghi, P., Wang, W., Henson, C., & Taylor, K. (2012). Semantics for the Internet of Things: Early progress and back. *International Journal on Semantic Web and Information Systems, 8*(1), 1–21. doi:10.4018/jswis.2012010101

Bastin, L., Buchanan, G., Beresford, A., Pekel, J. F., & Dubois, G. (2013). Open-source mapping and services for Web-based land-cover validation. *Ecological Informatics, 14,* 9–16. doi:10.1016/j.ecoinf.2012.11.013

Belgaum, M. R., Soomro, S., Alansari, Z., Musa, S., Alam, M., & Su'ud, M. M. (2017, November). Challenges: Bridge between cloud and IoT. In *2017 4th IEEE International Conference on Engineering Technologies and Applied Sciences (ICETAS)* (pp. 1-5). IEEE.

Belgaum, M. R., Soomro, S., Alansari, Z., & Alam, M. (2018). Article. Advance online publication. doi:10.1109/ICETAS.2017.8277844

Benedict, S. (2018). IoT-Cloud Applications for Societal Benefits – An Entrepreneurial Solution. *IEEE Web Hosting.* http://site.ieee.org/indiacouncil/files/2018/05/p59-p62.pdf

Benson, E. (2012). One infrastructure, many global visions: The commercialization and diversification of Argos, a satellite-based environmental surveillance system. *Social Studies of Science, 42*(6), 843–868. doi:10.1177/0306312712457851

Benson, E. (2015). Generating Infrastructural invisibility: Insulation, interconnection, and avian excrement in the Southern California power grid. *Environmental Humanities, 6*(1), 103–130. doi:10.1215/22011919-3615916

Compilation of References

Bharathi, R. J. (2020). *Paddy Plant Disease Identification and Classification of Image Using AlexNet Model*. Academic Press.

Bhardwaj, H., Tomar, P., Sakalle, A., & Sharma, U. (2021). Artificial Intelligence and Its Applications in Agriculture With the Future of Smart Agriculture Techniques. In Artificial Intelligence and IoT-Based Technologies for Sustainable Farming and Smart Agriculture (pp. 25-39). IGI Global.

Bhardwaj, A., & Tiwari, A. (2013, July). A novel genetic programming-based classifier design using a new constructive crossover operator with a local search technique. In *International Conference on Intelligent Computing* (pp. 86-95). Springer. 10.1007/978-3-642-39479-9_11

Bhardwaj, A., & Tiwari, A. (2013, July). Performance improvement in genetic programming using modified crossover and node mutation. In *Proceedings of the 15th annual conference companion on Genetic and evolutionary computation* (pp. 1721-1722). 10.1145/2464576.2480787

Bhardwaj, A., Tiwari, A., Bhardwaj, H., & Bhardwaj, A. (2016). A genetically optimized neural network model for multiclass classification. *Expert Systems with Applications*, *60*, 211–221. doi:10.1016/j.eswa.2016.04.036

Bhardwaj, A., Tiwari, A., Varma, M. V., & Krishna, M. R. (2014, July). Classification of EEG signals using a novel genetic programming approach. In *Proceedings of the Companion Publication of the 2014 Annual Conference on Genetic and Evolutionary Computation* (pp. 1297-1304). 10.1145/2598394.2609851

Bhattarai, K. P., Gautam, B. P., & Sato, K. (2018, October). Authentic Gate Entry System (AuthGES) by Using LBPH for Smart Home Security. In *2018 International Conference on Networking and Network Applications (NaNA)* (pp. 191-196). IEEE. 10.1109/NANA.2018.8648705

Bhattasali, T., Chaki, R., & Chaki, N. (2013). Secure and Trusted Cloud of Things. *2013 Annual IEEE India Conference (INDICON)*, 1–6. 10.1109/INDCON.2013.6725878

Bhosale, H. S., & Gadekar, D. P. (2014). A review paper on big data and hadoop. *International Journal of Scientific and Research Publications*, *4*(10), 1–7.

Bibri, S. (2015). *The Shaping of Ambient Intelligence and the Internet of Things: Historico-epistemic, Socio-cultural, Politico-institutional and Eco-environmental Dimensions*. Springer. doi:10.2991/978-94-6239-142-0

Biermann, F., Abbott, K., Andresen, S., Bäckstrand, K., Bernstein, S., Betsill, M. M., ... Gupta, A. (2012). Navigating the Anthropocene: Improving City system governance. *Science*, *335*(6074), 1306–1307. doi:10.1126cience.1217255 PMID:22422966

Biermann, F., Betsill, M. M., Vieira, S. C., Gupta, J., Kanie, N., Lebel, L., Liverman, D., Schroeder, H., Siebenhüner, B., Yanda, P. Z., & Zondervan, R. (2010). Navigating the anthropocene: The City System Governance Project strategy paper. *Current Opinion in Environmental Sustainability*, *2*(3), 202–208. doi:10.1016/j.cosust.2010.04.005

Birje, M. N., Challagidad, P. S., Goudar, R. H., & Tapale, M. T. (2017). Cloud computing review: Concepts, technology, challenges and security. *International Journal of Cloud Computing, 6*(1), 32–57. doi:10.1504/IJCC.2017.083905

Biswas, A. R., & Giaffreda, R. (2014, March). IoT and cloud convergence: Opportunities and challenges. In *2014 IEEE World Forum on Internet of Things (WF-IoT)* (pp. 375-376). IEEE.

Bodenheimer, T. (1999). The American health care system: The movement for improved quality in health care. *England Journal of Medicine, 340*(6), 488–492. doi:10.1056/NEJM199902113400621 PMID:9971876

Bolton, T., Goosen, L., & Kritzinger, E. (2020b, March 8). Security Aspects of an Empirical Study into the Impact of Digital Transformation via Unified Communication and Collaboration Technologies on the Productivity and Innovation of a Global Automotive Enterprise. Communications in Computer and Information Science, 1166, 99-113. doi:10.1007/978-3-030-43276-8_8

Bolton, A. D., Goosen, L., & Kritzinger, E. (2021a). Unified Communication Technologies at a Global Automotive Organization. In M. Khosrow-Pour (Ed.), *Encyclopedia of Organizational Knowledge, Administration, and Technologies* (pp. 2592–2608). IGI Global. doi:10.4018/978-1-7998-3473-1.ch179

Bolton, A., Goosen, L., & Kritzinger, E. (2016). Enterprise Digitization Enablement Through Unified Communication and Collaboration. In *Proceedings of the Annual Conference of the South African Institute of Computer Scientists and Information Technologists.* Johannesburg: ACM. 10.1145/2987491.2987516

Bolton, A., Goosen, L., & Kritzinger, E. (2020a). The Impact of Unified Communication and Collaboration Technologies on Productivity and Innovation: Promotion for the Fourth Industrial Revolution. In S. B. Buckley (Ed.), *Promoting Inclusive Growth in the Fourth Industrial Revolution* (pp. 44–73). IGI Global. doi:10.4018/978-1-7998-4882-0.ch002

Bolton, A., Goosen, L., & Kritzinger, E. (2021b). An Empirical Study Into the Impact on Innovation and Productivity Towards the Post-COVID-19 Era: Digital Transformation of an Automotive Enterprise. In L. C. Carvalho, L. Reis, & C. Silveira (Eds.), *Handbook of Research on Entrepreneurship, Innovation, Sustainability, and ICTs in the Post-COVID-19 Era* (pp. 133–159). IGI Global. doi:10.4018/978-1-7998-6776-0.ch007

Borgia, E. (2014). The Internet of Things vision: Key features, applications and open issues. *Computer Communications, 54*, 1–31. doi:10.1016/j.comcom.2014.09.008

Borthakur, D. (2007). The hadoop distributed file system: Architecture and design. *Hadoop Project Website, 11*, 21.

Botta, A., De Donato, W., Persico, V., & Pescapé, A. (2016). Integration of cloud computing and Internet of Things: A survey. *Future Generation Computer Systems, 56*, 684–700. doi:10.1016/j.future.2015.09.021

Brama, R., Tundo, P., Della Ducata, A., & Malvasi, A. (2014, March). An inter-device communication protocol for modular smart-objects. In *2014 IEEE World Forum on Internet of Things (WF-IoT)* (pp. 422-427). IEEE. 10.1109/WF-IoT.2014.6803203

Brooks, T. (2016). *Cyber-Assurance for the Internet of Things.* John Wiley & Sons. doi:10.1002/9781119193784

Bruun, H. P. (2018). *Building A Smart Sustainable Society.* Ramboll. https://de.ramboll.com/-/media/61247eef6e694d33886e9f54b20af51a.pdf

Bui, N., & Zorzi, M. (2011, October). Health care applications: a solution based on the internet of things. In *Proceedings of the 4th international symposium on applied sciences in biomedical and communication technologies* (pp. 1-5). 10.1145/2093698.2093829

Burhan, M., Rehman, R. A., Khan, B., & Kim, B. S. (2018). IoT elements, layered architectures and security issues: A comprehensive survey. *Sensors (Basel), 18*(9), 2796. doi:10.339018092796 PMID:30149582

Byers, C. C. (2017). Architectural imperatives for fog computing: Use cases, requirements, and architectural techniques for fog-enabled not networks. *IEEE Communications Magazine, 55*(8), 14–20. doi:10.1109/MCOM.2017.1600885

Bygrave, L., & Bing, J. (2009). *Internet Governance: Infrastructure and Institutions.* Oxford University Press. doi:10.1093/acprof:oso/9780199561131.001.0001

Campbell, P. (2013). *Connections Counter: The Internet of Everything in Motion.* Available online: https://newsroom.cisco.com/feature-content?articleId=1208342.

Canali, C., & Lancellotti, R. (2019, May). A Fog Computing Service Placement for Smart Cities based on Genetic Algorithms. In CLOSER (pp. 81-89). doi:10.5220/0007699400810089

Canali, C., & Lancellotti, R. (2019). GASP: Genetic algorithms for service placement in fog computing systems. *Algorithms, 12*(10), 201. doi:10.3390/a12100201

Carpenter, B. (2013). *Network Geeks: How They Built The Internet.* Springer Science & Business Media. doi:10.1007/978-1-4471-5025-1

Carroll, A. (2017). *How The Heat Generated by Data Centres can be Recycled?* https://lifelinedatacenters.com/data-center/heat-generated-by-data-centers-can-recycled/

Castanier, F. (2014). Reduce Cost and Complexity of M2M and IoT Solutions via Embedded IP and Application Layer Interoperability for Smart Objects. *Proceedings of the M2M Forum.*

Cavalcante, E., Pereira, J., Alves, M. P., Maia, P., Moura, R., Batista, T., Delicato, F. C., & Pires, P. F. (2016). On the interplay of Internet of Things and Cloud Computing: A systematic mapping study. *Computer Communications, 89*, 17–33. doi:10.1016/j.comcom.2016.03.012

Cerf, V. G., & Kahn, R. E. (1974, May). A protocol for packet network interconnection. *IEEE Trans. Comm. Tech, COM-22*(V 5), 627-641. doi:10.1145/1064413.1064423

Cerf, V., Dalal, Y., & Sunshine, C. (1974, December). *RFC0675: Specification of Internet Transmission Control Program.* Retrieved from https://dl.acm.org/doi/pdf/10.17487/RFC0675?casa_token=NOnU2L4MPPEAAAAA:sC4AvMV_LpQGCPPeiOjs8bp-OBj8vcme31lEY6nwAtnHosl8qLob9FvWde7lgublhEeaZJq4dtgU65Y

Cerf, V. G. (1979). DARPA activities in packet network interconnection. In *Interlinking of Computer Networks* (pp. 287–305). Springer. doi:10.1007/978-94-009-9431-7_17

Chakravorti, B., & Chaturvedi, R. S. (2017). The "Smart Society" of the Future Doesn't Look Like Science Fiction. *Harvard Business Review.* https://hbr.org/2017/10/the-smart-society-of-the-future-doesnt-look-like-science-fiction

Chandra, A. L., Desai, S. V., Guo, W., & Balasubramanian, V. N. (2020). *Computer vision with deep learning for plant phenotyping in agriculture: A survey.* arXiv preprint arXiv:2006.11391.

Chang, K. D., Chen, C. Y., Chen, J. L., & Chao, H. C. (2011, September). Internet of things and cloud computing for future internet. In *International Conference on Security-Enriched Urban Computing and Smart Grid* (pp. 1-10). Springer. 10.1007/978-3-642-23948-9_1

Chang, V., Kuo, Y.-H., & Ramachandran, M. (2016). Cloud computing adoption framework: A security framework for business clouds. *Future Generation Computer Systems, 57,* 24–41. doi:10.1016/j.future.2015.09.031

Chaudhary, R., Aujla, G. S., Garg, S., Kumar, N., & Rodrigues, J. J. (2018). SDN-enabled multi-attribute-based secure communication for smart grid in IIoT environment. *IEEE Transactions on Industrial Informatics, 14*(6), 2629–2640. doi:10.1109/TII.2018.2789442

Chen, D., Chang, G., Sun, D., Li, J., Jia, J., & Wang, X. (2011). *TRM-IoT: A trust management model based on fuzzy reputation for internet of things.* doi:10.2298/CSIS110303056C

Chen, I., Guo, J., Tech, V., Wang, D., & Al-hamadi, H. (2018). Trust-based Service Management for Mobile Cloud IoT Systems. *IEEE Transactions on Network and Service Management, 1.* doi:10.1109/TNSM.2018.2886379

Chen, K., Chen, K., Chang, Y., & Tseng, P. (2011). *Measuring the latency of cloud gaming systems Measuring The Latency of Cloud Gaming Systems.* doi:10.1145/2072298.2071991

Chen, C. C., McCarl, B. A., & Schimmelpfennig, D. E. (2004). Yield variability as influenced by climate: A statistical investigation. *Climatic Change, 66*(1–2), 239–261. doi:10.1023/B:CLIM.0000043159.33816.e5

Chen, I.-R., Guo, J., & Bao, F. (2016). Trust Management for SOA-Based IoT and Its Application to Service Composition. *IEEE Transactions on Services Computing, 9*(3), 482–495. doi:10.1109/TSC.2014.2365797

Chen, S., Xu, H., Liu, D., Hu, B., & Wang, H. (2014). A vision of IoT: Applications, challenges, and opportunities with china perspective. *IEEE Internet of Things Journal, 1*(4), 349–359. doi:10.1109/JIOT.2014.2337336

Chivilikhin, D., Patil, S., Cordonnier, A., & Vyatkin, V. (2019, July). Towards automatic state machine reconstruction from legacy PLC using data collection. In *2019 IEEE 17th International Conference on Industrial Informatics (INDIN)* (Vol. 1, pp. 147-151). IEEE. 10.1109/INDIN41052.2019.8972143

Christian, M., & Pierdicca, S. (2004). *Comparing and combining the capability of detecting earthquake damages in urban areas using SAR and optical data*. IEEE. doi:10.1109/IGARSS.2004.1368943

Collina, M., Corazza, G. E., & Vanelli-Coralli, A. (2012). Introducing the QEST broker: Scaling the IoT by bridging MQTTand REST. *2012 IEEE 23rd International Symposium on Personal, Indoor and Mobile Radio Communications*, 36–41.

Coskun, V., Ozdenizci, B., & Ok, K. (2013). A survey on near field communication (NFC) technology. *Wireless Personal Communications, 71*(3), 2259–2294. doi:10.100711277-012-0935-5

Crago, S., Dunn, K., Eads, P., Hochstein, L., Kang, D.-I., Kang, M., Modium, D., Singh, K., Suh, J., & Walters, J. P. (2011). Heterogeneous cloud computing. *2011 IEEE International Conference on Cluster Computing*, 1–8.

Crampin, S., Evans, R., & Atkinson, B. (1984). Earthquake prediction: A new physical basis. *Geophysical Journal of the Royal Astronomical Society, 76*(1), 147–156. doi:10.1111/j.1365-246X.1984.tb05030.x

Crezil, P. (2015). *Can the Internet of Everything Bring Back the High-Growth Economy?* Available online: https://www.progressivepolicy.org/issues/economy/can-the-internet-of-everything-bring-backthe-high-growth-economy

Curbera, F., Duftler, M., Khalaf, R., Nagy, W., Mukhi, N., & Weerawarana, S. (2002). Unraveling the web services web: An introduction to SOAP, WSDL, and UDDI. *Internet Computing, 6*, 86–93. doi:10.1109/4236.991449

Da Xu, L., He, W., & Li, S. (2014). Internet of things in industries: A survey. *IEEE Transactions on Industrial Informatics, 10*(4), 2233–2243. doi:10.1109/TII.2014.2300753

Dang, L. M., Piran, J., Han, D., Min, K., & Moon, H. (2019). *A Survey on Internet of Things and Cloud Computing for Healthcare*. doi:10.3390/electronics8070768

Daniya & Vigneshwari. (2019).A review on machine learning techniques for rice plant disease detection in agricultural research. *System, 28*(13), 49-62.

Das, S., Sismanis, Y., Beyer, K. S., Gemulla, R., Haas, P. J., & McPherson, J. (2010, June). Ricardo: integrating R and Hadoop. In *Proceedings of the 2010 ACM SIGMOD International Conference on Management of data* (pp. 987-998). 10.1145/1807167.1807275

Dastjerdi, A. V., Gupta, H., Calheiros, R. N., Ghosh, S. K., & Buyya, R. (2016). Fog computing: Principles, architectures, and applications. In Internet of things (pp. 61-75). Academic Press.

Dastjerdi, A. V., & Buyya, R. (2016). Fog computing: Helping the Internet of Things realize its potential. *Computer, 49*(8), 112–116. doi:10.1109/MC.2016.245

Dekhane, S., Mhalgi, K., Vishwanath, K., Singh, S., & Giri, N. (2019, January). GreenCoin: Empowering smart cities using Blockchain 2.0. In *2019 International Conference on Nascent Technologies in Engineering (ICNTE)* (pp. 1-5). IEEE. 10.1109/ICNTE44896.2019.8946014

Dell'Acqua & Gamba. (2012). Remote sensing and earthquake assessment: experiences and perspectives. IEEE.

Dell'Acqua, F., Christian, M. Gianni, D., & Salvatore. (2009). Earthquake damages mapping by satellite remote sensing data. IEEE.

Denair, G. (2016). *Disruptive Civil Technologies: Six Technologies with Potential Impacts on US Interests out to 2025*. Available online: https://fas.org/irp/nic/disruptive.pdf

Denardis, L. (2008). IPv6: Standards controversies around the Next-Generation Internet. In I. Inkster & J. Sumner (Eds.), *History of Technology* (Vol. 28). Continuum.

De-ren, L., Yuan, Y., & Zhen-feng, S. (2012). New mission for surveying, mapping and geomatics in Smart City era. *Science of Surveying and Mapping, 6*.

Dhivya & Sunitha. (2015). Article on Grid Computing Architecture and Benefits. *International Research Journal of Engineering and Technology, 2*(9), 1070-1074.

Di-Martino, B., Cretella, G., & Esposito, A. (2015). *Cloud Portability and Interoperability: Issues and Current Trends*. Springer.

Domdouzis, K. (2015). Sustainable Cloud Computing. In *Green Information Technology: A Sustainable Approach*. Elsevier. doi:10.1016/C2014-0-00029-9

Dong-Woo, L. (2016). A Study on Actual Cases & Meanings for Internet of Things. *International Journal of Software Engineering and Its Applications, 10*(1), 287–294. doi:10.14257/ijseia.2016.10.1.28

Dubey, H., Yang, J., Constant, N., Amiri, A. M., Yang, Q., & Makodiya, K. (2015). Fog data: Enhancing big telehealth data through fog computing. In *Proceedings of the ASE bigdata & social informatics 2015* (pp. 1-6). Academic Press.

Dubey, H., Monteiro, A., Constant, N., Abtahi, M., Borthakur, D., Mahler, L., & Mankodiya, K. (2017). Fog computing in medical internet-of-things: architecture, implementation, and applications. In *Handbook of Large-Scale Distributed Computing in Smart Healthcare* (pp. 281–321). Springer. doi:10.1007/978-3-319-58280-1_11

Duda, O., Kunanets, N., Matsiuk, O., & Pasichnyk, V. (2018). Cloud-based IT Infrastructure for "Smart City" Projects. In Dependable IoT for Human and Industry: Modeling, Architecting, Implementation. River Publishers.

Emeakaroha, V. C., Cafferkey, N., Healy, P., & Morrison, J. P. (2015, August). A cloud-based iot data gathering and processing platform. In *2015 3rd International Conference on Future Internet of Things and Cloud* (pp. 50-57). IEEE. 10.1109/FiCloud.2015.53

Escher. (2012). Bioanalytical Tools in water Quality Assessment. IWA Publishing Alliance.

Etherington, D. (2017). *Amazon AWS S3 outage is breaking things for a lot of websites and apps.* Academic Press.

European Commission. (2017). *LAB–FAB–APP, Investing in the European future we want: Report of the independent High Level Group on maximising the impact of EU Research & Innovation Programmes.* Directorate-General for Research and Innovation.

Evans, D. (2011). *The Internet of Things.* Cisco. http://blogs. cisco. com/news/the-internet-of-things-infographic/

Evans, D. (2017). *The Internet of Things: How the Next Evolution of the Internet is Changing Everything.* Available online: https://www.cisco.com/c/dam/en_us/about/ac79/docs/innov/IoT_IBSG_0411FINAL. pdf

Fan, W., & Bifet, A. (2013). Mining big data: Current status, and forecast to the future. ACM SIGKDD Explorations Newsletter, 14.

Farash, M. S., Turkanović, M., Kumari, S., & Hölbl, M. (2016). An efficient user authentication and key agreement scheme for heterogeneous wireless sensor network tailored for the Internet of Things environment. *Ad Hoc Networks, 36*, 152–176. doi:10.1016/j.adhoc.2015.05.014

Feller, G. (2011). The internet of things: In a connected world of smart objects. *Accenture & Bankinter Foundation of Innovation*, 24-29.

Ferdous, M. S., Hussein, R. K., Alassafi, M. O., Alharthi, A., Walters, R. J., & Wills, G. (2016). Threat taxonomy for cloud of things. In Internet of Things and big data analysis: Recent trends and challenges (pp. 149–190). Academic Press.

Ferentinos, K. P. (2018). Deep learning models for plant disease detection and diagnosis. *Computers and Electronics in Agriculture, 145*, 311–318. doi:10.1016/j.compag.2018.01.009

Ferrari, P., & Sisinni, E. (2017). *Evaluation of communication latency in Industrial IoT applications.* doi:10.1109/IWMN.2017.8078359

Fiorentino, G., & Corsi, A. (2014). Cyber Physical Systems give Life to the Internet of Energy. *ECRIM News, 98*, 39–40.

Fleisch, E., & Mattern, F. (Eds.). (2005). *Das Internet der Dinge—Ubiquitous Computing und RFID in der Praxis* (1st ed.). Springer. doi:10.1007/3-540-28299-8

Fleming, W. J. (2001). Overview of automotive sensors. *IEEE Sensors Journal, 1*(4), 296–308.

Floreano, D., & Wood, R. J. (2015). Robert J. Wood Science, technology and the future of small autonomous drones. *Nature, 521*(7553), 460–466. doi:10.1038/nature14542 PMID:26017445

Foresti, R., Rossi, S., Magnani, M., Bianco, C. G. L., & Delmonte, N. (2020). Smart Society and Artificial Intelligence: Big Data Scheduling and the Global Standard Method Applied to Smart Maintenance. *Engineering, 6*(7), 8835–8846. https://doi.org/10.1016/j.eng.2019.11.014

Forouzan, B. A. (2002). *TCP/IP protocol suite*. McGraw-Hill Higher Education.

Fortino, G., & Trunfio, P. (2014). *Internet of Things based on Smart Objects: Technology, Middleware and Applications*. Springer. doi:10.1007/978-3-319-00491-4

Friess, P. (2013). *Internet of Things: Converging Technologies for Smart Environments and Integrated Ecosystems*. River Publishers.

Gabrielov, A., & Newman, W. I. (1994). Seismicity modeling and earthquake prediction: A review. *Nonlinear Dynamics and Predictability of Geophysical Phenomena, 83*, 7–13. doi:10.1029/GM083p0007

Gadre, D. V., & Gupta, S. (2018). Universal Asynchronous Receiver and Transmitter (UART). In *Getting Started with Tiva ARM Cortex M4 Microcontrollers* (pp. 151–167). Springer. doi:10.1007/978-81-322-3766-2_12

Gaikwad, P. P., Gabhane, J. P., & Golait, S. S. (2015, September). 3-level secure Kerberos authentication for smart home systems using IoT. In *2015 1st International Conference on Next Generation Computing Technologies (NGCT)* (pp. 262-268). IEEE.

Gambi, E., Montanini, L., Raffaeli, L., Spinsante, S., & Lambrinos, L. (2016). Interoperability in IoT infrastructures for enhanced living environments. *2016 IEEE International Black Sea Conference on Communications and Networking, BlackSeaCom 2016*, 1–5. 10.1109/BlackSeaCom.2016.7901573

Gandhewar, R., Gaurav, A., Kokate, K., Khetan, H., & Kamat, H. (2019, June). Cloud Based Framework for IIOT Application with Asset Management. In *2019 3rd International Conference on Electronics, Communication and Aerospace Technology (ICECA)* (pp. 920-925). IEEE. 10.1109/ICECA.2019.8821897

Garg, R., & Sharma, S. (2018). Modified and improved IPv6 header compression (MIHC) scheme for 6LoWPAN. *Wireless Personal Communications, 103*(3), 2019–2033. doi:10.100711277-018-5894-z

Garg, R., & Sharma, S. (2020). Cooja Based Approach for Estimation and Enhancement of Lifetime of 6LoWPAN Environment. *International Journal of Sensors, Wireless Communications and Control, 10*(2), 207–216. doi:10.2174/2210327909666190409124604

Gautschi, G. (2002). Piezoelectric sensors. In *Piezoelectric Sensorics* (pp. 73–91). Springer.

Gavhale, K. R., & Gawande, U. (2014). An overview of the research on plant leaves disease detection using image processing techniques. *IOSR Journal of Computer Engineering (IOSR-JCE), 16*(1), 10-16.

Gazis, V., Manuel, G., Huber, M., Leonardi, A., Mathioudakis, K., Wiesmaier, A., & Zeiger, F. (2015). IoT: Challenges, projects, architectures. *2015 18th International Conference on Intelligence in Next Generation Networks*, 145–147.

Geller, R. J. (1997). Earthquake prediction: A critical review. *Geophysical Journal International*, *131*(3), 425–450. doi:10.1111/j.1365-246X.1997.tb06588.x

Geng, H. (2016). *Internet of Things and Data Analytics Handbook*. John Wiley & Sons.

Gershenfeld, N., Krikorian, R., & Cohen, D. (2004). The Internet of things. *Am. 2004, 291*, 76–81.

Gershenfeld, N. (1999). *When Things Start to Think* (1st ed.). Henry Holt and Company.

Ghasempour, A. (2016a). Optimum Number of Aggregators based on Power Consumption, Cost, and Network Lifetime in Advanced Metering Infrastructure Architecture for Smart Grid Internet of Things. *Proceedings of the IEEE Consumer Communications and Networking Conference (IEEE CCNC 2016)*, Las 9–12.

Ghasempour, A. (2016b). Optimized Advanced Metering Infrastructure Architecture of Smart Grid based on Total Cost, Energy, and Delay. *Proceedings of the 2016 IEEE Conference on Innovative Smart Grid Technologies (IEEE ISGT 2016)*, 1–6.

Ghasempour, A. (2016c) Optimum Packet Service and Arrival Rates in Advanced Metering Infrastructure Architecture of Smart Grid. *Proceedings of the 2016 IEEE Green Technologies Conference (IEEE GreenTech 2016)*, 1–5. 10.1109/GreenTech.2016.8

Ghasempour, A., & Gunther, J. H. (2016d). Finding the Optimal Number of Aggregators in Machine-to-Machine Advanced Metering Infrastructure Architecture of Smart Grid based on Cost, Delay, and Energy. *Proceedings of the 2016 13th IEEE Annual Consumer Communications & Networking Conference (IEEE CCNC 2016)*, 960–963.

Ghasempour, A. (2017). Advanced Metering Infrastructure in Smart Grid: Requirements, Challenges, Architectures, technologies, and Optimizations. In J. Lou (Ed.), *Smart Grids: Emerging Technologies, Challenges and Future Directions* (1st ed.). Nova Science Publishers.

Ghazal, B., Elkhatib, K., Chahine, K., & Kherfan, M. (2016). Smart traffic light control system. *2016 3rd International Conference on Electrical, Electronics, Computer Engineering and Their Applications, EECEA 2016*. 10.1109/EECEA.2016.7470780

Ghosh, A. M., Halder, D., & Hossain, S. A. (2016, May). Remote health monitoring system through IoT. In *2016 5th International Conference on Informatics, Electronics and Vision (ICIEV)* (pp. 921-926). IEEE. 10.1109/ICIEV.2016.7760135

GibbsW. (2002). *Autonomic Computing*. Retrieved from https://www.scientificamerican.com/article/autonomic-computing/

Gluhak, A., Vermesan, O., Bahr, R., Clari, F., Maria, T. M., Delgado, T., Hoeer, A., Bösenberg, F., Senigalliesi, M., & Barchett, V. (2016). *BDeliverable D03.01 Report on IoT platform activities - UNIFY-IoT*. Academic Press.

Gomes, M. M., Da Rosa Righi, R., & Da Costa, C. A. (2014). Future directions for providing better IoT infrastructure. *UbiComp 2014 - Adjunct Proceedings of the 2014 ACM International Joint Conference on Pervasive and Ubiquitous Computing*, 51–54. 10.1145/2638728.2638752

Goosen, L. (2015a). Educational Technologies for an ICT4D MOOC in the 21st Century. In D. Nwaozuzu, & S. Mnisi (Ed.), *Proceedings of the South Africa International Conference on Educational Technologies* (pp. 37 - 48). Pretoria: African Academic Research Forum.

Goosen, L. (2015b). Educational Technologies for Growing Innovative e-Schools in the 21st Century: A Community Engagement Project. In D. Nwaozuzu, & S. Mnisi (Ed.), *Proceedings of the South Africa International Conference on Educational Technologies* (pp. 49 - 61). Pretoria: African Academic Research Forum.

Goosen, L. (2016, February 18). *We don't need no education"? Yes, they DO want e-learning in Basic and Higher Education!* Retrieved from http://uir.unisa.ac.za/handle/10500/20999

Goosen, L. (2018a). Sustainable and Inclusive Quality Education Through Research Informed Practice on Information and Communication Technologies in Education. In L. Webb (Ed.), *Proceedings of the 26th Conference of the Southern African Association for Research in Mathematics, Science and Technology Education (SAARMSTE)* (pp. 215 - 228). Gabarone: University of Botswana.

Goosen, L. (2019c). Information Systems and Technologies Opening New Worlds for Learning to Children with Autism Spectrum Disorders. Smart Innovation, Systems and Technologies, 111, 134 - 143. doi:10.1007/978-3-030-03577-8_16

Goosen, L., & Mukasa-Lwanga, T. (2017). Educational Technologies in Distance Education: Beyond the Horizon with Qualitative Perspectives. In U. I. Ogbonnaya, & S. Simelane-Mnisi (Ed.), *Proceedings of the South Africa International Conference on Educational Technologies* (pp. 41 - 54). Pretoria: African Academic Research Forum.

Goosen, L., & Van Heerden, D. (2017). Beyond the Horizon of Learning Programming with Educational Technologies. In U. I. Ogbonnaya, & S. Simelane-Mnisi (Ed.), *Proceedings of the South Africa International Conference on Educational Technologies* (pp. 78 - 90). Pretoria: African Academic Research Forum.

Goosen, L. (2018b). Trans-Disciplinary Approaches to Action Research for e-Schools, Community Engagement, and ICT4D. In T. A. Mapotse (Ed.), *Cross-Disciplinary Approaches to Action Research and Action Learning* (pp. 97–110). IGI Global. doi:10.4018/978-1-5225-2642-1.ch006

Goosen, L. (2018c). Ethical Information and Communication Technologies for Development Solutions: Research Integrity for Massive Open Online Courses. In C. Sibinga (Ed.), *Ensuring Research Integrity and the Ethical Management of Data* (pp. 155–173). IGI Global. doi:10.4018/978-1-5225-2730-5.ch009

Goosen, L. (2018d). Ethical Data Management and Research Integrity in the Context of E-Schools and Community Engagement. In C. Sibinga (Ed.), *Ensuring Research Integrity and the Ethical Management of Data* (pp. 14–45). IGI Global. doi:10.4018/978-1-5225-2730-5.ch002

Goosen, L. (2018e). Students' Access to an ICT4D MOOC. In S. Kabanda, H. Suleman, & S. Jamieson (Ed.), *Proceedings of the 47th Annual Conference of the Southern African Computer Lectures' Association (SACLA 2018)* (pp. 183 - 201). Cape Town: University of Cape Town.

Goosen, L. (2019a). Technology-Supported Teaching and Research Methods for Educators: Case Study of a Massive Open Online Course. In L. Makewa, B. Ngussa, & J. Kuboja (Eds.), *Technology-Supported Teaching and Research Methods for Educators* (pp. 128–148). IGI Global. doi:10.4018/978-1-5225-5915-3.ch007

Goosen, L. (2019b). Research on Technology-Supported Teaching and Learning for Autism. In L. Makewa, B. Ngussa, & J. Kuboja (Eds.), *Technology-Supported Teaching and Research Methods for Educators* (pp. 88–110). IGI Global. doi:10.4018/978-1-5225-5915-3.ch005

Goosen, L. (2019d). *Innovative Technologies and Learning in a Massive Open Online Course.* In L. Rønningsbakk, T.-T. Wu, F. E. Sandnes, & Y.-M. Huang (Eds.), Lecture Notes in Computer Science (Vol. 11937, pp. 653–662). doi:10.1007/978-3-030-35343-8_69

Goosen, L. (2021). Organizational Knowledge and Administration Lessons from an ICT4D MOOC. In M. Khosrow-Pour (Ed.), *Encyclopedia of Organizational Knowledge, Administration, and Technologies* (pp. 245–261). IGI Global. doi:10.4018/978-1-7998-3473-1.ch020

Gope, P., & Hwang, T. (2015). Untraceable sensor movement in distributed IoT infrastructure. *IEEE Sensors Journal, 15*(9), 5340–5348. doi:10.1109/JSEN.2015.2441113

Granjal, J., Monteiro, E., & Silva, J. S. (2015). Security for the internet of things: A survey of existing protocols and open research issues. *IEEE Communications Surveys and Tutorials, 17*(3), 1294–1312. doi:10.1109/COMST.2015.2388550

Green, J. (2014). The internet of things reference model. In *Internet of Things World Forum* (pp. 1-12). Academic Press.

Grossman, R. L. (2009). The case for cloud computing. *IT Professional, 11*(2), 23–27.

Gubbi, J., Buyya, R., Marusic, S., & Palaniswami, M. (2013). Internet of Things (IoT): A vision, architectural elements, and future directions. *Future Generation Computer Systems, 29*(7), 1645–1660. doi:10.1016/j.future.2013.01.010

Guechi, F. A. (1955). Secure and Parallel Expressive Search over Encrypted Data with Access Control in Multi-CloudIoT. *2018 3rd Cloudification of the Internet of Things (CIoT)*, 1–8.

Guimaraes, P., Ferraz, L., Torres, J. V., Mattos, D., Alvarenga, I., Rodrigues, C., & Duarte, O. (2013). Experimenting content-centric networks in the future internet testbed environment. *IEEE International Conference on Communications Workshops (ICC)*, 1383-1387. 10.1109/ICCW.2013.6649453

Gunawi, H. S., Hao, M., Suminto, R. O., Laksono, A., Satria, A. D., Adityatama, J., & Eliazar, K. J. (2016). Why Does the Cloud Stop Computing? Lessons from Hundreds of Service Outages. *ACM Symp. Cloud Comput.*, 1–6. 10.1145/2987550.2987583

Guo, B., Zhang, D., Wang, Z., Yu, Z., & Zhou, X. (2013). Opportunistic IoT: Exploring the harmonious interactions between human and the internet of things. *Journal of Network and Computer Applications, 36*(6), 1531–1539. doi:10.1016/j.jnca.2012.12.028

Guo, H., Wang, L., Chen, F., & Liang, D. (2014). Scientific big data and digital City. *Chinese Science Bulletin, 59*(35), 5066–5073.

Guo, H., Wang, L., Chen, F., & Liang, D. (2014). Scientific big data and digital earth. *Chinese Science Bulletin, 59*(35), 5066–5073. doi:10.100711434-014-0645-3

Gupta, A., Christie, R., & Manjula, R. (2017). Scalability in Internet of Things: Features, techniques and research challenges. *International Journal of Computational Intelligence Research, 13*(7), 1617–1627.

Gupta, H., Bhardwaj, D., Agrawal, H., Tikkiwal, V. A., & Kumar, A. (2019). An IoT Based Air Pollution Monitoring System for Smart Cities. In *2019 IEEE International Conference on Sustainable Energy Technologies and Systems (ICSETS)* (pp. 173-177). IEEE. 10.1109/ICSETS.2019.8744949

Hamilton, H., & Alasti, H. (2017). Controlled Intelligent Agents' Security Model for Multi-Tenant Cloud Computing Infrastructures. *International Journal of Grid and High Performance Computing, 9*(1), 1–13. doi:10.4018/IJGHPC.2017010101

Han, Z., Member, S., Li, X., & Huang, K. (2018). *A Software Defined Network based Security Assessment Framework for CloudIoT.* doi:10.1109/JIOT.2018.2801944

Han, J., Choi, C. S., Park, W. K., Lee, I., & Kim, S. H. (2014). Smart home energy management system including renewable energy based on ZigBee and PLC. *IEEE Transactions on Consumer Electronics, 60*(2), 198–202. doi:10.1109/TCE.2014.6851994

Haqva, H. (2015). Smart water quality monitoring system. *2nd, Asia-Pacific World Congress on Computer Science and Engineering (APWC on CSE),* 1-6. 10.1109/APWCCSE.2015.7476234

Hargreaves, T., Wilson, C., & Hauxwell-Baldwin, R. (2018). Learning to live in a smart home. *Building Research and Information, 46*(1), 127–139. doi:10.1080/09613218.2017.1286882

Hasan, M. O., Islam, M. M., & Alsaawy, Y. (2019, June). Smart parking model based on internet of things (IoT) and TensorFlow. In *2019 7th International Conference on Smart Computing & Communications (ICSCC)* (pp. 1-5). IEEE.

Hayakawa, M., & Hobara, Y. (2010). Current status of seismoelectromagnetics for short-term earthquake prediction. *Geomatics, Natural Hazards & Risk, 1*(2), 115–155. doi:10.1080/1947 5705.2010.486933

Hayes, B. (2008). *Cloud computing.* Academic Press.

Heine, G., & Horror, M. (1999). *GSM networks: protocols, terminology, and implementation.* Artech House, Inc.

Hershey, S., Chaudhuri, S., Ellis, D. P., Gemmeke, J. F., Jansen, A., Moore, R. C., ... Wilson, K. (2017, March). CNN architectures for large-scale audio classification. In *2017 IEEE international conference on acoustics, speech and signal processing (icassp)* (pp. 131-135). IEEE.

Hey, A., & Pápay, G. (2014). *The Computing Universe: A Journey through a Revolution.* Cambridge University Press. doi:10.1017/CBO9781139032643

Hinden, R., & Deering, S. (2003). *Internet protocol version 6 (IPv6) addressing architecture.* RFC 3513. http://tools.ietf.org/ html/rfc3513

Holmes, A. (2012). *Hadoop in practice.* Manning Publications Co.

Holte, J., Talley, L. D., Gilson, J., & Roemmich, D. (2017). An Argo mixed layer climatology and database. *Geophysical Research Letters, 44*(11), 5618–5626.

Hong, Y.-M., Lin, H.-C., & Kan, Y.-C. (2011). Using wireless sensor network on real-time remote monitoring of the load cell for landslide. *Sensor Letters, 9*(5), 1911–1915. doi:10.1166l.2011.1522

Houze, R. A. Jr. (2014). *Cloud dynamics.* Academic press.

Hrestak, D., & Picek, S. (2014). Homomorphic encryption in the cloud. *2014 37th International Convention on Information and Communication Technology, Electronics and Microelectronics (MIPRO),* 1400–1404. 10.1109/MIPRO.2014.6859786

Huberman, B. A. (2016). Ensuring trust and security in the industrial IoT: The internet of things (ubiquity symposium). *Ubiquity, 2016*(January), 1–7. doi:10.1145/2822883

Hui, J. W., & Culler, D. E. (2008, November). IP is dead, long live IP for wireless sensor networks. In *Proceedings of the 6th ACM conference on Embedded network sensor systems* (pp. 15-28). 10.1145/1460412.1460415

Hummen, R., Henze, M., Catrein, D., & Wehrle, K. (2012, December). A cloud design for user-controlled storage and processing of sensor data. In *4th IEEE International Conference on Cloud Computing Technology and Science Proceedings* (pp. 232-240). IEEE. 10.1109/CloudCom.2012.6427523

Husmann, A., Betts, J. B., Boebinger, G. S., Migliori, A., Rosenbaum, T. F., & Saboungi, M. L. (2002). Megagauss sensors. *Nature, 417*(6887), 421–424.

IEEE Standards Committee. (2003). Part 15.3: Wireless Medium Access Control (MAC) and Physical Layer (PHY) Specifications for High Rate Wireless Personal Area Networks (WPANs). *IEEE Std, 802*(3).

Igarashi, Y., Altman, T., Funada, M., & Kamiyama, B. (2014). *Computing: A Historical and Technical Perspective.* CRC Press. doi:10.1201/b17011

International Telecommunication Union - ITU. (2017). *ITU-T Y.4455 - Internet of things and smart cities and communities – Frameworks, architectures and protocols Reference.* ITU.

Ishaq, I., Hoebeke, J., Moerman, I., & Demeester, P. (2012). Internet of things virtual networks: Bringing network virtualization to resource-constrained devices. *Proceedings - 2012 IEEE Int. Conf. on Green Computing and Communications, GreenCom 2012, Conf. on Internet of Things, IThings 2012 and Conf. on Cyber, Physical and Social Computing, CPSCom 2012*, 293–300. 10.1109/GreenCom.2012.152

Jabbar, S., Ullah, F., Khalid, S., Khan, M., & Han, K. (2017). Semantic interoperability in heterogeneous IoT infrastructure for healthcare. *Wireless Communications and Mobile Computing*, *2017*, 1–10. doi:10.1155/2017/9731806

Jadoul, M. (2015). The IoT: The next step in internet evolution. *Techzine*. Retrieved from https:// techzine. alcatel-lucent. com/iot-next-stepinternet-evolution

Jahan. (2019). Raspberry Pi Based Water Quality Monitoring and Flood Alerting System Using IoT. *International Journal of Recent Technology and Engineering, 7*(6S4), 640-643.

Jaiswal, S. (n.d.). *Cloud Computing Architecture*. https://www.javatpoint.com/cloud-computing-architecture

Jarvis, R., & Moses, P. (2019) Smart Grid Congestion Caused by Plug-in Electric Vehicle Charging. *Proceedings of the 2019 IEEE Texas Power and Energy Conference (TPEC)*, 1–5. 10.1109/TPEC.2019.8662152

Jensen, M., Schwenk, J., Gruschka, N., & Lo Iacono, L. (2009). On technical security issues in cloud computing. *CLOUD 2009 - 2009 IEEE International Conference on Cloud Computing*, 109–116. 10.1109/CLOUD.2009.60

Jiménez, C. E., Solanas, A., & Falcone, F. (2014). E-Government Interoperability: Linking Open and Smart Government. *Computer*, *47*(10), 22–24. doi:10.1109/MC.2014.281

Jin, J., Gubbi, J., Marusic, S., & Palaniswami, M. (2014). An information framework for creating a smart city through internet of things. *IEEE Internet of Things Journal*, *1*(2), 112–121. doi:10.1109/ JIOT.2013.2296516

Ji, Z., Ganchev, I., O'Droma, M., Zhao, L., & Zhang, X. (2014). A cloud-based car parking middleware for IoT-based smart cities: Design and implementation. *Sensors (Basel)*, *14*(12), 22372–22393.

Jogin, M., Madhulika, M. S., Divya, G. D., Meghana, R. K., & Apoorva, S. (2018, May). Feature extraction using convolution neural networks (CNN) and deep learning. In *2018 3rd IEEE International Conference on Recent Trends in Electronics, Information & Communication Technology (RTEICT)* (pp. 2319-2323). IEEE.

Kahn, R. (1972, Jan). *Communications Principles for Operating Systems*. Washington, DC: Bolt, Beranek and Newman (BBN).

Kajol, R., & Akshay, K. K. (2018). Automated agricultural field analysis and monitoring system using IoT. *International Journal of Information Engineering and Electronic Business*, *11*(2), 17.

Kalyani, G., & Chaudhari, S. (2019). An efficient approach for enhancing security in Internet of Things using the optimum authentication key An efficient approach for enhancing security in Internet of Things using the optimum authentication key. *International Journal of Computers and Applications, 0*(0), 1–9. doi:10.1080/1206212X.2019.1619277

Kamilaris, A., Trifa, V., & Pitsillides, A. (2010). The smart home meets the web of things. *International Journal of Ad Hoc and Ubiquitous Computing,* 1–12.

Kamvar, S. D., Schlosser, M. T., & Garcia-Molina, H. (2003). *The EigenTrust Algorithm for Reputation Management in P2P Networks.* Academic Press.

Kanniappan, J., & Rajendrin, B. (2017). Privacy and the Internet of Things. In I. Lee (Ed.), *The Internet of Things in the Modern Business Environment* (pp. 94–106). IGI Global. doi:10.4018/978-1-5225-2104-4.ch005

Kashyap, R., Azman, M., & Panicker, J. G. (2019, February). Ubiquitous mesh: a wireless mesh network for IoT systems in smart homes and smart cities. In *2019 IEEE International Conference on Electrical, Computer and Communication Technologies (ICECCT)* (pp. 1-5). IEEE. 10.1109/ICECCT.2019.8869482

Kassem, A., El Murr, S., Jamous, G., Saad, E., & Geagea, M. (2016, July). A smart lock system using Wi-Fi security. In *2016 3rd International Conference on Advances in Computational Tools for Engineering Applications (ACTEA)* (pp. 222-225). IEEE. 10.1109/ACTEA.2016.7560143

Kaswan & Dhatterwal. (2021c). *The use of Machine Learning for Sustainable and Resilient Building. Digital Cities Roadmap: IoT-Based Architecture and Sustainable Buildings.* Scrivener Publishing Press.

Kaswan, K. S., & Dhatterwal, J. S. (2021a). *Machine Learning and Deep Learning Algorithm IoD. The Internet of Drones: AI Application for Smart Solutions.* CRC Press.

Kaswan, K. S., & Dhatterwal, J. S. (2021b). *Implementation and Deployment of 5-G Drone Setups. The Internet of Drones: AI Application for Smart Solutions.* CRC Press.

Kaur, N., & Sood, S. (2015). Cognitive decision making in smart industry. *Computers in Industry, 74,* 151–161. doi:10.1016/j.compind.2015.06.006

Keilis-Borok, V. (2002). Earthquake prediction: State-of-the-art and emerging possibilities. *Annual Review of Earth and Planetary Sciences, 30*(1), 1–33. doi:10.1146/annurev.earth.30.100301.083856

Kelltontech. (n.d.). https://www.kelltontech.com/kellton-tech-blog/internet-of

Kempf, J., Arkko, J., Beheshti, N., & Yedavalli, K. (2011). *Thoughts on reliability in the Internet of Things.* Academic Press.

Kesavan, G., Sanjeevi, P., & Viswanathan, P. (2016, August). A 24 hour IoT framework for monitoring and managing home automation. In *2016 international conference on inventive computation technologies (ICICT)* (Vol. 1, pp. 1-5). IEEE.

Khan, Z., Pervez, Z., & Ghafoor, A. (2014, December). Towards cloud based smart cities data security and privacy management. In *2014 IEEE/ACM 7th International Conference on Utility and Cloud Computing* (pp. 806-811). IEEE.

Kharb, L. (2018). A Perspective View on Commercialization of Cognitive Computing. *2018 8th International Conference on Cloud Computing, Data Science & Engineering (Confluence).* 10.1109/CONFLUENCE.2018.8442728

Kharb, L. (2020). Proposing Real-Time Smart Healthcare Model Using IoT. In P. Raj, J. Chatterjee, A. Kumar, & B. Balamurugan (Eds.), *Internet of Things Use Cases for the Healthcare Industry.* Springer. doi:10.1007/978-3-030-37526-3_2

Kharb, L. (2021). "VISIO": An IoT Device for Assistance of Visually Challenged. In V. C. Pandey, P. M. Pandey, & S. K. Garg (Eds.), *Advances in Electromechanical Technologies. Lecture Notes in Mechanical Engineering.* Springer. doi:10.1007/978-981-15-5463-6_84

Kimiti, J. M., Odee, D. W., & Vanlauwe, B. (2009). *Area under grain legumes cultivation and problems faced by smallholder farmers in legume production in the semi-arid eastern Kenya.* Academic Press.

Kim, S.-M., Choi, H.-S., & Rhee, W.-S. (2015). IoT home gateway for auto-configuration and management of MQTT devices. *2015 IEEE Conference on Wireless Sensors*, 12–17. 10.1109/ICWISE.2015.7380346

Kiran Urs. (2018). Real-time Water Quality Monitoring using WSN. *3rd IEEE International Conference on Recent Trends in Electronics, Information & Communication Technology (RTEICT-2018),* 1152-1156.

Kleinrock, L. (1961, July). *Information Flow in Large Communication Nets.* RLE Quarterly Progress Report.

Kraemer, F. A., Braten, A. E., Tamkittikhun, N., & Palma, D. (2017). Fog computing in healthcare–a review and discussion. *IEEE Access: Practical Innovations, Open Solutions*, 5, 9206–9222. doi:10.1109/ACCESS.2017.2704100

Kranz, M. (2016). *Building the Internet of Things: Implement new Business Models, Disrupt Competitors, Transform Your Industry.* John Wiley & Sons.

Kshirsagar, R., Mudhalwadkar, R. P., & Kalaskar, S. (2019, April). Design and Development of IoT Based Water Quality Measurement System. In *2019 3rd International Conference on Trends in Electronics and Informatics (ICOEI)* (pp. 1199-1202). IEEE.

Kulwicki, B. M. (1991). Humidity sensors. *Journal of the American Ceramic Society*, 74(4), 697–708.

Kumari, A., Tanwar, S., Tyagi, S., & Kumar, N. (2018). Fog computing for Healthcare 4.0 environment: Opportunities and challenges. *Computers & Electrical Engineering*, 72, 1–13. doi:10.1016/j.compeleceng.2018.08.015

Kumari, S., Karuppiah, M., Kumar, A., Xiong, D., Fan, L., & Kumar, N. (2018). A secure authentication scheme based on elliptic curve cryptography for IoT and cloud servers. *The Journal of Supercomputing, 74*(12), 6428–6453. doi:10.100711227-017-2048-0

Lambert, L., Poole, H., & Woodford, C. (2005). *Internet: A Historical Encylopedia*. Moschovistis Group.

Lam, C. (2010). *Hadoop in action*. Manning Publications Co.

Landweber, L. H. (1992). Computer networking courses at the University of Wisconsin—Madison. *Computer Communication Review, 22*(1), 52–61. doi:10.1145/141790.141795

Laudon, K., & Traver, C. (2006). *E-commerce: business, technology, society*. Pearson Prentice Hall.

Lauter, K., Naehrig, M., & Vaikuntanathan, V. (2011). Can homomorphic encryption be practical? *Proceedings of the ACM Conference on Computer and Communications Security*, 113–124. 10.1145/2046660.2046682

Lazaro, A., Villarino, R., & Girbau, D. (2018). A survey of NFC sensors based on energy harvesting for IoT applications. *Sensors (Basel), 18*(11), 3746.

Lea, R., & Blackstock, M. (2014, December). City hub: A cloud-based iot platform for smart cities. In *2014 IEEE 6th international conference on cloud computing technology and science* (pp. 799-804). IEEE.

Lee, J., Lapira, E., Bagheri, B., & an Kao, H. (2013). Recent advances and trends in predictive manufacturing systems in big data environment. *Manufacturing Letters, 1*(1), 38–41. doi:10.1016/j.mfglet.2013.09.005

Levy, C., & Wong, D. (2014). *Towards a smart society*. Big Innovation Centre. https://www.biginnovationcentre.com/wp-content/uploads/2019/07/BIC_TOWARDS-A-SMART-SOCIETY_03.06.2014.pdf

Li, X. X., & Bian, F. L. (2010). The Research of Dynamic GIS. *Geomatics World, 6*.

Li, Z., Liang, M., O'Brien, L., & Zhang, H. (2013). The Cloud's Cloudy Moment: A Systematic Survey of Public Cloud Service Outage. *International Journal of Cloud Computing and Services Science, 2*(5), 1–15. doi:10.11591/closer.v2i5.5125

Liana, D. D., Raguse, B., Gooding, J. J., & Chow, E. (2012). Recent advances in paper-based sensors. *Sensors, 12*(9), 11505-11526.

Licklider, J. C. (1963, April). *The Intergalactic Computer Network*. Retrieved from http://imiller.utsc.utoronto.ca/pub2/licklider_intergalactic_1963.pdf

Li, F., Vögler, M., Claeßens, M., & Dustdar, S. (2013). Efficient and scalable IoT service delivery on Cloud. *2013 IEEE Sixth International Conference on Cloud Computing*, 1–8.

Ligthart, L., & Prasad, R. (2016). Role of ICT for Multi-Disciplinary Applications in 2030. Gistru: River Publishers.

Li, L. (2018). China's manufacturing locus in 2025: With a comparison of "Made-in-China 2025" and "Industry 4.0". *Technological Forecasting and Social Change, 135*, 66–74. doi:10.1016/j.techfore.2017.05.028

Lindsay, D. (2007). *International Domain Name Law: ICANN and the UDRP.* Bloomsbury Publishing.

Lin, J., & Ryaboy, D. (2013). Scaling big data mining infrastructure: The twitter experience. *SIGKDD Explorations, 14*(2), 2, 6–19. doi:10.1145/2481244.2481247

Liu, J., Xiao, Y., & Chen, C. L. P. (2012). Authentication and access control in the Internet of things. *Proceedings - 32nd IEEE International Conference on Distributed Computing Systems Workshops, ICDCSW 2012*, 588–592. 10.1109/ICDCSW.2012.23

Liu, J., Yu, X., Xu, Z., Choo, K. K. R., Hong, L., & Cui, X. (2017). A cloud-based taxi trace mining framework for smart city. *Software, Practice & Experience, 47*(8), 1081–1094.

Liu, Y., Dong, B., Guo, B., Yang, J., & Peng, W. (2015). Combination of Cloud Computing and Internet of Things (IOT) in Medical Monitoring Systems. *International Journal of Hybrid Information Technology, 8*(12), 367–376. doi:10.14257/ijhit.2015.8.12.28

Li, W., Cao, J., Hu, K., Xu, J., & Buyya, R. (2019). A trust-based agent learning model for service composition in mobile cloud computing environments. *IEEE Access: Practical Innovations, Open Solutions, 7*, 34207–34226. doi:10.1109/ACCESS.2019.2904081

Low, M. P., Chung, C., Ung, L., Tee, P., & Kuek, T.-Y. (2019). Smart Living Society Begins with A Holistic Digital Economy: A Multi-Level Insight. *7th International Conference on Information and Communication Technology (ICoICT)*, 1-7. 10.1109/ICoICT.2019.8835199

Lueg, C., & Fisher, D. (2012). *From Usenet to CoWebs: Interacting with Social Information Spaces.* Springer.

Lu, N., Cheng, N., Zhang, N., Shen, X., & Mark, J. (2014). Connected vehicles: Solutions and challenges. *IEEE Internet of Things Journal, 1*(4), 289–299. doi:10.1109/JIOT.2014.2327587

Lund, D., MacGillivray, C., Turner, V., & Morales, M. (2014). Worldwide and regional internet of things (iot) 2014–2020 forecast: A virtuous circle of proven value and demand. International Data Corporation (IDC). *Tech. Rep, 1*(1), 9.

Luo, L., Meng, S., Qiu, X., & Dai, Y. (2019). Improving failure tolerance in large-scale cloud computing systems. *IEEE Transactions on Reliability, 68*(2), 620–632. doi:10.1109/TR.2019.2901194

Luo, S., & Ren, B. (2016). The monitoring and managing application of cloud computing based on Internet of Things. *Computer Methods and Programs in Biomedicine, 130*, 154–161. doi:10.1016/j.cmpb.2016.03.024 PMID:27208530

Luttrell, R. (2016). *Social Media: How to Engage, Share, and Connect.* Rowman & Littlefield.

Macfarlane, J. (2007). *Network routing basics: Understanding IP routing in Cisco systems.* John Wiley & Sons.

Madakam, S., Lake, V., Lake, V., & Lake, V. (2015). Internet of Things (IoT): A literature review. *Journal of Computer and Communications, 3*(05), 164.

Madakam, S., Ramaswamy, R., & Tripathi, S. (2015). Internet of Things (IoT): A Literature Review. *Journal of Computer and Communications, 3*(5), 164–173. doi:10.4236/jcc.2015.35021

Mahalle, P. N., Anggorojati, B., Prasad, N. R., & Prasad, R. (2012). Identity establishment and capability based access control (IECAC) scheme for Internet of Things. *The 15th International Symposium on Wireless Personal Multimedia Communications,* 187–191.

Maharaj, P. K. G. B. T., & Malekian, R. (2016). A novel and secure IoT based cloud centric architecture to perform predictive analysis of users activities. *Multimedia Tools and Applications.* Advance online publication. doi:10.100711042-016-4050-6

Maharjan, K. L. (2013). Effect of climate variables on yield of major food-crops in Nepal: A time-series analysis. In *Climate Change, Agriculture and Rural Livelihoods in Developing Countries* (pp. 127–137). Springer. doi:10.1007/978-4-431-54343-5_9

Mahmud, M., Kaiser, M. S., Rahman, M. M., Rahman, M. A., Shabut, A., & Hussain, S. A. A. (2018). *A Brain-Inspired Trust Management Model to Assure Security in a Cloud Based IoT Framework for Neuroscience Applications.* Academic Press.

Maier, H. R. (2004). Use of artificial neural networks for predicting optimal alum doses and treated water quality parameters. *Environmental Modelling & Software, 19*(5), 485–494. doi:10.1016/S1364-8152(03)00163-4

Maksimović, M. (2017). Implementation of Fog computing in IoT-based healthcare system. *Jita-Journal Of Information Technology And Applications, 14*(2).

Malasinghe, L. P., Ramzan, N., & Dahal, K. (2019). Remote patient monitoring: A comprehensive study. *Journal of Ambient Intelligence and Humanized Computing, 10*(1), 57–76. doi:10.100712652-017-0598-x

Malik, A., & Om, H. (2018). *Cloud Computing and Internet of Things Integration : Architecture, Applications, Issues, and Challenges.* doi:10.1007/978-3-319-62238-5

Mansour, I., Sahandi, R., Cooper, K., & Warman, A. (2016). Interoperability in the heterogeneous cloud environment: A survey of recent user-centric approaches. *ACM International Conference Proceeding Series,* 1–7. 10.1145/2896387.2896447

Manyika, J., Chui, M., Bisson, P., Woetzel, J., Dobbs, R., Bughin, J., & Aharon, D. (2015). *The Internet of Things: Mapping the value beyond the hype.* Academic Press.

Marco. (2013). EARS (Earthquake Alert and Report System): Real Time Decision Support System for Earthquake Management. *KDD '14: Proceedings of the 20th ACM SIGKDD international conference on Knowledge discovery and data mining,* 1749–1758.

Margolis, M., & Resnick, D. (2000). *Politics as Usual: The Cyberspace Revolution*. SAGE Publications.

Martino, & ... . (2018). Internet of things reference architectures, security and interoperability: A survey. *Internet of Things*, *1*, 99–112. doi:10.1016/j.iot.2018.08.008

Masip-Bruin, X., Marín-Tordera, E., Alonso, A., & Garcia, J. (2016, June). Fog-to-cloud Computing (F2C): The key technology enabler for dependable e-health services deployment. In *2016 Mediterranean ad hoc networking workshop (Med-Hoc-Net)* (pp. 1-5). IEEE.

Masip-Bruin, X., Marín-Tordera, E., Tashakor, G., Jukan, A., & Ren, G. J. (2016). Foggy clouds and cloudy fogs: A real need for coordinated management of fog-to-cloud computing systems. *IEEE Wireless Communications*, *23*(5), 120–128. doi:10.1109/MWC.2016.7721750

Masoodi, F. S., & Bokhari, M. U. (2019). Symmetric Algorithms I. In *Emerging Security Algorithms and Techniques* (pp. 79–95). Chapman and Hall/CRC. doi:10.1201/9781351021708-6

Masoodi, F., Alam, S., & Siddiqui, S. T. (2019). Security & Privacy Threats, Attacks and Countermeasures in Internet of Things. *International Journal of Network Security & Its Applications*, *11*(02), 67–77. doi:10.5121/ijnsa.2019.11205

Mavromoustakis, C., Mastorakis, G., & Batalla, J. M. (2016). *Internet of Things (IoT) in 5G Mobile Technologies*. Springer. doi:10.1007/978-3-319-30913-2

Medvedev, A., Fedchenkov, P., Zaslavsky, A., Anagnostopoulos, T., & Khoruzhnikov, S. (2015). Waste management as an IoT-enabled service in smart cities. In *Internet of Things, Smart Spaces, and Next Generation Networks and Systems* (pp. 104–115). Springer.

Mehmood, R., Alam, F., Albogami, N. N., Katib, I., Albeshri, A., & Altowaijri, S. M. (2017). UTiLearn: A Personalised Ubiquitous Teaching and Learning System for Smart Societies. *IEEE Access: Practical Innovations, Open Solutions*, *5*, 2615–2635. doi:10.1109/ACCESS.2017.2668840

Meinel, C., & Sack, H. (2016). *Internetworking: Technological Foundations and Applications*. Springer Science & Business Media.

Mell, P., & Grance, T. (2011). *The NIST definition of cloud computing*. Academic Press.

Meng, X., & Feng, L. (2014). Research on application of internet of things technology to earthquake prevention and disaster reduction. *World Information on Earthquake Engineering*, *30*(2), 129–133.

Messier, R. (2014). *Collaboration with Cloud Computing: Security, Social Media and Unified Communication*. Elsevier.

Metternicht, G., Hurni, L., & Gogu, R. (2005). Remote sensing of landslides: An analysis of the potential contribution to geo-spatial systems for hazard assessment in mountainous environments. *Remote Sensing of Environment*, *98*(2), 284–303. doi:10.1016/j.rse.2005.08.004

Miao, Y., & Bu, Y. (2010). Research on the architecture and key technology of Internet of Things (IoT) applied on smart grid. *Proceedings of the International Conference on Advances in Energy Engineering (ICAEE)*, 69–72. 10.1109/ICAEE.2010.5557611

Miraz, M. H., Ali, M., Excell, P. S., & Picking, R. (2015). A review on Internet of Things (IoT), Internet of Everything (IoE) and Internet of Nano Things (IoNT). *2015 Internet Technologies and Applications, ITA 2015 - Proceedings of the 6th International Conference*, 219–224. 10.1109/ITechA.2015.7317398

Misra, P. (2016). *Build a scalable platform for high-performance IoT applications*. Academic Press.

Mital, M., Chang, V., Choudhary, P., Pani, A., & Sun, Z. (2016). TEMPORARY REMOVAL: Adoption of cloud based Internet of Things in India: A multiple theory perspective. *International Journal of Information Management*.

Moin, A. (2015). Sense-Deliberate-Act Cognitive Agents for Sense-Compute-Control Applications in the Internet of Things and Services. In *Internet of Things. User-Centric IoT: First International Summit, IoT360 2014, Rome, Italy, October 27-28, 2014, Revised Selected Papers, Part 1* (pp. 21-28). New York: Springer. 10.1007/978-3-319-19656-5_4

Mondal, Kumar, R. & Sarddar, D. (2015). Utility Computing. *International Journal of Grid and Distributed Computing*, *8*, 115–122. doi:10.14257/ijgdc.2015.8.4.11

Montori, Bedogni, L., Di Felice, M., & Bononi, L. (2018). Machineto-machine wireless communication Technologies for the internet of things: Taxonomy, comparison and open issues. *Pervasive and Mobile Computing*, *50*, 56–81. doi:10.1016/j.pmcj.2018.08.002

Moreno, M. V., Santa, J., Zamora, M. A., & Skarmeta, A. F. (2014, June). A holistic IoT-based management platform for smart environments. In *2014 IEEE International Conference on Communications (ICC)* (pp. 3823-3828). IEEE. 10.1109/ICC.2014.6883917

Moreno, M. V., Terroso-Sáenz, F., González-Vidal, A., Valdés-Vela, M., Skarmeta, A. F., Zamora, M. A., & Chang, V. (2016). Applicability of big data techniques to smart cities deployments. *IEEE Transactions on Industrial Informatics*, *13*(2), 800–809. doi:10.1109/TII.2016.2605581

Moskvitch, K. (2017). When machinery chats. *Engineering & Technology*, *12*(2), 68–70. doi:10.1049/et.2017.0209

Mouftah, H. T., Erol-Kantarci, M., & Rehmani, M. H. (2019). Communication Architectures and Technologies for Advanced Smart Grid Services. In Transportation and Power Grid in Smart Cities: Communication Networks and Services. Wiley.

Mrozek, D., Koczur, A., & Małysiak-Mrozek, B. (2020). Fall detection in older adults with mobile IoT devices and machine learning in the cloud and on the edge. *Information Sciences*, *537*, 132–147. doi:10.1016/j.ins.2020.05.070

Muhammad, Z. (2020) Smart Agriculture Using Internet of Things with Raspberry Pi. *2020 10th IEEE International Conference on Control System, Computing and Engineering (ICCSCE)*, 85-90. 10.1109/ICCSCE50387.2020.9204927

Murray, A. (2016). *Information Technology Law: The Law and Society*. Oxford University Press.

Muthukannan, K., Latha, P., Selvi, R. P., & Nisha, P. (2015). Classification of diseased plant leaves using neural network algorithms. *Journal of Engineering and Applied Sciences (Asian Research Publishing Network)*, *10*(4), 1913–1919.

Nachtigall, J., & Redlich, J.-P. (2011). Wireless alarming and routing protocol for earthquake early warning systems. In *4th IFIP International Conference on New Technologies, Mobility and Security*. IEEE. 10.1109/NTMS.2011.5720630

Naha, R. K., Garg, S., Georgakopoulos, D., Jayaraman, P. P., Gao, L., Xiang, Y., & Ranjan, R. (2018). Fog computing: Survey of trends, architectures, requirements, and research directions. *IEEE Access: Practical Innovations, Open Solutions*, *6*, 47980–48009. doi:10.1109/ACCESS.2018.2866491

Nanda, U., & Pattnaik, S. K. (2016, January). Universal asynchronous receiver and transmitter (uart). In *2016 3rd international conference on advanced computing and communication systems (ICACCS)* (Vol. 1, pp. 1-5). IEEE.

Narayani, N. (2014). *Protect the environment: Go plastic-free with these 11 easy everyday tips*. Retrieved from http://www.folomojo.com/protect-the-environment-go-plastic-free-with-these-11-easy-everyday-tips/

Nathan, S. (2019). *NIST Releases Final Version of Smart Grid Framework*. Available online: https://www.nist.gov/smartgrid/ upload/NIST-SP-1108r3.pdf

Ngugi, J., & Goosen, L. (2018). Modelling Course-Design Characteristics, Self-Regulated Learning and the Mediating Effect of Knowledge-Sharing Behavior as Drivers of Individual Innovative Behavior. *Eurasia Journal of Mathematics, Science and Technology Education*, *14*(8). doi:10.29333/ejmste/92087

Nitti, M., Atzori, L., & Cvijikj, I. P. (2013). *Friendship selection in the Social Internet of Things: challenges and possible strategies*. doi:10.1109/JIOT.2014.2384734

Nitti, M., Girau, R., & Atzori, L. (2014). Trustworthiness Management in the Social Internet of Things. *IEEE Transactions on Knowledge and Data Engineering*, *26*(5), 1253–1266. doi:10.1109/TKDE.2013.105

Nord, J., Koohang, A., & Paliszkiewicz, J. (2019). The internet of things: Review and theoretical framework. *Expert Systems with Applications*, *133*, 97–108. doi:10.1016/j.eswa.2019.05.014

Noura, M., Atiquzzaman, M., & Gaedke, M. (2019). Interoperability in Internet of Things: Taxonomies and open challenges. *Mobile Networks and Applications*, *24*(3), 796–809. doi:10.100711036-018-1089-9

O'Regan, G. (2013). *Giants of Computing: A Compendium of Select, Pivotal Pioneers*. Springer Science & Business Media. doi:10.1007/978-1-4471-5340-5

Odun-ayo, I., Okereke, C., & Orovwode, H. (2018). Cloud Computing and Internet of Things. *Issues and Developments, C, I.*

Okeyo, G., Chen, L., & Wang, H. (2014). Combining ontological and temporal formalisms for composite activity modelling and recognition in smart homes. *Future Generation Computer Systems, 39*, 29–43. doi:10.1016/j.future.2014.02.014

Pacheco-Torgal, F., Rasmussen, E. S., Granqvist, C., Ivanov, V., Kaklauskas, H. A., & Makonin, S. (2016). Start-Up Creation: The Smart Eco-efficient Built Environment. Sawton: Woodhead Publishing.

Padala, P., Zhu, X., Wang, Z., Singhal, S., & Sin, K. G. (2007). *Performance Evaluation of Virtualization Technologies for Server Consolidation.* http://137.204.107.78/tirocinio/site/tirocini/TirocinioZuluaga/Documents/virtualizzazione/Technologies%20for%20Server.pdf

Palmieri, F., Ficco, M., Pardi, S., & Castiglione, A. (2016). A cloud-based architecture for emergency management and first responders localization in smart city environments. *Computers & Electrical Engineering, 56*, 810–830.

Palvia, P., Baqir, N., & Nemati, H. (2015). ICT Policies in Developing Countries: An Evaluation with the Extended Design-Actuality Gaps Framework. *The Electronic Journal on Information Systems in Developing Countries, 71*. Advance online publication. doi:10.1002/j.1681-4835.2015.tb00510.x

Pandiyan, S., Ashwin, M., & Manikandan, R., KM, K. R., & GR, A. R. (2020). Heterogeneous Internet of Things organization predictive analysis platform for apple leaf diseases recognition. *Computer Communications, 154*, 99–110. doi:10.1016/j.comcom.2020.02.054

Pandow, B. A., Bamhdi, A. M., & Masoodi, F. (2020). Internet of Things: Financial Perspective and Associated Security Concerns. *International Journal of Computer Theory and Engineering, 12*(5), 123–127. doi:10.7763/IJCTE.2020.V12.1276

Patel, S., Shah, V., & Kansara, M. (2018). Comparative Study of 2G, 3G and 4G. *International Journal of Scientific Research in Computer Science. Engineering and Information Technology, 3*(3), 1962–1964.

Paul, H. C., & Bacon, K. A. (2016). A study on IPv4 and IPv6: The importance of their coexistence. *International Journal of Information System and Engineering, 4*(2).

Pavel, M. I., Kamruzzaman, S. M., Hasan, S. S., & Sabuj, S. R. (2019, February). An IoT Based Plant Health Monitoring System Implementing Image Processing. In *2019 IEEE 4th International Conference on Computer and Communication Systems (ICCCS)* (pp. 299-303). IEEE. 10.1109/CCOMS.2019.8821782

Peijiang, C., & Xuehua, J. (2008, December). *Design and Implementation of Remote monitoring system based on GSM. In 2008 IEEE Pacific-Asia workshop on computational intelligence and industrial application* (Vol. 1). IEEE.

Pei, L., Guinness, R., Chen, R., Liu, J., Kuusniemi, H., Chen, Y., & Kaistinen, J. (2013). Human behavior cognition using smartphone sensors. *Sensors (Basel), 13*(2), 1402–1424.

Perara, C., Zaslavsky, A., Christen, P., & Goergakopoulos, D. (2014). Context aware computing for the internet of things: A survey. *IEEE Communications Surveys and Tutorials, 16*(1), 414–454. doi:10.1109/SURV.2013.042313.00197

Persson, P., & Angelsmark, O. (2015). Calvin–merging cloud and iot. *Procedia Computer Science, 52,* 210–217.

Petnik, J., & Vanus, J. (2018). Design of smart home implementation within IoT with natural language interface. *IFAC-PapersOnLine, 51*(6), 174–179. doi:10.1016/j.ifacol.2018.07.149

Picozzi, M., Milkereit, C., Fleming, K., Fischer, J., Jaeckel, K., Bindi, D., Parolai, S., & Zschau, J. (2014). Applications of a low-cost, wireless, selforganising system (sosewin) to earthquake early warning and structural health monitoring. Early Warning for Geological Disasters, 263–288.

Pilli, S. K., Nallathambi, B., George, S. J., & Diwanji, V. (2015, February). eAGROBOT—A robot for early crop disease detection using image processing. In *2015 2nd International Conference on Electronics and Communication Systems (ICECS)* (pp. 1684-1689). IEEE.

Piyare, R., Park, S., Maeng, S. Y., Park, S. H., Oh, S. C., Choi, S. G., . . . Lee, S. R. (2013, October). Integrating wireless sensor network into cloud services for real-time data collection. In *2013 International Conference on ICT Convergence (ICTC)* (pp. 752-756). IEEE. 10.1109/ICTC.2013.6675470

Polato, I., Ré, R., Goldman, A., & Kon, F. (2014). A comprehensive view of Hadoop research—A systematic literature review. *Journal of Network and Computer Applications, 46,* 1–25.

Pothen, M. E., & Pai, M. L. (2020, March). Detection of Rice Leaf Diseases Using Image Processing. In *2020 Fourth International Conference on Computing Methodologies and Communication (ICCMC)* (pp. 424-430). IEEE. 10.1109/ICCMC48092.2020.ICCMC-00080

Pottoo, S. N., Wani, T. M., Dar, A., & Mir, A. (2018). IoT Enabled by Li-Fi Technology. International Journal of Scientific Research in Computer Science, Engineering and Information Technology, 1(4).

Prathibha, S. R. (2017). IoT Based Monitoring System in Smart Agriculture. *2017 International Conference on Recent Advances in Electronics and Communication Technology (ICRAECT),* 81-84. 10.1109/ICRAECT.2017.52

Purohit, A., Bhardwaj, A., Tiwari, A., & Choudhari, N. S. (2011, June). Removing Code bloating in crossover operation in genetic programming. In *2011 International Conference on Recent Trends in Information Technology (ICRTIT)* (pp. 1126-1130). IEEE. 10.1109/ICRTIT.2011.5972430

Puthal, D., Nepal, S., Ranjan, R., & Chen, J. (2016). Threats to networking cloud and edge datacenters in the Internet of Things. *IEEE Cloud Computing, 3*(3), 64–71. doi:10.1109/MCC.2016.63

Pye, A. (2016). Drives in the Internet of Things. *Engineering & Technology, 11*(3), 72–74. doi:10.1049/et.2016.0332

Qi, F., Yu, P., Chen, B., Li, W., Zhang, Q., Jin, D., Zhang, G., & Wang, Y. (2018). Optimal Planning of Smart Grid Communication Network for Interregional Wide-Area Monitoring Protection and Control System. *Proceedings of the 2018 IEEE International Conference on Energy Internet (ICEI)*, 190–195.

Qingkai, Schreier, Allen, & Strauss. (2015). *Smartphone-based Networks for Earthquake Detection*. IEEE.

Qin, J., Liu, Y., & Grosvenor, R. (2016). A categorical framework of manufacturing for industry 4.0 and beyond. *Procedia CIRP*, *52*, 173–178. doi:10.1016/j.procir.2016.08.005

Qin, L., Feng, S., & Zhu, H. (2018). Research on the technological architectural design of geological hazard monitoring and rescue-after-disaster system based on cloud computing and internet of things. *International Journal of Systems Assurance Engineering and Management*, *9*(3), 684–695. doi:10.100713198-017-0638-0

Rabkin, A., Arye, M., Sen, S., Pai, V., & Freedman, M. J. (2013). *Making Every Bit Count in Wide-Area Analytics*. Academic Press.

Rafiei, S., & Bakhshai, A. (2012). A review on energy efficiency optimization in Smart Grid. *Proceedings of 38th Annual Conference on IEEE Industrial Electronics Society*, 5916–5919. 10.1109/IECON.2012.6389115

Rahman, H., Rahmani, R., Kanter, T., Persson, M., & Armundin, S. (2013). Reasoning Service Enabling SmartHome Automation at the Edge of Context Networks. In Á. Rocha, A. M. Correia, H. Adeli, L. P. Reis, & M. Teixeira (Eds.), *Advances in Information Systems and Technologies* (Vol. 1, pp. 777–795). Springer.

Rajiv, P., Raj, R., & Chandra, M. (2016). Email based remote access and surveillance system for smart home infrastructure. *Perspectives in Science*, *8*, 459–461. doi:10.1016/j.pisc.2016.04.104

Rani, S., Ahmed, S. H., & Rastogi, R. (2019). Dynamic clustering approach based on wireless sensor networks genetic algorithm for IoT applications. *Wireless Networks*, 1–10.

Rashid, B., & Rehmani, M. H. Applications of wireless sensor networks for urban areas. *Journal. of Network & Computer Applications, 60*.

Ray P., (2018). A survey on internet of things architectures. *Journal of King Saud University - Computer and Information Sciences, 30*(3), 291–319.

Ray, P. P. (2017). Internet of Things for Smart Agriculture: Technologies. *Practices and Future Direction, 1*(Jan), 395–420.

Refaat, S. S., Abu-Rub, H., Trabelsi, M., & Mohamed, A. (2018). Reliability evaluation of smart grid system with large penetration of distributed energy resources. *Proceedings of the 2018 IEEE International Conference on Industrial Technology (ICIT)*, 1279–1284. 10.1109/ICIT.2018.8352362

Reid, M. E., & Lahusen, R. G. (1998). Real-time monitoring of active landslides along highway 50, el dorado county. *California Geology*, *51*(3), 17–20.

Rittinghouse, J., & Ransome, J. (2016). *Cloud Computing: Implementation, Management, and Security*. CRC Press.

Roberts, L. (1967, October). Multiple Computer Networks and Intercomputer Communication. *ACM Gatlinburg Conference*. Gatlinburg: ACM.

Robison, P., Sengupta, M., & Rauch, D. (2015). Intelligent energy industrial systems 4.0. *IT Professional*, *17*(3), 17–24. doi:10.1109/MITP.2015.48

Rodrigues, L., Guerreiro, J., & Correia, N. (2016). RELOAD/CoAP architecture with resource aggregation/disaggregation service. *IEEE International Symposium on Personal, Indoor and Mobile Radio Communications, PIMRC*, 1–6. 10.1109/PIMRC.2016.7794607

Roman, R., Zhou, J., & Lopez, J. (2013). On the features and challenges of security and privacy in distributed internet of things. *Computer Networks*, *57*(10), 2266–2279. doi:10.1016/j.comnet.2012.12.018

Rose, K., Eldridge, S., & Chapin, L. (2015). The internet of things: An overview. *The Internet Society (ISOC), 80*, 1-50.

Russell, A. (2014). *Open Standards and the Digital Age: History, Ideology and Networks*. Cambridge University Press. doi:10.1017/CBO9781139856553

Sahoo, K. C., & Pati, U. C. (2017, May). IoT based intrusion detection system using PIR sensor. In *2017 2nd IEEE International Conference on Recent Trends in Electronics, Information & Communication Technology (RTEICT)* (pp. 1641-1645). IEEE. 10.1109/RTEICT.2017.8256877

Sakalle, A., Tomar, P., Bhardwaj, H., & Sharma, U. (2021). Impact and Latest Trends of Intelligent Learning With Artificial Intelligence. In Impact of AI Technologies on Teaching, Learning, and Research in Higher Education (pp. 172-189). IGI Global.

Sakr, S., Liu, A., Batista, D. M., & Alomari, M. (2011). A survey of large scale data management approaches in cloud environments. In IEEE Communications Surveys and Tutorials (Vol. 13, Issue 3, pp. 311–336). doi:10.1109/SURV.2011.032211.00087

Salehi, A., & Aberer, K. (2007, January). *GSN, quick and simple sensor network deployment*. In *4th European conference on Wireless Sensor Networks*, Delft, The Netherlands.

Salim, F., & Haque, U. (2015). Urban computing in the wild: A survey on large scale participation and citizen engagement with ubiquitous computing, cyber physical systems, and Internet of Things. *International Journal of Human-Computer Studies*, *81*, 31–48. doi:10.1016/j.ijhcs.2015.03.003

Samie, F., Bauer, L., & Henkel, J. (2016). IoT technologies for embedded computing: A survey. *2016 International Conference on Hardware/Software Codesign and System Synthesis, CODES+ISSS 2016*, 1–10. 10.1145/2968456.2974004

Sammer, E. (2012). *Hadoop operations*. O'Reilly Media, Inc.

Sanislav, T., Zeadally, S., & Mois, G. D. (2017). A cloud-integrated, multilayered, agent-based cyber-physical system architecture. *Computer*, *50*(4), 27–37. doi:10.1109/MC.2017.113

Sanjeevi, P., & Viswanathan, P. (2017). NUTS scheduling approach for cloud data centers to optimize energy consumption. *Computing*, *99*(12), 1179–1205. doi:10.100700607-017-0559-4

Santos, C., Mehrsai, A., Barros, A. C., Araújo, M., & Ares, E. (2017). Towards Industry 4.0: An overview of European strategic roadmaps. *Procedia Manufacturing*, *13*, 972–979. doi:10.1016/j.promfg.2017.09.093

Santos, M., & Oliveira, J. (2017). A big data system supporting bosch braga industry 4.0 strategy. *International Journal of Information Management*, *37*(6), 750–760. doi:10.1016/j.ijinfomgt.2017.07.012

Sarma, S., Brock, D. L., & Ashton, K. (2000). *The Networked Physical World*. Auto-ID Center White Paper MIT-AUTOID-WH-001.

Sathi, A. (2016). *Cognitive (Internet of) Things: Collaboration to Optimize Action*. Palgrave Macmillan. doi:10.1057/978-1-137-59466-2

Saxena, A., Tyagi, M., & Singh, P. (2018, February). Digital Outing System Using RFID And Raspberry Pi With MQTT Protocol. In *2018 3rd International Conference On Internet of Things: Smart Innovation and Usages (IoT-SIU)* (pp. 1-4). IEEE. 10.1109/IoT-SIU.2018.8519923

Schoenberger, C. R. (2002). The Internet of things. *Forbes*, 155-160.

Sciforce. (2020). *Smart Farming: The Future of Agriculture*. Retrieved from https://www.iotforall.com/smart-farming-future-of-agriculture

Seel, P. (2012). *Digital Universe: The Global Telecommunication Revolution*. John Wiley & Sons.

Senyo, P. K., Addae, E., & Boateng, R. (2018). Cloud computing research: A review of research themes, frameworks, methods and future research directions. *International Journal of Information Management*, *38*(1), 128–139. doi:10.1016/j.ijinfomgt.2017.07.007

Sethi, S. R. S. (2017). *Internet of things: architectures, protocols, and applications*. https://www.hindawi.com/journals/jece/2017/9324035

Shah, S. A., Seker, D. Z., Hameed, S., & Draheim, D. (2019). The rising role of big data analytics and IoT in disaster management: Recent advances, taxonomy and prospects. *IEEE Access: Practical Innovations, Open Solutions*, *7*, 54595–54614.

Shannon, M. A., Bohn, P. W., Elimelech, M., Georgiadis, J. G., Mariñas, B. J., & Mayes, A. M. (2008). Science and technology for water purification in the coming decades. *Nature*, *452*(7185), 301–310. doi:10.1038/nature06599 PMID:18354474

Sharma, P. (2020). Intrusion Detection and Security System. In *Big Data Analytics and Intelligence: A Perspective for Health Care*. Emerald Publishing Limited. doi:10.1108/978-1-83909-099-820201011

Sharma, P., & Kamthania, D. (2019). Intelligent object detection and avoidance system. In *International Conference on Transforming IDEAS (Inter-Disciplinary Exchanges, Analysis, and Search) into Viable Solutions* (pp. 342-351). Macmillan Education.

Sharma, S., Chang, V., Tim, U. S., Wong, J., & Gadia, S. (2019). Cloud and IoT-based emerging services systems. *Cluster Computing, 22*(1), 71–91.

Sherki, Y., Gaikwad, N., Chandle, J., & Kulkarni, A. (2015). Design of real time sensor system for detection and processing of seismic waves for earthquake early warning system. *Conference: 2015 International Conference on Power and Advanced Control Engineering (ICPACE)*, 285–289. 10.1109/ICPACE.2015.7274959

Shi, Y. G., & Bian, F. (2011). The study of public service for remote sensing information based on cloud platform. *Geomatics World, 3.*

Shin, H. C., Roth, H. R., Gao, M., Lu, L., Xu, Z., Nogues, I., Yao, J., Mollura, D., & Summers, R. M. (2016). Deep convolutional neural networks for computer-aided detection: CNN architectures, dataset characteristics and transfer learning. *IEEE Transactions on Medical Imaging, 35*(5), 1285–1298. doi:10.1109/TMI.2016.2528162 PMID:26886976

Shrivastava, V. K., Pradhan, M. K., Minz, S., & Thakur, M. P. (2019). Rice plant disease classification using transfer learning of deep convolution neural network. *International Archives of the Photogrammetry, Remote Sensing & Spatial Information Sciences.*

Shvachko, K., Kuang, H., Radia, S., & Chansler, R. (2010, May). The hadoop distributed file system. In *2010 IEEE 26th symposium on mass storage systems and technologies (MSST)* (pp. 1-10). IEEE.

Sicari, S., Rizzardi, A., Grieco, L. A., & Coen-Porisini, A. (2015). Security, privacy and trust in Internet of things: The road ahead. *Computer Networks, 76*(October), 146–164. doi:10.1016/j.comnet.2014.11.008

Simmhan, Y., Kumbhare, A. G., Cao, B., & Prasanna, V. (2011). An analysis of security and privacy issues in smart grid software architectures on clouds. *Proceedings - 2011 IEEE 4th International Conference on Cloud Computing, CLOUD 2011*, 582–589. 10.1109/CLOUD.2011.107

Simon, H. A. (1963). *The heuristic compiler*. Rand Corporation.

Singh, Kumar, & Chandana, (2020). A Review on PDIS (Plant Disease Identification Systems). *International Journal of Engineering Research & Technology, 8*(10).

Singh, P. P., Kaushik, R., Singh, H., Kumar, N., & Rana, P. S. (2019, December). Convolutional Neural Networks Based Plant Leaf Diseases Detection Scheme. In *2019 IEEE Globecom Workshops (GC Wkshps)* (pp. 1-7). IEEE.

Singh, R. S. S., Ibrahim, A. F. T., Salim, S. I. M., & Chiew, W. Y. (2009, November). Door sensors for automatic light switching system. In *2009 Third UKSim European Symposium on Computer Modeling and Simulation* (pp. 574-578). IEEE.

Singh, D., Tripathi, G., & Jara, A. J. (2014). A survey of Internet-of-Things: Future Vision, Architecture, Challenges and Services. *Proceedings of the 2014 IEEE World Forum on Internet of Things (WF-IoT)*, 287–292. 10.1109/WF-IoT.2014.6803174

Singh, J., Pasquier, T., Bacon, J., Ko, H., & Eyers, D. (2016). Twenty Security Considerations for Cloud-Supported Internet of Things. *IEEE Internet of Things Journal*, 3(3), 269–284. doi:10.1109/JIOT.2015.2460333

SinghT. (2020). A Survey on Intelligent Techniques for Disease Recognition in Agricultural Crops. Available at SSRN 3616700. doi:10.2139srn.3616700

Singh, T., & Kumar, A. (n.d.). Survey on Characteristics Of Autonomous System. *International Journal of Computer Science and Information Technologies, 8.*

Singh, T., Kumar, K., & Bedi, S. S. (2021). A Review on Artificial Intelligence Techniques for Disease Recognition in Plants. *IOP Conference Series. Materials Science and Engineering, 1022*(1), 012032. doi:10.1088/1757-899X/1022/1/012032

Singh, U. P., Chouhan, S. S., Jain, S., & Jain, S. (2019). Multilayer convolution neural network for the classification of mango leaves infected by anthracnose disease. *IEEE Access: Practical Innovations, Open Solutions, 7*, 43721–43729. doi:10.1109/ACCESS.2019.2907383

Singhvi, R. K., Lohar, R. L., Kumar, A., Sharma, R., Sharma, L. D., & Saraswat, R. K. (2019, April). IoT basedsmart waste management system: india prospective. In *2019 4th International Conference on Internet of Things: Smart Innovation and Usages (IoT-SIU)* (pp. 1-6). IEEE.

Slama, D., Puhlmann, F., Morrish, J., & Bhatnagar, R. (2015). *Enterprise IoT: Strategies and Best Practices for Connected Products and Services*. O'Reilly Media.

Smart Society. (2019). [REMOVED HYPERLINK FIELD]https://www.azbil.com/top/pickup/whitepaper/pdf/Azbil_Smart_Society_WP_12022020.pdf

Smartcity. (2018). *Smart Cities Need To Be On The Cloud To Speed Up Sustainable Development.* https://www.smartcity.press/cloud-computing-benefits/

Smart, P., Heersmink, R., & Clowes, R. (2016). The cognitive ecology of the internet. In S. J. Cowley & F. Vallée-Tourangeau (Eds.), *Cognition Beyond the Brain: Computation, Interactivity and Human Artifice* (2nd ed., pp. 251–282). Springer International Publishing.

Sobin, C. C. (2020). A Survey on Architecture, Protocols and Challenges in IoT. In Wireless Personal Communications. Springer US. doi:10.100711277-020-07108-5

Son, S. C., Kim, N. W., Lee, B. T., Cho, C. H., & Chong, J. W. (2016). A time synchronization technique for coap-based home automation systems. *IEEE Transactions on Consumer Electronics, 62*(1), 10–16. doi:10.1109/TCE.2016.7448557

Sood, S. K. (2019). Mobile fog based secure cloud-IoT framework for enterprise multimedia security. *Multimedia Tools and Applications*. Advance online publication. doi:10.100711042-019-08573-2

Stallings, W., & Prentice, P. (2002). *Communications and Networks*. doi:10.1109/PACIIA.2008.195

Stankovic, J. A. (2014). Research directions for the internet of things. *IEEE Internet of Things Journal, 1*(1), 3–9. doi:10.1109/JIOT.2014.2312291

Stanley, M. (2020). *75 Billion Devices Will Be Connected to The Internet of Things By 2020*. Available online: https://www.businessinsider.com/75-billion-devices-will-be-connected-to-the-internet-by-20202013-10

Stergiou, C., Psannis, K. E., Kim, B. G., & Gupta, B. (2018). Secure integration of IoT and Cloud Computing. *Future Generation Computer Systems, 78*, 964–975. doi:10.1016/j.future.2016.11.031

Stojmenovic, I., & Wen, S. (2014). The Fog computing paradigm: Scenarios and security issues. *2014 Federated Conference on Computer Science and Information Systems, FedCSIS 2014*, 1–8. 10.15439/2014F503

Sturken, M., Thomas, D., & Ball-Rokeach, S. (2004). *Technological Visions: The Hopes and Fears that Shape New Technologies*. Temple University Press.

Sundmaeker, H., Guillemin, P., Friess, P., & Woelfflé, S. (2015). *Vision and challenges for realising the Internet of Things*. European Commission. Retrieved from http://www.internet-of-things-research.eu/pdf/IoT_Clusterbook_March_2010.pdf

Supply Chain Council. (2012). Supply Chain Operations Reference Model 11.0. In *Supply Chain Operations Management*. doi:10.1108/09576059710815716

Suryadevara, N. K., Mukhopadhyay, S. C., Wang, R., & Rayudu, R. K. (2013). Forecasting the behavior of an elderly using wireless sensors data in a smart home. *Engineering Applications of Artificial Intelligence, 26*(10), 2641–2652. doi:10.1016/j.engappai.2013.08.004

Suzuki, Saruwatari, Kurata, & Morikawa. (2007). *Demo abstract: A high-density earthquake monitoring system using wireless sensor networks*. Academic Press.

Takeshi, Makot, & Yutaka. (2013). *Tweet Analysis for Real-Time Event Detection and Earthquake Reporting System Development*. Academic Press.

Takeshi, Makot, & Yutaka. (2013). *Tweet Analysis for Real-Time Event Detection and Earthquake Reporting System Development*. Academic Press.

Tan, J. (2018). *Cloud Computing Is Crucial To The Future Of Our Societies*. https://www.forbes.com/sites/joytan/2018/02/25/cloud-computing-is-the-foundation-of-tomorrows-intelligent-world/?sh=483139c64073

Tao, M., Zuo, J., Liu, Z., Castiglione, A., & Palmieri, F. (2018). Multi-layer cloud architectural model and ontology-based security service framework for IoT-based smart homes. *Future Generation Computer Systems*, *78*, 1040–1051. doi:10.1016/j.future.2016.11.011

Tay, S. I., Lee, T. C., Hamid, N. Z. A., & Ahmad, A. N. A. (2018). An overview of industry 4.0: Definition, components, and government initiatives. *Journal of Advanced Research in Dynamical and Control Systems*, *10*(14), 1379–1387.

Techahead. (2021). https://www.techaheadcorp.com/knowledge-center/evolution-of-iot/

Tei, K., & Gürgen, L. (2014, March). ClouT: Cloud of things for empowering the citizen clout in smart cities. In *2014 IEEE World Forum on Internet of Things (WF-IoT)* (pp. 369-370). IEEE.

Thanh, N. C., & Singh, B. (2006). Constraints faced by the farmers in rice production and export. *Omonrice*, *14*, 97–110.

The role of ICT in the proposed urban suatainable development goal. (2014). https://www.ericsson.com/assets/local/news/2014/9/the-role-of-ict-in-the-new-urban-agenda.pdf

Thibaut, M. (2018). Convolutional network for earthquake detection and location. *Science Advances*, *4*(2), 2. doi:10.1126ciadv.1700578 PMID:29487899

Thorat, A., Kumari, S., & Valakunde, N. D. (2017). An IoT-based smart solution for leaf disease detection. In *2017 International Conference on Big Data, IoT and Data Science (BID)*, (pp. 193-198). IEEE. 10.1109/BID.2017.8336597

Thota, C., Sundarasekar, R., Manogaran, G., Varatharajan, R., & Priyan, M. K. (2018). We have a centralized fog computing security platform for IoT and cloud in the healthcare system. In *Fog computing: Breakthroughs in research and practice* (pp. 365–378). IGI Global. doi:10.4018/978-1-5225-5649-7.ch018

Tian, J., & Jing, X. (2019). A lightweight secure auditing scheme for shared data in cloud storage. *IEEE Access: Practical Innovations, Open Solutions*, *7*, 68071–68082. doi:10.1109/ACCESS.2019.2916889

TJB, D. D., Subramani, A., & Solanki, V. K. (2017). Smart City: IOT Based Prototype for Parking Monitoring and Management System Commanded by Mobile App. *Annals of Computer Science and Information Systems*, *10*, 341–343.

Tjensvold, J. M. (2007, September). Comparison of the IEEE 802.11, 802.15. 1, 802.15. 4 and 802.15. 6 wireless standards. IEEE, 18.

Tomlinson, R. (2009). *The first network email.* Retrieved from Raytheon BBN Technologies: https://www.raytheon.com/sites/default/files/news/rtnwcm/groups/public/documents/content/rtn12_tomlinson_email.pdf

Tripathi, K. (2015). Optimizing Operational and Migration Cost in Cloud Paradigm (OOMCCP). In P. Sharma, P. Banerjee, J.-P. Dudeja, P. Singh, & R. K. Brajpuriya (Eds.), *Making Innovations Happen* (pp. 83–91). Allied Publishers.

Tseng, C. W., & Huang, C. H. (2014, April). Toward a consistent expression of things on epcglobal architecture framework. In *2014 International Conference on Information Science, Electronics and Electrical Engineering* (Vol. 3, pp. 1619-1623). IEEE. 10.1109/InfoSEEE.2014.6946195

Tuli, S., Mahmud, R., Tuli, S., & Buyya, R. (2019). FogBus: A blockchain-based lightweight framework for edge and fog computing. *Journal*, 22-36.

Turečková, K., & Nevima, J. (2020). The Cost Benefit Analysis for the Concept of a Smart City: How to Measure the Efficiency of Smart Solutions? *Sustainability, 12*, 2663. doi:10.3390u12072663

Uma, S., Eswari, R., Bhuvanya, R., & Kumar, G. S. (2019). IoT based voice/text controlled home appliances. *Procedia Computer Science, 165*, 232–238. doi:10.1016/j.procs.2020.01.085

United Nations, Department of Global Communications. (n.d.). *The 17 goals.* https://sdgs.un.org/goals

United States Congress Committee on Commerce, Science and Transportation. (1991). *High-Performance Computing and Communications Act of 1991: hearing before the Subcommittee on Science, Technology, and Space of the Committee on Commerce, Science, and Transportation, United States Senate, One Hundred Second Congress, first session, on S.* Washington, DC: Congress of the U.S.

Urfalıoğlu, O., Soyer, E. B., Toreyin, B. U., & Cetin, A. E. (2008, April). PIR-sensor based human motion event classification. In *2008 IEEE 16th Signal Processing, Communication and Applications Conference* (pp. 1-4). IEEE.

Usman, A., Bukht, T. F. N., Ahmad, R., & Ahmad, J. (2020). Plant Disease Detection using Internet of Things (IoT). *Plant Disease, 11*(1).

Van Voorthuijsen, G., van Hoof, H. A. J. M., Klima, M., Roubik, K., Bernas, M., & Pata, P. (2005, October). CCTV effectiveness study. In *Proceedings 39th Annual 2005 International Carnahan Conference on Security Technology* (pp. 105-108). IEEE. 10.1109/CCST.2005.1594815

VanderZee, M., Fisher, D., Powley, G., & Mohammad, R. (2015). Scada: Supervisory control and data acquisition. *Oil and Gas Pipelines*, 13-26.

Varadharajan, V., & Bansal, S. (2016). Data Security and Privacy in the Internet of Things (IoT) Environment. In Z. Mahmood (Ed.), *Connectivity Frameworks for Smart Devices: The Internet of Things from a Distributed Computing Perspective* (pp. 261–280). Springer. doi:10.1007/978-3-319-33124-9_11

Velastin, S. A. (2009, November). CCTV video analytics: Recent advances and limitations. In *International Visual Informatics Conference* (pp. 22-34). Springer. 10.1007/978-3-642-05036-7_3

Venkataramanan, A., Honakeri, D. K. P., & Agarwal, P. (2019). Plant disease detection and classification using deep neural networks. *International Journal on Computer Science and Engineering, 11*(08), 40–46.

Compilation of References

Verma, P. K., Verma, R., Prakash, A., Agrawal, A., Naik, K., Tripathi, R., ... Abogharaf, A. (2016). Machine-to-Machine (M2M) communications: A survey. *Journal of Network and Computer Applications*, *66*, 83–105.

Verma, P., & Sood, S. K. (2018). Cloud-centric IoT based disease diagnosis healthcare framework. *Journal of Parallel and Distributed Computing*, *116*, 27–38.

Vermesan, O., & Friess, P. (2015). Building the Hyperconnected Society: Internet of Things Research and Innovation Value Chains, Ecosystems and Markets. Gistrup: River Publishers. doi:10.13052/rp-9788793237988

Vermesan, O., Friess, P., Guillemin, P., Gusmeroli, S., Sundmaeker, H., Bassi, A., ... Doody, P. (2011). Internet of things strategic research roadmap. *Internet of Things-Global Technological and Societal Trends, 1*(2011), 9-52.

Villars, R. L., Cooke, J., & MacGillivray, C. (2015). Impact of internet of things on datacenter demand and operations. *Special Study*, 255397.

Vincenti, G. (2010). *Teaching through Multi-User Virtual Environments: Applying Dynamic Elements to the Modern Classroom: Applying Dynamic Elements to the Modern Classroom.* IGI Global.

Voas, J. (2016). Demystifying the internet of things. *Computer*, *49*(6), 80–83. doi:10.1109/MC.2016.162

Voas, J. (2016). Networks of 'things'. *NIST Special Publication*, *800*(183), 800–183.

Vorster, J., & Goosen, L. (2017). A Framework for University Partnerships Promoting Continued Support of e-Schools. In J. Liebenberg (Ed.), *Proceedings of the 46th Annual Conference of the Southern African Computer Lecturers' Association (SACLA)* (pp. 118 - 126). Magaliesburg: North-West University.

Voss, A. (2010). *Cloud computing.* Academic Press.

Wang & Ni. (2012). Wireless sensor networks for earthquake early warning systems of railway lines. *Lecture Notes in Electrical Engineering, 148*, 417–426.

Wang, Y., & Scott, S. (2007). *U.S. Patent Application No. 11/282,001*. US Patent Office.

Wang. (2011). Online Water Monitoring System Based on ZigBee and GPRS. Key Laboratory of Advanced Process Control for Light Industry (Ministry of Education). *Procedia Engineering, 15*, 2680-2684.

Water, S. (2016). Managing the water distribution network with a Smart Water Grid. *Smart Water*. doi:10.118640713-016-0004-4

Wazid, M., Das, A. K., Bhat, V., & Vasilakos, A. V. (2020). LAM-CIoT: Lightweight authentication mechanism in cloud-based IoT environment. *Journal of Network and Computer Applications, 150*, 102496. doi:10.1016/j.jnca.2019.102496

Weiser, M. (1991). The Computer for the 21st Century. *Am. 1991, 265*, 66–75.

White, T. (2012). *Hadoop: The definitive guide.* O'Reilly Media, Inc.

Whitmore, A., Agarwal, A., & Da Xu, L. (2015). The Internet of Things—A survey of topics and trends. *Information Systems Frontiers, 17*(2), 261–274. doi:10.100710796-014-9489-2

Wieser, M. (1991). The computer for the 21st century. *Scientific American, 265*(3), 94–104. doi:10.1038cientificamerican0991-94 PMID:1675486

Witham, M. D., Argo, I. S., Johnston, D. W., Struthers, A. D., & McMurdo, M. E. (2006). Predictors of exercise capaCity and everyday activity in older heart failure patients. *European Journal of Heart Failure, 8*(2), 203–207.

Wu, L., Xu, Y. J., Xu, C. N., & Wang, F. (2013). Plug-configure-play service-oriented gateway: For fast and easy sensor network application development. *SENSORNETS 2013 - Proceedings of the 2nd International Conference on Sensor Networks*, 53–58. 10.5220/0004271700530058

Wu, Q., Ding, G., Xu, Y., Feng, S., Du, Z., Wang, J., & Long, K. (2014). Cognitive internet of things: A new paradigm beyond connection. *IEEE Internet of Things Journal, 1*(2), 129–143. doi:10.1109/JIOT.2014.2311513

Wu, Y.-M., & Kanamori, H. (2008). Development of an earthquake early warning system using Real-Time Strong Motion Signals. *PMC Article, 8*(1), 1–9. doi:10.33908010001 PMID:27879692

Xu, B., Da Xu, L., Cai, H., Xie, C., Hu, J., & Bu, F. (2014). Ubiquitous data accessing method in iot-based information system for emergency medical services. *IEEE Transactions on Industrial Informatics, 10*(2), 1578–1586. doi:10.1109/TII.2014.2306382

Yadav, E. P., Mittal, E. A., & Yadav, H. (2018, February). IoT: Challenges and issues in indian perspective. In *2018 3rd International Conference On Internet of Things: Smart Innovation and Usages (IoT-SIU)* (pp. 1-5). IEEE.

Yadav, P., & Vishwakarma, S. (2018, February). Application of Internet of Things and big data towards a smart city. In *2018 3rd International Conference On Internet of Things: Smart Innovation and Usages (IoT-SIU)* (pp. 1-5). IEEE.

Yasuura, H., Kyung, C. M., Liu, Y., & Lin, Y. L. (Eds.). (2017). *Smart sensors at the IoT frontier.* Springer International Publishing.

Yin-Min. (1999). *Development of an integrated Earthquake Early Warning System Case for the Hualien Area Earthquakes.* Academic Press.

Yong, C. Y., Sudirman, R., & Chew, K. M. (2011, September). Motion detection and analysis with four different detectors. In *2011 Third International Conference on Computational Intelligence, Modelling & Simulation* (pp. 46-50). IEEE. 10.1109/CIMSim.2011.18

Youssef, Y. El-Sheimy, & Noureldin. (2007). A novel earthquake warning system based on virtual mimo-wireless sensor networks. Academic Press.

Compilation of References

You, Z., & Feng, L. (2020). Integration of industry 4.0 related technologies in construction industry: A framework of cyber-physical system. *IEEE Access: Practical Innovations, Open Solutions*, *8*, 122908–122922. doi:10.1109/ACCESS.2020.3007206

Yue, H., Guo, L., Li, R., Asaeda, H., & Fang, Y. (2014). DataClouds: Enabling community-based data-centric services over the Internet of Things. *IEEE Internet of Things Journal*, *1*(5), 472–482. doi:10.1109/JIOT.2014.2353629

Zahmatkesh, H., & Al-Turjman, F. (2020). Fog computing for sustainable smart cities in the IoT era: Caching techniques and enabling technologies-an overview. *Sustainable Cities and Society*, *59*, 102139. doi:10.1016/j.scs.2020.102139

Zambrano, P. Palau, & Esteve. (2014). Quake detection system using smartphone-based wireless sensor network for early warning. Academic Press.

Zambrano, Perez, Palau, & Esteve. (2017). Technologies of internet of things applied to an earthquake early warning system. *Future Generation Computer Systems*, *75*, 206–215.

Zaslavsky, A., Perera, C., & Georgakopoulos, D. (2012). Sensing as a Service and Big Data. *International Conference on Advances in Cloud Computing (ACC)*, 1–8.

Zelnick, B., & Zelnick, E. (2013). *The illusion of Net Neutrality: Political Alarmism, Regulatory Creep and the Real Threat to Internet Freedom*. Hoover Press.

Zhang, F., Liu, G., Fu, X., & Yahyapour, R. (2018). A survey on virtual machine migration: Challenges, techniques, and open issues. *IEEE Communications Surveys and Tutorials*, *20*(2), 1206–1243. doi:10.1109/COMST.2018.2794881

Zhang, G., Li, Y., & Lin, T. (2013). Caching in information centric networking: A survey. *Computer Networks*, *57*(16), 3128–3141. doi:10.1016/j.comnet.2013.07.007

Zhang, P., Zhou, M., & Fortino, G. (2018). Security and trust issues in fog computing: A survey. *Future Generation Computer Systems*, *88*, 16–27. doi:10.1016/j.future.2018.05.008

Zhang, Y., & Tao, F. (2016). *Optimization of Manufacturing Systems Using the Internet of Things*. Academic Press.

Zhang, Z., Zhang, Y. Q., Chu, X., & Li, B. (2004). An overview of virtual private network (VPN): IP VPN and optical VPN. *Photonic Network Communications*, *7*(3), 213–225. doi:10.1023/B:PNET.0000026887.35638.ce

Zhao, L., Matsuo, I. B. M., Zhou, Y., & Lee, W. J. (2019). Design of an industrial IoT-based monitoring system for power substations. *IEEE Transactions on Industry Applications*, *55*(6), 5666–5674. doi:10.1109/TIA.2019.2940668

Zhao, Z., & Chen, G. (2018). An Overview of Cyber Security for Smart Grid. *Proceedings of the 2018 IEEE*.

Zhou, J., Cao, Z., Dong, X., & Vasilakos, A. V. (2017). Security and privacy for cloud-based IoT: Challenges. *IEEE Communications Magazine*, *55*(1), 26–33.

Zhou, J., Leppanen, T., Harjula, E., Ylianttila, M., Ojala, T., Yu, C., ... Yang, L. T. (2013, June). Cloudthings: A common architecture for integrating the internet of things with cloud computing. In *Proceedings of the 2013 IEEE 17th international conference on computer supported cooperative work in design (CSCWD)* (pp. 651-657). IEEE. 10.1109/CSCWD.2013.6581037

Zhu, Y. J., Li, Q., & Feng, X. (2014). Study on technological framework of Smart City based on Big Data. *Science of Surveying and Mapping*, (8), 17.

Zuckerman, E. (2013). *Digital Cosmopolitans: Why We Think the Internet Connects Us, Why It Doesn't, and How to Rewire It*. W.W. Norton & Company.

About the Contributors

Pradeep Tomar is working as Assistant Professor in the School of Information and Communication Technology, Gautam Buddha University, Greater Noida, U.P., India since 2009. Dr. Tomar earned his Ph.D. from MDU, Rohtak, Haryana, India. Before joining Gautam Buddha University, he worked as a Software Engineer in a multi-national company, Noida and lecturer in M. D. University, Rohtak, Haryana and Kurukshetra University, Kurukshetra, Haryana. Dr. Tomar has good teaching, research and software development experience as well as vast administrative experience at university level on various posts like research coordinator, examination coordinator, admission coordinator, programme coordinator, time table coordinators, proctor and hostel warden. Dr. Tomar is also a member of Computer Society of India (CSI), Indian Society for Technical Education (ISTE), Indian Science Congress Association (ISCA), International Association of Computer Science and Information Technology (IACSIT) and International Association of Engineers (IAENG). Dr. Tomar has qualified the National Eligibility Test (NET) for Lecturership in Computer Applications in 2003, Microsoft Certified Professional (MCP) in 2008, SUN Certified JAVA Programmer (SCJP) for the JAVA platform, standard edition 5.0 in 2008 and qualified the IBM Certified Database Associate - DB2 9 Fundamentals in 2010. Dr. Tomar has been awarded with Bharat Jyoti Award by India International Friendship Society in the field of Technology in 2012 and Bharat Vikas Award by Institute of Self Reliance in National Seminar on Diversity of Cultural and Social Environment at Bhubneswar, Odisha, in 2017. He has been awarded for the Best Computer Faculty award by Govt. of Pondicherry and ASDF society. His biography is published in Who's Who Reference Asia, Volume II. Dr. Tomar has been awarded distinguished Research Award from Institute for Global Business Research for his work in "A Web Based Stock Selection Decision Support System for Investment Portfolio Management in 2018. Several technical sessions in national and international conferences had been chaired by Dr. Tomar and he delivered expert talks at FDP, workshops, national and international conferences. Three conferences have been organized by Dr. Tomar: one national conference with COMMUNE group and two international conferences, in which one international ICIAICT 2012 was organized by CSI, Noida Chapter and second international conference 2012 EP-PICTM was organized in collaboration with MTMI, USA, University of Maryland Eastern Shore, USA and Frostburg State University, USA at School of Information and Communication Technology, Gautam Buddha University, Greater Noida, India. Apart from teaching, he is running a programming club for ICT students and he is guiding various research scholars in the areas of Software Engineering, reusability of code, soft computing technique, big Data and IoT. His major current research interest is in Component-Based Software Engineering. He is working as Co investigator in sponsored research project in High throughput design, synthesis and validation of TALENs for targeted Genome Engineering, funded by Department of Biotechnology, Ministry of Science and Technology Government of India New. Two books "Teaching of Mathematics" and "Communication and Information Technology" at national levels and Examining Cloud Computing Technologies through the Internet of Things (IoT) at international level have been authored by Dr. Tomar. He has also contributed more than 100 papers/articles in national/international journals and conferences. He served as a member of the editorial board and reviewer for various Journals and national/international conferences.

* * *

Iram Abrar is currently pursuing M.tech in the Department of Computer Science, University of Kashmir. Prior to this, she has completed her B.tech in computer science and engineering from Islamic university of science and technology. Her basic research interests include network security, IoT and machine learning.

Hadi Alasti received his PhD in Electrical Engineering with concentration on communications and signal processing from University of North Carolina. He is an assistant professor at School of Polytechnic, at Purdue University Fort Wayne. Previously, he has taught as full-time teaching professor at East Coast Polytechnic Institute, and as adjunct faculty in Johnson C. Smith University and University of North Carolina at Charlotte. He has taught undergraduate courses, and graduate courses in Purdue University Fort Wayne, and University of North Carolina at Charlotte. Dr. Alasti is a member of ASEE, a senior member of IEEE, and member of several IEEE societies such as communication society, and signal processing society. He has had several years of industry work experience in power system companies and field experience in power system communications.

Alwi M. Bamhdi is an assistant professor in the Department of Computer Sciences, Umm Al-Qura University, Saudi Arabia. He received his MSc and Ph.D. in computer science in 2014 from Heriot-Watt University, UK. His research interests include mobile ad hoc networks, wireless sensor networks, information security, internet of things, cyber security, computer vision and simulation and performance evaluation.

Jai Prakash Bhati is working as Assistant Professor in Department of Computer Science and Engineering, School of Engineering and Technology, Noida International University, Greater Noida, Uttar Pradesh, India since August 2013. He has earned his master's degree, M.Tech. (Specialization in Intelligent Systems and Robotics) from School of Information and Communication Technology, Gautam Buddha University, Greater Noida, U.P., India. Prior to his masters he has worked in various domains like ERP, technical support and software development around four years. Also he has worked as a guest faculty in the School of Information and Communication Technology, Gautam Buddha University, Greater Noida, U.P., India Apart from teaching experience he has administrative experience at university level on various posts like examination coordinator, registration coordinator, course coordinator, University Tech Fest coordinator, training and placement coordinator, sports event coordinator, academic tour coordinator. Mr. Bhati has organized and coordinate many workshops, seminars and quiz competitions in university. He has been member of organizing committee for national and international conferences at university level. Mr. Bhati has also contributed 03 papers in national/international journals and conferences. He is serving as reviewer for various national and international journals. His areas of interest are artificial intelligence, expert systems, soft computing, artificial neural network, Big Data, Cloud and DBMS.

Aditya Bhattacharyya is presently working as Assistant Teacher of a School and has completed his MCA degree from Vidyasagar University. He has numerous research papers in the domain of Cryptography and Network Security among which many has been awarded with "Best Paper Award."

Anthony Bolton is a PhD candidate in the School of Computing at the University of South Africa. He is also Chief Information Officer (CIO) and Chief Technical Officer (CTO) Global Telecom, End User Infrastructure & Services, Immersive Technology Development and Engineering at General Motors in Ireland.

Jagjit Singh Dhatterwal is presently working as Assistant Professor, School of Computing Sciences & Applications, PDM University, Haryana. He received a Master of Computer Application from Maharshi Dayanand University, Rohtak (Haryana). He is also a Member of Computer Science Teacher Association (CSTA), New York, USA, International Association of Engineers (IAENG), Hong Kong, IACSIT (International Association of Computer Science and Information Technology, USA, professional member Association of Computing Machinery, USA, IEEE, and Life Member, Computer Society of India, India. His area of interest includes Artificial Intelligence and Multi-Agents Technology. He has a number of publications in International/National Journals and Conferences.

Harsh Garg is an engineering student in the Department of Electrical Engineering, Delhi Technological University (Formerly Delhi College of Engineering), Delhi, India. He is working in various technologies like IoT, Electric Vehicle, and Robotics. He has work experience with engineering teams, Startups while building multiple products from the ground up.

Ruchi Garg is a faculty member in Gautam Buddha University, SOICT, department of computer science and engineering, Greater Noida. She is having more than 12 years of experience in teaching students of graduate and post-graduate levels. She is pursuing her Ph.D. from Maulana Azad National Institute of Technology (MANIT), India, and her thesis is submitted. Her research interest includes low power wireless sensor networks, the Internet of Things (IoT), and Cloud Computing. She has authored three books with titles "Operating Systems", "Operating Systems golden solutions" under BPB Publications, and "Computer Organization" with Gold publishers. She has published various research papers in SCIE and SCOPUS indexed journals. She has also attended various other national and international conferences and presented research papers in them.

Leila Goosen is a full professor in the Department of Science and Technology Education of the University of South Africa. Prof. Goosen was an Associate Professor in the School of Computing, and the module leader and head designer of the fully online signature module for the College for Science, Engineering and Technology, rolled out to over 92,000 registered students since the first semester of 2013. She also supervises ten Masters and Doctoral students, and has successfully completed supervision of 43 students at postgraduate level. Previously, she was a Deputy Director at the South African national Department of Education. In this capacity, she was required to develop ICT strategies for implementation. She also promoted, coordinated, managed, monitored and evaluated ICT policies and strategies, and drove the research agenda in this area. Before that, she had been a lecturer of Information Technology (IT) in the Department for Science, Mathematics and Technology Education in the Faculty of Education of the University of Pretoria. Her research interests have included cooperative work in IT, effective teaching and learning of programming and teacher professional development.

Payel Guria is presently working as Assistant Professor of Department of Computer Science, Vidyasagar University. Along with her academic experiences, she has guided several dissertation, projects and published several research articles.

Kuldeep Singh Kaswan is presently working as an Associate Professor, School of Computing Sciences & Engineering, Galgotias University, Uttar Pradesh. He received a Doctorate in Computer Science under the Faculty of Computer Science at Banasthali Vidyapith, Rajasthan. He received his Master of Technology in Computer Science and Engineering from Choudhary Devi Lal University, Sirsa (Haryana). His area of interests includes Software Reliability, Soft Computing, and Machine Learning. He has published a number of research papers, books, book chapters, and patents at the national and international level.

Latika Kharb has been working as a Professor in the Jagan Institute of Management Studies (JIMS), Delhi, India. She has been Editor of numerous book titles viz. Learning Python, Research with Software Engineering, Communications in Computer and Information Science with Springer. She is one of the shortlisted candidate for UGC organized Commonwealth Fellowship tenable in U.S.A. (2004). Dr. Kharb has been awarded with International Professional of the Year award by IBC, Britain in 2012. Several technical sessions in national and international conferences had been chaired by Dr. Kharb and she has organized and participated in various FDP, workshops, national and international conferences. Apart from teaching, researches in the areas of software engineering, Artificial Intelligence, Cyber Laws, Bioinformatics, Mobile Computing, Data Analytics, Computer Forensic Science, Nanotechnology, Cyber Medicine & Dentistry, Data Analytics are being carried over by Dr. Kharb. She has also contributed more than 164 papers/articles/chapters in national/international journals, books and conferences. She has contributed several Chapters in Scopus Indexed Books with Elsevier, CRC, Taylor & Francis, IGI Global, Emerald, EAI-Springer with International and National Editors.

Elmarie Kritzinger joined the University of South Africa's College of Science, Engineering and Technology (CSET) in 2000 and currently holds the position of full professor in the School of Computing. Prof Kritzinger completed her PhD in 2006 and Post Graduate Certificate in Education in 2012. She also recently successfully completed her Master's in Education (Online Technology). Her research primarily focuses on Cyber Safety awareness, training and education for school learners, teachers and schools. The main aim is to establish and promote social responsibilities within communities to establish and grow a cyber-safety culture within South Africa. Prof. Kritzinger has established herself as a mature researcher and has published in accredited national and international journals, contributed to various chapters in books and presented at peer-reviewed conferences across the globe. Prof Kritzinger currently holds a National Research Foundation C3 rating within her research field.

Krishan Kumar is presently working as Assistant Professor, Department of Computing Science & Engineering, KCC Institute of Technology and Management, Greater Noida, UP. He received a Master of Technology in computer science from GJU Hisar (Haryana). He is also a Member of the Computer Science Teacher Association (CSTA), New York, USA, International Association of Engineers (IAENG),. His area of interest includes Wireless Networks and Multi-Agents Technology. He has a number of publications in International/National Journals and Conferences.

Faheem Syeed Masoodi is currently working as an assistant professor in the Department of Computer Science, University of Kashmir. Earlier, he served College of Computer Science, University of Jizan, Saudi Arabia as an assistant professor. Prior to that, he performed his duties as a research scientist at NMEICT-Edrp project sponsored by Ministry of HRD, Govt. of India in 2015. He was awarded PhD in the domain of network security & cryptography by the Department of Computer Science, Aligarh Muslim University India in year 2014 and did his masters in computer sciences from University of Kashmir. His basic research interests include cryptography & network security; and internet of things (IOT). He is a professional member of many cryptology associations and has published multiple research papers in reputed journals and conferences. He has been awarded fellowship for summer training "Conference effective moduli spaces and application to cryptography" organized by Centre Henri Lebesgue, Rennes, France in 2014 and was also awarded fellowship for summer school "SP-Ascrypto-2011 Advance School of Cryptography" at University of Campinas, Sao Paulo, Brazil in 2011. He was also awarded Maulana Azad National Fellowship for his doctorate programme by UGC New Delhi. His teaching interests include cryptography and network security, theory of computation and design and analysis of algorithms.

Sahil Nazir Pottoo received the M.Tech. degree in Wireless Communication Engineering in 2020 from the I. K. Gujral Punjab Technical University, India with distinction and ranked 1st in the batch. He received the B.Tech. degree in Electronics and Communication Engineering in 2018 from the Baba Ghulam Shah Badshah University, India with distinction and ranked in the top 2% among all the undergraduate students. His master's thesis titled "Design and Analysis of M-Ary Modulation Driven Free Space Optical Transceiver using Coherent Detection and DSP Algorithms" involved primary research on the design and numerical simulations of coherent optical communication transceivers for 5G and beyond applications. He has published his research findings in various SCI journals and IEEE international conferences. He is acting as the technical reviewer for the Journal of SPIE – Optical Engineering, Journal of Optical Communications, and is an accredited reviewer of The Optical Society (OSA). His research interests are B5G/6G, IoT, and free-space optics.

Aditi Sakalle has a B.E in Electrical and Electronics Engineering from RGPV University Bhopal M.P, Mtech in Modelling and Simulation Savitri Bai Phule University Pune MH.

Prerna Sharma is a diligent developer. Have worked in full-stack development, mainly working in Python and JS. Have a knack for IoT.

Jaswinder Singh is working as an Associate Professor in the Department of Computer Science & Engineering at Guru Jambheshwar University of Science & Technology, Hisar, Haryana. He has completed his Ph.D in Computer Science & Engineering from Deenbandhu Chhotu Ram University of Science and Technology, Murthal, Sonepat, Haryana and completed his M.Tech in Computer Science & Engineering from Kurukshetra University, Kurukshetra, Haryana. He has teaching experience of more than 17 years and he has published more than 25 research papers in international journals and conferences.

Pooja Singh received her PhD degree form Gautam Buddha University in Computer Science and Engineering in the year 2020. She completed her M.Tech (Computer Science) from Banasthali University, Rajasthan. Currently she is working as an Assistant Professor in Shiv Nadar University, Greater Noida, Uttar Pradesh.

Dimpal Tomar is pursing Ph.D from School of Information and Communication Technology, Gautam Buddha University, Greater Noida, U.P., India with the specialization in Internet of Things. She also worked as a Asst. Professor in Dept of CSE, School of Engineering and Technology, Noida International University, Greater Noida, U.P., India since Sept 2014. She has earned his master's degree M.Tech. (Specialization in Software Engineering) from School of Information and Communication Technology, Gautam Buddha University, Greater Noida, U.P., India. Ms. Dimpal has good teaching experience as well as administrative experience at university level. Also she has worked as a guest faculty in School of School of Information and Communication Technology, Gautam Buddha University, Greater Noida, U.P., India. Ms. Dimpal has coordinated many workshops, seminars and quiz competitions. She has been member of organizing committee for international conference at university level. Ms. Dimpal has also contributed 07 papers & 03 book chapters in national/international journals and conferences. His areas of interest are IoT, Big Data, Data Structures, DBMS, Compiler, Analysis and Design of Algorithms.

Index

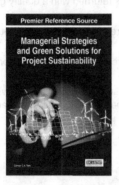

IGI Global Author Services

Providing a high-quality, affordable, and expeditious service, IGI Global's Author Services enable authors to streamline their publishing process, increase chance of acceptance, and adhere to IGI Global's publication standards.

Benefits of Author Services:

- **Professional Service:** All our editors, designers, and translators are experts in their field with years of experience and professional certifications.
- **Quality Guarantee & Certificate:** Each order is returned with a quality guarantee and certificate of professional completion.
- **Timeliness:** All editorial orders have a guaranteed return timeframe of 3-5 business days and translation orders are guaranteed in 7-10 business days.
- **Affordable Pricing:** IGI Global Author Services are competitively priced compared to other industry service providers.
- **APC Reimbursement:** IGI Global authors publishing Open Access (OA) will be able to deduct the cost of editing and other IGI Global author services from their OA APC publishing fee.

Author Services Offered:

English Language Copy Editing
Professional, native English language copy editors improve your manuscript's grammar, spelling, punctuation, terminology, semantics, consistency, flow, formatting, and more.

Scientific & Scholarly Editing
A Ph.D. level review for qualities such as originality and significance, interest to researchers, level of methodology and analysis, coverage of literature, organization, quality of writing, and strengths and weaknesses.

Figure, Table, Chart & Equation Conversions
Work with IGI Global's graphic designers before submission to enhance and design all figures and charts to IGI Global's specific standards for clarity.

Translation
Providing 70 language options, including Simplified and Traditional Chinese, Spanish, Arabic, German, French, and more.

Hear What the Experts Are Saying About IGI Global's Author Services

"Publishing with IGI Global has been **an amazing experience** for me for sharing my research. The **strong academic production** support ensures quality and timely completion." – **Prof. Margaret Niess, Oregon State University, USA**

"The service was **very fast, very thorough, and very helpful** in ensuring our chapter meets the criteria and requirements of the book's editors. I was **quite impressed and happy** with your service." – **Prof. Tom Brinthaupt, Middle Tennessee State University, USA**

Learn More or Get Started Here:

For Questions, Contact IGI Global's Customer Service Team at cust@igi-global.com or 717-533-8845